The authors of this book have developed a new and stimulating approach to the analysis of the transitions of Bulgaria, the Czech Republic, Hungary, and Slovakia to democracy and a market economy. They integrate interdisciplinary theoretical work with elaborate empirical data on some of the most challenging events of the twentieth century. Three groups of phenomena and their causal interconnection are explored: the material legacies, constraints, habits, and cognitive frameworks inherited from the past; the erratic configuration of new actors, and new spaces for action; and a new institutional order under which agency is institutionalized and the sustainability of institutions is achieved. The book studies the interrelations of national identities, economic interests, and political institutions with the transformation process, concentrating on issues of constitution making, democratic infrastructure, the market economy, and social policy.

INSTITUTIONAL DESIGN IN
POST-COMMUNIST SOCIETIES

THEORIES OF INSTITUTIONAL DESIGN

Series Editor
Robert E. Goodin
Research School of Social Sciences
Australian National University

Advisory Editors
Brian Barry, Russell Hardin, Carole Pateman, Barry Weingast,
Stephen Elkin, Claus Offe, Susan Rose-Ackerman

Social scientists have rediscovered institutions. They have been increasingly concerned with the myriad ways in which social and political institutions shape the patterns of individual interactions which produce social phenomena. They are equally concerned with the ways in which those institutions emerge from such interactions.

This series is devoted to the exploration of the more normative aspects of these issues. What makes one set of institutions better than another? How, if at all, might we move from the less desirable set of institutions to a more desirable set? Alongside the questions of what institutions we would design, if we were designing them afresh, are pragmatic questions of how we can best get from here to there: from our present institutions to new revitalised ones.

Theories of institutional design is insistently multidisciplinary and inter-disciplinary, both in the institutions on which it focuses, and in the methodologies used to study them. There are interesting sociological questions to be asked about legal institutions, interesting legal questions to be asked about economic institutions, and interesting social, economic and legal questions to be asked about political institutions. By juxtaposing these approaches in print, this series aims to enrich normative discourse surrounding important issues of designing and redesigning, shaping and reshaping the social, political and economic institutions of contemporary society.

Institutional Design in Post-communist Societies

Rebuilding the Ship at Sea

JON ELSTER, CLAUS OFFE, AND
ULRICH K. PREUSS

with

FRANK BOENKER, ULRIKE GOETTING, AND
FRIEDBERT W. RUEB

PUBLISHED BY THE PRESS SYNDICATE OF THE UNIVERSITY OF CAMBRIDGE
The Pitt Building, Trumpington Street, Cambridge CB2 1RP, United Kingdom

CAMBRIDGE UNIVERSITY PRESS
The Edinburgh Building, Cambridge, CB2 2RU, United Kingdom
40 West 20th Street, New York, NY 10011-4211, USA
10 Stamford Road, Oakleigh, Melbourne 3166, Australia

First published 1998

Printed in the United Kingdom at the University Press, Cambridge

Typeset in 10.5/12 Minion [CE]

A catalogue record for this book is available from the British Library

Library of Congress Cataloguing in Publication data

Elster, Jon, 1940–
Institutional Design in Post-communist Societies / Jon Elster, Claus Offe, Ulrich K. Preuss;
with Frank Boenker, Ulrike Goetting, Friedbert W. Rueb.
    p.   cm. – (Theories of institutional design)
Includes bibliographicl references (p.   ) and index.
ISBN 0 521 47386 1 (hard). – ISBN 0 521 47931 2 (pbk.)
1. Europe, Eastern – Politics and government – 1989–
2. Democracy – Europe, Eastern. 3. Europe, Eastern – Economic policy – 1989–
4. Post-communism – Europe, Eastern.
I. Offe, Claus. II. Preuss, Ulrich Klaus, 1939–   . III. Title. IV. Series.
JN96.A58E57   1997
943′.0009717–dc21   96-50073 CIP

ISBN 0 521 47386 1 hardback
ISBN 0 521 47931 2 paperback

Contents

Acknowledgements

The topics that we deal with in this book have two things in common: they are evidently of great consequence for the evolution of a new socio-political and economic order in Central East Europe, and these consequences, as well as the mechanisms that bring them about, are largely uncertain and untested. Also, the authors of this book share two features: their interest in Central East European transformations has been relatively recent, and they therefore had to operate (as is the case with quite a number of recent authors in the emerging field of "transitology") without the benefit of the comprehensive experience, expertise, and linguistic competence that has normally been accumulated throughout a career by "area specialists."

It is for these kinds of deficiencies that we had to start with, that we depended on the help of others to an uncommon extent in the conduct of our research. Gathering data in the countries under study, conducting interviews, tracking down key agents and key events, making contact with the "local" theories about the trajectories of change in post-state-socialist societies, and refining our typologies and interpretations were all tasks that could not be accomplished, or accomplished to the extent to which we actually succeeded, without the assistance of people who, within as well as outside of academia, were willing to help with the tasks of data collection, with sharing their knowledge and insight, and with following the project with critical attention as its findings emerged. We wish to express our sincere gratitude to all of them, while none of them should be blamed for the shortcomings of our analysis.

Not all of them, however, can be mentioned here. A number of senior academic colleagues contributed their helpful advice. These include Attila

Agh, László Bruszt, Wolfgang Eichwede, Zsuzsa Ferge, Robert A. Goodin, Leslie Holmes, Stephen Holmes, Wiktor Osiatynski, Harry Rigby, and Hans Juergen Wagener.

Much greater was the number of people who helped through locating sources of data, making contacts, and generously sharing the results of their own research and reflection. We wish to express our gratitude to Albena Azmanova, Snezhana Botusharova, András Bozóki, Monika Cambalikova, Tanya Chavdarova, Waska Dimitrova, Georgi Georgiev, Teodoritchka Gotovska, Hans Hermann Hertle, Milan Horacek, Berthold Kohler, Rumyana Kolarova, Miriam Kotrusova, János Köllö, Jiri Kral, Ivan Kristev, Erika Kvapilová, Darina Malova, Zuzana Müllerova, Alena Nesporova, Kinga Petervari, Martin Potucek, Todor Radev, Klaus Schrameyer, Georgi Spassov, Alexander Stoyanov, Zsuzsa Széman, Sonya Szomolányi, Jiri Vecernik, Ivan Vejvoda, Helena Wolekova, Milan Zemko.

The research was conducted at the Center for European Law and Policy Research at the University of Bremen (ZERP) which received a generous grant of the Volkswagen-Stiftung.

Other institutions which have supported our work include the Center for Social Policy Research at the University of Bremen, the Research School of Social Sciences at the Australian National University in Canberra, the Collegium Budapest, and the Central European University at Prague, the last three of which have hosted members of the project team as well as meetings.

We have also tried to compensate for our collective lack of long-standing "area-expertise" by designing a rather elaborate scheme of specialization and division of labor among the six persons – three senior and three junior by age and academic seniority – that have (hopefully) cumulatively cooperated in writing this volume. Thus drafting responsibilities were allocated for the individual chapters. The chapters were drafted, before undergoing a lengthy process of joint discussion and subsequent revisions, by the following persons: Offe (chapter 1), Boenker, Goetting and Preuss (chapter 2), Elster and Preuss (chapter 3), Rueb (chapter 4), Boenker (chapter 5), Goetting (chapter 6), Offe (chapter 7) and Preuss (chapter 8).

April 1996
Bremen, Berlin, New York

F.B. C.O.
J.E. U.K.P.
U.G. F.W.R.

Abbreviations

AG TRAP	Arbeitsgruppe Transformationsprozesse der Max-Planck-Gesellschaft
CEPR	Centre for Economic Policy Research
CERGE-EI	Centre for Economic Research and Graduate Education Charles University, Economics Institute of the Academy of Science of the Czech Republik
CEE	Central Eastern Europe
CEU	Commission of the European Union
CMEA	Council for Mutual Economic Aid
EBRD	European Bank for Reconstruction and Development
ECO	Economic Co-operation Organization
ECPR	European Consortium for Political Research
EECR	East European Constitutional Review
EUI	European University Institute, Florence
ILO-CEET	International Labour Office / Central East European Team
IMF	International Monetary Fund
IPSA	International Political Science Association
iw-trends	Institut der deutschen Wirtschaft-Trends
NBER	National Bureau of Economic Research
OECD	Organisation for Economic Co-operation and Development
RFE/RL	Radio Free Europe/Radio Liberty
SSRC/ACLS	Social Science Research Council/American Council of Learned Society

UCEMET	University Council for Economic and Management Education Transfer
UN	United Nations
UNDP	United Nations/Development Programme
UNICEF	United Nations International Children's Emergency Fund
UNICEF-ICDC	UNICEF – International Child Development Centre
WIIW	Wiener Institut für Internationale Wirtschaftsvergleiche
WZB	Wissenschaftszentrum Berlin
ZERP	Zentrum für Europäische Rechtspolitik an der Universität Bremen

1

Introduction: agenda, agency, and the aims of Central East European transitions

The breakdown of the European regimes of state socialism and the subsequent efforts to establish a new social order in its former domain are arguably the most consequential, as well as most fascinating, historical events in the authors' adult lifetime. What we want to understand in this comparative study is not so much the breakdown of the old order, but the problematic emergence of the new. To that end, we look at three groups of phenomena and their causal interconnection. These phenomena can be located on a time axis. First, we have the material legacies, constraints, and set of habits and cognitive frames that are inherited from the past regime (as well as the social and cultural conditions preceding it), as well as from the mode of its sudden and unpredicted disintegration. Second, we see a turbulent configuration of new actors and new opportunities for action; they emerge as the old regime loses its repressive grip on society. Third, we see – or rather still partly anticipate – a new consolidated institutional order under which agency is institutionalized and a measure of sustainability (or "consolidation") of these agency-shaping institutions is achieved. Thus the breakdown, transformation actors, and new and (more or less) consolidated regimes are the three phenomena we encounter along the transformation path. The causal links that connect the (in)stabilities of institutional outcomes to actors, and actors to the constraints, opportunities, and preferences inherited from and inherent in the original conditions of the breakdown of the old regime will together form the focus of this book.

Events along this path, and the demise of the state socialist system in particular, can at best be explained with the benefit of hindsight; they had not been predicted beforehand, other than in the way of idiosyncratic guesswork by non-academics, as opposed to robust social or economic theories about the sustainability of the state socialist social order. There is a somewhat ironical symmetry of cognitive failure: while the official doctrine of state socialism *included* a theory about the necessary eventual demise of democratic capitalism which so far has *not* occurred, social science in the West had *no* established theory about the crisis and breakdown of state socialism before it actually *did* occur. Apart from the fact that the social sciences have not been very strong in predicting macro-events (partly because such predictions tend to trigger forces that render them self-destroying, as was arguably the case with Marx' prediction concerning the future of capitalism), there are a number of ways to account for this specific failure of predictive theory (see Lipset and Bence 1994).

First, Western theorists may have been blinded either by their tacit hopes for state socialism being eventually able to sustain itself through learning and reform or, more likely, by the fears of what would happen to the post-World War II world order if state socialism were to crumble. A syndrome of left liberal "anti-anti-communism" may have lead a generation of observers who grew up under Cold War conditions to take the permanence of the Soviet empire for granted. Conversely, on the part of those who would have wished the Soviet "kingdom of evil" to disappear from the map the self-censorship mechanism of counter-wishful thinking may have played an inhibiting role.

Second, the fate of state socialism was actually exceedingly hard to predict, given the systemic opacity of this social order, i.e., its inability to monitor itself and provide reliable information about the state of its critical variables not only to Western observers and the mass of East European populations, but even to Eastern elites themselves. State socialism, in other words, is a system that does not generate knowledge, least of all *public* knowledge, about indicators of its own malfunctioning.

Third, accurate prediction may be said to have been impossible, as the events of 1989–91 were essentially triggered by contingent and erratic personal decisions at the top level of the Soviet elite that followed no known rule or pattern whatsoever and in the absence of which the system might well have survived for some undeterminable span of life. Whatever the right explanation is, the lack of prediction and anticipation about what happened *before* it happened, as well as, partly as a result of this lack, lack of plans and guidelines for future action *after* it happened, is a pervasive element of post 1989. That situation is hence replete with surprise, panic, unpatterned turbulence, and disorientation. Note that the failure to predict does not end with the end of the old regime. For who has predicted (and if so, on the basis of which kind of social theory?) the eruption of ethnic conflicts in many of the post-communist states, the resurgence of communist elites in some of them, or the adoption by the latter of rather liberal (but in some cases also nationalist) policies that were at variance with their electoral promises?

1 The particular character of the Central and East European transitions

The best we can therefore hope to do is to disentangle the drama and make explanatory sense of the subsequent chain of events in an *ex post* perspective, relying on information that the actors could not possibly possess at the point of their action.

The chain of causation from original conditions to political and economic "transformation actors," and from actors to a new and more or less consolidated and institutionalized social order comprises the cycle of systemic transition. Rather than studying it on a global level – i.e. all post-communist societies in all aspects of their reorganization – we propose an approach that is more disaggregate and comparative. We thus focus upon four countries – Bulgaria, the Czech Republic, Hungary, and Slovakia – and upon the building of four vital (as well as intensely interacting) institutional components within each of them – constitution-building, the formation of political institutions, the privatization and marketization of the economy, and the new institutional forms that emerge in the field of social security, poor relief, and social services. We hope that this comparative approach brings us closer to an understanding of why actors involved in the transition do what we see them doing, and why they accomplish – or fail to achieve – the desired outcome of a new and sustainable political, social and economic order. Each of these sectoral transition trajectories will be linked to the specifics of the "original position" in which the countries found themselves when the old regime collapsed in 1989.

In contrast to much of the political science literature on transitions to democracy, we explore and emphasize those aspects of the post-communist experience that are *different* from transitions to democracy that took place at other times and places in the course of the twentieth century. The most significant of those post-communist specificities and singularities will be discussed in the present chapter. They are seen (1) in the *non-military* and non-violent nature of the collapse and transition, (2) in the *absence of "revolutionary"* counter-elites, ideologies, and blueprints, as well as in the absence of reasonably unified political agents rooted in socio-economic cleavages and conflicts, (3) in the *simultaneity* with which the tasks of political, economic, and territorial reform and reconstitution appear on the rather overcrowded transformation agenda, and (4) in the *revolutionary and universalist* pretenses of the now defunct old regime. In the concluding part of this chapter, we (5) offer a conceptual discussion of the key criterion of a successful transition, namely institutionalized agency within a "consolidated" social and political order.

The object of our study is specified in time and space. As far as time is concerned, the historically unique nature of the transformation that occurred after 1989 in the Central East European countries, as well as subsequently in the former Soviet Union and the former Yugoslav Republic and Albania, becomes evident if we compare its patterns with those waves of transition from authoritarian rule to democracy that took place earlier in the twentieth century. These earlier waves which resulted in the adoption of full and equal adult voting rights, free competition between parties, and representative government within the framework of institutional guarantees of rights were those (a) after World War I (e.g., Germany, Britain), (b) after World War II (Germany, Italy, Austria, Japan), and (c) in the period 1974–85 in the (mostly) "Latin" countries of Southern Europe and South America (Greece, Portugal, Spain; Brazil, Uruguay, Argentina). We are concerned with the specificities of the post-1989 wave.

This book deals with political and economic transformations that occurred in a *subset*, to be located in space, of the countries that underwent the regime change of 1989. This subset is defined by eliminating from the universe of communist countries, as it existed in the 1980s, a number of countries that we are not concerned with here for partly pragmatic, partly systematic reasons. Communist – or synony-mously "state socialist" – countries are defined by their monopolistic ruling socialist party and its ideology and by their largely state controlled economies. Our focus is here on former state socialist *transformation* countries in which a sharp rupture of the political and economic regime occurred in the period 1989–91. This leaves a choice among only those (but at the same time all of those) for which the capital is located in Europe (Mongolia being a possible exception), excluding at any rate the People's Republic of China, Cuba, Vietnam, as well as African varieties of state socialism (where Ethiopia would be a possible exception). Second, we have excluded all cases which were *not* part of the economic (CMEA) and military (Warsaw Pact) *alliances* dominated by the Soviet Union, which eliminates non-aligned Yugoslavia and Albania from our set and leaves all the European CMEA countries in it. A third step is to look at only those states that, while being *dependent participants* in the two alliances (which eliminates the Soviet Union itself), at the same time were *formally sovereign* states throughout the period after World War II, which eliminates the Baltic and other newly independent republics, but leaves the Czech Republic and Slovakia in the sample, as these two now independent states together formed a sovereign nation state throughout the communist period. This operation leaves us with six countries (in 1990) which will be called the Central East European (or CEE) countries in this study. These countries are Rumania, Bulgaria, Hungary, Poland, German Democratic Republic (merged with West Germany in 1990), and the Czech and Slovak Socialist Republic. Finally, we concentrate in this study on a *subset* of the CEE countries – our sample countries – which are Bulgaria, the Czech Republic, Hungary, and Slovakia, leaving out of the sample just Rumania, Poland, and the former GDR which became part of the German federal state in 1990.

Although limited in number, this set is still rich in diversity. *Common* features of the three countries include the fact that they are all former components of the Soviet empire (Warsaw Pact, CMEA); this implies their former military, ideological, political as well as trade dependency upon the imperial power. The respective communist regimes were imposed upon all of the countries in non-revolutionary ways as a consequence of World War II. The breakdowns of the old regimes occurred simultaneously in all the (then) three countries within a few weeks at the end of 1989. All of them have, subsequent to the breakdown, officially embarked upon transitions to liberal democracies and market economies based on private property – but with one of them, Hungary, with preparations to this transition adopted semi-officially much earlier. A process of constitutional reform or innovation has been initiated in all of the four countries, with freely elected parliaments functioning as constitutional assemblies. Finally, all of the countries, if to sharply differing degrees, are characterized by inferior economic performance compared to – as well as massive future economic dependency upon – the West European core. All of the countries have applied for EU membership as well as for military integration into the NATO alliance.

Major *differences* between the countries include: two of them, Bulgaria and Slovakia, contain deep ethnic cleavages, the two others do not according to their present ethnic composition. Three of them, Bulgaria, Czech Republic and Slovakia, were among the more harshly repressive communist regimes, whereas Hungary was relatively liberal for a long time. Two, Hungary and the Czech Republic belong to the economically most advanced of the former communist countries, whereas the two other are more backward and with a greater share of their economies agrarian. While Hungary, the Czech Republic and Slovakia have been the scene of spectacular popular uprisings against communist rule in 1956 and 1968, respectively, Bulgaria is the only country within the former CMEA system where opposition to the Soviet Union and/or established domestic communist rule has been conspicuously absent, both at the elite and at the mass level. The breakdowns that occurred in all of our countries in 1989 differ: in Hungary they resulted from *internal cleavages* within the communist party elite, in the Czech Republic and Slovakia from sudden *mass mobilization* and popular protest, and in Bulgaria from a small urban *dissident intelligentsia* (of mostly ecologists) who relied upon the strong "amplifier effects" of the international media and organizations – in this country, also repression of the Turkish minority had undermined international and domestic support for the old regime. One of the countries (Hungary) had a small enterprise sector and a sizeable "informal economy" which has been allowed to develop since the seventies, whereas both Czechoslovakia and Bulgaria had a centralized regime of economic planning imposed upon virtually all economic activity. Bulgaria has a religious history of affiliation with the Russian Orthodox Church (as well as a political history of having been part of the Ottoman Empire), while both Slovakia and Hungary, as well as, to a lesser extent, the Czech Republic, are strongly Roman Catholic countries, with the latter two having a sizeable Protestant-Calvinist minority.

2   The role of military force and conflict

2.1   Its conspicuous absence

If we compare the CEE countries, and more generally, the CMEA and other transformation countries with the countries that have been the scene of earlier transition waves, one striking negative feature must be noted that defines the post-communist condition: transitions were peaceful. The negative feature is thus the absence of ("hot") war and *military* defeat of the old regimes as the trigger of transformation (as in the post-World War I and post-World War II cases, also in Argentina 1983 and Portugal 1974) or democratic victory over a previously ruling *military* regime (Brazil, Greece, to some extent also Spain). The two transformation cases in which military force played some role in the post-communist transitions, namely the death penalty sentenced on part of the old leadership by a military court in Rumania in December 1989 and – outside the CEE universe – the killing of a still contested number of White House occupants in Moscow, October 1993, were highly ephemeral and both of a nature that helped to strengthen (albeit to a very limited extent) the new regime and made its advent more irreversible by abolishing (rather than restoring) remnants of the old regime.

Correspondingly, there is a conspicuous absence in 1989 of the *armed forces as an agent* trying to prevent the breakdown of the old or to obstruct the emergence of the new regimes (as in Spain, Argentina). Again, the attempted coup (executed by a party-military alliance) against Soviet President Michael Gorbachev in August 1991 stands out as the only exception at the level of the universe of post-communist transformation countries, with no exception having occurred at the level of CEE countries.

The only case for which this generalization raises apparent difficulties at the CEE level is the Polish case with the introduction of martial law in 1981. This corresponds to another Polish exception (see below), namely the country being the only one in which a sizeable opposition movement ("Solidarnosc") which effectively challenged the political and economic order of state socialism and its ideology, ever emerged. Yet a martial law regime is different from the actual use of military force (which never occurred in Poland). Poland under martial law in 1981 still differed from a military regime in that after the first days of putting the leaders of the opposition into internment and threatening society by the show of force the tanks were not in the streets, but remained in the barracks. By virtue of this fact, the Polish martial law regime was significantly different from the instances of military intervention that had occurred in 1953, 1956, and 1968 in other CEE countries. Moreover, this regime took office under the premise that foreign military resources (coming from the Soviet Union or the GDR) would not be part of any conceivable course of events. This semi-official assurance of foreign non-intervention, in turn, did a lot to undermine the credibility of the military threat of the Polish generals and their forces, as the preparedness of the Polish Army to take military action against Polish workers could never be seriously counted upon. In the absence of any conceivable "fraternal help" from across the Polish borders, the martial law regime was bound to remain a mere facade of a military regime.

Yugoslavia is included in the universe of transformation countries, but excluded from the CMEA/Warsaw Pact universe. The dramatic extent to which military conflict has in fact accompanied the political (and rather prevented the economic) transformation of this country must be accounted for in terms of exactly its "non-aligned" status, i.e., the absence of a transnational security structure (such as was provided by the Warsaw Pact to the other transformation countries) and the manifest failure of NATO or, for that matter, UN forces to substitute for the absence of the restraining and the disciplinary potential of such a security structure. Several factors are responsible for the glaring "Yugoslav exceptionalism," as far as the role of military violence is concerned. First, Yugoslavia, on account of its 1974 constitution, was hardly a "state," but an ethnically structured federation characterized by an extreme degree of devolution of powers, with the communist party being the only supposedly unifying force. Second, the defense forces of the country were split into a (nominally) unitary army, the Yugoslav Peoples Army (JNA), and Territorial Defense Forces, with the command structures of the latter (together with the media) being organized at the level of the Republics, a pattern inspired by the heroic model of guerilla warfare in World War II. Third, after the definitive abdication of the communist party as a unitary force, the JNA remained the only federal institution. Without, however, an accountable civilian-political supreme command, as the only agency of common Yugoslav statehood, the party, had effectively "withered away". At the same time, the Territorial Defense forces were effectively appropriated by separatist forces at the level of the Republics. Taken together, the non-aligned position of the country, its extreme internal divisions which were partly nurtured by the memories of ethnic hostilities during World War II, the lack of clarity as to whom to defend the country against (the imperialist West? the Warsaw Pact? other Republics?), the parallel organization of defense, and the lack of effective federal leadership all contributed to a situation in which the end of the monopoly of the communist party meant the manifest dissolution of the state itself. In all other cases, including those of the CSFR and the GDR, statehood remained sufficiently robust after the demise of the monopolistic party to allow for a civilian and negotiated process of redefining the territory (through "velvet divorce" and "unification," respectively). Under the Yugoslav exceptional conditions, in contrast, military force, being split, decapitated, and up for grabs to the proponents of ethno-nationalist forces, remained the only resource to be employed for the purpose of territorial reorganization.

Before the regime breakdown, and unless the military itself assumes authoritarian governing powers, the military can either repress the forces of rebellion (PR China) or play an active role in the breakdown itself (Portugal). Once the breakdown has occurred, the military can play a violent role in the consolidation of the new regime and support its elite (Moscow 1993) or try to subvert it (as repeatedly attempted by the *carapintadas* in Argentina after 1985). A striking feature of the CEE transitions is that *none* of these four options was chosen by the armed forces of these countries.[1]

---

[1] The only exceptions to the rule of pre- as well as post-breakdown military inaction (and even of organized civilian violence) are to be found outside the CEE world, namely the Soviet/Russian case (with its ingredients of the Afghanistan defeat, regional nationality conflicts in some of the (former) southern republics, the Chechnya war, and the attempted and failed coup of August 1991). Saying

2.2   Political implications

What must be considered, moreover, as a decisive element in the causation of the 1989 demise of CEE state socialist regimes is the *anticipatory reliance*, on the part of masses, on the elites' military inaction. Not only did military violence play no role; it was largely expected to play no role. The fact that "fraternal help," as it was administered by Warsaw Pact forces before, was expected to be not forthcoming in 1989 resulted partly from Gorbachev's reassurances, but partly also from the fresh memory of the devastating international response to the military crushing of the Chinese democracy movement on June 4, 1989. This event and its aftermath gave rise to some critical measure of confidence that the military option was spent everywhere, and that "they can't afford to do it again and do it here."[2]

Whatever the accurate and complete explanation is of the conspicuously limited role of the military in the 1989 breakdown of the CEE regimes, these comparative observations strongly suggest that the distinctively "peaceful" course of the breakdowns and the subsequent transformations are essential determinants of the agenda and the actual course of these regime transformations, and that this peacefulness sets them apart from both the countries involved in earlier waves of transition and from post-communist transformation countries outside the CEE domain. Ironically, it is most conspicuously at the point of their demise that the state socialist regimes, at least at the CEE level (which also has been the scene of the notorious "fraternal help" incidents), seem to have redeemed what they had always enunciated as their supreme value: the preservation of domestic and international peace.

---

this, we do not mean to rule out the possibility that the actual or perceived economic requirements of the arms race and the Cold War had weakened both the economic effectiveness and political legitimacy of the Warsaw Pact countries beyond any potential recovery.

[2] As far as the military non-intervention in the GDR is concerned, the following considerations have played a "civilizing" role in the ranks of the leadership: First, fresh evidence of the devastating international repercussions of a "Chinese solution" made military repression, even if successful as such, appear an act of political suicide, particularly given the grim economic realities which the GDR elite could only hope to overcome through Western credits. Second, even military success was far from certain, as (a) the Soviet leadership was clearly committed to non-intervention and as (b) the dissolution of morale and discipline within the armed forces of the GDR had rendered any reliance on this means of last resort illusory. This dissolution, in turn, was strongly inspired by the negative example of the Chinese "June events." (For a detailed analysis of Soviet and East German elite moves between October 7 and November 11, 1989 (see Hertel 1994)).

Now, the thoroughly peaceful nature of the post-1989 breakdown and transition in the CEE countries is likely to shape a very different, as well as paradoxically more difficult, agenda and course of events. In previous transitions to democracy, the experience of war and military dictatorship has been a powerful catalyst of successful transformative efforts. In the case of the mass transitions to democracy that occurred after the two world wars, war-related parameters such as defeats, thorough elite delegitimation, massive destruction of human lives and material resources, occupation regimes, international control, and the territorial reorganization accomplished through peace treaties were all essential and helpful devices in abolishing the old and defining the new regimes, as well as in constraining the range of conflicts that erupted in the process. Although the peaceful nature of the breakdown in the CEE countries has been welcomed with deep relief and amazement (and the bizarre exception to this rule, the televised Romanian Christmas killings of 1989, watched with horror), it also involves a number of subsequent problems that were unknown in earlier transitions. These include the following distinctive implications of peaceful transitions.

First, in a peaceful regime change, the old elite is not discredited to the same extent that tends to be the case after a military defeat (cf. Germany after 1918 and after 1945), or where defeat is combined with the exposure of military elites having committed (or having been part of) massive human rights violations (cf. again Germany 1945) and, on top of that, having been defeated in war (Argentina). The problem of exchanging elites is more easily solved after wars than after civilian breakdowns.

Second, in peaceful breakdowns, there is no occupation regime of victorious allies or some other transnational agency that could impose by force a new institutional order and control the rise of new military conflict over ethno-territorial issues. The peace treaty with new externally enforced territorial settlements that comes at the end of wars does not have a civilian equivalent in the case of a non-military regime breakdown. On the contrary, the breakdown *without* war provided windows of opportunity for unilateral territorial reorganization (secession). As military control had evaporated with the breakdown of the regime itself, rather than being defeated in war, this vacuum of physical force has encouraged, if only outside the CEE universe, a variety of small-scale military enterprises in the multi-ethnic federal states of former Yugoslavia and the Soviet Union. Hence the inversion of the familiar sequence: world wars did not trigger regime transformations and transitions to democracy, but regime transformations (and subsequent regime decompositions) triggered local wars.

Finally, post-war conditions have often been the historical moment of vigorous political and institutional innovations. An outburst of public creativity generates new constitutions, new social and political rights, new social policy claims and institutions. The exercise of solidarity generated under conditions of common danger in war, as well as the collective sense of relief over having escaped its horrors, translates into a public-minded reconstruction effort, in which inter-class zero-sum games can be suspended for a while. As the peaceful mode of extrication does not generate these sentiments to the same extent, it appears to be less creative in terms of institutional innovation.

3 The political context: weak agents, diverse aspirations

The second major characteristic of the post-communist breakdown, in addition to its peaceful character, is its "non-revolutionary" nature. In order to speak of a "revolution," one would have to point to the action of an internal elite that brought about the regime change; in the CEE case, it makes much more sense to point to the declared *inaction* of an *external* elite as the major causal factor. Saying this we mean to emphasize another negative feature of the CEE transitions: organizationally weak and ideologically diverse agency. What actually happened (the demise of the old regime) was of course in some way caused by actors, but neither intended nor anticipated by them – nor often even believed to be within the range of the possible! There was no counter-elite, no theory, no organization, no movement, no design or project according to whose visions, instructions, and prescriptions the breakdown evolved. Rather than agents intentionally causing the outcome, the events that foreshadowed the ultimate outcome *gave rise* to and encouraged agents, movements, and projects. Apart from narrow and rather ineffectual circles of dissidents that could never effectively break out of their marginal habitat of academic, artistic, or religious institutions (if not prisons), oppositional movements were largely, with due consideration for Polish exceptionalism, a by-product of the regime's decay rather than its antecedent cause. State socialism does not appear to conform to the stereotype of a system that systematically raises a swelling class of active grave-diggers and breeds the social conflicts to which it eventually falls victim. On the contrary, the social contradictions it systematically breeds (such as consumer dissatisfaction) can relatively easily be coped with by a mix of concession and repression, while those contradictions they have in fact fallen victim to are not easily, even in retrospect, deciphered as "systemic" ones; at least to a large extent, these contradictions may well be read as an ultimately fatal chain of accidental and contingent occurrences.

3.1 Lack of a transformative vanguard

At any rate, and leaving this thorny question to future historians for the moment, it seems safe to observe that a transformative vanguard (understandably strong interests in its retrospective invention notwithstanding) was not a significant part of the old regime's dynamic of breakdown and of the shaping of subsequent events, neither above ground nor underground, neither civil nor military, neither organizationally nor intellectually (at least in terms of ideas that had any chances of "capturing" the masses). This absence of ideas and agents having been formed in the womb of the old order is the core of another momentous peculiarity that sets the post-1989 CEE experience[3] apart from the pattern we find in most of the previous transitions to democracy.

Turning for a moment to a transition country outside the domain of CEE proper, namely the Soviet Union, we encounter a case of indisputably strong agency which, however, was also marked by a blatant incongruity of intentionality and causation. In the Soviet Union, as in Hungary, the initiative of change originated in the second half of the 1980s within the highest ranks of the party, probably mostly with Gorbachev himself. Not even his worst enemies, however, would probably attribute to him what he actually *caused* to happen, as a long-term consequence of his sweeping reform initiatives, as his *intentional design*. Initiating an economic, political, and foreign policy reform initiative of the scope that Gorbachev actually advocated (and which he respectively termed "perestroika," "glasnost," and "Common European House") has by itself three momentous consequences that may well turn, as they doubtlessly did in the case under discussion, against the intentions of their author. First, the proclamation of these initiatives sends out, to the population in general and to sectoral elites in particular, the ambiguous message that the system and its established mode of operation is deeply in trouble and lacking the forces within civil society whose assistance would have been crucial, which is the only conclusion to be drawn from the fact that such incisive reforms are deemed necessary by the leaders themselves.

[3] It also sets this experience apart from the experience of the transformation countries outside of CMEA (Yugoslavia, Albania) and the countries outside of CEE, e.g., the Caucasus republics of the Soviet Union. In all of these areas, repressed and dormant ethno-nationalist aspirations erupted *prior* to the transition and contributed their share to the weakening and demise of the old regime. As far as the CEE universe is concerned, Bulgaria and Romania partake in this pattern, as it was failed attempts to repress internal minorities (of Turkish and Hungarian ethnic origin, respectively) that heralded the beginning of the end in these two countries.

By advertising such reform initiatives, top elites allow themselves to be seen as having lost faith in the system and its shibboleths. Second, a system that is exposed by the leadership as being so deeply in trouble is not easily trusted as to its capability of actually performing the bootstrapping act that the reformers at the top unexpectedly call for. Third, the actors that are most directly targeted by the reform proposals will be rightly alarmed, as well as provoked to respond in ways that will protect their privileges and obstruct the proposed reforms. Taken together, such images and responses can do more harm than good. Gorbachev's policies provide a striking example of the paradox that, at least under certain unfavorable conditions and beyond a certain state of disrepair, the most devastating thing one can do to an old regime is try to subject it to groundshaking reforms.[4]

Nor is the weakness of organized centers and ideological patterns of transformative agency hard to explain, neither at the elite nor at the mass level. Turning to the latter, reformist opposition of any strategic significance had virtually evaporated. While the experience of the state socialist system has everywhere, if in differing degrees, eroded popular support for communism, it has also rendered sterile and disorganized civil society to an extent that no reasonably potent idea of a systemic alternative could emerge. Authors such as Hankiss, Kolakowski, Staniszkis, Fehér, and many others (cf. diPalma 1990: 65f.) have again and again stressed the stultifying and demeaning communicative and associative conditions and, as a consequence, the widespread "semantic incompetence," "cognitive confusion," and "self-doubt" that stood in the way of any formation of agency and made most people most of the time actually cooperate in their own repression. They became "apathetic about collective aspirations" and were forced into a passive and fatalistic "semi-loyalty." (diPalma 1990: 66f.) The other side of the medal of apathy is *informalism*. Where associative activities occurred, they were escapist, inward-looking micro-groups of individuals trusting each other, helping each other in the coping with everyday problems, and creating some space for intellectual survival through clandestine ("samizdat") publications. There was no public space in which members of these informal networks, let alone formal associations, could challenge the right of the ruling powers to rule. The spectacular if short-lived popular mobilization of the last months of 1989 and the first months of 1990 *followed* and *confirmed* the self-

---

[4] "Had [the consequences of Gorbachev's reform initiatives] been known in advance, it would have encouraged such bunker mentality that no change would have been attempted. Differently put, Gorbachev destroyed state socialism perfectly because he was blind" (Hall 1995: 34).

abandonment of the ruling powers, rather than being the *cause* of their resignation.

The two cases that appear to come closest to being an exception to the rule of the weakness and sterility of transformative agency are those of Poland and Hungary, at least if we limit our attention to the period after the late 1970s. There cannot be any denying of the fact that in Poland a potentially revolutionary mass movement had formed in the late 1970s whose combination of traditional political and human rights claims, with nationalist, religious, and workers' control appeals, and the resulting political and economic demands, constituted the most serious challenge any state socialist regime ever had to face. But even here, this nascent center of transformative (and *only* in this case: potentially revolutionary) agency was to a large degree contained by repression through the martial law regime after 1981. The Hungarian case had even less that would justify calling it a "revolutionary" process. To be sure, there was, prior to 1989, a long history of economic, and partly also political, reformist openings in this country. But they were initiated and executed from within the ruling party and economic elite, not by any mass opposition movement. In all the other CEE countries, transformative agency emerged in the climate of, and was encouraged by the course of, precipitous events unfolding domestically and internationally, rather than the other way round.

3.2 The search for orientations

In the case of any successful revolution, a new center of power and agency emerges which undertakes to shape the future of society and relies on the means of repression and/or hegemony and the charismatic legitimacy of a person, an organized group, or set of ideas. In contrast, the case of a non-revolutionary transition does not generate a comparable measure of social and political integration and capacity for action. Counter-elites are small, poorly organized, ideologically confused, and lacking a strategic vision as much as a mass base. What we therefore find in the post-communist polities of the CEE variety is, soon following the liberating outburst of the months after the breakdown, a widespread disaffection, alienation, and cynicism concerning elites and their politics of change. Neither the breakdown of the old regime nor the construction of the new can be attributed to the design of some coherent and reasonably powerful counter-elite, and neither can it be attributed to the intentional action of international forces. Both the destructive and the constructive outcomes must be seen, instead, as being brought about through rather anonymous contingencies that follow a logic of "all causation, (almost) no intention." It is this peculiarly "subjectless" process in which the old system disintegrated, as well as the vegetative mode in which it is being replaced by new economic and political mechanisms, which make the question of agency, intentionality, and purpose so hard to answer beyond the very short period of oppositional mass mobilization during the winter of 1989.

There is no clearly dominant plan or project of transformation because there is no victorious counter-elite (as in revolutions in the proper sense) that prevailed over the old regime and that can derive unequivocal legitimacy and a mandate for action from this accomplishment. As there is no clear answer to the question who exactly "made" the old system go away, their is no answer as to who is entitled to lead the society into some better future. Hence the desirable shape of the new regime, the institutional patterns to be adopted in its consolidation, are deeply contested among the poorly organized proponents of three divergent orientations. These three orientations or ideas focus, respectively, on the *distant past*, the *"modern"* West, and what is still deemed, increasingly, the accomplishments of the *immediate past* of the state socialist system. Each of them comes with a specific assessment of the *virtues* of the new system and the *vices* of the old.

The Western-oriented modernizers base their claim to leadership on a consequentialist reading of the institutional setup of the OECD world. They conclude that representative democracy and a market economy yield *prosperity*, and as prosperity is evidently the highest, at any rate the most urgent priority, all "we" need to do is imitate and transplant Western patterns – above all in order to motivate the provision of urgently needed Western assistance and cooperation. Even if the imitation of such models is not aimed at genuinely and for their own sake, the dependence of new post-communist regimes upon Western-dominated transnational actors and the loss of credit of the old regime leave no alternative to at least paying lip-service to the institutional patterns of democratic capitalism. Among the modernizers, the negative assessment of the old regime is this: We want to be a "normal country," and the long period of communist rule has prevented us from becoming one. The old regime must be blamed for its *authoritarian inefficiency*.

In contrast to the modernizers, the "traditionalist" political forces draw upon the national culture and history and propose to reactivate, if not reinvent, institutional models (often including the monarchy) that were in place at some time prior to the communist takeover after World War II and usually work with strong appeals to *religious and ethno-national* identities. They look for cultural, economic, and political models that can be adopted from the respective country's pre-communist tradition. Their underlying intuition is something like this: We want to be "ourselves," and the rapid and indiscriminate adoption of Western economic, political and cultural patterns must be checked, as it will rather destroy the prospects of that project. Western patterns are suspected as being not suitable for "us." The old regime must be blamed for its quality of *"foreign domination"* and alienation from the authentic national culture.

Proponents of the third position, the ex-communist reformers, experience a remarkable surge in political strength in CEE countries[5] and opt for economic marketization and privatization (if with a variety of reservations) while maintaining and preserving at least some of the accomplishments of state socialism and the notions of social justice through *social and employment security* provided by it. The increasingly plausible and appealing political claim is that "we" want to do at least as well as we did five years ago, and this has not been accomplished anywhere by the post-communist regimes in terms of GNP, income distribution, or employment. The old regime must be blamed for "mistakes" and "errors" that were committed by its elites, and for having failed to make good its political and economic promises. According to the proponents of this orientation, the breakdown of the old regime should not be mistaken for any conclusive proof of its basic faults, but as the consequence of *endogenous failures* and deformations for which the leaders of the old regime are to be personally held responsible and which should – and in fact can – be avoided in the future.

Given these three poles of the political universe of post-communism, and also given the fact that governments in post-communist countries tend to be coalition governments,[6] because no single political camp is strong enough to win and maintain clear-cut majorities, there are three potential alliances of political forces. Each of which can occur in the form of either a governing coalition or a negative oppositional alliance. First, there is a *left-liberal alliance* composed of reformed communist parties and pro-market liberal forces, of which the Horn government in Hungary is the prominent example. Second, there is a *socialist-nationalist alliance* of the kind that we find in Slovakia under Meciar. Third, there is a possible coalition of *national-conservative and liberal* forces, of which both the Hungarian government led by Antall and the Czech government under Klaus are examples.

---

[5] This holds with the notable exception of the Czech Republic, which also happens to be the only country where the respective party has not changed its "communist" name into some socialist or social democratic designation.

[6] In this respect, the Bulgarian BSP government is an exception.

These three vague ideological orientations that together make up the universe of post-communist politics are by no means yet embodied in solidly established political parties, but rather represented by numerous, fuzzy, overlapping, and often short-lived organizational initiatives. Typically, what representative actors and political entrepreneurs say is different from what they believe, and what they do is again different from both of these. The course of political events suffers from all the symptoms of an immature system of parties and party politics: low membership, low electoral turnout, and a high degree of volatility not only of voters, but also of deputies shifting parties, splitting parties, or starting new ones. As parties are insufficiently consolidated to send clear-cut programmatic messages to voters and competing elites, the political discourse tends to be tinged by charismatic pretenses and personal loyalties. Ironically, the cognitive frame inherited from the old regime, namely the polarizing division of the political world into "us" (the faithful supporters of some "correct line") and "them" (the "enemies of the people") continues to be adhered to, particularly among the staunchest opponents of state socialism. This cognitive pattern often gives rise to the passionate display of personal hatred and hostility (often amounting to mutual accusations of corruption and/or involvements with the old regime), rather than to the quiet and routinized pursuit of "normal politics" through oligarchically controlled mobilization, issue raising, agenda setting, coalition building, and compromise bargaining within a framework of procedures and institutions that are largely accepted as given. In sum, and for all these reasons, political agency seems to be extremely fragmented, incoherent, ambiguous, and short-lived – albeit to an extent that differs between the countries under consideration and that will provide us with clues for an explanation of country-specific trajectories of transition.

4 The agenda: economic interests, political institutions, national identities

In spite of the weakness of agency, there cannot be a misreading among political elites concerning the set of tasks that must be solved in the process of transformation. First, a vast institutional reorganization of economic life must be accomplished, involving the steps of privatization, marketization, and stabilization. Second, a democratic constitutional government must be established which grants rights to citizens and prescribes rules for the future conduct of politics and policies, as well as judicial enforcement mechanisms backing those rights and rules. Third, a territorial nation state must be consolidated, which involves a definition of undisputed borders recognized by neighboring states, as well as by the international community, and the definition of the nation in terms of citizenship and minority rights.

4.1 The poor institutional legacy of the old regime

These three formidable items on the post-communist agenda have in common that they can be largely accomplished by legislation, including the law-making activities with which constitutional assemblies and the parties to international treaties are concerned. But there are also many changes, widely considered as urgently required, which cannot be, or not fully, accomplished by legislative means alone. This pertains to social, economic and cultural initiatives of citizens which new laws may facilitate and encourage, but do not determine their outcomes. At any rate, the warning seems to be in place that transformation and systemic change is something that is only to a limited extent a matter of law making. Cultural patterns, identities and legacies, associative practises that help or hinder the solution of collective goods problems, and the vigor with which entrepreneurial and other economic interests are pursued are among those determinants of change that cannot easily legislated into – or out of – being. Not only is political agency weak and fragmented in an *absolute* sense; even if it were strong, resourceful, and united, agents would have to face the fact that many of the changes that need to be accomplished in order for the transformation to succeed are beyond the reach of political and economic elites, as they are entrenched in the "habits of the hearts" and "frames of mind" of masses and elites alike. Seen from this angle, post-communist political elites are weak relative to the transformative challenges with which societies emerging from state socialism are confronted.

The giant proportions of the legislative tasks pertaining to the main three items on the transition agenda – economy building, polity building, and nation building – become evident when we realize that hardly any of the *institutional* elements of the old order can be relied upon, i.e., is considered (or, for that matter, openly advocated as being) worthy of preservation for more than a transitory period, or recognized as a worthy legacy.[7] Virtually everything must go and be replaced by something new. On the other hand, many of the *factual* conditions and residues of the old order appear unrelentingly entrenched, i.e., not easily nor rapidly alterable by intentional action, even if the political will and the administrative

[7] Examples include not only the design of political and economic institutions, but also the vast social policy and social service functions that were assigned to industrial enterprises under the old regime.

capacity to implement change could be presupposed. Virtually everything is affected by the long arm of the past and the ruinous conditions and habits the old regime has left behind. More specifically, this *fixity of inherited constraints* affects three conditions: (1) the state of material resources and their organization, levels of productivity, and environmental conditions; (2) The "inner environment" of mental residues, including the cognitive and normative culture, human capital, work habits, and social and political aspirations, collective identities and their potential for social conflict; and (3) the established elites and their informal power resources – the agents of the old regime, except for the narrow circle of leading figures, have not been physically liquidated, defeated, or effectively discredited, which is partly due to the fact that the breakdown occurred in the "civilian" mode.

Taken together, the situation was *tabula rasa* in institutional terms, *massive constraints* in "empirical"[8] terms, or, to use Max Weber's distinction, no authority (*Herrschaft*), all amorphous, scattered, and institutionally unsettled power (*Macht*).

Our ambition in this study is to explain deviations from these model assumptions. What we want to understand is how and to what extent the fluidity of institutionally unsettled power relations that we find in the immediate post-breakdown situation of each of our four countries congeals into reasonably solid, well-enforced, and reliable patterns of the new political and socioeconomic order of post-socialist nation states.

4.2   The problem of simultaneity

As the agents involved in the transition process cannot afford to follow the golden rule of "one thing at a time," but are forced to act simultaneously on all three tasks, two particularities arise that are unknown from other transitions. First, mutual incompatibilities or adverse interaction effects are to be expected to evolve between the three tasks of reconstruction. This historically rather unique simultaneity makes the desired overall outcome more uncertain, as well as the means to bring it about more controversial, as there are no successful models that can be unequivocally relied upon. Second, the three reform tasks entail widely diverging time horizons for their completion. In a sense (and disregarding for the moment the maturation time that a well-functioning political order may require), building the formal-legal pre-

---

[8] The term "empirical" connotes here, as it does in the Kantian terminology, "blind" facticity and normative unintelligibility of acts and events actors encounter in social life.

requisites of a new political order can be done within a year – simply by abolishing the political monopoly of the party and proclaiming a Bill of Rights, thereby vastly increasing the "voice" resources (elections, party competition, media, etc.) at the disposal of civil society. The building of a consolidated nation state that is securely recognized by its neighbors, as well as universalistically self-recognized by its citizens, may take a century. Economy building is a process of intermediate duration.[9]

We now want to address the mildly counter-intuitive question of why these tasks, given their formidable complexity and the uncertainty of success, need to be performed at all, and all three of them at the same time? Couldn't at least one of them wait until one of the other two is successfully resolved? Although the idea of such a macro-sequencing is suggested by Western patterns of political and economic modernization (first the nation state as a necessary precondition of capitalism, and finally mass democracy on the basis of capitalist growth and prosperity), it is unlikely to work in the case of post-communist transitions. Designs of orderly sequencing or "controlled decompression" have not worked anywhere in the region. The idea of first rebuilding the economy under the umbrella of temporarily preserved authoritarianism, then allow for a democratic opening and finally, say, addressing issues of nationhood appears grotesquely inadequate in a situation where no agent controls the power that is required to hold back the supposedly "later" issues until the "earlier" ones are settled.

For what puts all three items on the agenda in equally urgent and irrefutable ways is not just the "pull" of anticipated and desired outcomes of each of three reforms, but also the "push" that results from the powerlessness of those who might in fact want to keep any particular one of our three items off the agenda, but are unable to do so. What is lacking is the kind of power that manifests itself in the capacity for selective and sequential agenda setting. For instance, advice that could be taken from the Chilean example might be: Let's hold back on constitutional democracy while concentrating all efforts, for the time being, on economic modernization and recovery. It is evident that the "Chilean formula" of

---

[9] Concerning the temporal pattern of economic reconstruction and "normalization," the several features of the proverbial "valley of transition" may make for very different trajectories and durations. If this valley is anticipated to be deep and wide, and if the positive difference between what "we have now" and what we "might get once the new plateau is reached" is perceived to be unimpressive, the dynamics of economic transformation is likely to be rather sluggish. In contrast, the perception of limited sacrifices and the anticipation of steep progress may both work as powerful accelerators. These factors will help to explain differences between countries in their paths of economic reconstruction.

sequencing economic reform and political opening cannot work in the post-communist situation, mainly for the simple reason that there is no one who could assemble the military, economic, ideological or other resources to actually "hold back" on democratization or, for that matter, on any of the other two reforms. Seen from this perspective, the reform agenda is enormous not because of the grandiose aspirations of elites; it is enormous by default, due to the weaknesses of elites, including their incapacity to limit the active role that political and economic actors in the West play in setting the agenda of reform.

The haste with which the issues of democratization and constitution building should be taken up, as well as those of territorial reorganization and ethnic issues of minority citizenship, must be traced to the new elites' lack of staying power. Neither their civilian nor military resources are any longer sufficient to hold the line and to check the rise of citizens' and new elites' claims for participation, nor for the rise of so far repressed nationalist claims for ethnic "self-determination." Not only do political elites typically lack a strategic vision of priorities and approaches; even if such a vision were available and widely shared, the lack of institutionally legitimated authority renders governing elites defenseless as they are exposed to the "flooding" of their political agenda with a vast variety of issues, problems and demands that they must simultaneously respond to. While, from the point of view of any liberal political value perspective, the old regimes' loss of "staying power," authoritarian agenda-setting capacity, as well of its repressive ability to impose "non-decisions" can only be most emphatically welcomed, the price that comes in terms of a pervasive paralysis of political agency and governing capacity should not be overlooked. This paralysis is epitomized by the inability of elites to limit their agenda to manageable proportions and to extract from their societies both the political support and the economic resources required for the successful accomplishment of the tasks of constitution making and the building of a polity, economy, and nation.

5   The demise of European state socialism

If "the 'Autumn of the People' was a dismal failure of political science" (Przeworski 1991:1), i.e., of the academic discipline supposedly equipped but actually unable to predict significant political change, the science of mainstream economics celebrates the triumph of its wisdom that state socialism could not have worked in the first place. Thus, what was *ex ante* deemed a virtual impossibility by one academic discipline is held *ex post* to be a virtual necessity by the other. While the former of the two has to explain socialism's breakdown, the latter would have to come to terms with its apparent viability for over 74 or, respectively, 41 years. There is no clear explanation to either of these two questions. What economists need to come to terms with is the question why state socialism not only worked, but performed rather well, compared with other known and practised institutional methods of modernizing backward economies – at least for a time. What, in turn, political scientists need to understand is the declining part of state socialism's life cycle. "It is unclear what did not work under socialism: was the root of the crisis in the system of legitimacy, or in the economy, was it induced by domestic or international, economic or military processes?" (Szelenyi and Szelenyi 1994: 214).

5.1   Hypothetical explanations

What was seen happening in the period 1989–1991 was the effective disestablishment of (all European, but so far only the European instances of) an authoritarian regime whose original ideological claim of "applied Marxism" was universalistic, i.e., the claim to provide a permanently viable model for the future of all countries and all mankind. This claim distinguishes our case from those other authoritarian or, for that matter totalitarian, regimes which have broken down in modern times. For none of those other regimes has ever pretended to be capable of generalizing itself in time and space.

Moreover, and as far as the economic aspect of transformation is concerned, post-communist societies are now in the process of adopting a "capitalist" order, i.e., an order whose rejection and critique was the very cornerstone of the official theory of the old regime. Not only must the universalist claim be given up, but the presumed historical sequence of "stages" of social formations literally inverted. What was depicted as the dark past of an anarchic and exploitative social order is now being envisaged as the shining, if difficult to accomplish, future condition.

Even in retrospect, we are far from a proven explanation of this amazing turn of history. Arnason (1993: chapter 4) has suggested a useful categorization of four broad explanatory hypotheses worth pursuing. Two of them refer to internal and two to external causes, i.e., two to problems of "system integration" and two to those of "social integration," or legitimation. As to the internal-systemic hypotheses, the focus is upon the endemic problems of the systems integration of state socialist societies, i.e., the functional failures and lack of effectiveness of totalitarian regimes in steering and coordinating demand and supply, the polity and the economy, the civilian and the military sectors, etc. Doubts concerning this quasi-Marxist model of built-in self-destructive tendencies are raised, first, by the fact that the Soviet regime has in fact been capable not only of an unparalleled success in modernizing a backward society (Therborn 1992), but also of winning victory in a murderous war, as a consequence of which it was able to absorb and integrate the vast resources of the CEE countries. The iron grip of the centralized and monopolistic command of a party elite was exactly what the theorists of totalitarianism used to employ as an explanation of the *stability* of the system; it is not clear why the same structural feature should also serve to account for its demise brought about by somehow "excessive" control. Second, the internal-legitimation hypothesis, in short, states that state socialism was unable to create "socialist men". In the words of Hall (1995: 21–2; cf. also Przeworski 1991): "Whole societies [as opposed to religious or revolutionary elites] have difficulties supporting . . . generalized heroism and enthusiasm for very long. Accordingly, state socialist regimes can be judged to have placed excessive demands on their citizens" – both, we might add, in terms of what citizens are supposed to do and what they are supposed to endure. While the observation of a pervasive lack of heroism, if not outright cynicism, lethargy, and passive obstruction is certainly valid, it is not clear how this could have led to the regime's demise – given the fact that both its repressive and redistributive capacities were sufficient to check, once again disregarding the Polish exception, the formation of opposition forces (be it of "civil society," be it of "class antagonism") that might have challenged the regime from within for its failure to live up to its own (or anyone else's) standards of moral and political justice.[10] It actually appears in retrospect that the breakdown could only take place after would-be counter-elites had embraced "anti-politics" and the last traces of oppositional visions and projects of a "socialism with a human face" had exhausted themselves.

Turning, third, to the external-legitimation hypothesis, the asymmetry has been pointed out that while the Warsaw Pact (putatively) threatened Western democracies through the missiles pointed at them, the West threatened the Comecon countries by its mere existence, i.e., by undermining the loyalties of state socialist citizens through the deeply subversive, media-mediated demonstration effect of the images and realities of prosperity, freedom, and democracy. Yet, again, no opposition within the

---

[10] Incidentally, where oppositional forces have at all played a limited role in triggering the decomposition of communist rule, their ideological resources and motivations were not of a nature that we would commonly associate with the idea of a "civil society." To wit, they were nationalist and religious in Poland's "Solidarnosc" movement and ethnic in the minority upheavals of the Bulgarian Turks and the Hungarians in Romania – to say nothing about the fundamentalist Islamic Mujahedin guerilla in Afghanistan.

state socialist regimes can be pointed at that would have accomplished the breakdown by advocating the emulation of such Western models and perceptions. Finally, the external-systemic hypothesis must be mentioned. It cites cumulatively effective strains and cracks within the "Second World" of state socialism (beginning with the repressive CEE interventions of the fifties and sixties, the Sino-Soviet rift, the uneven economic developments and centrifugal tendencies within the Comecon, the vast network of patronage and assistance extended to the socialist Third World of African and Caribbean states, the ethno-nationalist and religious independence movements in the southern Republics of the Soviet Union, and finally the Afghanistan war) as symptoms of imperial overstretching and the resulting failure of the Center to control, accommodate, and coordinate the divergent parts of an increasingly differentiated whole. This reading of the regime's breakdown makes sense, however, only if we assume that the ruling elite of the center has itself understood and appreciated the situation in those terms – and had voluntarily capitulated and abdicated its claim to power as a result of this insight. For, alternatively, there is no evidence that the determined use of violence, both internally and externally, could not have considerably extended the span of life of the empire had its leadership *defied* the suggestion that holding fast to imperial ambitions was an ultimately hopeless project.

Whichever of the above four main hypotheses – or which combination of them – may be found to be valid by future historians as an explanation of the systemic breakdown of the core power of World War II, the event of this breakdown cannot be fully understood without reference to one highly contingent, "subjective" factor: the "loss of nerve" of key leaders, the willingness to admit failure (as opposed to the equally conceivable and psychologically perhaps more likely stubborn determination to repress and deny it), the preparedness to let a sudden decompression occur even in the absence of any well-supported hope that in response to it forces within civil society would spontaneously emerge capable to serve as allies in the accomplishment of a basic though still "immanent" reform. The almost frivolous preparedness to let, according to Gorbachev's famous dictum, "life" administer those punishments, even to what were nominally still close allies, that it holds out for those that "come late" is a clear indication of the sense of futility and exhaustion, and ultimately the resignation of the empire's core leadership. With this open and willful act of abdication and self-abandonment on the part of the Soviet leadership, resistance on the part of less insightful elites of the GDR, the CSSR, Bulgaria, and Romania was also doomed to fail, whereas the Polish and the Hungarian elites had occasion to learn much earlier that a new set of rules for the economic and political game was called for, and to prepare for their installation.

5.2 The *Tabula Rasa* of 1989

This brief review of the main alternative ways to account for the causes of the breakdown of the old regime has served here just to demonstrate three constituent elements of the new situation as it emerged after 1989.

First, no constituted authority survived the old regime, as its liquidation was accomplished through the self-liquidation and abdication of power of the old regime. What it left behind was, in institutional terms, a *tabula rasa*. As the "leading role of the party" was stricken from the rulebook, nothing was at hand to fill that leading role – or to generate actors to do so. The question of the moment was not "What is to be done?" but "Is there anyone who might be able to do anything – including defining what needs to be done?" (a question that only in the German case was quickly answered by the West German government stepping in).

Second, once the repressive grip of the old regime was removed, the hope of some, most likely naive from the beginning, that the constructive voices of civil society would fill the gap, came up for manifest disappointment. Again, the German example is instructive for its extremity: in the interval between the crumbling of the old and the externally engineered construction of the new regime, it was largely exit, not voice, that reigned the hour (Hirschman 1993). To the extent society involved itself at all in the reconstruction of political authority, initiatives were feeble, mobilization low, concepts and programs muddled, and organizational patterns splintered; and it was often deceptive or inapplicable Western models, rather than autochthonous preparatory work performed by the opposition to the old regime, that dominated the scene of an embryonic political discourse. Nor is this lack of crystallized political agency surprising, as the old regime had consistently and successfully repressed its emergence, and also because the regime had, in sharp contrast to all earlier cases of transition to democracy, rather successfully prevented the emergence of socio-economic cleavages (such as countryside versus city, workers versus employers, the oligarchy versus the poor) which now would have provided a fertile soil for the formation of representative collective actors. What the regime had left behind, instead, was the atomized and politically decapacitated mass of ex-clients of state socialism, accustomed to the authoritarian (as well as largely egalitarian) provision of the means of subsistence and the rules according to which life had to be conducted.

Third, while there were few (if any) residues of past authority, as well as an almost total lack of the structural predisposition and a reasonably unified will to create new centers of authority and modes of legitimation, this *tabula rasa* metaphor applies to *authority* alone, not to *power*. As far as social power is concerned, everything boils down, in the absence of effective institutional and legal parameters, to the empirical question of who, together with which others, is capable of employing whatever resources in order to protect himself and take advantage of others. As individual actors made their transition from the old to the new, all of them retained and kept hold of their skills, their positions and the material resources attached to them, their formal and informal ties to other agents, their memories of their own and other people's past actions, their habits and frames, feelings of guilt and pride, loyalties and hostilities, fears and hopes – all of which can now be employed in the struggle for social power and the defense against that power. Unsurprisingly, the dynamics of such extra-institutional power struggles, sometimes reminiscent of the state-of-nature nightmare of seventeenth century political theorists, appears to be the stuff of social life in at least some sectors of some post-communist countries for some time after 1989.

As the people of state socialist societies had not "made" the breakdown of the old regime but just "experienced" it with the same degree of surprise and amazement as outside observers, they had remained "the same" while the institutional shell of their society was crumbling. This coincidence of macro-change with micro-continuity on the individual level, together with the sense of panic, urgency, and uncertainty resulting from the former, led individual as well as nascent collective actors to making the best possible use of the assets and orientations acquired under the old regime. Needless to say, some of these residues, material as well as non-material, are more easily converted into individually useful resources, thus generating positions of power and advantage unregulated by legal rules, while others may turn out as individual handicaps or collectively harmful obstacles to the formation of a new institutional order of social, political, and economic life. Depending on the particular configuration of these residues, there are transition winners and transition losers, both among citizens within post-communist countries as well as, collectively, among the countries themselves.

Equally needless to say, the situation of panic, surprise, extravagant aspirations as well as paralyzing uncertainties, triggered by the sudden breakdown, is not the most conducive one to furthering the huge constructive and cooperative effort of institution building that society is now challenged to perform. On the contrary, we would not be surprised in this situation to see actors use the resources available to them either according to a logic of "life boat behavior" (with an extremely shrunken horizon for future-regarding and other-regarding capacities) or, alternatively, to a logic of "bunker-building" with the dominant intention to avoid, postpone and ignore the need for institutional reconstruction (i.e., of seeking shelter in the perhaps even partly restored ruins of the old order) for as long as possible.

The story that we want to relate in this book is the story of how – against these odds and in which cases – the constructive challenge of rebuilding the damaged boat essentially through the efforts of its passengers and in the "open sea" can be met and in fact has been met, though to widely varying extents according to the conditions we find in the four countries under study. Before we embark on this task, however, we need to specify the criteria by which we judge the success of these efforts – the criteria of institutional consolidation.

6   Consolidating the new order by institutionalizing agency: who shall be in charge?

In a reasonably well-ordered society, actors have a recognized license or mandate for what they are doing. They can, whatever they happen to be doing, state recognized and legitimating rules that allow or mandate them to do it. Most actors conform to these institutional frameworks in their activities most of the time. We might also speak of the institutional encapsulation of agency, with the rules and demarcation lines according to which freedoms and responsibilities are assigned to agents, are themselves arrived at in institutionally regulated forms, e.g., an orderly and legitimate procedure of law making or contract making. We believe that the successful and complete institutionalization of agency also applies as a criterion of consolidation of post-communist regimes. Let us consider what happens if consolidation fails, or gets stuck before it has been reached in full. The symptoms of such failure are ubiquitous, uncontroversial, as well as easy to recognize: the core symptom of failed institutionalization is *violence*, which may take the forms of international war, civil war, violent repression, or "civic" violence of ordinary crimes. In all these cases, the essence of violence is the absence of legitimating rules to which actors can refer – in that sense the silence that prevails when only the gun "speaks." Failure of transformation is failure to provide effective protection to the three things any "social order" that is embodied in a state is supposed to protect: life, property (as well as other material life chances), and liberty. Transition and transformation are usually seen as aiming at, but do not necessarily in fact reach, an equilibrium point of "consolidation," at which, once it is reached, violence has become an exceptional event that is not to be "reckoned with," as domains and limits of agency have been demarcated in legitimate – and can be enforced in effective – ways.

6.1 Criteria of consolidation

Turning to the concept of "consolidation"[11] or (equivalently) "institutionalization," we propose to distinguish a "vertical" and a "horizontal" dimension of the process in which consolidation occurs. A well-institutionalized social order is one in which the (contingent, "non-natural") rules according to which political and distributional conflicts are carried out are relatively immune from becoming themselves the object of such conflict. In such a social order, even the temptation of actors to embark upon a dangerous *regressus ad infinitum* (in the course of which controversies over rules spill over to controversies over the rules of rule making and further to the question of the ultimate authority – or rather the factual power! – to settle such issues) is a rare occurrence. There is, in other words a solid hiatus between rules and decisions, or regimes and elites: decision-makers take rules as valid, and even in the rare cases where they do not, they still are prepared to accept the rules of rule validation and rule interpretation (e.g., through the court system) as valid. Even as rules are contested, the rules of carrying out that contest are not – be it out of traditional reverence for the rules as they are or be it out of the calculating consideration of the prohibitive efforts that are anticipated by the actor in case he were to challenge those second-order rules as well.

Such quasi-automatic mechanisms of acceptance of rules (or at least second-order rules) "as they are" are typically absent in new regimes. After all, or so an actor dissatisfied with the rules must be disposed to think, the rules in question do not date back to some point of original rule making that is hidden in the mist of the distant past, but the rules are of recent making – and hence can be easily undone and changed. Moreover, as the makers of those rules have made them under conditions of a deep rupture and discontinuity, the rules must have been made not with obliging principles and time-honored traditions, but with consequences and specific pay-offs in mind. Moreover, being of recent and well-remembered origin, these rules have not yet "sunk in," which circumstance would evidently make it easier for the would-be challenger of the

---

[11] A more parsimonious notion of consolidation would simply frame it in negative terms and equate it to "irreversibility" of some basic features of the new regime. But operationally, in order to ascertain "irreversibility," one would have to await the test of time. "Consolidation," says diPalma (1990:35) is the process in which "the temptation of essential players to boycott the game. . . is rendered inoperative." Which leaves us with the question what exactly the features of the new regime are that frustrate such temptations, thus endowing it with a measure of resilience. It is the answer to this question that our conceptual construct of "vertical" and "horizontal" differentiation is meant to provide.

rule, to find like-minded allies, particularly as the rule makers' claim to universal beneficence and fairness of the particular set of rules in question has not yet been tested and confirmed by experience. Or the original rule makers, in anticipation of such controversies, may have taken resort to intentionally fuzzy and ambiguous or incomplete formulations of the rule which are designed to postpone conflict, which in turn may encourage the exploitation of such weak spots at the earliest point in time in order to discredit the entire rule-making endeavor as non-binding. All of this suggests that the costs are moderate and the potential personal gains significant from an effort to have the rules revised according to "my" liking, even if that may require the deployment of a means of power and violence to implement the change. It seems to follow from these considerations that new regimes depend on the rapid, in fact sometimes hasty, adoption of new rules; that these rules (unless backed up by strong sanctioning powers, such as an occupation regime) are relatively transparent as to their origin and originating intentions; that they are not yet tested, proven, or widely supported; and that therefore structural inhibitions to embark upon a new round of rule making are weak, especially if the political or economic pay-offs are expected to be significant by the challengers. All of which leads us to expect that "new" regimes are likely to get involved in a never-ending process of rule making and rule revision without ever reaching a state of stability. The policy areas in which this dynamic of constant flux has been observed in various post-communist polities include such core areas as the division of government and presidential powers, the control over the secret services, the media regime, the governing of higher education, minority rights, and, perhaps most significantly, the privatization process and property rights.

In contrast to such fluidity of rule making, in consolidated regimes the defining presence of a robust hiatus between rules and decisions means that virtually all decisions take place "under" accepted rules and in accordance with the domains of action assigned through such rules to private and public actors. After all, the fact that rules have existed for a long time suggests that they have allowed for at least viable outcomes. At the same time, the cost–benefit ratio of changing them becomes incalculable. As the result of these two considerations, rules become "stickier" the longer they have been in force, and the system governed by them path dependent (which, to be sure, may in turn itself constitute a rigidity with potentially de-consolidating consequences).

What are the formal properties of "consolidated" institutional systems? Our preliminary answer to this question comes in two parts. Using the spatial metaphors of the "vertical" and the "horizontal" dimension, we look at the two ways in which domains of action are demarcated.

(1) As far as the *vertical* dimension is concerned, consolidated systems are those to which the following property applies: every actor's decision making is constrained by higher-order decision-making rules, i.e., rules that are not at the disposition of the actor himself, but to which the actor can refer as a license for or legitimation of his own decision making. For example, parliaments may decide on a piece of legislation, but not, at least not at the same time and often not even with the same (simple) majority, on the rules that govern law making itself. These rules are of a somehow "higher" order of validation and durability than the rules resulting from simple law making. The problem here is that, as hierarchies cannot indefinitely be extended upwards, agents must be capable of performing *self*-supervisory functions. They must develop the capacity to decide on rules that are meant to be self binding, and to comply with these rules, once adopted, *as if* they had been imposed and enforced by some hierarchically superior actor. To be sure, the authority (or capacity to bind) of "our" past decisions is thoroughly fictitious. The hiatus between the contingent and the non-contingent is in many instances not an objective, but an imagined and recognized one. The fact is that "we" could easily change the rules according to changing majorities or changing preferences. The authority of the rules is thus equivalent to the capacity of agents *to overcome such opportunistic temptations* to revise the rules according to present expediency, which in turn is a function of the *opportunity costs* of compliance (i.e., of the amount of utilities I forego by complying) and the *trust* "we" lodge in other actors (i.e., the expected probability that they, too, will be able to overcome opportunistic inclinations and comply in analogous cases). The "vertical" authority of self-imposed rules, even though they do not in fact derive from some higher level of authority (such as, ultimately, the will of God), does thus appear to ultimately reside in the nature of the distributional game actors are involved in (positive versus constant sum), the distributional gains expected to be made by individual actors, and the trusting expectation that others will reciprocate compliance. This trust, understood as a robust background assumption of some basic benevolence and the cooperative dispositions of other people, can be the sedimented result of many rounds of successful interaction that have occurred in the past. In case consolidation is strong (or, which amount to virtually the same: if civility is developed), a spill-over is unlikely to occur from disagreement about rules to disagreement about those second-order rules that are supposed to govern the condition of our disagreement on the rules. All of which yields the prediction that the authority of self-imposed rules will be weak, and therefore consolidation difficult, if much is at stake for the parties involved, if growth is perceived to be zero or negative, and if trust is

poorly developed. Inversely, and to complete the vicious circle, all these negative conditions are much more likely to prevail if the effectiveness of self-binding mechanisms is (perceived to be) low.

(2) *"Horizontal"* differentiation is our second conceptual criterion for consolidation. A measure of such differentiation is the degree of insulation of institutional spheres from each other and the limited convertibility of status attributes from one sphere to the other. State socialism is an institutional order that systematically obstructs horizontal differentiation and maximizes inter-domain convertibility of resources, thereby creating a pattern of "tight coupling" of domains. Without discussing the issue whether and to what extent state socialist societies have actually been "monolithic" in reality, it is safe to assume that they have tried to maximize their "unitary" (and in this sense "totalitarian") quality according to their own guiding theory and self-image, beginning with formulae such as the "leading role of the party" or the "unity of economic and social policy," etc. If the state executive can directly mandate investment decisions, or if, conversely, large investors can "buy" seats in the legislature or positions in the administration, we deal with instances of "tight coupling" which is the opposite of a "consolidated" social order. The same applies when political power controls the pro-duction of scientific truth and science in turn, by virtue of its pretense to "scientific socialism," claims to legitimate political strategies. For one thing, what makes tight coupling, or the convertibility of media, a precarious social arrangement is the fact that shock waves that occur in one institutional sphere are easily and dangerously transmitted across feeble or non-existing demarcation lines. For another, tight coupling nurtures irresponsible behavior as it provides ample opportunity, as well as incentives, to either blame others if things go wrong or to positively exploit others (as in the case of "soft budget constraints"). What we have in mind here as a contrasting model of institutional pluralism is a rich diversity of domains, each of them "staffed" with competent actors that are capable of performing the specific function assigned to them without being under the dictate of, corrupted by, or otherwise subject to binding premises set by the agents within other sectors or domains.

6.2   Rules, resources, recognition

Much of the ongoing transformation process can actually be concep-tualized in terms of the splitting up of encompassing and multi-functional institutional compounds into smaller and functionally more specific units. Investment decisions are being separated from the state, the state from the party, the media from state control, social services from the enterprise, local governments from central governments, etc. This, at least, is the declared intention of post-communist regimes. Separating, circumscribing, and demarcating spheres of permissible and mandated activity, however, presupposes a complex set of legal rules which provide answers to questions such as: Who has access to a position? How are the activities to be performed and regulated? Who decides in case of conflict? Moreover, in order to consolidate demarcated spheres of action, actors within that sphere must be granted access to material resources, as well as information and human capital. Finally, a reasonably plausible justification for the location of demarcation rules must be available which helps in the understanding and recognition (insiders as well as outsiders) of why, for instance, a certain case is to be processed by a Federal rather than a District court, or why a certain kind of medication must be administered by doctors rather than nurses. All three of these conditions – call them *rules, resources, and recognition* – must be provided for before we can speak of "institutionalized" or "consolidated" agency. In order for domains of agency to become independent, they must be constituted as such through the allocation of legal and other resources. Political inaction is not enough for horizontal differentiation to unfold.

Assigning specified institutional locations for actors and functions and endowing them with resources, rules, and recognition is the opposite of what is otherwise easily confused with the process of differentiation "from below." This opposite is perhaps best captured by the distinction of "devolution" versus "appropriation." Differentiation through the unregulated appropriation of desired (or the abandonment of undesired) domains of activities is the dominant impulse that drives actors subsequent to the decomposition of the old regime – but before any new regime has taken hold. In contrast, the task of the new regime is to see to it, through a difficult and precarious strategy of institution building, power sharing, and the devolution of power, that domains become operative, that they do not dominate or obstruct each other, and that boundaries between domains are effectively enforced. In other words, what we mean by horizontal differentiation as one of the essential aspects of consolidation is the opposite of a largely passive and retreatist government allowing powerful social actors to grab those spheres of activity that they are capable of and interested in bringing under their control.

The activity of governments and law makers when building institutional domains and assigning adequately endowed and recognized actors to them is arguably the most demanding and most precarious step that must be performed in the process of transformation. The problem is that such demarcation of domains, as well as allocation of agents to those domains, is an act of "investment" of political power, whereas the nascent centers of political agency in post-communist societies (parliaments, parties, presidencies, governments) typically seem to see the situation as one in which it is imperative for them to bring as many resources and spheres of action under their control. Power is simply too scarce for any of it to be invested, rather than consumed in the interest of enabling the power holder to extract the resources that enable him to stay in power. Power spending in order to maximize control – rather than power investing in the interest of devolution, institution building, and eventually power sharing – is the order of the day. The temptation appears almost irresistible for governments to bring the media, the educational system, the trade unions, strategic sectors of former state industry, or local governments under their control rather than to concede and assign to them a space of autonomous agency. Again, it is the characteristic strategic exigencies of the forces and incentives that prevail under the conditions of breakdown and transformation that render the achievement of consolidation, understood here as the creation of relatively autonomous spheres of action, so exceedingly difficult.

The obsession with discretionary power spending appears to be as rational in its motivation as it is tragic in its consequences. It is rational because the making of rules and the granting of autonomous domains of action are, in an environment of massive de-institutionalization and equally massive time pressure, things that enjoy very low priority, particularly if rules are anticipated to be short lived and poorly enforced. For spending governing capacity not on the allocation of immediate and tangible benefits through decree, but in the making of rules is typically not seen as rewarding, particularly as rule making always involves not only the *self-binding* of the rule maker, but also *empowering* or *enabling* others, i.e., power sharing. Binding oneself to rules, giving up discretionary powers involves always the granting of some freedom of action to others. Given the perception of an environment that is both hostile and uncertain, the holders of power are *too weak to share and to delegate it* by investing it in rule making. Post-communist power holders have in fact often very good reasons to believe that, in order to stay in power, they cannot afford to share it with others, as no enforcement mechanism, neither formal nor informal, is in place which could generate some confidence that sharing power would not turn into the outright abandonment of power.

As a consequence, establishing binding rules and entering into lasting arrangements must appear virtually suicidal to any holder of economic or political resources in an institutionally insecure and low trust environment. What results is the pathology of permanent *ad-hoc* tinkering through an often hyper-centralized practise of ruling by unilateral decrees, rather than authority building through self-binding and other-empowering rules that concede and demarcate spaces for autonomous action. Power holders are too weak to engage in the development of horizontal differentiation and power sharing, although a richly differentiated arrangement, at least if combined with channels for consultation and bargaining linking and mediating between constituent domains, might well increase the overall governing capacity the system generates. Again, a vicious circle model suggests itself: because their governing capacity is so limited, holders of political power tend to rely on decrees rather than institution building and power sharing, which in turn will render political control more contested and more precarious.

The pathologies of "decreeism" obviate both what we have called here "vertical" differentiation, according to which conflict is embedded in a recognized framework of rules and procedures that prescribe how it is to be carried out, and the "horizontal" differentiation of relatively autonomous domains of action and the pursuit of interest.[12] Because society is so intensely felt to be in a state of disorder and fragmentation, the authoritarian impulse, so firmly rooted in the political culture of CEE societies, of resorting to some "iron fist" can become irresistible – with the tragic result of perpetuating the very conditions of "disorder" that activate that impulse. What this study attempts to demonstrate is both the reality of these vicious circles and the conditions and forces that have helped post-communist societies, if to a widely varying extent, to extricate themselves from their impact.

---

[12] A conceptualization that is remarkably similar to the two axes of differentiation proposed here can be found in Higley and Pakulski 1995.

Mapping Eastern Europe

1 Introduction

It is a truism to say that the present and its continuation into the future are determined by the past. Post-communist societies, however, have multiple pasts. We may think of, at least, three different pasts exercising their causal influence on the present: the communist period, the more remote pre-communist period, and the very immediate period of extrication from the communist regimes. The critical question then becomes how and to what extent these three pasts have shaped the national transformation paths.

The most popular argument in "transitology" is certainly the one which points at the negative impact of 40 years of communism on mentalities and political culture. People in Eastern Europe, it is argued, have become used to patronage and protection under the old regime; they deeply distrust legal procedures and political elites; they tend to be skeptical of anything new and, thus, resist changes. The egalitarian ideologies of Marxism, sometimes bordering on a culture of envy, are supposed to be an obstacle to economic reforms that will inevitably make some groups better off than others. It is assumed that those attitudes and patterns of behavior will continue at least during the early transition and constrain the speed and direction of reform. Likewise, the economic legacies of communism are supposed to impede current reform efforts. Post-communist societies inherited, among other things, an outdated capital stock, distorted sectoral structures, oversized firms, arbitrarily allocated credits, a substantial monetary overhang, and a huge foreign debt from the past regime. Those "legacies of Leninist rule" (Jowitt

1992a) will render a transition to democratic capitalism rather difficult in Eastern Europe.

Yet the communist decades may well turn out to have been a brief historical episode without a lasting impact. According to the "return of history" argument, the cultural and institutional heritage of the pre-communist period may prove to be momentous to the processes of consolidation in the region.[1] Traditional values and orientations which hibernated during the communist period may emerge again and determine the future of post-communist societies. Likewise, nationalist movements and old ethnic conflicts will revive and spread throughout the region. In this view, the countries of "Central Europe," which had strong cultural and institutional ties to Western Europe before the communist takeover, appear to be in a much better position to establish democracy and capitalism on a permanent basis than other transition countries. At the same time, the importance of communist legacies can be questioned by pointing at the decisive role of the choices and outcomes of the national extrication processes (Bruszt and Stark 1991). Agreements and decisions made in the short "historical moment" when the political regime change was brought about may exercise a causal influence on the speed and direction of later policy choices.

The aim of this chapter is to present comparative profiles of the three (respectively four) countries under analysis at the outset of transformation.[2] We shall provide some background information for subsequent chapters on transformation paths as well as justifying the selection of the country sample. We shall briefly compare the socio-economic and political development of the countries prior to 1989 and try to identify the cultural and legal traditions they share. In order to sharpen the country profiles, the chapter covers all CEE countries: Bulgaria, Czechoslovakia, the GDR, Hungary, Poland, and Romania. We argue that the popular distinction between East Central and South Eastern Europe captures only a small part of the inter-country variations in economic, political, social, and cultural dimensions. Moreover, because of the striking affinities between Czechoslovakia and the GDR, between Hungary and Poland, and between Bulgaria and Romania, our three countries are in fact representative of the whole region.

Section 2 covers the entire period before 1989 and deals with both the pre-communist and the communist periods of the CEE countries. Section

[1] See, e.g., Putnam's instant classic (1993) which convincingly demonstrates the importance of "civic traditions" deriving from the last centuries for successful democratic governance in Italy today.
[2] In this chapter, Czechoslovakia is treated as one entity. Yet we try to hint at the differences between the two republics.

3 focuses on the "annus mirabilis" of 1989 and compares the extrication processes in the six countries. Here, the purpose is to identify patterns of regime breakdown which may have shaped the character of the new political order. Section 4 tries to spell out some of the mechanisms by which the "three pasts" have contributed to the transformation processes.

2 Bulgaria, Czechoslovakia, and Hungary at the outset of transformation: comparative country profiles

2.1 The pre-communist period

World War I brought the defeat of the German, Habsburg, Ottoman, and Russian empires which had dominated the region. These four empires were replaced with a dozen newly created, recreated or reshaped nation states. Czechoslovakia and Hungary were carved out of the Habsburg empire. Hungary became the biggest territorial loser of World War I. With the Trianon Treaty, the country lost about two thirds of its territory. Poland was restored by merging former German, Habsburg, and Russian territories. Bulgaria and Romania which had been independent states since 1878 saw sweeping territorial changes, too. Whilst Romania was significantly enlarged, Bulgaria had to cede territories.

The new territorial settlement was fraught with problems (Rothschild 1993: chapter 1). The new states were heterogenous and suffered from problems of national integration. They were highly involved in quarrels over borders and the treatment of ethnic minorities. In addition, they were in various ways caught between Germany and Russia. The demise of the old empires was also associated with a number of economic problems (Dornbusch 1992; Teichova 1988). New currencies had to be introduced in a turbulent economic environment. Trade and production had to be adjusted to the new borders.

Although they shared a number of problems, the countries in the new Central and Eastern Europe also differed in many ways. Two main division lines ran across the region. On the one hand, there was a fundamental socio-economic and political divide between Czechoslovakia (and Germany) and the other countries. A second demarcation line, located further to the East, separated the Latin part of Eastern Europe from Bulgaria and Romania.

In the inter-war period, Czechoslovakia was the only industrialized country in the region.[3] GDP per capita reached about two-thirds of the

[3] Within Czechoslovakia, however, a huge gap between the Czech lands and the more backward Slovakia existed. In socio-economic terms, the Slovak parts of

German level. In contrast, the other countries clearly belonged to the European economic periphery.[4] Hungary and Poland and even more so Bulgaria and Romania were agrarian economies which suffered from stalled land reforms and a chronic shortage of capital. Due to its more advanced state of economic development, Czechoslovakia was the only country in the region where sizeable and politically conscious bourgeois and working classes as well as mature civil societies existed. It also scored significantly better on socio-economic indicators, such as school enrollment and life expectancy. Finally, Czechoslovakia was also the East European country with the most liberal foreign trade regime and the best stabilization performance during the inter-war years.

This economic divide corresponded with differences in democratic consolidation. All East European countries saw the introduction of the universal ballot after World War I. However, Czechoslovakia was the only country in the region where democracy was not brought to an end from within, but by outside intervention. Even before the shift to authoritarian rule, democracy and parliamentarism remained largely formal outside Czechoslovakia and Germany. The other countries were democratic in form, but essentially bureaucratic in character. They were effectively run by the state bureaucracy which was generally able to produce the desired election results. The existing socio-economic stratification, the weak national integration of the new states, and the prevalence of political-cultural traditions such as the acceptance of state supremacy, messianic concepts of political change, and the disregard of institutions, proved to be inimical to a consolidation of democracy (Bibó 1946; Stokes 1989; Schöpflin 1993: chapter 1).

A second division line separated Czechoslovakia, Hungary, and Poland from Bulgaria and Romania (Giaro 1993; Wieacker 1990: 7f.). Whereas the former countries enjoyed a long tradition of affiliation with the Latin Church and Roman Law and were part of the Austrian sphere of legislative power, the latter had close ties with the East Roman Empire, the Byzantine version of Roman Law, and the Greek Church. The Balkan states turned toward West European constitutional and legal thought and practice no earlier than the second half of the nineteenth century. They took part in the European-wide move toward codification in the late nineteenth century and adopted a body of law built upon West European

---

Czechoslovakia came closer to the other countries than to Bohemia and Moravia.

[4] Estimates of inter-war GDP regularly arrive at the same ordinal country ranking. Yet it is not clear whether Polish GDP was closer to the (higher) Hungarian or to the (lower) Bulgarian and Romanian level. For different estimates, see Harrison 1994.

models. Yet their law was more eclectic and less firmly established than in the two other countries.

In the inter-war period, standardization and codification of law were seen as essential elements of state building in most East European countries. This particularly applied to the states which had been newly created or significantly enlarged after World War I and had inherited a number of different legal orders. Yet in most of the countries the process never became fully consolidated (Korkisch 1958: 201–5). Standardization and codification were not completed before the sovietization of the countries, thus leaving pre-communist law in a somewhat preliminary state.[5] Hungary, for example, did not even have a written constitution until 1949.

The disparities in socio-economic development and differences in legal traditions also manifested themselves in the inter-war social policy arrangements. Czechoslovakia inherited Austria's social insurance system addressed to the needs of the industrial working class from the Danube Monarchy. The social security net was substantially improved, especially in terms of coverage, during the inter-war period. Czechoslovakia was almost in step with the pioneer country Germany at that point of time (Bohata 1990). In Hungary and Poland, too, inter-war social reforms were essentially patterned on the German–Austrian model. Yet owing to the lower level of socio-economic development, the coverage ratio was much lower in both countries. The schemes covered mainly urban wage earners, while the vast majority of the population working in agriculture remained unprotected in the 1920s. In Bulgaria and Romania, too, the social security system remained very patchy before the communist take-over and left the agrarian population practically uncovered.[6]

2.2 The legacies of communism

The end of World War II was again associated with sweeping territorial changes. Germany was eventually divided. Poland was "moved" to the West. Czechoslovakia lost the Carpatho-Ukraine, Romania Bessarabia, and northern Bukovina to the Soviet Union. Bulgaria and Hungary were

[5] For a synopsis of inter-war legal provisions, see Heitger et al. 1992: 124–36, 175–92.
[6] Take, e.g., the health insurance coverage. In countries, like Germany, Austria, or Great Britain, more than 30 percent of the population were covered by the national health insurance schemes in the mid twenties. In Czechoslovakia the respective figure amounted to nearly 20 percent, in Hungary to 12 percent, in Poland to 7 percent, and in Bulgaria less than 5 percent of the population were protected (no data available for Romania, see ILO 1927: 182–87).

more or less restored in their inter-war borders. The territorial changes and the related massive resettlements changed the countries' ethnic composition and their balance of internal and external minorities (table 2.1).[7] Poland became internally homogeneous. Relevant internal minorities have continued to exist in Bulgaria (Turks), Romania (Hungarians), and Slovakia (Hungarians). With a quarter of ethnic Hungarians living abroad, Hungary has by far been the most externally heterogeneous country.

The end of World War II brought Eastern Europe under Soviet control (Rothschild 1993: chapter 3; Swain and Swain 1993: chapters 2 and 3). Between 1944 and 1949, communist regimes were installed in all countries. The sovietization of the region meant the forced adoption of a uniform model of communism. The East European countries were incorporated into a system of Soviet-controlled supra-national organisations, such as Cominform or CMEA. The national constitutions were modelled upon the Soviet Constitution of 1936. The planning offices which had been established to handle post-war reconstruction were transformed into Gosplan-type Planning Commissions. Nationalizations were further extended. Save for Poland, agriculture was collectivized. All countries embarked upon forced industrialization along Soviet lines. After Stalin's death, Soviet control loosened and a limited "return to diversity" (Rothschild 1993) set in which gained further momentum in the 1980s. However, this process left the essentials of the system untouched. The suppression of workers in the GDR in 1953 and in Poland in 1956, the invasions of Hungary in 1956 and Czechoslovakia in 1968, and the declaration of martial law in Poland in 1981 again and again stressed the limits to reform.

All countries experienced a massive social upheaval under communism. The industrialization of the East European economies led both to a massive sectoral reallocation of labor and to rapid urbanization. Save for Czechoslovakia and the GDR, the Central and East European countries witnessed a transformation from primarily rural, agricultural societies to industrial, urban ones. The property reforms sealed the end of the old economic elites. Highly stratified societies were transformed into more egalitarian ones with a low degree of stable social differentiation. Although the political leadership formed a new type of elite, the nomenklatura, unlike earlier elites it was not based on the possession of inheritable property. Political power could to some extent be handed down from one generation to the next, but the inheritance was much less secure.

---

[7] For the distinction between internal and external minorities, see Elster 1991: 450f.

Table 2.1. *External and internal minorities in the CEE countries (millions)*

	Bulgaria (1987)	Czech Republic (1991)	Slovak Republic (1991)	Hungary (1987)	Poland (1992)	Romania (1987)	Others	Total	External minorities (%)
Bulgarians	7.65	–	–	–	–	0.01	0.14	7.80	1.9
Czechs	–	9.40	0.06	–	0.01	–	0.01	9.48	0.8
Germans	–	0.07	–	0.22	0.35	0.54	–	78.11	–
Hungarians	–	–	0.60	9.56	–	1.93	0.66	12.75	25.0
Poles	–	0.08	0.01	–	37.00	–	1.88	38.97	5.1
Romanians	0.01	–	–	0.01	–	19.52	0.29	19.83	1.7
Slovaks	–	0.30	3.99	0.12	0.02	0.02	0.01	4.46	10.5
Turks	0.82	–	–	–	–	–	–	–	–
Gypsies	0.16	0.40	0.40	0.50	0.15	0.50	–	–	–
Others	0.36	0.05	0.21	0.29	0.77	0.22	–	–	–
Total Population	9.00	10.30	5.27	10.70	38.30	22.74	–	–	–
Internal Minorities (%)	15.00	8.70	24.00	10.66	3.40	14.17	–	–	–

Source: Brunner 1993: Annex 1; Kubiak 1993: Table 1; own calculations.

At the same time, however, the traditional economic hierarchy within the region remained largely intact (Ehrlich 1991, 1993; János 1994: 3–6).[8] In the second half of the 1980s, per-capita incomes in Czechoslovakia and the GDR were still significantly higher than in the other countries. At the same time, the gap between Czechoslovakia and the GDR, on the one hand, and the developed OECD countries had widened (Havlik 1992). The greatest leaps forward were accomplished by Bulgaria and Slovakia. Within Czechoslovakia, the economic gap between the two republics was drastically reduced. Whilst in 1948 per-capita income in Slovakia was 40 percent lower than in the Czech lands, this gap was down to 13 percent in 1988 (OECD 1994a: 44).[9] In the 1980s, Bulgaria surpassed Poland in terms of per-capita income and Hungary with regard to life expectancy and health care.[10]

In the political realm, the communist takeovers meant the installation of autocratic regimes. These regimes basically persisted until 1989. Yet governments exercised their rule in different ways and differed in their strategies of regime stabilization and legitimation.

In the 1980s, repression was harshest in Romania, the last totalitarian regime in our sample. The Hungarian and Polish regimes clearly were the most liberal ones, even after the imposition of martial law in Poland in 1981. In both countries, first tendencies toward a separation of state and party occurred. However, the nature of political pluralism differed: whereas in Poland there existed a strong autonomous opposition, pluralism in Hungary was largely confined to the communist party (Frentzel-Zagórska 1990: 762–6). Bulgaria, Czechoslovakia, and the GDR ranked somewhere in between.[11] In Czechoslovakia, the mass exodus in the wake of the suppression of the Prague spring led to a lasting weakening of the oppositional potential. In the GDR, the proximity of the Federal Republic had a similar effect. Also, in both these countries state repression was very harsh.

Bulgaria and Romania were set apart from the other countries by

[8] From a comparative perspective, convergence within the Eastern bloc was apparently less pronounced than convergence among the industrialized market economies (Baumol 1986: 1079f.).

[9] Other estimates arrive at an even stronger equalization of incomes. According to Myant (1993: 222), Slovakia's per-capita income in 1989 amounted to 94 percent of the Czech level. Wolchik (1991: 187–91) reports that an earlier 66:100 ratio was reduced to a mere 96:100.

[10] In 1987, the United Nations' Human Development Index which combines per-capita income with socio-economic indicators was thus higher for Bulgaria than for Hungary (UNDP 1990). For a critical assessment of this index, see Srinivasan 1994.

[11] This ranking is confirmed by various civil liberties indexes (for an overview, see Scully and Slottje 1991).

certain "sultanistic" tendencies and a stronger reliance on nationalist mobilization. In Romania, the personalization of power gave rise to a strange blend of "dynastic socialism" (Tismaneanu 1985). In Bulgaria, similar, albeit less pronounced, tendencies came to a halt with the death of Liudmila Zhivkova in July 1981. Both governments also shared a strong commitment to nationalism (Troebst 1992; Verdery 1991). In the late 1980s, they aggressively promoted the forced assimilation of ethnic minorities.

Outside Bulgaria and Romania, conditions were less favorable to nationalist mobilization. Czechoslovakia and the GDR were countries with a low degree of national integration. The GDR government feared that any tinkering with nationalism would automatically raise the delicate issue of German unification. Likewise, the Czechoslovak government was confronted with the tensions between Czechs and Slovaks which had been present ever since the foundation of Czechoslovakia. In Hungary and Poland, the countries with the highest level of national integration, playing the nationalist card was complicated by the existence of external minorities in communist "brethren" states[12] and the traditional anti-Russian element in Hungarian and Polish nationalism.

In the economic realm, communist regimes remained characterized by the dominance of state ownership and bureaucratic allocation. The insistence upon the maintenance of a political monopoly affected all moves toward market socialism (Kornai 1992). Yet substantial inter-country differences could be observed in the political field. The deceleration of economic growth which set in in the 1970s gave room for economic experiments and tinkering with economic reforms. As the legitimation of the communist regimes became increasingly based upon the promise of a steady increase in material well-being, communist governments desperately looked for a way out. In the late 1980s, differences with regard both to the reform stance and to macro-economic performance loomed large (Fischer and Gelb 1991: 92–4).

As for economic reforms, a clear divide emerged in the 1980s. Whilst the Polish and, in particular, the Hungarian government embarked on economic reforms in order to increase economic performance, the other countries' governments remained resistant to reforms and committed to the traditional notion of a centrally planned economy. Economic reforms in Hungary and Poland mainly aimed at the decentralization of economic decision making. Core elements included the liberalization of private

---

[12] The increasing international isolation of Romania made it easier for the Hungarian government to rally domestic support by protesting against the treatment of the Hungarian minority in Romania.

economic activities, a greater tolerance toward the so-called "second economy," the strengthening of enterprise autonomy and self-management, price reform and subsidies reduction, as well as liberalization of trade and a gradual opening of the economy. From a comparative point of view, reforms were more consistent and comprehensive in Hungary than in Poland (Kozminski 1992: 315–18). In Hungary, economic reforms were initiated in 1968. After a period of recentralization and reform abortion in the 1970s, these reforms were resumed in the late 1970s and gained further momentum in the mid 1980s (Berend 1990; Révész 1990). Among other things, reforms brought the creation of a two-tier banking system in 1987 and the adoption of the Western-style company, bankruptcy, competition, and tax law. In Poland, the post-martial law governments stressed their commitment to economic reforms along Hungarian lines. The reforms introduced in 1982, 1986, and 1988 remained, however, half-hearted (Myant 1993: 59–80).

In contrast, the Bulgarian, Czechoslovak, East German, and Romanian economies remained fairly unreconstructed planned economies until the end of 1989. Here, the measures which were adopted since the early 1970s aimed at the "perfectioning" of the system and were largely limited to the reorganization of the planning bureaucracy and the merging of firms. Consequently, these economies were characterized by smaller private sectors, higher degrees of monopolization, less autonomous enterprises, and higher shares of CMEA trade than in Hungary and Poland.

Whereas the GDR and Romania resisted reforms until the bitter end, the Czechoslovak and, especially, the Bulgarian governments, in response to Gorbachev's "perestroika" and the increasingly visible deterioration of the economic situation, announced and initiated some reforms along Hungarian lines in the late 1980s. The Bulgarian reform attempts culminated in the adoption of the famous Decree 56 which introduced a rudimentary Western-style company law, enlarged the scope for private economic activity, and outlined first steps toward the creation of a capital market, in January 1989 (Wyzan 1991: 85–9). These reforms, as well as their much more timid Czechoslovak counterparts (Myant 1993: 155–67; Wolchik 1991: 239–48), were, however, never really implemented before the end of 1989.

The differences in commitment to central planning partly manifested themselves also in the field of civil law (Brunner 1992: 41f.; Giaro 1993: 342; Westen 1993: 13f.). Ironically, the countries which went furthest in giving up the traditional unity of civil law were the most "Western" ones, Czechoslovakia and the GDR. In Czechoslovakia, even a special Business Code for economic transactions within the socialist sector was adopted. In contrast, Hungary and Poland remained more strongly committed to the Western (and their own pre-communist) legal tradition.

East European countries also differed with regard to their macro-economic records in the late 1980s. These differences were only loosely related to the inclination toward economic reform. Whilst Czechoslovakia and the GDR scored relatively well, reform-resistant Bulgaria faced severe macro-economic imbalances in the second half of the 1980s, as did Poland. Hungary, the forerunner of economic reforms, took an intermediate position. As budget deficits indicate, macro-economic policy in the second half of the 1980s was tighter in Czechoslovakia, the GDR, and Romania than in Bulgaria, Hungary, and Poland. Due to price reforms and the softening of wage policy, open inflation was highest in Hungary and Poland. In the other countries, inflation remained repressed. In Bulgaria, macro-economic imbalances led to the accumulation of a huge monetary overhang.

The deteriorating economic situation of the East European countries also manifested itself in the rise of the foreign debt. With the exception of Romania, all East European countries saw a massive increase in foreign debt in the second half of the 1980s. This particularly applied to Bulgaria where net foreign debt nearly quadrupled between 1985 and 1988. In the late 1980s, Bulgaria, Hungary, and Poland belonged to the group of the most indebted countries in the world. In contrast, Czechoslovak foreign debt, albeit increasing, remained modest. The GDR benefitted from its special relationship with the Federal Republic which provided privileged access to foreign credit. The Romanian Ceaucescu government followed a historically unique policy of repaying its foreign debt ahead of schedule at all cost which resulted in an exhaustion of the economy and a dramatic lowering of the population's living standards.

In Hungary and Poland, economic reforms were accompanied by certain cautious social policy reforms. While the Czechoslovak, Bulgarian, Romanian, and East German social policy systems remained fairly unchanged till the end of communist rule, some gradual changes in employment policies could be observed in Hungary and Poland in the 1980s. Well before the demise of the communist regime, a sort of unemployment benefit was set up and a number of employment promotion measures, although insignificant in quantitative terms, were introduced. From the mid 1980s on, the Hungarian and the Polish governments became more open-minded and honest concerning the problems of poverty and hidden unemployment (Ferge 1989: 99f.; Sziráczki 1990: 717f.; Szurgacz 1991: 298).

The Czechoslovak and the Bulgarian social policy systems remained closely oriented toward the Soviet model, set up in the early 1950s, during the communist period. Hungary, by contrast, was the country that went furthest in departing from this model. In particular, Hungary blazed a trail in family policies. The country was the first in the region to set up a system of paid child-care leave (already in 1967) and, altogether, had a very generous family benefit system (Voirin 1993: 39). This family policy record provides one important explanation, as to why Hungary had by far the lowest female labor force participation rates among the East European countries in the 1980s.[13]

There was a close correlation between reform-readiness and greater income inequalities. Economic reforms tended to allow for wider income differentials within and between state enterprises. Moreover, chances to engage in lucrative private sector activities were unevenly distributed. Hungary and Poland were thus set apart from their neighboring countries by their relatively inegalitarian income distribution. According to most estimates, gross earnings as well as net household incomes were more equally distributed in the latter countries than in the former (cf. Atkinson and Micklewright 1992). Moreover, in Hungary and Poland the level of poverty was significantly higher than in Czechoslovakia (cf. Sipos 1992).

2.3 Summary assessment

The analysis leads to the question whether the similarities and differences mentioned permit a clear-cut clustering of the six countries. In the literature an "invisible map" drawing a distinction between East Central and South Eastern Europe plays a prominent part.[14] It underlies the Visegrád cooperation as well as the traditional segmentation of research on Eastern Europe, with most comparative studies being confined either to East Central European or to the Balkan countries. However, the evidence presented above suggests that this distinction with its familiar discriminatory connotations[15] is a rather shaky basis for

---

[13] While in Czechoslovakia and Bulgaria well over 70 percent of the women at employable age were integrated into the labor market in the eighties, female participation rates amounted to slightly over 60 percent in Hungary; Poland and Romania were equally ranked in between (Boeri and Sziráczki 1993: 244).

[14] For useful summaries of the extensive literature on "Central Europe" which has mushroomed since the mid 1980s, see Fehér 1989; Judt 1990; Miszlivetz 1991.

[15] Agh (1993: 235f.), for example, distinguishes between the Eastern part of Central Europe and "Eastern Europe proper," thus clearly confirming Miszlivetz's observation: "To be a Central European means to be neither an East European nor the citizen of a Balkan state. It means to be better than the Russians, the Bulgarians, the Montenegrines. Central Europe became a program which allowed one to distinguish oneself from the 'barbarians'". (Miszlivitz 1991: 975) The authors also recall the mixture of surprise and indignation with which several Czech and Hungarian colleagues reacted when being confronted with the fact that the research project provided for a comparison of their countries with Bulgaria.

comparative research on East European transitions. This is not to deny the existence of different cultural traditions in the region. Nor is it to neglect the role of geography which clearly favors the Visegrád countries as against the Balkan states. Due to their geographical location, they are in a better position to benefit from West European economic growth and to attract Western financial support. Yet the distinction captures only a small part of the relevant initial conditions of societal transformation. On the one hand, it abstracts from the different – and not unequivocally positive – pre-communist legacies in Czechoslovakia, Hungary, and Poland. On the other hand, the map neglects the lasting impact of 40 years of communism on these societies, the effective "desertification" (Schöpflin 1993: 256) of traditional ideas, values, institutions, and solidarities under communist rule.

Taking the communist period into account, Hungary is set apart from Czechoslovakia and Bulgaria in having a long tradition of economic reforms and irresolute attempts to liberalize society. Kádár's "reform communism" had a formative influence on society and paved the way for more far-reaching reforms in the late 1980s. By contrast, Czechoslovakia and Bulgaria were "tough" communist regimes in the 1970s and 1980s. In both cases, the communist leadership remained strongly committed to central planning and authoritarian rule. Yet the imprint of communism on Bulgarian society was much stronger than in the Czechoslovak case (and within Czechoslovakia on the Slovaks than on the Czechs). The reason was that Czechoslovak society experienced the communist take-over at a different stage of socio-economic and political development than Bulgaria. Czechoslovakia had been a highly industrialized and democratic country in the inter-war period sharing the cultural and legal traditions of Western Europe. In contrast, Bulgaria did not catch up with the industrialized world until communist rule and significantly improved its relative socio-economic position in that period. Bulgaria had never truly experienced democracy in its history before the breakdown of the communist regime and was culturally separated from its Western neighbors. Inter-war Hungary has to be located somewhere in between. Like Bulgaria, it had been an agrarian society and lacked a democratic political culture. But Hungary had always had strong cultural ties to Western Europe.

Altogether, both Czechoslovakia and Hungary appear to be in a rather fortunate position at the outset of the transformation process: Czechoslovakia because of its pre-communist traditions and its favorable economic balance sheet in 1989, Hungary because of its reform communist legacies. Bulgaria initially was facing extremely bad conditions: it could not refer to a "golden" pre-communist period, it did not experience reform communism, and it was severely hit by macro-economic imbalances at the outset of transformation.

Hence, this study's country sample appears to be representative, as it covers relevant variations in important variables that are supposed to determine national transformation paths. To be sure, the discrepancy between the small number of countries and the large number of variables prevents any causal testing in the strict sense. But our sample at least allows us to consider various hypotheses which have been developed within "transitology." In addition, the three cases may be regarded as representative, as it is possible to construct "affinity pairs" (Jowitt 1992: 186f.) of countries which share a large number of relevant characteristics. It seems that for each East European country included in the analysis a complementary country outside the sample exists: Czechoslovakia and the GDR, Hungary and Poland, Bulgaria and Romania make up "twin pairs" prior to 1989 (for this argument, see also Offe 1994: 241–9). Needless to say that affinities at the outset of transformation must not turn into commonalities in overall transformation records.

3 The demise of communist rule: modes of extrication

3.1 Systemic and political revolutions

Among past periods which have left traces on the structure of the newly emerging polities, the period of extrication is the most short-lived one. Yet, its short duration is probably offset by its density and intensity, which are habitual features of revolutionary situations. Frequently they form the basis of long-lasting elements of the new order. When we speak of extrication we refer only to the political order, not to the economic and much less to the cultural sphere. Extrication means the countries' disentanglement from the main political properties of communist regimes, such as the dominant power position of the communist parties, the pervasive role of the security apparatus, or the comprehensive state and party control and streamlining of the public sphere. Hence, this period started out when the regime was challenged for the first time in full public view by opposition groups, however small, weak, and disorganized they may have been. It was the beginning of the end, the juncture where the old regime lost its total grip on the public sphere and its monopoly to define the field of political action. The period ended when the main features of the new order were established and worked, i.e., immediately after the first free elections of parliaments or presidents, as the case may be. In Poland this period began with the opening of the RTT on February 6, 1989 and ended in October 1991, the time of the first entirely free elections (Rothschild 1993: 227 ff.; Banac 1992a).[16] In Hungary it lasted from March 1989 (the first huge anti-systemic demonstrations on the anniversary of the revolution of 1848) until March/April 1990 (Bozóki 1993: 277 f.), in Bulgaria from about October 1989 (the first street demonstrations of *Ecoglasnost)* until June 1990, in (what was then) Czechoslovakia from November 1989 until June 1990, and in Romania from December 15, (the first spontaneous anti-regime rally in Timisoara) until May 20, 1990, (the day of the elections of both the president and the parliament) (Rothschild 1993: 226 ff.; Banac 1992).

The impact of this short period of extrication in terms of the risks and chances of creating a consolidated democratic political order cum market economy is ambiguous. There is, of course, the negative historical experience of the last 300 years which teaches us that the overthrow of an existing regime by a violent revolution tends to produce quite unstable democratic systems (Dahl 1991: 13; see also Karl and Schmitter 1991: 280). But this does not tell us whether the non-violent modes of extrication from the communist regimes which have been characteristic of the CEE countries are likely to contribute to the consolidation of the newly emerging polities. In order to understand the contribution of this particular period it seems appropriate to make use of the distinction between systemic and political revolutions offered by Zygmunt Bauman. According to this distinction, political revolutions adjust a political regime to the requirements of the socio-economic system and are launched by agents who represent more or less established collective "transformative" interests which cannot find an appropriate institutional expression in the extant political structure; these interests will immediately gain from the change of the political regime. In contrast, the agents of a systemic revolution do not only dismantle an old regime, but find themselves in the situation that a new society and its actors have still to be constructed (Bauman 1993).

Evidently it is this "systemic" brand which characterizes the regime transitions in the post-communist societies of the CEE. In none of the CEE countries did the old regime generate interests and actors that could easily slip into the institutional forms hastily created after the breakdown of the old regime. Everywhere it was not only necessary to produce new spaces of action and new rules of action, but at the same time the actors who were capable of making use of these new openings. This has several important implications. First, the forces which brought the old system down are not

---

[16] It might also be claimed that the extrication period ended on December 9, 1990, the date of the runoff presidential elections where Walesa was elected president. Yet we believe that the free election of the parliament is a more significant criterion for the establishment of a new political order.

likely to be those which will benefit from the "revolution," because they represent merely the dissatisfaction with the old regime which, in contrast to the conditions of a political revolution, does *not* yet bear the new order in its womb. Second and consequently, it is not likely that those united forces which brought the old regime down will continue to be united in the vision of a new order or will be satisfied with the outcomes which the new order yields for them (Bauman 1993: 5 f.). In other words, there is no determinate relation between the forces which dismantled the old regime and the character of the emerging new order. Third, systemic revolutions create an empty space which is left over after the fall of the old regime and onto which the new order has not yet had the chance to instill its mark. In this extremely open situation the actors are truly acting behind a veil of ignorance: they have no knowledge about the actual distribution of power, about the motives, interests, and actions of other (internal or external) actors, and they find themselves in the situation where huge masses of people are easily mobilized, without knowing the focal point of mobilization other than the purely negative resentment against the old regime.

Thus, actions and decisions which in the situation of a political revolution would be ephemeral and negligible because they do not meet the requirements of the "transformative" constituencies and interests, may acquire a thoroughly disproportionate relevance and exercise a lopsided influence on the evolution of the new order simply because there are no forces and structures which would assign them their relative weight(lessness). Conversely, there may be discernible patterns of the downfall of the old regime which pre-establish the boundaries and perhaps even the main elements of the space in which the actors of the extrication make their choices which then may predetermine future structures. These patterns are likely to have been shaped by the particular historical traditions of the relevant countries which, as it were, fill the vacuum which has been left by the waning regime. Hence, it can be surmised that the modes of extrication, by defining the starting point for the creation of the new polity, served as a vehicle for the transfer of historical legacies into the future. Both interpretations suggest that it cannot be ruled out that the distinct modes of extrication in the several CEE countries do matter for the character of the future political order and obtain an importance which is perhaps not inferior to the influence of the pre-communist and the communist pasts.

3.2 Different character of the breakdowns, identical causes

In saying this, we presuppose that the regime breakdowns in the diverse countries did not have the same political character, the same meaning and the same consequences in all pertinent countries. Before 1989 it was justified to speak of a "Soviet Bloc," a term which referred to the homogeneity which had been imposed on the East and Central European countries by the Soviet Union after World War II (Comisso 1991: 123 f.; v. Beyme 1994: 52). After 1989 it became obvious that the homogeneous bloc had encapsulated rather diverse countries. Given the diversity of the pre-communist countries in terms of socio-economic development, political and legal traditions and cultural orientations, the extent to which the Soviet system had been compatible with the respective host societies diverged considerably. For instance, the much appreciated historical role which Russia played in the liberation struggles of Bulgaria against the Ottoman empire, the fact that after World War II Soviet troops were never stationed in the country (Todorova 1992: 159; Rothschild 1993: 212), and that the communist regime has rightly been credited for its industrialization made the imposition of the Soviet system far more acceptable to the Bulgarians than in, say, Poland where strong anti-Russian resentments and feelings of superiority have been common for a long time. Likewise, Slovakia as a more traditional society was more receptive to the "real socialist" system than the more industrialized Czech lands. Thus, the gradual weakening and final abandonment of the coercively homogenizing force of Soviet power did not only allow these countries to retrieve their regional differentiation and to "return to diversity" (Rothschild 1993), but to pursue quite different paths of extrication.

On the other hand, it is of course not by mere accident that all East and Central European communist regimes collapsed almost simultaneously. This suggests the assumption that they all died from the same disease. As has been expounded in more detail in the introductory chapter, these countries were part of a project which aimed at the historically predetermined liberation of mankind from the yoke of capitalism and imperialism. This entailed the establishment of social structures (institutions, habits, values, modes of thinking, etc.) which claimed to be universally valid and beneficial for all peoples and which, consequently, were very much the same in countries which lived under Soviet-type regimes, irrespective of their economic, political, cultural, and historical diversity and geographical dispersion. These common properties have been called the "Leninist legacy." It was imprinted on all pertinent countries and created a number of shared institutional, ideological, economic and social elements (like, e.g., the preference for large-scale heavy industry or the absence of a politically integrating national public realm and of a shared public identity as citizens) (Jowitt 1992a; cf. also Machonin 1993).

There were essentially three common causes which finally led to the breakdown of the communist socio-policical systems. First, there was massive economic inefficiency. Second there was a complete collapse of the ideological legitimation of the systems. Third, there was a structural incapacity to adjust to new problems due to the lack of institutional devices for observing and learning. The economic failure of the system, well-known to experts both from the West and the East, became squarely visible for the East European masses through the pictures and information conveyed by the international electronic mass media. Still, economic inefficiency as such need not cause a system to collapse as long as it is accepted as either inevitable or legitimate. The view that the ill-performance of the socialist economy was widely accepted as the price which had to be paid for economic and social equality – one of the pivotal elements of the socialist ideology – is hard to validate empirically. But even if this trade-off was ever accepted as a justification for economic frugality, it lost credibility during the eighties when the principle of equality increasingly failed to meet the test of reality. The gap between the economic and political elite which had privileged access to society's resources and the masses who lived far below the mass consumption standards of the populations of the West became more and more visible (Jowitt 1992a; v. Beyme 1994: 54 ff.).

In itself the erosion of the basic legitimation of weak economic productivity did not necessarily doom the regimes to their eventual breakdown. The most serious problem which they could not solve and which finally left them unprotected was the lack of institutional learning devices which would provide them with the appropriate means to overcome their problems or at least keep them at bay. The communist regimes have become the victims of their alleged strength: the omniscience of the party and the omnipotence of the state deprived them of the capacity to learn, i.e., to adapt themselves to social change and to challenges which could not be answered in the language of state power. Gorbachev's often-invoked decision to refuse the Soviet Union's "fraternal help" for its satellite regimes finally removed a crucial constraint which up until this time had discouraged and repressed opposition tendencies which to different degrees and in different social, cultural, and political forms had emerged during the eighties; after this decision the causes which had undermined the systems long before could become operative (Przeworski 1991: 5 ff.).

Thus, the crises of the communist regimes in East and Central Europe had essentially identical causes. Yet the manifestation and intensity of the reactions were specific to the host country. The questions, then, are whether the mode of extrication in the respective countries led to the expression of particular "transformative" interests and the emergence of particular constituencies, whether it determined the political, social, religious, or economic actors who controlled the course of events and who survived the extrication period, and whether it has left lasting institutional traces on the new polity.

Poland was the only country where a broad social movement not controlled by the regime could emerge and maintain a considerable strength under the communist regime.[17] For the first time in a communist country a device of power sharing between the regime and the opposition emerged, and the novel institution of a Round Table was invented and established. During the transition period it was the main source of legitimate institutional change. Among other things, it produced – also for the first time in a communist state – the recognition of an independent workers' union, parliamentary elections whose results were not entirely predetermined by the monopoly of the communist party, i.e., an, if limited, electoral competition to which the communists were exposed under equal conditions, and finally a non-communist government in a satellite state of the Soviet Union. Poland remained the only CEE country with a genuine counterforce of the regime rooted in the society. Paradoxically, Poland was also the only country in which initially the negotiations between the regime and the opposition were not designed to abolish the regime altogether, but to reform it, the primary (non-revolutionary) request of the opposition being the legal recognition of the Solidarity Union. Consequently, the disastrous communist performance in the semi-contested elections of June 4 and 18, 1989 created a situation in which the country's politico-institutional framework was still largely communist, although the spirit of the regime was clearly broken.

In all other countries the opposition consisted of "a set of weak, diverse, and fragmented organizations" (Bruszt and Stark 1992: 30, with respect to Hungary) which could even not think of challenging the power of the regime, much less participate in anything like a power-sharing structure. Yet, in all countries they had an influence on the course of events. In *Hungary* the regime was pulled down mainly by the interplay of a powerful reform wing of the communist party and the opposition which was able to mobilize huge masses in critical moments. The reformers had emerged during a period of gradual economic reform which had been inaugurated at the beginning of the eighties and whose limited results had convinced them of the necessity for major politico-

---

[17] We dismiss the Catholic Church, another important actor on the Polish scene, because it cannot be counted as an anti-regime force which struggled directly for a downright change of government.

institutional reforms. The opposition had, as in Bulgaria, been organized mainly around environmental causes. Mutual support between the reform wing of the party and the weak opposition was essential to the Hungarian way of extrication. The former needed the voice (and at least the appearance of strength, as expressed in their capacity to mobilize more masses in the streets than the regime) of the latter in their struggle against the orthodox hardliners of the party, and the latter needed the protection of the reformers within the party for their survival (Bruszt 1991; Bruszt and Stark 1992; Bozóki 1992). As in Poland, these interactions took place (at least initially) under the shadow of possible Soviet intervention.

The *GDR*, suffering from the congenital defect that it was not an entrenched nation-state ruled by a communist regime, but rather a communist regime ruling over a more or less randomly shaped territory and its population, had to cope with two difficulties which were absent in the other countries: first, it had to prove itself successful in order to legitimize not only the regime, but the existence of the country itself as an independent state; second, it was exposed to the unique threat of an attractive exit option for its citizens, namely the alternative to escape the rule of the regime without at the same time being forced to take the heavy burden of emigration into a foreign country. The impossibility to draw a distinction between the regime and the country, i.e., between ideological and national interests may be one of the reasons why after 1961 the communist party of the GDR did not generate a reform wing that struggled for liberalization of the regime. Not surprisingly, the regime finally became the victim of this particular weakness, viz. mass exit which merged with mass mobilization in the streets.

While the GDR was probably the regime most dependent upon the Soviet Union's promise of "fraternal help," in contrast, the *Bulgarian* regime was least vulnerable to Gorbachev's abandonment of this guarantee. Due to the traditionally friendly relations between Bulgaria and Russia, the communist regime was not seen as being imposed by an unfriendly foreign power and therefore did not stir up questions of national sovereignty and anti-Russian sentiments. Also its authoritarian character was barely challenged. The opposition was extremely weak, consisting of a loose coalition of small groups with almost no national organization, incompatible political goals and platforms and more or less amateurish leaders (Todorova 1992; Rothschild 1993: 250 ff.; Kolarova and Dimitrov 1994). Hence, the turnabout of the regime started with what was largely regarded as a coup, namely the deposition of Zhivkov on November 10, 1989. Despite the establishment of Round Table Talks between the regime and the opposition, the change was by and large pursued as the politics of perestroika, i.e., as a reform of the regime from above.

In *Czechoslovakia* the regime was as orthodox, rigid and inflexible, and at the same time clearly as vulnerable to the Soviet Union's abandonment of its survival guarantee as that of the *GDR*. Thus it is not surprising that this regime, being the second last domino to fall (just before Romania), was the only one which simply capitulated before peaceful mass rallies in the streets and simply collapsed. It is part of the weakness both of the regime and of the opposition that the negotiations which they conducted during the short period between November 17 and mid-December did not deal with the institutional structures of the transition period, but with the changes in the party leadership, the executive and the parliament. Another reason which would put this country still closer to the GDR may also apply. Whilst the regime breakdown in the GDR gave rise to the dissolution of the state and its unification with the Federal Republic, which was regarded as the single legitimate German nation-state, in Czechoslovakia the same regime collapse was soon overshadowed by the conflicts between the new Czech and Slovac political elites over the appropriate structure of a Czechoslovakian bi-national state. Eventually the overthrow of the regime entailed the separation of the Czech and the Slovak parts of the country into two distinct nation-states. For some it was simply a secession. At any rate, as in the case of the GDR the breakdown of the regime caused the foundering of the state itself.

Romania was the only country among the communist regimes of East and Central Europe which did not enjoy a completely non-violent path of transition to a democratic form of government. One may even doubt whether this country is really an exception to the rule, since it is plausible to assume that the formerly communist character of the Romanian dictatorship had changed into a personal, almost sultanistic dictatorship in which not the party and its historical mission, but the "individual leader is the source of the authority" (Huntington 1992: 581). Perhaps the personal character of the dictatorship is the reason why the old regime did not surrender peacefully. The official version of the events claims that in December 1989 a popular uprising was supported by the army which heroically defended the people against the armed and brutal attacks of the notorious *Securetate* which had remained loyal to Ceaucescu. According to a less heroic assessment the popular uprising was successful only because it was supported by a simultaneous *coup d'état* conducted by the alienated elites of the old regime (Verdery and Kligman 1992; Rothschild 1993: 247 ff.).

3.3   Institutional effects

This sketchy overview shows that the CEE countries clearly add to the diversity of the modes of extrication from authoritarian rule which have occurred in the twentieth century in other parts of the world. A few general observations seem appropriate. First, in the broad scope of configurations of extrication – involving cases with strong independent actors who were already prominent under the old regime and the opposite cases of the complete absence of such actors even in the advanced phases of the extrication process (viz., Poland and Romania, respectively), or cases with and without major mass mobilization in the streets (viz., Czechoslovakia and Bulgaria, respectively) – it is not easy to identify cases where the political actors of the opposition, who had played a major role in the overthrow of the regime, survived and became the representative of "transformative interests." Characteristically "the opposition" had consisted of umbrella organizations of the Forum-type (Hungary, Czechoslovakia, GDR, Bulgaria) which soon after the first free elections disintegrated into small and often irrelevant groups. This fate even fell on the Solidarity Movement which under the old regime had mainly represented workers' interests and which one would have expected would most easily and most likely represent "transformative interests," i.e., become the core of a workers' party in the framework of the newly emerging democratic government.

A second observation pertains to the institutional heritage of the extrication period. Some authors have claimed that the particular mode of extrication in a country is an important explanatory variable for the institutional outcomes which eventually shape the new polity (Bruszt and Stark 1992; Alexander and Skapska 1993). Indeed, it may be part of the paradoxical character of the "systemic" revolutions in the CEE countries that in the absence of entrenched transformative interests and constituencies the contingencies of the extrication process and its events may have a more significant influence on the institutional structure of the new order than would be the case in "genuine" revolutions.

The most profound institutional trace which is conceivable is of course the dissolution of the state itself as an effect of the breakdown of the regime. This is likely to happen after a violent change of regime, be it a war or a civil war. In our sample of countries which includes only peaceful transitions (Romania being no real exception) two such cases occurred (GDR, Czechoslovakia). It is striking that these two countries were also those in which the regime simply collapsed, i.e., was overturned without negotiating the institutional conditions of the change. There is obviously an interdependence between the downfall of a regime and the dissolution of a country. The precarious status of the country as an entrenched nation-state weakened the regime's capacity and resources to defend itself by arranging at least a negotiated transition which would include basic institutional provisions. Conversely, the regime was the major force to maintain the country as an independent state. When the regime eventually collapsed, there was (almost) nothing left to keep up the state.

Leaving these two extreme cases of state dissolution aside, the mode of extrication may positively affect the institutional devices of the polity under construction. The hypothesis that initial institutional choices are not easily changed once a new system has been established (Lijphart 1992: 99) has clear implications for the fate of the new polity. Did the particular mode of extrication create specific institutional devices that imposed a distinct logic on the decisions of the actors? There is one element of the extrication process which all countries with the exception of Romania have in common, namely Round Table Talks. These had considerable influence, albeit to varying degrees in the respective countries, both on the extrication process itself and on the institutional fate of the future polity. With regard to the former, they helped to avoid violent forms of the downfall of the old regime and hence provided the most important conditions for the peaceful formation of a democratic order. Moreover, in many cases they laid the institutional foundations for the future order, most visibly by creating the institutional framework for free, fair and competitive elections. Hence, so far the answer to the question whether the mode of extrication has affected the structure of the newly created polities is affirmative. Although this result is not surprising, the more interesting question is whether the particular mode of extrication in the several countries have generated particular institutional outcomes.

Of course, in all countries we can identify decisions or actions which were shaped by the particularity of the situation. For instance, the decision of the Civic Forum in Czechoslovakia to opt for proportional rather than for majority voting for the parliamentary election in 1990, although the latter would have guaranteed a clear victory for the Civic Forum and the choice of the former would have guaranteed the survival of the communists, or the decision to limit the term of the first assembly to two years (Elster 1995), did not reflect strategic interests of any of the involved individuals, groups or constituencies. Both decisions were the result of the transitory situation of extrication which did not necessarily follow from the particular mode of extrication in Czechoslovakia. A quite similar counter-intuitive decision with regard to the electoral system can be observed in Romania. According to a well-established hypothesis (Rokkan 1970: 157 ff.; Lijphart 1992; see also Rüb 1994) one would have expected that the successors of Ceaucescu would choose a majority voting system cum a strong presidency. Whilst in fact a strong presidency was established, the National Salvation Front (NSF) which inherited the communist party and which could expect to gain a sweeping electoral victory with majority voting, opted for an extreme version of PR, thus favoring the access of a huge number of parties to the electoral race. This decision has been interpreted as the result of the NSF's concern to avoid an excessive and self-discrediting electoral victory (Stefoi 1994: 55). These examples, to which others could certainly be added, give sufficient evidence that the extrication period leads to actions and decisions which are thoroughly contingent upon individual persons, situations, and circumstances and hence unaccessible to structural explanations.

Having said this, the question is still open as to whether we can observe structural affinities between a particular mode of extrication and particular institutional outcomes or features of the newly emerging political and economic order. There are some striking correlations which may reflect causal mechanisms. For instance, is there such a causality between the radical break with the communist past in Czechoslovakia and the formidable economic performance and political stability in the Czech Republic? Could one explain this correlation by arguing that where the obstacles of the old regime are pushed away most radically the field is free for the establishment of the most efficient economy? Could one explain the political stability of the Czech Republic in a like manner? The hypothesis seems to be corroborated if we look at Bulgaria, where the extrication period has been more dominated by the principle of continuity. Our analysis shows that the country ranks lowest in terms of economic performance (chapter 5). The recurring government crises also show that the country cannot be credited for political stability. One of the reasons could be that the extrication process was not radical enough in abolishing the structures which discourage the establishment of an efficient economy and, consequently, of interests and constituencies which organize along socio-economic cleavages (chapter 4). On the other hand, Slovakia which experienced the very same extrication process as the Czechs does far less well in terms both of economic performance and political stability. Evidently other factors must have played an important role.

Some authors have offered typologies of modes of extrication in order to better understand their relevance for the further political development of the countries which they compared (Share and Mainwaring 1986; Huntington 1992: 583). Karl and Schmitter (1991) offer an analytical distinction of four ideal types which result from a table whose y-axis covers a continuum which ranges from unilateral recourse to force to

multi-lateral willingness to compromise, and whose *x*-axis comprises
actions from below and actions from above. Thus, there is a transition by
pact when "elites agree upon a multilateral compromise among themselves"; by *imposition,* when "elites use force unilaterally and effectively to
bring about a regime change against the resistance of the incumbents"; by
reform, "when masses mobilize from below and impose a compromised
outcome without resorting to violence"; and by *revolution* when "masses
rise up in arms and defeat the previous authoritarian rulers militarily."

With respect to Hungary, Kis (1995) distinguishes between revolution,
reform and regime change, the property of the latter being that it changes
the basis of legitimacy without affecting the continuity of legality, while
revolutions change both legitimacy and legality and reforms neither. In a
broader comparative perspective Bruszt and Stark (1992: 16 ff.) in their
analysis of the regime transitions of 1989 in Eastern Europe distinguish
four forms of confrontations between the regime and society, namely *use
of violence* by the regime (China), *capitulation* of the regime (GDR,
Czechoslovakia), *compromise* of the regime with the opposition (Poland),
and constrained or unfettered *electoral competition* (Bulgaria, Romania,
Albania for the former, Hungary for the latter). Finally, v. Beyme (1994:
95 f.) offers a classification which focuses on the ideological formation of
socialism as the essential element of the old regimes in Eastern Europe. In
his matrix the *y*-axis ranges from *regulation from above* to *pressure from
below,* and the *x*-axis comprises all cases reaching from *pragmatic
muddling through* to *ideologically motivated innovation of socialism.* As a
result, he identifies four cases: (1) change of the character of socialism
(Bulgaria, Romania), (2) rejuvenation of socialism (perestroika in the
Soviet Union), (3) erosion of socialism (Poland, Hungary), and (4)
collapse of socialism (Czechoslovakia, GDR).

Since we are mainly interested in the potential role which the
particular mode of extrication in the several countries has played for the
creation of the basic elements of a new social and political order and of
independent agency in particular, our account of the modes of extrication
in the CEE countries produces a somewhat different classification. As we
stated earlier, in all CEE countries, with the possible exception of Poland,
the communist rule disintegrated in an anonymous and subjectless
process which did not generate a powerful counter-elite which had the
clear mandate to lay the ground for the new order. The resulting new
space for action and the potential for innovation which emerged –
gradually or suddenly – could have been exploited in quite different ways.
It could have been "invested" into the creation of new institutions, or it
could have been "consumed" for the accumulation of power and the
ad-hoc dealing with new problems. Furthermore, both alternatives are

Table 2.2

	Exclusion of old elites	Inclusion of old elites
'investive' use of new space of action	GDR Czech Republic (1)	Poland Hungary (2)
'consumptive' use of new space of action	Czechoslovakia Slovakia (3)	Romania Bulgaria (4)

conceivable as either excluding or including the elites of the old regime. If we combine these possibilities, table 2.2 ensues, the insertions being mere hypotheses at this stage of our analysis:

Case (1) represents the most uncompromising attempt to construct an entirely new polity, while case (2) represents different forms of cooperation and compromise between old and new political elites with regard to the construction of the new polity. Cases (3) and (4) represent political games in which the actors are less concerned with rules, institutions, structures than with the distribution of power, be it contested almost exclusively among the new political elites (3) or between old and new (4). The following analysis of the constitutional, political, economic and social policy elements of the transformation processes will provide us with more detailed information that may allow us to validate the insertions in the table and to draw some conclusions about the relation between the mode of extrication and the chances of consolidation.

4   The shadow of the past: methodological remarks

The "triple past" of post-communist societies influences the present in manifold ways. This section tries to isolate four causal mechanisms that may be at work in the political and economic reform processes in Eastern Europe: (1) The past can shape values, beliefs, habits, and frames of the peoples in CEE. (2) Past choices can serve as a constraint on political actors' behavior. (3) Past regimes may serve as models or focal points in the search for new economic and political institutions. (4) The past provides a repertoire of arguments that can be used in political discourse. Sometimes, an influence from the past has a positive effect, in the sense of making survival or adoption of past institutions more likely. At other times, the influence has a negative effect, leading to "reactive institution building."

(1) One mechanism by which the past makes itself felt in the present is socialization and cultural tradition. Citizens in post-communist societies developed their beliefs and desires, values and frames, roles and routines in past periods of life, that is under the communist regime or even earlier. We cannot expect those value patterns and ways of thinking to change all at once. They will continue to be pervasive after the political regime change, at least for a certain period of time. "Mental residues of communism" are usually stereotyped in the following way: people in Eastern Europe developed, under the old regime, bad work habits, a contempt for effort and initiative, a fear of innovation, and an inclination to trade the expression of their loyalty for patronage and protection. Egalitarian and envious attitudes create reactions both against excessive poverty and excessive wealth. Due to their experiences under communist rule, citizens do not believe in the rule of law, tend to distrust political elites, and they are rather skeptical that political and economic reforms will bring about the desired outcomes. Conversely, we should bear in mind attitudes and skills unofficially cultivated under the old regime. People in Eastern Europe developed virtues such as self-reliance, flexibility, effort, and inventiveness in order to cope with the vast inefficiencies of the past system. Those "unofficial virtues" turn out to be well-suited to the needs of a market economy. In addition, we can observe the survival of pre-1949 attitudes throughout the region. Traditional values such as religion or various craft traditions which were preserved during the communist period could become important again. Likewise, traditional animosities between ethnic groups may reemerge.

(2) Even if the past had no influence on individual motives and attitudes, it could still play an important role in post-communist politics as a constraint on behavior. This applies, in the first place, to the communist past. The economic legacies of communism, for instance, form serious obstacles to current efforts to achieve stabilization and restructuring. Governments have to contend with macro-economic imbalances resulting from previous policies. Part of the inheritance is also a particular structure of ownership, production, and trade with which post-communist reforms have to deal. Likewise, the legal and political apparatus that is in place in 1989 will constrain efforts to change the system, including changes in that apparatus itself. The existing constitution-making framework, for example, may turn out ill-suited for designing new constitutions, in that it is not sufficiently flexible to allow for rapid, massive changes. Consider also the old administrations. The administrative apparatus was highly centralized and used to a top–down style of governance under the old regime. Those administrative structures are

likely to constrain the design and implementation of reforms at the start of transition. Further constraints for current policy making may result from the very recent past, the period of extrication. Contingent choices early in the reform process, for example, the decision for a particular election system, will influence later developments, such as the formation of party systems.

(3) In addition, the past can play a role as a cognitive point of reference or focal point in the search for new institutions. Reformers may choose to model constitutional provisions, economic laws, or the social policy framework on institutional arrangements that have existed during the inter-war period. In a situation where options are numerous and everything must be accomplished at once, the return to the "golden" pre-communist past can serve as a clue to come to an agreement. However, pre-communist traditions providing a sense of direction seem rarely strong enough to override interest-based preferences. Only when interest is relatively weak, such as in the choice between a three-fifth or a two-third majority for constitutional amendment, can we expect tradition to emerge as an independent causal force.

(4) Moreover, the past provides an arsenal of arguments in the processes of institution building. Political actors will make continuous reference to the past, so as to disguise more partisan motives. Solutions may be rejected on the grounds that they smack of central planning or authoritarian rule, others may be explicitly justified by appeal to the "golden" pre-communist era.[18] To sell institutional designs as copies of past regimes (and/or the West) is to pose them as superior to other solutions and to generate trust in the quality of the new institutions.

The following chapters that expound and analyze the political and economic changes in Bulgaria, the Czech Republic, Hungary, and Slovakia will provide empirical evidence for the shadow of the past in post-communist politics.

[18] Admittedly, it is hard to reconstruct *ex post* whether institutional choices are modelled or only alleged to be modelled on historical precedents.

3

Constitutional politics in Eastern Europe

Constitutions did not play an important role under communism. Although in all countries of our study constitutional texts were formally in force, they were not meant to constrain and to obligate the power elites. They had little, if anything, to do with the idea of constitutionalism. Constitutionalism is the philosophical source and the institutional embodiment of political freedom (McIlwain 1966; Friedrich 1974); obviously political freedom was not the inherent principle of the soviet-type communist regimes. Thus, after 1989 constitutions evolved into emblems of political liberation in most of the post-communist East and Central European countries. At the same time they were rediscovered as symbols of the renaissance of these countries as independent sovereign nations. These two reasons for the regeneration of constitutionalism do not necessarily go together, much less so right after the absolute breakdown of an economic and political order. Hence, the task of the framers was to find a concord of political freedom and national sovereignty under the pressure of simultaneously creating new political and economic actors. However, fortunately this task has been solved; the mere fact that since 1989 constitutions matter again in the countries of East and Central Europe is in itself already a major achievement in the transition process.

Constitution making exemplifies an "investive" use of the energies which normally are released after the collapse of an old regime.[1] Hence, the choices which the relevant actors – the *pouvoir constituant* – make are likely to have long-lasting effects. This chapter deals with two issues: (1) the first part gives an account of the political procedures, the forces and

[1] See Chapter 2, section 3.3.

the political issues which shaped the process of constitution making. It complements the analysis of the modes of extrication developed in the previous chapter. (2) In the second portion of this chapter we change our perspective on the constitution. Rather than reconstructing the political *context* of the constitution, i.e., the dynamics and the political forces of the process which generated the constitution in the first place, we deal with constitutions in their quality as legal *texts*. The constitution embodies the political substance of a polity; if the constitution consists of a written text, its political essence is encapsulated in its textuality. Hence, in order to understand its meaning it has to be deciphered by way of interpretation of the legal text.

1 Constitution making

1.1 Introduction

Between the fall of 1989 and the fall of 1992, all but one of the countries in our study adopted new constitutions. This exception is Czechoslovakia, where the failure to create a new constitution was closely related to the failure to keep the country together.[2] Hungary created a new constitution in 1989–90 by a series of patchwork amendments that added up to a wholly new document. Bulgaria adopted its constitution in July 1991, Slovakia in September 1992, and the Czech Republic in December 1992. Prior to the constitution-making process there had been quasi-constitutional Round Table Talks in Hungary, Bulgaria, and Czechoslovakia.[3] The present chapter begins by discussing these first steps, and then goes on to describe the constitution-making process proper.

The impact of the constitution-making process on ordinary politics has several aspects. Most obviously, the product of that process – the Constitution – defines the ground rules within which day-to-day legislation and government are to be conducted. Moreover, the perceived legitimacy of the process will be one determinant of the extent to which those rules are actually obeyed. There is also a more indirect effect: the constitution-making process may bring to the forefront divisive issues that might otherwise have been accommodated by less conflictual means. Sometimes, *non*-constitution making may be the wiser choice.[4]

---

[2] See also Elster 1995a.
[3] See the articles in Elster (ed.) 1996.
[4] This may be an important part of the explanation of Poland's reluctance to adopt a wholly new constitution: the actors wanted to avoid taking a stand on the issue of abortion and more generally on Church–State relations.

Some observers argue that it was a big mistake for Czechoslovakia to decide to adopt a new constitution in the first democratic parliament, elected for two years only. If the process had been more open-ended, the country might have survived as a federation.

The substance of the new constitutions is surveyed in chapter 3, section 2 below. The present, process-oriented section of this chapter will be organized as follows. First, we discuss the Round Table Talks that took place in Bulgaria, Czechoslovakia, and Hungary. Next, we consider the constitution-making process proper, in the same countries and in the two successor states to Czechoslovakia. We conclude with some comparative remarks on the forces and mechanisms that were at work in these processes.

1.2 The Round Table Talks

The spring of 1989 was decisive and fateful for communism, a time of confrontation between the regimes and the emerging democratic oppositions. In China, the regime crushed the opposition and set the clock many years back.[5] In Poland, the Round Table Talks (RTT) between Solidarity and the regime set in motion a domino process that within a year led to the fall of all the communist regimes in Eastern Europe. As part of this process, Round Table Talks, in chronological order, also took place in Hungary, East Germany, Czechoslovakia, and Bulgaria. Because of our focus on a subset of the countries in the region, we do not discuss the RTT in Poland and in East Germany.

In *Hungary*, the RTT in the summer and fall of 1989 were greatly inspired by the Polish example. The crushing defeat of the communists in the Polish elections of June 1989 was a shock to communists everywhere through the region, and contributed decisively to their demoralization and paralysis. The tactics adopted by Solidarity, notably the insistence on publicity, also inspired the negotiators in the Hungarian opposition. Most importantly, perhaps, the passivity of the Soviet Union in the face of the Polish earthquake suggested to the Hungarians that a military intervention was unlikely. Against this, the Hungarian opposition suffered from the disadvantage that it was not based on a tight, effective organization such as Solidarity. As in Bulgaria, the opposition in Hungary originated in ecological pressure groups. By the time of the RTT, a few political parties had emerged, but not with the broad civic basis that could give them the threat potential of Solidarity. They could,

---

[5] For an analysis of the "Beijing Spring" of 1989, see the contribution of Tang Tsou 1996.

at most, play on the regime's fear of mass demonstrations on the occasion of various commemorations. Also, the oppositional groups were divided among themselves, and some refused to sign the final agreement of the RTT.

The main thrust of the agreement was the creation of a multi-party constitutional democracy. The two most contentious issues were the electoral procedure and the presidency. As in Bulgaria, the regime and the opposition had opposed preferences on the issue of proportional versus majoritarian elections. The communists believed they would do better with majoritarian elections, as they had the more visible candidates. Conversely, the opposition thought they would benefit more from running on a party list. And, as in Bulgaria, the outcome was a compromise: roughly half of the deputies would be elected by the proportional method and half by the majoritarian system.[6] The Bulgarian elections showed that the communists had been right in their calculations. In Hungary, however, they were saved by their opponents, insistence on proportionality. Having 75 percent of the seats filled in single-member districts, as they had originally proposed, would have hurt them badly (Lijphart 1992a: 215). Here, as in Poland, both the communists and the opposition vastly underestimated the lack of electoral support for the regime.

With regard to the presidency, there were three issues at stake: the mode of election of the president (direct or indirect), the timing of the presidential election (before or after the election of a new parliament), and the powers of the presidency. In reality, the main issue was whether the opposition would accept Imre Potzgay, a reformist communist leader, as president. Because of the extreme fluidity of the political situation, the questions were never definitely settled, and the eventual outcome differed from what had been expected by most participants.

From the point of view of the communists, the alternatives were assessed as follows. If the president was elected by the obedient parliament then in session, their candidate was a certain winner – but his legitimacy might suffer. If he was elected by referendum before the elections to the new parliament, Potzgay's visibility and popularity made it likely that he would win. Although slightly more risky, this option offered the advantage of greater legitimacy. Election by referendum after the parliamentary elections was probably a more attractive idea than having the president elected by the new parliament. Both options, however, were highly risky.

---

[6] Bulgaria chose a simple system: each voter cast two votes, one for a party list and one for a single district candidate. The more complicated system adopted in Hungary is described in Hibbing and Patterson 1990.

From the point of view of the opposition, the main demand was to delay the election of the president until after the election of the new parliament. A secondary demand, based on the assumption that Potzgay was in fact likely to be elected, was for a strict limitation of the powers of the presidency.

In the course of negotiations, the communists made several concessions aimed at creating a consensus for Potzgay. In August, they offered that, in exchange for the acceptance of his candidacy, they would dissolve the Workers Defense, a paramilitary communist organization. In September, they also offered to have the new president elected by referendum. This was presented as a concession, as they could easily have elected the president by the parliament then in session. Yet, as mentioned, this course also offered the advantage of greater legitimacy. Faced with these proposals, the opposition was unable to reach internal agreement. At least three oppositional groups favored a presidential referendum before the parliamentary elections, thus in effect accepting Potzgay as president. Others, notably the Free Democrats under the leadership of Janos Kis, insisted that the presidency be offered to the communists, but only after the parliamentary elections, so that it could be used as a bargaining chip. Although the former got their way, the latter kept their options open by refusing to sign the final agreement on September 18.

At that time, the general expectation was that there would be an early election of Potzgay. The calculations were upset by a major unforeseen event. When the communist party dissolved itself and created a new socialist party to take its place, a majority of the members failed to join the new party. Not even a majority of members of parliament – selected for their blind loyalty – joined up. Moreover, the expected election of Potzgay as president of the new party also failed to materialize. These events created a severe demoralization in the regime. In the ensuing power vacuum, the government was able to be a surprisingly active force, and to push through a number of constitutional amendments with minimal resistance in parliament. The free democrats and their allies called for a referendum on the presidential elections and obtained, by a narrow margin, that the president be elected after parliament. When a later referendum (called by the ex-communists) for direct elections of the president failed to get the necessary quorum, the final result was the very opposite of the implicit deal of the RTT agreement. Instead of a communist candidate chosen in direct elections before the election of a new parliament, the presidency went to a politician from the opposition elected by the new parliament.

In *Czechoslovakia*, the most important precedent-setting event was the collapse of East Germany. These two regimes were by far the most repressive within the communist bloc, and their leaders probably saw their fates as more closely linked to each other than to the reformist regimes of Poland and Hungary. The fact that the Soviets had not intervened in the latter countries was not necessarily a sign that they would also keep on the sidelines in the former. The decisive event, therefore, may have been Gorbachev's statement on October 7, during the celebrations of the fortieth anniversary of the German Democratic Republic, that "Whoever comes late will be punished by life itself." Then, subsequent weeks saw ever-larger rallies in the streets of Leipzig and other cities, until the regime caved in on November 9. The RTT began on December 7. On November 17 there were demonstrations in Prague, inspired by the events in East Germany. A week later the Czechoslovak regime also collapsed.

Whereas the Polish and to a smaller extent the Hungarian RTT had been genuine negotiations, the RTT in Czechoslovakia (and even more in the GDR) were more like a unilateral imposition of terms by the victorious opposition on the defeated regime. In retrospect, one may argue that the leaders of Civic Forum and their Slovak Counterpart, Public Against Violence could have obtained even more than they got. Like their Hungarian and Polish counterparts, they overestimated popular support for the party and did not realize the full extent of its demoralization. At the time, however, the balance of forces was shrouded in uncertainty, leading to elements of compromise in the RTT agreement.

The main decisions in the Prague RTT were the election of Havel as president, the formation of a coalition government with elements both from the party and the opposition, and the recall of between one third and one half of deputies from the Federal Assembly and their replacement by members of Civic Forum and Public Against Violence. New elections were set for June 1990. Unlike what happened elsewhere, the electoral laws were not part of the RTT compromise, but were set unilaterally by Havel and his group of close advisors. As in the other countries, the question was whether to adopt a proportional system or a majority system with single-member districts (see chapter 4, section 2 below).

The decision to adopt proportional voting was taken in a way that had a curious and possibly momentous side effect. When the electoral system was discussed in a meeting between Havel and some of his associates, it became clear that they were close to persuading him to adopt proportional representation. To clinch the matter, one of them added that the decision was not a definitive one: they could always change the system later. It was in that experimental spirit that the idea of having the first parliament elected for two years rather than four first came up. That was an idea that Havel appreciated on other grounds, too. He had been reluctant to serve as president for four years, and this proposal would allow him to serve for two years only. Many believe today that it was a mistake to think that the new federal constitution could be written in two years. One centrally placed politician also said so at the time: a constitution can be written in three months or in ten years, but not in two years. Although he did not advocate the idea of pushing through the constitution immediately, while a window of opportunity still existed, he did oppose the two-year parliament. Although there were other centrally placed actors who shared his opinion, the two-year option won out. The argument Havel made in public – as distinct from what may have swayed him initially – was that a parliament elected in 1990 would mainly reflect the rejection of the old regime and not allow the expression of pluralism.

In Bulgaria, the setting for the RTT differed in one important respect. Alone among all the communist regimes in Eastern Europe, Bulgaria did not harbor strong anti-Soviet feelings. On the contrary, they were seen in a friendly perspective, because of what was perceived as the progressive role of Russia in liberating the Bulgarians from "the Turkish yoke." Because it was not perceived as betrayer of national interest and national independence, the communist party had much stronger popular support than elsewhere. The RTT therefore, as in Poland (although for very different reasons), took the form of real negotiations rather than a unilateral dictate of terms by the opposition. The main issues of the RTT were the timing of the first free elections, the choice of an electoral system, and the election of a new president. The opposition wanted to delay the elections, so as to gain time to organize themselves. The party negotiators, preferring early elections, got their way. As mentioned earlier, the electoral system involved a compromise between majority voting and proportional voting, the latter a concession to the opposition in exchange for the early timing of the elections. The opposition obtained a weak presidency, on the assumption that it would be filled by the communist candidate. However, President Mladenov had to resign soon after taking power, when it turned out that during the demonstrations in Sofia on December 16 he had said, on camera, "Let the tanks come." He was replaced by the leading politician in the opposition, Z. Zhelev.

A most delicate issue in the Bulgarian RTT was the political role to be played by the Turkish minority. Although invited to join the talks, they did not (for reasons still not fully understood) take part in them. Although the RTT usually took place with full publicity and openness, the session devoted to the place of "social movements," notably the Turkish Movements for Rights and Freedoms, was held behind closed doors. An agreement was reached to ban ethnically based parties, but the ban was not respected.

1.3   The making of the new constitutions

In Hungary, the constitution that is currently in force was adopted in October 1989 through a series of individual amendments. In Bulgaria and Czechoslovakia, the RTT were soon followed by the elections in June 1990 of new assemblies with the task of writing entirely new constitutions. These assemblies also served as ordinary legislatures. The Bulgarian assembly succeeded in its task, adopting a new constitution in July 1991. The Czechoslovak assembly failed, and the country broke up in the fall of 1992. The Slovak and Czech Republics then adopted new constitutions in, respectively, September and December 1992.

Before we discuss these processes in more detail, a general comment may be in order. In all countries in the region some constitutional changes took place immediately after the collapse or overthrow of the communist regimes, usually to delete all references to socialism and the leading role of the party. In Hungary, as noted, these changes were so extensive as to amount to a wholly new constitution. In Czechoslovakia many important constitutional acts were also adopted by the first democratic parliament, independently of the constitutional commissions that had been set up. In particular, parliament adopted a bill of rights and defined the competencies of the federation and of the two member republics. Below we consider both piecewise and wholesale constitution making, emphasis depending on the circumstances of each country.

In *Hungary*, we find the only example in the region of an enduring democratic constitution created by a parliament that had not been democratically elected.[7] By the fall of 1989, the Hungarian communists were thoroughly demoralized, by a series of internal and external events. The newly emerging parties, supported by the Minister of Justice Kalman Kulcsar, used the occasion to push through a series of constitutional reforms that established wholly new rules of the political game. The most fundamental change was the creation of a multi-party system and of free competitive elections. A constitutional court – which later turned into a very powerful institution – was set up. A presidency was created that, although strong on paper,[8] has tended to be the loser in an ongoing struggle with the prime minister. There are some remnants of communist ideology, notably in the provisions that stipulate the "right to emolument that corresponds to the amount and quality of the work performed"

---

[7] For an analysis of the October 1989 amendments, see Adam 1990.

[8] McGregor 1994, ranks the Hungarian presidency as the most powerful in the region, on the basis of the formal powers ascribed to it in the constitution. The index is somewhat inadequate, however in that it does not take account of the mode of election of the president.

(Art.70/B) and "the right to the highest possible level of physical and mental health" (Art.70/C). Presumably these were token concessions to the communists that were never intended to be implemented.

The Hungarian constitution-makers exploited a "window of opportunity" – a short period during which the communists remained demoralized and the opposition was not yet seriously divided. In Poland, some members of Solidarity pushed for a similar strategy, but failed (Elster 1993).

In *Czechoslovakia*, the same opportunity may have existed. Given the overwhelming moral victory of the Civic Forum and the abject state of the communists, it would probably have been possible to push through a wholly new constitution within a short time. In that way, the breakup of the country might also have been avoided. These are mere speculations, with the benefit of hindsight. When the decision was made in January 1990 to have elections to a parliament that would adopt a new constitution, the fear of a breakup had not yet crystallized.

The first parliament was dominated by a protracted struggle to define the division of powers between the federation and the two constituent republics. Although the original idea had been to resolve this issue as part of the general process of establishing a new constitution, it soon became clear that the Slovaks wanted an immediate solution. Tripartite talks between the federal government and the governments of the two republics took place from August to December 1990, culminating on December 12 with the adoption by the Federal Assembly of a constitutional amendment on power sharing. The amendment went quite far in meeting Slovak demands, including a somewhat absurd provision that the governorship of the central bank would alternate annually between a Czech and a Slovak.[9] Yet it soon became clear that it did not go far enough.

To understand the escalating conflicts over the nature of the federation, it is important to know the options that were being debated, e.g., by considering the alternatives presented at the opinion polls. In June 1990, these were:

common state, with large powers vested in central government;
common state with large powers vested in Czech and Slovak governments;
confederation;
two completely independent states.

There was a gradual shift in the alternatives. Initially, the debate

[9] It is a commonplace in the economic theory of central banks (i) that to carry out their task properly they need to be independent of the government and (ii) that a long tenure for the Governor is a necessary condition for independence (see Cukierman 1992).

concerned the division of powers between the federal and the national governments. Next, the main opposition was between a federation (as defined for instance by the December 12 amendment) and a more loosely structured confederation. Finally, the idea of confederation was progressively diluted so that in the end it became almost indistinguishable from the creation of two independent states.

We shall not attempt to give a blow-by-blow account of this process, but only sketch the main mechanisms that propelled it forward. Some of these were rooted in Czech-Slovak relations. There was a strong element of Slovak brinkmanship, embodied in Vladimir Meciar. After the Czech Prime Minister Petr Pithart publicly referred to the threats that Meciar had made in their private negotiations, the latter was locked into an aggressive position from which he could not back down. Also, in the perceptions of many Czechs there was little difference between Slovak nationalism and Slovak separatism, a suspicion that easily became self-fulfilling. Other mechanisms were linked to intra-Slovak relations, as Meciar for electoral purposes had to demarcate himself from his Slovak rivals. The separatist position was already occupied by the Slovak National Party. The federative position was occupied by Jan Carnogursky and his Christian Democratic Party, although with the curious twist that in their program the federation was supposed to last only ten years, until the time when the Czech and Slovak Republics could enter the European Union as two separate entities.[10] The only position left to Meciar was the confederative one. He found that a strategy with great appeal was to pay lip service to the idea of keeping the country together while at the same time demanding Slovak independence in more and more domains. Thus, before the elections of June 1992 he proposed the adoption of a Slovak constitution before the federal one, the election of a Slovak president,

---

[10] Meciar's demand for a confederation within which each republic would have virtually all the attributes of an independent state was one of the strange ideas launched in this period. Another was Carnogursky's idea of the "federation for ten years." In interviews with Slovak politicians who advocated this proposal, we regularly asked the following question. "Suppose that in a marriage, one spouse announces to the other that he or she will seek a divorce in ten years. Don't you think that marriage would collapse immediately? And wouldn't the same psychological mechanism of anticipating and immediately consuming the announced divorce hold for the proposal of a federation that is to end in ten years?" We never got an answer that we could understand. A third convoluted idea that originated in Slovakia was the proposal of a "state treaty" between the two republics (RFERL 7.6.1991), a procedure that might have required the momentary dissolution of the federation shortly followed by its reemergence on the basis of an agreement between the two states.

the creation of a Slovak central bank, and even an independent foreign service.

At the constitutional level, the most notable achievement was the adoption in 1991 of a federal bill of rights. There was a conspicuous failure, however, to adopt a new federal constitution. The nature of the federation or confederation was the main stumbling block. There was also failure to reach agreement on the relations between government, parliament, and the president. A "little constitution" regulating these relations was submitted to the Federal Assembly in the spring of 1992, but failed by two Slovak votes in the upper house.

The role of President Havel in the constitution-making process was complex, and possibly counterproductive. Many close observers explained his behavior in terms of his background as a playwright. According to one, Havel lived in "dramatic time," not understanding that parliamentary politics takes place in "epic time." He wanted long periods to be condensed into short, dramatic moments. According to another, Havel saw himself as an actor, acting in a play written by himself. He had no feeling of being subject to constraints. By the time he understood how normal politics worked, valuable time had been lost. The same observers emphasized that Havel's overall contribution to the Czechoslovak transition was immensely positive, and that, moreover, his positive achievements stemmed from the same character traits that in other situations made him an obstacle to conflict resolution. Sometimes, disregard for consequences has good consequences; sometimes, not.

Havel's direct constitutional initiatives invariably failed, largely because of bad tactical judgement. He repeatedly asked parliament to increase the powers of the presidency. His constitutional draft of March 5, 1991, for instance, gave the president the right to declare a state of emergency, to dissolve parliament, and to call referendums. Apparently, he did not understand that such proposals, coming from the very office whose powers were to be enhanced, were likely to meet with suspicion.[11] He repeated the same proposals in a televised speech on November 17, 1991. Between these two proposals for constitutionalizing the presidential right to call referendums, Havel had also tried to push a bill on referendum on separation through the Federal Assembly. A petition was organized that gathered almost 2.5 million signatures, and there were big demonstrations in Prague to put pressure on parliament. Whether or not the latter were called by Havel – a point on which observers disagree – they probably had the effect of strengthening resistance in parliament to the bill. It failed when most Slovak and virtually all communist deputies voted against it.

---

[11] For a discussion of such "reactive devaluation," see Ross 1995.

In Bulgaria, the Grand National Assembly began its work on the new constitution in the summer of 1990. Among all the constituent assemblies in the region, this was the only one that had a majority of communist members (the Romanian National Salvation Front had a similar but more ambiguous status). As a consequence, the constitution-making process was dominated by the Bulgarian Socialist Party (the ex-communists). The BSP delayed the proceedings of the constitutional committee, in a successful attempt to postpone the next round of elections beyond the established date of May, 1991. In protest against these tactics and against the constitutional draft prepared by the Socialists, 39 members of the oppositional Union of Democratic Forces walked out of the Assembly on May 14, 1991. When the constitution was adopted on July 12, 1991 after an unsuccessful hunger strike by some members of the opposition, it was the first wholly new constitution to be adopted in the region. There was no popular referendum to ratify the constitution, largely because of fears among the Socialists that the "Group of 39," supported by President Zhelev, would mobilize the population against it.

The legislature worked extremely rapidly in the last stages, because of a deadline of July 17 set by the president. As a consequence, the document has more than its share of ambiguities and inconsistencies. In some respects, it is also quite illiberal, reflecting the communist dominance in the Assembly. The rights of ethnic minorities, for instance, receive much less protection than in any other country in the region. Ethnically based parties are forbidden (a provision that is not enforced, however) and minorities have the right only to be taught their own language, not (as required by the Council of Europe) the right to be taught any subject *in* their own language. It has been claimed, moreover, that some provisions are directly inspired by the desire of the former communists to protect themselves against criminal prosecution and demands for restitution of property.[12]

In Slovakia, the constitution adopted on September 1, 1992 was the last document in a series of evolving draft constitutions for the Slovak Republic within the Federation. This continuity led, among other things, to the Slovaks retaining the Federal bill of rights in their constitution. It has been said that it "owed much to [the earlier] proposals; but even more of the constitution's provisions were based on the winning party's own conceptions."[13] Reading the constitution, it seems to owe even more to the need to put something together in a hurry. It is a clumsily formulated document, with a number of ambiguities and technical flaws

[12] RFE/RL Research Report 16.8.1991.
[13] RFE/RL Research Report 30.10.1992.

(see Jicinsky and Mikule 1994; also Mates 1992). The most unusual (and unusually vague) provision is Art. 106, which allows parliament to recall the president with a three-fifths majority (the same needed to elect him) for "conduct aimed to destroy the democratic and constitutional regime."[14] Parliament is thus placed in the strange role of having power to elect and remove both executives, the prime minister and the president. Although himself vulnerable to parliament, the president can dismiss the prime minister on his own initiative, not only when the government fails to retain the confidence of parliament.

As we do not know much of what went on behind the scenes, it is difficult to trace specific provisions in the Slovak constitution to the ideas or interests of its creators. It is possible to say a bit more about *the making of the Czech constitution*. It was clearly a result of compromise. The constitution needed 121 votes to be passed. The coalition headed by Vaclav Klaus had 105 members. An additional 12 votes from the Moravian party were obtained by means of vague promises to do something for Moravia. Votes of former communists and social democrats were obtained by including a reference to the Czechoslovak bill of rights, which has a strong emphasis on social and economic rights.

At the level of overt argument, references to the constitution of the First Republic were used both to justify specific provisions (the creation of a senate, proportional representation in elections to the lower house, one-third quorum, three-fifths majority for constitutional amendments) and to exclude others (the constructive vote of no confidence). In addition to the force of precedent, other reasons may have operated or perhaps even been more decisive. Klaus wanted a simple majority for amending the constitution, understandably enough as his party had more than a half but less than three-fifths of the deputies. When formulating this demand he had no hope that it would be accepted, yet it gave him something to give up in exchange for concessions on other issues (Jicinsky and Mikule 1994: part I, p.26). The actual reason why parliament did not accept the constructive vote of no confidence certainly had something to do with the fact that this mechanism leads to a weakening of parliament *vis-à-vis* government. The creation of the senate may owe less to the precedent of the First Republic than to the mundane facts that we now go on to describe.[15]

As we further discuss below, unicameral constituent assemblies tend to create unicameral constitutions, bicameral assemblies to create bicameral

---

[14] In March 1994, pro-Meciar deputies wanted to use the provision to remove President Kovacs from office for no other reason than his criticism of Meciar (RFE/RL Research Report 1.4.1994).

[15] See also Cepl and Franklin (1993).

constitutions (Elster 1993: 183, 212). The unicameral Czech assembly created a bicameral constitution, for reasons well stated by Jiri Pehe:

> In December 1992 the Czech parliament adopted a constitution providing for the creation of a two-chamber Czech parliament. The upper chamber – the Senate – was to be made up entirely of Czech deputies from the Federal Assembly after the dissolution of the federation. The parliament's decision to create the Senate was widely seen – particularly by the media – as an incentive offered to Federal Assembly deputies to pass a constitutional law abolishing the federation; it was argued that without such an incentive, deputies of the federal parliament, fearing the loss of their mandates, would reject the law – a development that could torpedo efforts to dissolve Czechoslovakia peacefully.[16]

If the origin of the Czech Senate was mundane, the continuation of the story is downright sordid. As Pehe goes on to say, "after the abolition of the federation, the Czech parliament changed its mind." According to many observers, he writes, "what had really prompted many deputies to change their minds was the realization that, if not given new political roles in the Senate, most former Federal Assembly deputies – their political rivals – would disappear from the media spotlight, which would then automatically be focused on the deputies of the existing Czech parliament" (Pehe 1993). Finally, after a protracted dispute between President Havel and Prime Minister Klaus the Senate was constituted by the end of 1996, and elections were held in November 1996. In the meantime the lower house has been carrying out its duties, in accordance with the constitution.

Less is known about the constitutional bargaining over the presidency.[17] After Havel's resignation from the federal presidency, it was reported that he might accept the presidency of the Czech republic if that office was vested with more than symbolic powers. He was also said to prefer direct elections of the president. The latter wish was not fulfilled. If we compare the power of the presidencies in the ex-communist countries, as measured by an index based on their formal attributions, that of the Czech presidency falls in the lower half (McGregor 1994). It is well known, however, that the real power of the president may deviate from the formal attributions, either because of accumulated traditions[18] or because of the personality of the office holder. For both reasons, Havel's real power is certainly greater than as measured by the formal index. The tradition from the First Republic that the president is heavily involved

[16] RFE/RL Research Report 12.11.1993.
[17] For some general comments on this issue, see Elster 1994.
[18] See for instance the chart in Duverger 1992: 147.

with foreign policy still lives on. Needless to say, Havel's personal stature also enhances his influence. One may conjecture that one reason why the formal powers of the presidency are relatively weak is that the framers anticipated these effects.

1.4   Forces and mechanisms

Generally speaking, we may think of the constitution-making process as shaped by two forces: *arguing* and *bargaining* (Elster 1995). On the one hand, the framers offer impartial arguments for their proposals, in terms of the common interest, the public good, individual rights and democratic values. On the other hand, self-interested framers may also resort to threat-based bargaining in order to get their way.

Actually, the situation is more complicated. Although interest may be the most important motivation in most constituent assemblies, it will not always dare to speak its name. Especially when the process is under strong scrutiny from the public, the parties will feel constrained to present their argument in terms of the common good or the public interest. Self-interest, in other words, may induce the speakers to adopt non-self-interested language. Small parties, when arguing for proportional voting, appeal to democratic values rather than to the interest of small parties. Conversely, large parties tend to rest their case for majority voting on the claim that it is more likely to produce a stable government. Equity in the former case, efficiency in the latter, are put forward as impartial disguises for partiality. Similarly, when deputies argue for a strong legislature, they appeal to the need to respect and embody the popular will and not to their institutional interest. Conversely, when the executive power is involved in the constitution-making process, its representatives will argue for a strong executive on the seemingly non-self-serving grounds of stability and efficiency.

As we said, the pressure to disguise self-interest as public interest will be stronger when the process is under public scrutiny. One might wonder whether the disguise matters. Given the large pantheon of plausible-sounding impartial values, it might seem that any actor would be able to find a public-interest justification that coincides with his private interest. Three considerations tend to mitigate this conclusion. First, some private interests probably do not have *any* plausible impartial equivalent. Second, a *perfect* match between an obvious private interest and an impartial equivalent will often be perceived as too crude to be taken seriously. Third, even if an actor could find an impartial argument that might advance his interest in a given situation, he may be prevented from using it by the stand he has taken on previous occasions. These arguments suggest the idea of the *civilizing force of hypocrisy*: when discussing under public scrutiny, actors may be forced or induced to pull their punches and refrain from the most blatant expressions of self-interest. Against this positive effect of publicity, we must balance a number of negative effects: the opportunity for strategic precommitment, vanity-induced reluctance to back down, as well as the irreversibility of publicly stated positions.

These propositions can be illustrated by some examples from the RTT and the constitution-making processes considered above.

(i) The importance of publicity was repeatedly demonstrated by the RTT. The Hungarian and Bulgarian oppositions, in particular, got much of their clout from the fact that the negotiations were open rather than closed.

(ii) The negative effects of publicity are illustrated by the Czech-Slovak negotiations over the future of the Federation. As noted above, once Pithart had made public Meciar's use of threats in their private talks, the latter was locked into an uncompromising situation. Conversely – and more conjecturally – the peaceful divorce of the Czech and Slovak Republics may have been due to the fact that it was engineered in private talks between Klaus and Meciar.

(iii) In bargaining situations, the party who can afford to walk away from the bargaining table has an advantage. As Rumyana Kolarova observes, this mechanism applied to the RTT in Bulgaria: "It was generally believed that the electoral chances of UDF would be enhanced by delaying the elections. This knowledge was an important bargaining card in the negotiations, as UDF could credibly threaten to break off negotiations – they had nothing to lose from delays" (Kolarova 1996).

(iv) The RTT in the three countries under study here were to some extent shaped by threats (or warnings[19]) about external interventions. According to one observer, "hardliners in the [Czechoslovak] leadership were being paralyzed by President Michail Gorbachev's support for reform and by the presence of about 85,000 soldiers in Czechoslovakia."[20] In Bulgaria and Hungary, the ability of the opposition to draw crowds – and to control them – was an important asset.

(v) *Time* was an important factor in the constitution-making processes. The defects of the Bulgarian and Slovak constitutions are due to the fact that they were put together in a hurry. The failure to create a Czechoslovak constitution may be related to the tight time limit of two years.

[19] For this distinction, see Elster 1995.
[20] *Radio Free Europe Research*, December 8, 1989. In the Polish RTT, needless to say, the fear of Soviet intervention strengthened the negotiators of the regime rather than the oppositions.

(vi) The role of *personal self-interest* in shaping the constitution-making process is evident in several cases. Most obviously, both the Czech deputies in the upper house of the Federal parliament and the members of the Czech parliament were moved by their self-interest when the former voted for the break-up of the federation in exchange for places in the Czech senate and the latter then broke their promise to create these places. Also, some provisions in the Bulgarian constitution may owe their existence to the desire of communist framers to protect themselves against legal action in the future.

(vii) *Group interest* was crucial in shaping electoral laws in Bulgaria and Hungary. Czechoslovakia, by contrast, offers an important counter-example. Similarly, both in Bulgaria and Hungary the opposition negotiated a relatively weak presidency[21] because they thought – wrongly as it turned out – that the position would be occupied by a communist.

(viii) *Institutional self-interest* can matter when one or more of the organs to be regulated by the constitution – notably the legislature and the executive – are also active as constitution makers. In Bulgaria, the strong role of parliament in the constitution may be seen in light of the fact that the constituent assembly also served as an ordinary legislature. In the Czech Republic, the defeat of a proposal for a constructive vote of no confidence was related to the fact that this institution would have weakened parliament.

(ix) To the extent that the constitution makers genuinely tried to find the arrangement that would best further society's interest in an impartial perspective, they have relied extensively on foreign models and models from the pre-communist past. The German constitution, with a strong Constitutional Court, has been especially influential. The adoption in Hungary of the constructive vote of no confidence was also a borrowing from Germany. The Czech constitution is on several points modeled on the constitution of the First Republic. It is difficult to tell, however, whether the earlier models had a direct causal influence or were simply used to rationalize interest-based preferences.

(x) The constitution making was also shaped by the past in another, more direct sense. In Hungary and – especially – in Czechoslovakia, society was rebuilding the boat in the open sea. When trying to change the

---

[21] The characterization of the Hungarian presidency as weak is not inconsistent with the conclusion of the article cited in note 10 above. In the fall of 1989, the communists thought they might be able to retain their power through a communist president endowed with very wide powers, similar to those of Jaruzelski in Poland. The presidency that emerged was weak compared with this ambition, but not necessarily when compared with other presidencies in the region.

constitutional framework they had to use that framework itself. Hungary benefitted from the fact that constitutional amendments were easily made. Czechoslovakia was arguably destroyed by the fact that the communist constitution of 1968 gave the Slovaks unusually strong veto powers.

2 Constitutional structure and provisions

2.1 Introduction

In the following sections we turn, as announced above, to the analysts of the legal quality of the constitutions, i.e., to their texts.

Given the diversity of historical legacies, the different character of the modes of extrication, and the dissimilarities of the constitution-making processes proper in the several countries under study – to say nothing about manifold contingencies like the role of eminent personalities or the more or less accidental availability of constitutional experts of a particular Western country – it could be expected that the enacted constitutions vary considerably in their substance. However, once the essentials of constitutionalism are taken seriously and constitutions effectively impose legal obligations on all relevant actors in the polity and provide legally enforceable rights for the citizens, the scope of possible constitutional choices which the relevant actors could make is not unlimited. The options ranged between the two extreme points of simply copying one of the ready-mades easily available from the "world market" of (mostly Western) constitutions, or the creative re-invention of constitutionalism for the particular conditions of post-communist societies on their way to a constitutional democracy-cum-market economy.

Not surprisingly, none of the countries "bought" one of the most current constitutional models wholesale, be it the Westminster model of parliamentary sovereignty, the French idea of a unitary homogeneous état-nation, the pluralist–societal US concept of constitutionalism, or the German hybrid which amalgamates statist and societal elements into a neo-corporatist socio-political arrangement. Nor did any of them develop a thoroughly new country-specific kind of constitutionalism. Rather, the new constitutional designs combine the selectively traditional elements of the different Western constitutional traditions with sometimes quite idiosyncratic "local," as it were, properties which lend them a genuine character.

In what follows we shall investigate the most distinctive elements of constitutions which at the same time account most for the particular character of the polity, namely, first, the scope and character of individual rights, second, the concept of citizenship, third, the explicit or implicit concept of democracy and the resulting structure of government, fourth, the function of constitutional courts, and, finally, the amendment rules. In a concluding section we shall evaluate the constitutions under study with respect to their contribution to the process of consolidation.

2.2 The scope and character of individual rights

All the constitutions under study contain an extensive catalogue of rights.[22] In view of the dissident groups' quest for human and civil rights this comes as no surprise. What is more illuminating is the character of the rights which prevail in the new constitutions. Generally legal scholars classify fundamental rights into negative and positive rights. The former include the rights which protect the individual against the state's interference in his or her freedom, like the traditional rights to life, liberty, and property, to religious freedom, freedom of speech, and the like. They are "negative" not because they do not require positive state action – evidently the rights to life or to property require resourceful state activity – but because they protect what Georg Jellinek called the status negativus of an individual, i.e., his or her status as an independent individual who makes the claim on the society not to be disturbed (Jellinek 1963: 94 ff.). Positive rights, by contrast, are an individual's legal claims to the state's provision of certain benefits, like education, shelter, free medical care, social security, or an opportunity for paid work. Sometimes these rights are also called social and economic or plainly welfare rights (Schwartz 1992). Since negative rights are judicially enforceable, they are universally recognized as genuinely legal rights. By contrast, the character of positive rights as rights is largely disputed because their enforcement requires complex policy choices by the legislative and executive branches of government. They are regarded as mere policy goals whose realization is contingent upon the political process. They inspire and stimulate political action, while traditional constitutional rights are devised in order to constrain the political process. Hence some authors consider the stipulation of positive rights in the constitution as undermining the legal force of the constitution altogether (cf. Sunstein 1992, 1993, 1995).

There is even talk of so-called "third generation" rights which stipulate either individual claims to collective goods – like the right to a healthful environment – or claims of collectivities to collective well-being, like the

---

[22] The text of the Czech constitution does not explicitly contain a bill of rights; yet, in its Article 3, it declares the Charter of Fundamental Rights and Freedoms, passed by the Federal Assembly of the Czech and Slovak Federal Republic in 1991, "part of the constitutional order of the Czech Republic."

right of individuals to peace or the right of peoples to development
(Henkin 1985). Apparently here the boundaries between policy goals and
rights in their traditional meaning of judicially enforceable entitlements
are blurred.

From a purely legal point of view both positive rights and the so-called
"third generation" rights are not only prone to obscure the concept of
rights, but may even undermine the functional differenciation and the
ensuing equilibrium of the state powers in that constitutional courts may
be pushed into the role of policy makers for which they are not qualified.
This shift of competency is likely to jeopardize not only the authority of
the democratically elected legislature, but ultimately the legitimacy of the
constitutional court itself. One author even made the claim that positive
rights plus constitutional court equals socialism redivivus (Sájó 1996). In
sum, the extension of the concept of individual rights may have
disintegrative effects.

However, a purely legal understanding of a constitution is perhaps too
narrow. As has been pointed out, frequently constitutions embody the
political aspirations of a people and serve as a means of integrating a
fragmented society into a political community (Schwartz 1992; Preuss
1995a: 25 ff.). Moreover, the traditional concept of separation of powers
may be too traditional and prevent us from recognizing or developing
new constitutional designs which are more responsive to new social and
political needs than the old ones.

Viewed against this background of different philosophical conceptions
of the constitution and given the plurality of political forces who
participated in the framing process it cannot be expected that the
constitutions and the concepts of rights which finally came about were
devised according to one homogeneous philosophical model. Thus, the
following account of the rights discourse of the post-communist constitutions displays a broad spectrum of provisions. However, there is one
tendency where the constitutions broadly conform to each other, namely
the tendency to overstep the boundaries of traditional Western liberal
constitutionalism and, consequently, to politicize the concept of rights.

2.2.1   NEGATIVE RIGHTS   All constitutions under study contain the
traditional negative rights of the individual versus the state, namely the
rights to life, liberty, and property. Yet, in all the constitutions their
negative character has been enlarged by a positive and protective dimension. We may speak of their "trans-liberal" character in that they tend to
include the right to the basic institutional preconditions which are
required for their implementation. Thus, in the Bulgarian constitution
the right to life is embedded in a state guarantee to protect human life

and to punish any attempt upon human life.[23] In the Czech and in the Slovak Republics the abortion issue, which has proved to be highly divisive in countries as different as Poland, Germany, and the US, has been left open. In both countries "human life deserves to be protected already before birth,"[24] without defining the exact time when human life begins. Thus, in the Czech Republic the Czechoslovak law of 1986 which allowed abortion within the first 12 weeks after conception on the request of the pregnant woman and which is still in force is nowhere regarded as violating the constitution. In Hungary the Constitutional Court pursued a procedural direction. It contented itself with declaring the Ministry of Health's communist-era regulations on abortion to be unconstitutional and inconsistent with Art. 54 because the constitution requires rules affecting abortion to be enacted by parliament (see Klingsberg 1993: 47).

The right to life is only the most prominent case where the purely negative dimension of rights is held to no longer meet the requirements of appropriate protection. In the constitutions under study the guarantees for private property have also gone far beyond the purely liberal notion of the individuals' right to possess and to dispose of. Property has been acknowledged as a complex social institution. This is most strikingly expressed in the Hungarian constitution where the right to property is not stipulated in the chapter on Fundamental Rights and Duties, but in the first chapter which contains "General Provisions" which the drafters regarded as basic for the whole polity. Here the right to property is only one element in a comprehensive institutional setting: the Hungarian economy is defined as a market economy "where public and private ownership shall be equally respected and enjoy equal protection" and where the right of undertaking and free economic competition are safeguarded.[25] In Bulgaria this institutional aspect is defined in the rule that the economy should be "based on free economic initiative";[26] the Slovak constitution stipulates that the economy should be based on "the principles of a socially and ecologically oriented economy" in which competition is protected and encouraged.[27] A similar rule is lacking in the Czech constitution.

Particular attention is paid to the sensitive question of exclusive state property. Apart from an explicit determination of certain natural resources (e.g., underground water, mineral resources) or assets (like railway and telecommunication networks) as state property in the Bulgarian and the Slovak constitutions respectively,[28] in all countries the

---

[23] Art. 4 II, 28.   [24] CZ Charter Ch. II, Art. 6 para. 1; Sl. Art. 15 para. 1.
[25] Art. 9.   [26] Art. 19.   [27] Art. 55.
[28] Art. 18 BG; 4, 20 II Slo.

legislature is authorized to demarcate the fields where the exclusive property of the state may be established.[29] Art. 52 para. 5 of the Bulgarian constitution is exceptional in that it decrees that the state shall exercise control over the production of and trade in pharmaceuticals, biologically active substances (sic!), and medical equipment. Given the huge problems of privatization and the difficulties of transition to a market economy the attempt to control the dynamics of the economic process by a constitutional fiat appears somewhat naive. A more distrustful interpretation could suspect that these rules serve as a pretext for not privatizing all of the state-owned industries. It is very much in line with this presumption that the constitutions explicitly state that all classes of ownership enjoy the same protection.[30]

2.2.2 INSTITUTIONAL GUARANTEES In order to better understand the "trans-liberal" character of the right to property predominant in the East and Central European constitutions under study a brief excursion seems in place. Under the Weimar constitution the German constitutional doctrine developed the concept of the "institutional guarantee" which has become also part of the constitutional reasoning under the Basic Law (Preuss 1995: 105 ff.). An institutional guarantee, rather than containing entitlements to particular freedoms or benefits to individuals contains the state's obligation to protect, to care, and to foster a particular social domain and its network of social relations as a whole.

For instance, the freedoms of speech and of the press are individual rights in many liberal constitutions; in order that they can unfold their particular social and political significance they must be embedded in an institutional and cultural setting of a pluralist public sphere. Since its spontaneous emergence cannot be taken for granted in all societies, it can (or must) become the object of a particular state responsibility – this is essentially the idea of an "institutional guarantee." Thus, the German Basic Law contains, in addition to the individual rights to the freedoms of speech and of the press, the guarantee of the institution of the free press which entails the state's responsibility for a minimum degree of diversity of the print media. Consequently, the state obligations created by the institutional guarantee require manifold policy choices and primarily legislative and administrative activities while their judicial enforceability is weak at best.

Sometimes the boundaries between an individual right and an

---

[29] Art. 19 BG; 20 II Slo; 10 II H; 11 II C. Charter. The Czech constitution itself makes a qualification in that its Art. 7 confines itself to the state's obligation to see to it "that natural resources are used economically and natural wealth is protected."

[30] Art. 11 Czech Rep., 19 II Bulgaria, 20 I Slovak Rep., 9 I Hungary.

institutional guarantee are blurred, as in the case of private property. In the modern society the individual right of the owner to enjoy his or her property is highly dependent upon economic, social, cultural, and legal preconditions which remain far beyond the control of the individual and hence cannot become the object of an individual property *right*. Instead, they are embodied in the concept of private property as an institution. Its appropriate protection requires extensive legislation on issues such as competition, establishment of corporations, credit, banking, liability, trade marks, etc., and skilfull economic, fiscal, and budget policies of the executive, the central bank and other public economic actors. Thus, the shape of the guarantee of private property in the new constitutions is likely to tell us a lot about the character of the envisaged new political and economic order.

The brief excursus on the idea of the institutional guarantee has been prompted by the observation that in fact a strikingly large number of this quite peculiar constitutional construction can be found in the constitutions under study.

Starting with property, first of all notable differences in the wording of the guarantee occur. Whereas the Hungarian and the Bulgarian constitutions establish "the right to property,"[31] the Czech Charter, and in its wake the Slovak constitution, lays down that everyone "has the right to own property."[32] In the former text the aspect of property as a social institution predominates, whereas the latter clearly emphasizes the individual's subjective right to own property. Interestingly, the Bulgarian constitution is the only one which also regards labor as an institution which shall become subject to protection through the law.[33]

Apart from the afore-mentioned self-declaration of the Hungarian economy as a "market economy"[34] and the similar stipulation in the Bulgarian and the Slovak constitutions[35] several other institutional guarantees manifest themselves. According to Art. 15 of the Hungarian constitution the state shall "protect the institutions of marriage and family," similar stipulations exist in the other countries' constitutions.[36] The same pattern applies in other social fields one of which merits particular attention. The Bulgarian, the Slovak, and the Czech constitutions commit themselves to the principle of "political competition" or "political plurality."[37] The Hungarian constitution points in the same direction, although less explicitly, in that it assigns to "the parties" the

---

[31] Art. 17 and 13 respectively. [32] Art. 11 I, 20 I respectively.
[33] Art. 16. [34] Art. 9. [35] Art. 19, 55 respectively.
[36] Art. 14, 46, 47 BG; 32 Czech Charter; 41 Slo.
[37] Art. 31 Slovakia, 11 I Bulgaria, 22 Czech Charter, 5 Czech Constitution.

function of taking part in forming and expressing the will of the people –
this is an implicit institutional guarantee of a multi-party system.[38] In
contrast, the Czech constitution, evidently the most individualistic one
among those examined here, limits itself to the traditional liberal view on
political parties as private associations. The Charter does not speak of the
functions of political parties but of the right of citizens to form political
parties.[39] A notable institutional guarantee is contained in Art. 13 III of
the Bulgarian constitution which declares Eastern Orthodox Christianity
to be the "traditional religion in the Republic of Bulgaria" while at the
same time it asserts the separation of religious institutions from the
state.[40]

2.2.3   POSITIVE RIGHTS A further hallmark of the post-communist
constitutions is the broad scope of positive rights which they encompass.
All constitutions under study contain concurrently the rights to work[41] or
to unemployment benefits respectively,[42] and to education.[43] With the
exception of Hungary they provide the right to medical care through
different schemes of public insurance,[44] while Hungary proclaims the
"right to physical and mental health care of the highest possible standard"
to be provided, amongst other means, directly through health institutions
and medical care.[45] Other positive rights include, e.g., the right to healthy
working conditions,[46] to welfare subsistence for the needy,[47] and to old
age provisions.[48] Noteworthy is the right to "an income corresponding to
the quantity and quality of the work performed"[49] and the right to "equal
pay for equal work" which is established only in the Hungarian constitution.[50] Contrary to what one would expect none of the constitutions
explained here stipulates the right to shelter, whereas all of them contain
the aforementioned "third generation" right to a "healthy" and/or
"favorable" environment.[51]

---

[38] Art. 3 II.   [39] Art. 20 II Charter.   [40] Art. 13 II.
[41] Art. 70/B II (H); 26 II (Cz); 35 III (Slo); 48 I (Bg.).
[42] Art. 70/E I (H.); 26 III (Cz.); 35 III (Slo.); 51 II (Bg.).
[43] Art. 70/F I (H); 33 (Cz.); 42 (Slo.); 53 I (Bg.).
[44] Art. 31 (Cz.); 40 (Slo.); Art. 52 I (Bg.).
[45] Art. 70/D.   [46] Art. 36 lit. c, d (Slo.); 48 V (Bg.).
[47] Art. 70/E I, and 17 (H); 30 II (Cz.); 39 II (Slo.); 51 I (Bg.).
[48] Art. 70/E I (H.); 30 I (Cz.); 39 I (Slo.); 51 III (Bg.; note here the rather extreme
       version of the subsidiarity principle!).
[49] Art. 70/B III (H); less explicit, but betraying a similar tendency Art. 28 (Cz: "fair
       remuneration"); 36 lit. a) (Slo.: "compensation for the work performed to secure
       a dignified standard of life") and 48 V (Bg.: "remuneration for the actual work
       performed").
[50] Art. 70/B II.   [51] Art. 18 (H); 35 (Cz); 44 (Slo); 55 (Bg., see also 15).

Most of these rights are not justifiable because they require policy choices by the legislative and executive branches of government. The constitutions recognize that. Thus, both the Czech Charter and the Slovak constitution explicitly stipulate that the positive rights which they grant "may be claimed only within the scope of the laws implementing these provisions."[52] The Hungarian and the Bulgarian constitutions are less explicit and less systematic. With respect to the rights to health care, social security, and education the Hungarian constitution specifies the institutional means through which the right has to be realized (e.g., by health institutions, social insurance, or primary and secondary schools),[53] whereas the rights to work, to equal pay for equal work, or to rest and leisure and paid holidays do not contain any implementation mechanism. The Bulgarian constitution generally lays down that the state has either to provide the conditions for the exercise of the particular right, or to establish those conditions by law.[54] In all these cases it is more appropriate to speak of state goals in order to make it clear that the obligations of the state cannot be enforced by the courts but need legislative activity.

Generally speaking the study of the post-communist constitutions gives rise to the observation that the boundaries between traditional negative rights and their "trans-liberal" expansion, institutional guarantees, and positive rights are in flux. The order of this spectrum mirrors a decreasing degree of judicial enforceability and of an increasing necessity for political and administrative discharge of the respective state obligations. Moreover, a great number of institutional guarantees and positive rights causes the institutional after-effect of a shift of state authority from the courts to the other branches of government, primarily to the executive branch; we shall come back to this question in the section about the structure of government.

2.3   The concept of citizenship

The preference of the framers of the EEC constitutions for positive rights gives rise to a close analysis of their concepts of citizenship. For the first time for two generations the political system in these countries has been based on the principle of equal national citizenship. This makes social integration a complex undertaking. Thus, positive rights may have appeared to them as a useful device to strengthen the bonds between the citizens and their polity.

---

[52] Art. 41 I Czech Charter, almost the same wording Art. 51 Slovak constitution.
[53] See Art. 70/D II, 70/E II, 70/F II.
[54] For instance Art. 48 I (right to work), 48 V (right to healthy, etc. working conditions), 52 II (medical care).

The concept has two dimensions: nationality and citizenship proper. The former is a purely legal status which embodies the legal bond of affiliation of an individual to a particular state and which has to be respected by other states according to the rules of international law. By contrast, citizenship proper defines the role of the individual as a competent member of the polity, that is, as a person who due to his and her rights and duties participates actively in the formation of the political will and the significant decisions of the polity. Roughly speaking, the concept of nationality applies in the international sphere, whereas the concept of citizenship is relevant in the domestic sphere of the polity. Note, however, that the two concepts are inseparably connected in that today to the best of our knowledge no single state grants the rights and benefits of citizenship (and imposes citizenship duties) on individuals who do not possess its nationality (while the reverse case – nationals of a particular state are excluded from rights and duties of citizenship of this state – has been a frequent case throughout modern history).

Both nationality and citizenship become a problem in the cases of external and internal minorities. An external minority is a group of individuals who possess the nationality and are citizens of the state in which they reside, but who belong to an ethnos which forms the (majority of the) population of another state, e.g., the ethnic Hungarians living in Slovakia, viewed from Hungary. Viewed from the Slovak government, the ethnic Hungarians, although Slovak nationals and citizens, form an internal minority. The political problem with both external and internal minorities is about a real or alleged split of loyalties of the members of the minorities: is it stronger to the government of the state whose nationals and citizens they are, or do they, rather, behave as a bridgehead of the government of the state in which their ethnos predominates? In order to pre-empt this potentiality, should they receive particular rights and benefits, or, on the contrary, should they be treated with suspicion? Given the ethnic plurality of the countries under study, it comes as no surprise that the constitutions under study deal quite extensively with these questions.

An essential point is the definition of how the nationality (and consequently the citizenship) of the state is acquired. Only the Bulgarian constitution explicitly states the '*ius sanguinis*' as the primary principle of acquiring nationality, whereas both the Czech and the Slovak Republics leave this question (as most countries in the world) to statutory rule.[55] Hungary and Bulgaria care about their respective external minorities, i.e.,

---

[55] Art. 25 BG, 12 Czech Constitution, 5 Slov. Hungary's constitution does not mention this issue at all.

about the Hungarians and Bulgarians abroad in that both countries grant them the constitutional right to return to their homeland.[56] Susceptible to tensions with the respective host countries is Bulgaria's ruling according to which Bulgarian citizens are vested with all rights and obligations of the constitution (including the duty to military service) irrespective of their residence. Given the rather easy acquisition of Bulgarian citizenship by birth from at least one parent holding Bulgarian citizenship this may encompass a considerable amount of persons holding the nationality of another country.

Like many other countries whose nationality is based on the "ius sanguinis" principle, Bulgaria too pledges a right of every Bulgarian citizen to return to the country. Hungary is less explicit in that it contents itself with the affirmation that the Hungarian Republic "recognizes its responsibilities toward Hungarians living outside the borders of the country" which apparently points mainly to Slovakia and to Romania. But also Hungary grants all Hungarian citizens the right to return home from abroad at any time.[57] It is not clear whether this refers to the minorities in Slovakia and Romania or rather to the many refugees after the breakdown of the popular uprising of 1956.

All constitutions under study include the guarantee of equal rights and opportunities for each citizen and the prohibition of any discrimination on grounds of sex, race, color of the skin, birth, language, faith, religion, ethnic, national or social origin, membership of a national or ethnic minority, political or other conviction.[58] Hungary goes even two steps further in that it obligates the legislature, first, to make any prejudicial discrimination on the aforementioned grounds a punishable act, and, second, to take actions aiming at eliminating inequalities of opportunity. This could be read as a constitutional recognition of affirmative action programs. Yet it is striking that apart from the general ban on discrimination on, among others, the grounds of sex and the Hungarian guarantee of equal pay for equal work, none of the constitutions contains explicit precepts as to the equality of men and women. In several Western constitutional states a stipulation of this kind is frequently invoked as the source for far-reaching anti-discriminatory legislation in almost all fields of social life. The absence of this element in the countries under study may reflect the weak role of women's movements in the process of constitutional transformation in these countries.

Another sensitive issue of equal citizenship is the equal access to public

[56] Art. 35 II BG; 69 II H.
[57] Art. 69 para. 2.
[58] Art. 70/A (H.); 6 (BG); 3 (Czech Charter); 12 II (Slo.).

offices. This is safeguarded in Hungary[59] and in the Czech and the Slovak Republics, but not in Bulgaria. There is reason to suspect that this lacuna may not be purely accidental. The ethnic connotations of citizenship are most strongly marked in the Bulgarian constitution. Art. 3 declares Bulgarian the official language of the Republic; moreover, Art. 36 para. 1 makes the study and use of the Bulgarian language a duty which is only slightly mitigated (not offset) by the right of citizens whose mother tongue is not Bulgarian to study and use their own language under the terms of the law.[60] It should be noted in passing that in this respect the Slovak constitution, the second in our sample which establishes an official national language, is much more generous toward minorities. Part of the obvious tendency of the Bulgarian constitution toward ethnic homogeneity is the prohibition to form parties along, among others, ethnic lines[61] which obviously pertains to the Turkish minority and their party. The attempt to have this party declared unconstitutional by the Constitutional Court failed,[62] yet the stipulation itself is a permanent threat to this minority. This tendency seems equally to apply to the stipulation of Art. 12 II which forbids citizens' associations, including the trade unions, any kind of political activity. Thus, it is not surprising that the Bulgarian constitution contains no guarantee of group rights for minorities, contrary to the other three constitutions under study.[63] This deficiency may be partially offset by a unique individual guarantee, namely the individual right to develop one's own culture "in accordance with his ethnic self-identification";[64] it is unclear what this could mean in view of the absence of constitutional protection for ethnic groups which are the main cultural humus for individual development. The concern of the framers of the Bulgarian constitution with ethnic homogeneity is also revealed in the exclusion of foreigners from the right to acquire ownership over land[65] and in a significant non-inclusion: according to Art. 19 III all investment and economic activities of Bulgarians and foreign persons shall enjoy the protection of the law – the omission of the adjective "equal" may give rise to second thoughts.

The concept of citizenship is not only associated with rights. Duties may also play a role, depending on the idea of citizenship (see Bellamy 1993; Preuss 1995; Selbourne 1994). According to a thoroughly liberal-universalist pattern of constitutionalism – one extreme point on a broad

---

[59] Although only in an indirect manner, see Art. 70 IV; more explicit with respect to the principle of equality Art. 21 IV Czech. Charter, 30 IV Slovak Constitution.
[60] Art. 36.   [61] Art. 11 para. 4.
[62] Cf. the report about the opinion of the Bulgarian Constitutional Court in EECR Summer 1992, pp. 11–12.
[63] Art. 68 (H.); 25 Czech Charter, 34 (Sk.).   [64] Art. 54 I.   [65] Art. 22.

scale – duties of individuals consist generally of the reverse side of the equal right to specified freedoms which everybody is granted with the proviso that he or she has to respect the equal freedom of others. These boundaries of the rights are determined by law, and hence the only duty of the individual in this model of constitutionalism is to obey the laws. According to this idea citizenship is based on rights, while duties are entirely derivative from rights. At the other extreme a concept of citizenship is conceivable which is essentially based on the idea that the individual owes a debt of responsibility to the society in which he or she lives (see Kymlicka and Norman 1994).

According to the latter idea duties would be primary, and rights would be derivatives from duties. None of the constitutions under study subscribes to either of these variants, but there are significant tendencies in both directions. The Czech constitution (constitution plus charter) comes closest to the former extreme, the Bulgarian to the latter. The Czech constitution itself does not contain any single independent duty but contents itself with the procedural rule that duties may be imposed only by law and within the boundaries of the fundamental individual rights and freedoms. Thus, rights and freedoms are antecedent to duties and define their scope. The Czech Charter avoids even the most common and least debatable duty which is stipulated in quite unsuspicious constitutions like the German Basic Law, namely the duty of parents to care for their children and to raise them. Instead, it proclaims the *right* of the parents to care and bring up their children, and the *right* of the children to parental upbringing and care.[66] In a strictly liberal manner the duties of the parents are constructed as the reflection of their children's rights. In all other cases duties are constructed as limitations of constitutional rights which require the form of the law: in Art. 9 para. 2 lit. b) and c) the duties to do military service and to perform services in cases of natural disaster, accidents, etc. surface only indirectly, namely as constraints on the right not to be subjected to forced labor or service, permissible only in the limits set by law.

The Bulgarian constitution points in the opposite direction. It stipulates the duty of parents to raise their children (which is simultaneously their right),[67] the duties to do military service,[68] to pay taxes,[69] to "assist the state and society in the case of natural or other disaster,"[70] and to "protect the environment."[71] Above all it determines the quite general

---

[66] Art. 32 para. 4.   [67] Art. 47 para. 1.
[68] Art. 59.   [69] Art. 60.   [70] Art. 61.
[71] Art. 55.

and extremely ambiguous duty of the citizens "to observe and implement (!) the Constitution and the laws" and at the same time "respect the rights and the legitimate interests of others."[72] This suggests the priority of duties over rights. This supposition is corroborated by the fact that the right to conscientious objection – the exemption from a civic duty – is only indirectly mentioned and essentially left to the largely discretionary regulation of the legislature.[73] This reluctance to recognize the constitutional right to exemption from a constitutional duty may originate in an egalitarian spirit which is revealed in the constitution's admonition that "obligations established by the Constitution and the law shall not be defaulted upon on grounds of religious or other convictions."[74]

Hungary and the Slovak Republic figure somewhere between these opposite variants. They include elements which can be found in both of them. Thus, Hungary establishes the parental duty to instruct their minor children,[75] whereas the Slovak constitution, not quite consistently with its general approach, has largely borrowed from the Charter in that it, too, speaks only of the rights of parents and of children. With respect to the right to conscientious objection the Slovak constitution concurs with the Czech Republic's ruling,[76] while the Hungarian constitution's reluctance is much the same as that of the Bulgarian.[77] They concur also inasmuch as both contain the duty to pay taxes[78] which does not exist in either the Czech or the Slovak constitution. With regard to the duty to perform services in cases of natural disasters, accidents, etc., Slovakia has adopted the model of the Charter and hence concurs with the Czech Republic, while this duty is not mentioned in the Hungarian constitution.

The four constitutions reveal quite different conceptions of citizenship. The most extreme version of a liberal rights-based concept is embodied in the Czech Charter, whereas its more "communitarian" antipode, the Bulgarian constitution, seems very much concerned with potential disintegrative forces originating from ethnic diversity so that they conceive of a largely homogeneous citizenry. In contrast, the Hungarian constitution tends to discard the potentially divisive elements of the Republic

---

[72] Art. 58 para. 1.
[73] Art. 59 para. 2.
[74] Art. 58 para. 2.
[75] Art. 70/J.
[76] Art. 25 para. 2.
[77] Art. 70/H para. 2.
[78] Art. 70/I (H.), 60 (BG).

and to find a compromise between the values of a liberal democracy and the heritage of the old system (e.g., in the case of conscientious objection, or in the use of the instruments of both criminal law and positive state action in order to implement the principle of equal citizenship, or the establishment of a Commissioner for National and Ethnic Minority Rights). The Slovak constitution seems to be torn by two rivaling and incompatible principles – the priority of rights or of duties – which makes it difficult to find a consistent concept of citizenship altogether.

2.4   The concept of democracy and the structure of government

2.4.1   THE CONCEPT OF DEMOCRACY Given the power prerogative of the communist parties, based on the idea of the historical vanguard role of the working class, it comes as no surprise that all post-communist constitutions unequivocally take precautions against any kind of privileged access of any group, class or party to power. Thus, the Bulgarian and the Hungarian constitutions, obviously referring to the famous constitutional source of the principle of equal citizenship as stipulated in all French constitutions since 1791,[79] explicitly state that no part of the people shall usurp the expression of popular sovereignty and that no state party or ideology should be allowed.[80] In addition, all constitutions commit themselves to the principle of political pluralism and competition[81] – a peculiarity of constitutional design already mentioned earlier. However, this principle is variously interpreted in the different constitutions. The Hungarian and the Slovak constitutions state that the people exercises its sovereignty "through its elected representatives as well as directly."[82] This may be a not so distant echo from the era of the communist constitutions when the elected powers had supreme authority from which the other powers were derived and to which they were inferior and dependent.[83]

---

[79] Art. 3 para. 3 of the constitution of 1958 reads: "No section of the people, nor any individual, may arrogate to themselves or to him, or herself the exercise [of national sovereignty]."

[80] Art. 1 para. 3, 11 para. 2 (BG), 2 para. 3, 3 para. 3 (H.).

[81] Art. 3 I, II (H.); 11 I (BG.); 5 (Cz. const.); 31 (Slov.).

[82] Art. 2 II; almost same wording Art. 2 I Slovak const.

[83] According to Article 10 paras. 1 and 2 of the Hungarian constitution of 1949 "the National Assembly is the highest organ of state authority in the Hungarian People's Republic" which "exercises all the rights resulting from the sovereignty of the people." Note the slightly changed wording of today: according to Art. 19 para. 2 the National Assembly exercises "its rights deriving from popular sovereignty" – the word "its" has been substituted for "all the."

Among the constitutions of our sample the Czech constitution is the only one which excludes all forms of direct democracy. Yet, it is questionable whether the other constitutions' stipulations about direct democracy embody a higher level of citizens' direct political participation. Only the Slovak constitution includes a separate chapter on referenda prescribing their minimum procedural requirements. Those of Bulgaria and Hungary content themselves with delegating the whole issue to the legislature, the potential law-giving competitor of the people. Moreover, neither Hungary nor Bulgaria establish the right of citizens to initiate a referendum. In Hungary the initiative rests with both the National Assembly and the President,[84] in Bulgaria it is only with the National Assembly.[85] Thus, plebiscites may well be misused as purely acclamative instruments for political control. The Slovak constitution is somewhat different in that it establishes the citizens' right to initiate a referendum. But it provides the same right for the parliament and, indirectly, even for the government. Obviously, this power of the political elites is a strong incentive to stimulate passive mass acclamations rather than active civic participation.

Democracy allows different forms of democratic government. While ideally the former requires the identity of the rulers and the ruled, the latter, contrariwise, presupposes a gap between the rulers and the ruled. Consequently, it includes basically the ideas and institutional devices about the legitimacy and accountability of the rulers *vis-à-vis* the ruled. While some consider this gap a necessary precondition for the good quality of democracy, others regard it as a major restraint to genuine democracy and try to realize the democratic ideal of the identity of the rulers and the ruled in the institutions of democratic government to the farthest possible degree. Thus, one can distinguish two different basic concepts underlying the rich variety of institutional patterns of democratic government: one system of democratic government aims at the most authentic expression of the sovereign unitary and homogeneous popular will through the institutions of the polity; it draws much on the French concept of the democratic republic. The opposite idea presumes a fragmentaion of the people in a plurality and diversity of social categories and groups and aspires to organize the government as a system of mutual checks and balances of different social forces who compete for political power; this model refers to the US idea of constitutional democracy. The former model tends to invest the sovereignty of the people in one state organ, be this an executive organ (presidentialism), be it the (usually

---

[84] Art. 19 para. 5, 30/A para. 1 lit. g).
[85] Art. 42 para. 2, 84 No. 5.

unicameral) legislature (Parliamentary sovereignty). The latter type
regards popular sovereignty as incarnated – and diffused – in the
functionally differentiated dynamic system of interactions, checks and
balances of the manifold forces which participate in the government and
its process of policy making. In both models the basic devices of the
separation of powers will occur, but in the former the institution which is
supposed to embody the popular will holds sway over the others, while
the latter is likely to establish a balanced system in which no organ can
impose its will on anybody. Thus, government systems may range
between two extremes, from an executive which is nothing but a
committee of the omnipotent parliament to the reverse case where the
parliament is a mere appendix of the popularly elected (executive)
president. In between we may find the genuinely constitutional model,
according to which all organs, their competencies, and consequently their
democratic legitimacy are equally rooted in the constitution itself.

In our sample none of these conceptions occur in a pure version, but
among the hybrids which we traced we discovered different tendencies.

2.4.2 THE STRUCTURE OF GOVERNMENT All constitutions establish the parliamentary form of government; presidentialism or semi-
presidentialism has been dismissed in all countries of our sample. Yet the
conceptions of parliamentarism differ considerably.[86] The idea to preserve popular sovereignty in one single organ is very much alive in the
Hungarian constitution. It declares the National Assembly the "supreme
organ of state power and popular representation."[87] The other constitutions avoid this hierarchical connotation and establish their parliaments
as the main legislative body with significant additional political functions.
Quite in line with the "popularist" understanding of the parliament the
Hungarian constitution lacks an explicit and unequivocal guarantee, the
so-called free mandate, i.e., the deputies' freedom from any kind of
instructions, it avoids clear determinations of the conditions for their
immunity, and it is entirely silent on the issue of their indemnity.[88]

---

[86] The Czech Republic is the only country with a bicameral parliament. However,
due to protracted political struggles about the details of the electoral mode of
election the first elections to the Senate did not occur earlier than in November
1996. According to Art. 106 para. 2 of the constitution, the Chamber of Deputies
exercises its functions, so that until the end of 1996 both *de facto* and *de jure* also
the Czech Republic had a unicameral parliament.
[87] Art. 19 para. 1.
[88] Art. 20 paras. 2, 3; this law, however, requires a two-thirds majority of the
attending representatives, see para. 6. As to the free mandate see Art. 67 (BG.), 26
(Cz. const.), 73 II (Slov.); to immunity and indemnity Art. 70, 69 (BG.), 27 (Cz.
const.), 78 (Slov.). Note the unique stipulation of Art. 27 para. 4 Czech

On the other hand, the Hungarian National Assembly's competencies and powers are unmatched by the parliaments of the other countries. It shall "guarantee the constitutional order of society and shall determine the structure, orientation and conditions of government,"[89] and it is assigned the extraordinary and paradoxical double role as both a constituted and the constituent power.[90] This ambiguous constitutional situation is further complicated by the fact that certain laws and decisions which the drafters of the constitution deemed particularly important require a two-thirds majority of the National Assembly representatives,[91] and in a number of other instances, particularly in the field of Fundamental Rights and Duties, of two-thirds of the attending representatives.[92] Since amendments to the constitution require the vote of two-thirds of the representatives,[93] the constituent power, the power to amend the constitution, and the function of ordinary legislation are blurred.

However, the main test of the parliament's power is the character of its relations to the other organs. As regards the relationship between the parliament and the executive branch in our sample of constitutions, the scope of possible devices runs from a high degree of dependency of the cabinet upon the will of the parliament, making it almost its executive committee, to the reverse constellation where the government is to a great extent shielded against the potential instability of the parliament. The criteria by which this can be assessed are the modes of electing governments, and the conditions under which the parliament can express its confidence or lack of confidence in the government. All constitutions determine the right of parliament to choose the head of government, although this may take different forms. In Hungary the prime minister is elected by the vote of the majority of all members of the National Assembly upon the instigation of the president.[94] In view of the pre-eminent role of the National Assembly, it is surprising that the other members of the government are not elected, but appointed (and removed) by the president at the suggestion of the prime minister.[95] Consequently, a vote of no confidence in an individual minister is not

---

constitution which grants immunity not just for the period of the mandate, but "forever."
[89] Art. 19 para. 2.   [90] Art. 19 para. 3 lit. a.
[91] Art. 19 para. 4, 19/A para. 4, 76 para. 3.
[92] Art. 19 para. 5, 32/A para. 6, 40/A para. 2, 40/B para. 4, 44/C, 50 para. 4, 60 para. 4, 61 para. 4, 62 para. 2, 63 para 2, 65 para. 3, 68 para. 5, 69 para. 4, 70/C para. 3, 70/H para. 3, 71 para. 3.
[93] Art. 24 paras. 3 and 5. It is evidently due to a technical error that the paras. 3 and 5 have almost the same wording.
[94] Art. 33 para. 3.   [95] Art. 33 para. 4.

admissible, although each is accountable not only to the government, but to the National Assembly as well. Still, their political survival depends on the prime minister. Even more striking is the buttressing of the power of the prime minister *vis-à-vis* the National Assembly in that he (or she) can only be removed by a constructive vote of no confidence which requires the vote of the majority of the members of the National Assembly.[96] By contrast, the prime minister only requires the majority of the attending representatives – the quorum being more than half of all members of parliament – when he himself requests a vote of confidence.[97] Thus, the prime minister is in a strong position both *vis-à-vis* the National Assembly and the government.

The institutional relationship with the second element of the executive power, the president, is more equivocal. The president is elected by the National Assembly. Hence his legitimacy derives from the same source as that of the prime minister. It is certainly strong if he is elected in the first or second ballot, which require a two-thirds majority, while it is likely to be considerably diminished if he succeeds only after the third ballot, in which a simple majority of votes cast suffices.[98] Given this indirect (and possibly even rather weak) parliamentary legitimacy, his functions and powers are quite remarkable. While it is common that the president represents the unity of the nation, it is exceptional that he shall "safeguard the democratic functioning of the State Organization"[99] in the presence of a Constitutional Court with the power of judicial review.[100] The competencies are even more obscured by the above-mentioned National Assembly's task to "guarantee the constitutional order of society."[101] This unclear allocation of an essential function is likely to cause serious constitutional conflicts. Actually the conflict between the Antall government and President Göncz over the appointment of the heads of the public broadcasting bodies, of radio and television, was partly prompted by the constitution's ambiguity.

Generally the Hungarian constitution tends to assign to the president functions and powers which one would expect for a popularly elected president and which therefore appear out of proportion to the indirect mode of his election. Thus, the president has the power to declare a state of war or a state of emergency whenever the National Assembly is unable to make such a decision; in a period of crisis, he sets up and presides over the Council of Defence, which combines most of the legislative and executive powers of the state. Even then, certain important decisions (like

---

[96] Art. 39/A para. 1.   [97] Art. 39/A paras. 3, 4/24 paras. 1, 2.
[98] Art. 29/B paras. 2–4.   [99] Art. 29 para. 1.
[100] Art. 32/A.   [101] Art. 19 para. 2.

the deployment of the armed forces or the issuance of decrees) are reserved for him personally.[102] Apart from these emergency powers he has, among others, the right to effect the convocation of the National Assembly, to adjourn its session,[103] to instigate legislation,[104] and to initiate plebiscites.[105] As mentioned earlier, this constitutional incoherence derives from the particular circumstances in which the articles about the presidency originated, devised initially as they were on the lines of the presidential systems of France and the US. The present hybrid reflects the constitutional compromise between the then significant political forces of the opposition who preferred a purely parliamentary system and the reform wing of the old regime which hoped to preserve as much of their power as possible by opting for a presidential system (cf. Mink 1994).

Bulgaria is the other country in our sample in which the parliament elects the prime minister upon the designation of the president (which, however, does not mean much, as we will see immediately). He or she requires the simple majority of the present members, the quorum being more than half of the members of parliament.[106] Thus, a prime minister could be elected with only the support of slightly more than one-quarter of the members of parliament. In contrast, recall of the prime minister is much more difficult, in that a vote of no confidence requires the absolute majority of the members of parliament.[107] This puts the government in a rather strong position vis-à-vis parliament. This is corroborated by Art. 112 para. 1 which determines that the vote of confidence which the government may request with respect to its overall policies or on a specific issue requires the absolute majority of the votes of the present members of parliament, i.e., again a potentially rather weak majority. In other words, it is relatively easy to become a prime minister, and relatively difficult to be removed by a vote of no confidence. The political standing of the prime minister is further bolstered both vis-à-vis the parliament and the other members of the Council of Ministers in that the latter are elected and dismissed at his instigation.[108] Consequently, a motion of no confidence can be initiated only against the prime minister or against the Council of Ministers as a whole, not against an individual minister.[109] Thus far the constitutional construct, with its approximation of a constructive vote of no confidence (similar to that of the Fifth French Republic), gives the impression of a coherent pattern which guarantees

---

[102] Art. 19/A, 18/B, 19/C.
[103] Art. 22 paras. 3, 4.   [104] Art. 25 para. 1.
[105] Art. 30/A para. 1 lit. g.   [106] Art. 84 No. 6, 81 paras. 1 and 2.
[107] Art. 89 para. 1.   [108] Art. 84 No. 6.
[109] Art. 89 para. 2, 111 para. 1, No. 1a.

the stability, continuity and discipline of the executive in preference to the expression of democratic plurality in parliament.

This impression is compromised, however, by the nature of the presidential institution, in which the Hungarian problem of the discrepancy between legitimacy and authority appears in reverse. Here the president seems to be over-legitimized in relation to his (or her) competencies. He (or she) embodies the unity of the nation[110] and is elected by direct popular vote[111] and could thus play an important role as arbiter in potential conflicts between parliament and government. Instead, his (or her) powers are rather limited: although the National Assembly can only elect a prime minister designated by him, he is not free to form a sustainable majority and to designate its political leader as prime minister but is obliged to follow the order as established in Art. 99 which renders him more or less a subaltern emissary of the parliamentary groups. Even in the case where the procedure established in Art. 99 does not yield an agreement on the formation of a government, he has no political discretion on how to resolve the crisis. He has to dissolve the parliament and to appoint a caretaker government.[112] He is even denied the potentially disciplining weapon of the right to dissolve the National Assembly when a vote of confidence in the government is requested and refused.[113] His only major power *vis-à-vis* the National Assembly is the power to veto its bills;[114] but since the veto can be overruled by the majority of the members of the National Assembly, it is essentially suspensive. The president is equally powerless *vis-à-vis* the government. Most of his acts need the countersignature of the prime minister or the minister concerned. Obviously the seed for constitutional conflict lies in the discrepancy between the popular election and the resulting strong national legitimacy of the president with his/her relatively weak competencies and lack of means to instigate political initiatives in the case of political crisis.[115]

In the Czech and the Slovak Republics the prime minister is not elected by the parliament, but appointed by the president. In turn, the president can appoint only ministers who have been proposed by the prime minister. Hence, the political judgment of the prime minister has priority over that of the Chamber of Deputies and the National Council respectively, whose vote of confidence the government has to request within thirty days.[116] In

---

[110] Art. 92 para. 1. [111] Art. 93 para. 1. [112] Art. 99 para. 5.
[113] Art. 112 para. 2. [114] Art. 101.
[115] A brief account of the history of the presidency in Bulgaria and the factual role of President Zhelev is given in the two contributions of Poshtov and Ganev 1994: 61–4.
[116] Art. 68 paras. 1, 2 (Cz. const.), 110 para. 1, 111, 113 (Slov.).

this construction, the vote is indirectly also a vote on the political standing of the president. The majority required both for this mandatory vote of confidence and for those which can be requested by the government at any time[117] is rather low: the absolute majority of the attending representatives, the quorum in the Czech Republic being the lowest among all the constitutions under study, namely just one third of the members of the Chamber of Deputies, in Slovakia it is the majority of the members of the National Council.[118] By contrast, a vote of no confidence requires the majority of all members of parliament in both countries.[119] Thus, in both countries it is relatively easy to establish and rather difficult to overthrow the government.

Beyond these concurrences there are some significant differences between the constitutions of the two countries. Firstly, according to the Czech constitution the government as a body is accountable to the Chamber of Deputies and hence only as a body is exposed to a vote of no confidence.[120] This is a further reinforcement of their position against the threats which particular discontents in the Chamber of Deputies may pose. The individual ministers who have been appointed at the suggestion of the prime minister can only be dismissed on his proposal.[121] They owe their loyalty primarily to him. By contrast, according to the Slovak constitution, an individual member of the government can be dismissed either at the suggestion of the prime minister or following a vote of no confidence. Only the vote against the prime minister entails the dismissal of the whole government.[122] Thus, individual ministers' loyalties are torn between the prime minister and the majority of the parliament, a fact that may jeopardize the overall stability of the government. Secondly, since neither the Czech nor the Slovak constitutions establish a constructive vote of no confidence, a situation may arise in which no government gets a vote of confidence. In this case a crisis-solving mechanism is required.

The solution adopted by the Czech constitution consists in the right of the president – this time at the suggestion of the chairman of the Chamber of Deputies – to dissolve the Chamber of Deputies after the third attempt to establish a government has failed.[123] This threat of dissolution is evidently intended to discipline the Chamber of Deputies. As the president is not accountable for the discharge of his office and can only stand trial on charges of high treason initiated by the Senate and conducted before the Constitutional Court[124] the Chamber of Deputies

---

[117] Art. 71 (Cz. const.), 114 paras. 2, 3 (Slov.).
[118] See Art. 39 paras. 1, 2 and 68 para. 3 (Cz. const.), 84 paras. 1, 2, 113.
[119] Art. 72 para. 2 (Cz. const.), 88 para. 2 (Slov.).   [120] Art. 68 para. 1, 72.
[121] Art. 74.   [122] Art. 116 paras. 3–5.
[123] Art. 68 para. 4, 35 para. 1 lit. a).   [124] Art. 65 para. 2.

can neither pre-empt nor retaliate in any way. The Czech president is not vulnerable to the sanction of the Chamber of Deputies. For those decisions which require the countersignature of the prime minister or of an individual minister the government is accountable to the Chamber of Deputies.[125] Given that the competencies of the president which do not require countersignature or which can be taken independently of other state organs are relatively weak, and that those competencies which do carry some political weight are dependent upon the co-operation primarily of the government,[126] the president's formal authority is not very great. This distances him from political conflict and may help him to develop the informal authority requisite to the solution of serious political crises (see Cepl and Gillis 1994).

In this respect the Slovak constitution differs considerably. The role of the president in a political crisis is very weak. According to Art. 102 lit. d) the president may dissolve parliament, after consultations with its chairperson, if it has refused a vote of confidence in the government three times. Amazingly, this right exists only within six months of the elections, leaving all crises thereafter unsolved. Moreover, the president is vulnerable to sanctions of the parliament which can initiate, at any time, a motion calling for his resignation, permitted by Art. 106, on the rather vague grounds, amongst others, that the president acted in a manner which "aimed at destroying the democratic and constitutional regime in the Slovak Republic."[127] While the ousting of the president requires a three-fifth majority of the members of the National Council, Art. 107 permits the additional possibility of an indictment for treason before the Constitutional Court by the majority of the attending deputies. Given the quorum of the majority of all members, in extreme situations this indictment could be pursued by as few as 39 out of the 150 deputies.[128] Thus, the author of the crisis can even undo the constitutional means of its solution.

The Slovak constitution is the only one in our sample in which the removal of the president is not effected through a procedure before the Constitutional Court and conducted solely on legally specified grounds.[129] But there are also other peculiarities (see Holländer 1992: 16–17). In addition to the already mentioned intitiative in the process of government formation, the president has a number of other significant

[125] Art. 63 para. 3.
[126] The rather important right to appoint the judges of the Constitutional Court is dependent upon the consent of the Senate, see Art. 84 para. 2.
[127] Art. 106.
[128] Cf. Art. 73 para. 1, 84 paras. 1, 2, 107.
[129] Cf. Art. 31 para. 4, 31/A (H.); 103 (BG.); 65 para. 2 (Cz. const.).

powers such as the authority to negotiate and ratify international agreements, the right to appoint and remove the principal officers of national bodies, to grant amnesty, or to preside over the meetings and require reports from the government or from individual ministers.[130] He can exercise these (and all other powers) without the endorsement of the government as a whole or of an individual minister because the institution of countersignature does not exist in the Slovak constitution. On the other hand, he must exercise a suspensive veto on bills of the National Council at the request of the government.[131] Given these instances and his vulnerability to parliamentary sanctions, the entire construct of the machinery of government appears unbalanced and liable to create rather than to avoid or resolve political crises.

2.5 The role of Constitutional Courts

All the countries under study have established Constitutional Courts although, with the exception of Czechoslovakia, none of them has a tradition in the field of constitutionalism (Schwartz 1993: 28). Constitutional jurisdiction is most frequently established in politically fragmented systems, particularly in federal states, where the idea of a neutral arbiter between equally entitled protagonists is an obvious solution to political conflicts (v. Beyme 1988). Moreover, these polities are more inclined to the concept of constitutional supremacy, which in turn nourishes the idea of a neutral judiciary enforcing the constitution in a depoliticized manner. By contrast, political systems which adhere to the idea of popular or of parliamentary sovereignty are reluctant to adopt either federalism or constitutional jurisdiction. It is against this general theoretical background that we can better understand that the two successor states of Czechoslovakia have a different conception of their respective Constitutional Courts to that of Hungary and Bulgaria, which have no tradition in either federalism or constitutional jurisdiction.

Neither in the Bulgarian nor in the Hungarian constitution is the Constitutional Court devised as part of the judiciary. In the systematic order of the Hungarian constitution the chapter concerning the Constitutional Court ranks below the chapters on the National Assembly and the President of the Republic but before the chapters on government, local self-government, and the judiciary. Equally, in the Bulgarian constitution the Constitutional Court is dealt with outside the chapter on judicial power. This places the Constitutional Courts closer to political than to judicial institutions. In the Hungarian case this is affirmed by the

---

[130] Art. 102.   [131] Art. 87 para. 4.

selection of the judges: they are nominated by a committee of the National Assembly comprising one member of each of the groups of representatives of the parties with seats in the National Assembly, and elected with a two-thirds majority of the members of the National Assembly. This ensures that the broadest possible spectrum of political forces are represented in the Court.[132] The Bulgarian constitution's selection mechanism for the judges of the Constitutional Court reflects the political character of the Court more indirectly in that it is more committed to the principle of checks and balances between interested political actors. One third each of the judges are elected by the National Assembly and the justices of the country's supreme courts of justice, and one third are appointed by the president.[133]

Both the Czech and Slovak constitutions establish the Constitutional Courts as special courts within the judicial power of the state. They are explicitly defined as a "judicial body" and as an "independent judicial authority" respectively.[134] Consequently, the Czech constitution attempts to depoliticize the office of the constitutional justices in that they are appointed by the president at the proposal of the Senate, whose political power is fairly limited and in which, due to the majority vote on which it is based, the influence of the political parties is restricted.[135] In the unicameral Slovak system the ten judges are appointed by the President from among twenty candidates nominated by the National Council.[136] Although both the Czech and Slovak constitutions stick to the European concept of constitutional jurisdiction, institutionalizing it in distinct courts which do not deal with ordinary lawsuits, the scope of its competencies is not limited to constitutional issues *strictu senso*. Matters of administrative adjudication are included, among which the control of regulations of bodies of territorial self-administration are particularly important.[137] Experience shows that it is the parochialism of the local sphere which is most likely to jeopardize human and civil rights.[138]

Despite the different systematic ranking in the constitution and the differing selection methods for the judges in Bulgaria and Hungary, on the one hand, and in the Czech and Slovak Republics, on the other, the respective competencies are rather similar. The most important and most

---

[132] Art. 32/A.   [133] Art. 147.
[134] Art. 83 ff. (Czech Rep.), 124 ff. (Slov. Rep.).
[135] Art. 84. As we mentioned earlier, until the end of 1996 *de facto* also the Czech Republic had a unicameral legislature.
[136] Art. 134.
[137] Art. 87 para. 1 lit. b), d), see also para. 2 (Czech Rep.); 125 lit. c), d).
[138] See Constitutional Watch in EECR Spring 1993, pp. 5 f. (Czech Rep.), Summer/ Fall 1994, pp. 21 f. (Slov. Rep.).

controversial is the power to declare laws unconstitutional and void, which is most appropriate in political systems in which the supremacy of the constitution over all branches of government, including the people themselves and the legislature, is established. All of the constitutional courts in our sample possess this authority.[139] But their significance is not always the same.

Paradoxically, in the Hungarian constitution two seemingly incompatible elements are assembled, namely the sovereignty of the National Assembly and its role as guarantor of the constitutional order[140] is at odds with the declaration of the constitution as the "Fundamental Law of the Republic of Hungary," with binding force upon all organizations within the society and on all state organs and citizens,[141] from which the power of the Constitutional Court emanates to abrogate laws on grounds of their unconstitutionality.[142] The situation is even more complicated by the stipulation that according to Art. 29 para. 1 the President is also the guarantor of the "democratic functioning of the State organization." This ambiguity of the constitution may account for the fact that among all Constitutional Courts in the region, that of Hungary has been the most involved in the political struggles of parliament, government and president, and that it has become the Court which has left by far the most visible traces on the political life of the country (Klingsberg 1993).

Bulgaria's constitution also makes the explicit statement that the constitution shall be the supreme law and that no other law shall contravene it.[143] Consequently, it establishes, among others, the Court's power to declare laws unconstitutional.[144] In contrast to the constitutions of Hungary and the Czech and Slovak Republics, individual citizens have no access to the Constitutional Court in Bulgaria. Only institutional actors like the government or one-fifth of all members of the National Assembly are able to initiate the proceedings of the Court.[145] Thus, in Bulgaria the Constitutional Court is more a "government tribunal" with special competencies in the sphere of government than a general guardian over the constitutional order, much less a court which, as in the American system, adjudicates disputes between private parties, with the merely incidental task of constitutional review. Its competencies – e.g., the check of the constitutionality of international acts of the government prior to their ratification, and of domestic laws with

---

[139] Art. 32/A para. 2 (H.); 149 para. 1 No. 2 (BG.); 87 para. 1 lit. a (Czech Rep.); 125 lit. a (Slov. Rep.).
[140] Art. 29 para. 2. [141] Art. 77. [142] Art. 32/A para. 2.
[143] Art. 5 para. 1. [144] Art. 149 para. 1 No. 2. [145] Art. 150.

international law – render the Bulgarian Constitutional Court a primarily political institution whose functions place it closer to the role of the French Constitutional Council than to that of a Constitutional Court in the American or post-World War II German understanding of this institution. In fact, since in most cases the Court has been appealed to by a parliamentarian minority which had been overruled, an observer familiar with the political life of Bulgaria noted that "in a sense the Court has acted as a second chamber of parliament, resolving conflicts within the legislature" (Kolarova 1993: 49). However, the decisions of the Court, mostly in the field of highly divisive issues (e.g., laws on de-communization, or on the status of the party of the Turkish minority) reveal its efforts to act as a moderator rather than as an active participant in the political game. In the Czech and the Slovak Republics the Constitutional Courts have played a minor political role. Given the inherently instable character of the Slovak constitution it may damage this country's long-term stability that no institutional mechanism for the solution of political crises is available.

2.6 Amendment rules

Amendment rules are not merely technical devices. They are rules about changing the outcome of the constituent power which gave birth to the constitution and which, as in the cases examined here, acted in an extraordinary, quasi-revolutionary situation. Amending the constitution means revising and redrafting the founding act of the constituent powers in a non-revolutionary spirit in that the changes are performed according to the rules which the constitution has already established. Amendment rules embody the compromise between the tendency towards social and political innovation which struggles for the adjustment of the political system to new conditions, and the opposite impetus to guarantee legal, economic, and social stability and predictability by keeping certain issues apart from normal politics and the fluctuations of changing majorities. This is why normally, amendments to the constitution are rendered difficult by specific requirements such as, e.g., supermajorities, burdensome, and time-consuming procedures, the necessity of a special convention, or a referendum.

Generally speaking, it follows that the distinction between amending the constitution and ordinary law making is the more marked the more the constitution is conceived as the supreme law, which imposes its rules even on the will of the sovereign, and vice versa. However, as already mentioned earlier, in the Hungarian constitution we find both the declaration of the constitution as the fundamental law which imposes its force on all state bodies (including the National Assembly),[146] and a blurring between ordinary legislation and constitutional amendments. Not only does it assign the power to enact (!) the constitution to the National Assembly,[147] but it also confines itself to requiring a two-thirds majority of the members of the National Assembly for amendments to the constitution without determining any further procedural conditions.[148] No essentials, such as the democratic form of government and certain human rights, are protected from elimination via constitutional amendments. Since the two-thirds majority is also required for several other acts of the legislature, the symbolic boundaries between normal and constitutional politics are quite indistinct.

The same is true for the Czech and the Slovak constitutions. For them, amendments to the constitution are no more than the enactment of a law which requires a larger than normal majority, namely a three-fifths majority of all members of the National Council in Slovakia[149] and the same majority in the Czech Chamber of Deputies whilst a less demanding majority of three-fifths of the present members is required in the Senate.[150] Until the end of 1996 the functions of the Czech Senate were performed by the Chamber of Deputies,[151] the situation was *de facto* the same in both successor states of Czechoslovakia. No further procedural requirements are established, even a provision stating the inadmissability of an amendment which aims at the elimination of the essential tenets of the constitution is lacking.

By contrast, the amendment rules of the Bulgarian constitution appear more consistent with its self-declared character as the supreme law.[152] For the adoption of a new constitution and for several specified amendments of particular significance, the election of a special convention, of the Grand National Assembly, is necessary whose powers expire after it has performed the task for which it was elected.[153] To pass a bill the Grand National Assembly requires the rather high majority of two-thirds of all members in three ballots on three different days.[154] Since the Grand National Assembly acts as a Constituent Assembly, it follows that it is free to resolve any issue without restrictions.[155] Other amendments can be resolved by the (legislative) National Assembly through an equally burdensome procedure: only the president or a quarter of the members of

---

[146] Art. 77.
[147] Art. 19 para. 3 lit. a.   [148] Art. 24 paras. 3, 5.   [149] Art. 84 para. 3.
[150] Art. 39 para. 4.   [151] Art. 106 para. 2 sentence 2.   [152] Art. 5 para. 1.
[153] Art. 157–62.   [154] Art. 161.
[155] See Art. 158 which renders even the form of state structure, the form of government or the irrevocability of the fundamental civil rights at the disposition of the Grand National Assembly.

the National Assembly can initiate an amendment procedure, and the bill can only be adopted if it has acquired the necessary majority of three-quarters of the votes of all members of the National Assembly in three ballots on three different days.[156] This is an extreme version of a deliberation requirement which tends to make changes to the constitution almost prohibitively difficult. Yet, there is an alleviating alternative which permits a two-thirds majority in exchange for delaying the draft by no less than two and no more than five months.[157]

2.7 Conclusions

All constitutions under study reveal a strong commitment of their drafters to the legally binding force of the constitution, i.e., to the essential idea of constitutionalism. Given the merely symbolic character of communist constitutions this marks the most radical break with the past. The existence of positive rights (largely identified with so-called social and economic or welfare rights) in all constitutions under study, even in the most radical-liberal Czech constitution, should not be regarded as counter-evidence. True, they do not have the force of judicially enforceable entitlements; but they are not merely political declarations without any legal significance either. They are declared outright as requiring legislative action (and administrative implementation), and this sets them close to the French model of constitutional rights (see Preuss 1996). One of the consequences characteristic of the constitutions under study is the less important role of the judicial branch of government. This is consistent with the continental European tradition which had more trust in the parliaments than in the courts as the defenders of the rights and interests of the individuals (Henkin 1989). Hungary is the rare case of a combination of numerous institutional guarantees and positive rights with an activist role of the constitutional court. Not accidentally this amalgam has been criticized as distorting both the rule of law and the welfare state (Sajo 1996).

Despite this questionable Hungarian experience it is safe to assume that positive constitutional rights as such are not likely to weaken the idea of constitutionalism in these countries. This hypothesis is supported by the fact that all countries strongly emphasize the stability of the government *vis-à-vis* the potentialities of fluctuating and unstable majorities in the parliaments. Hungary goes farthest in this direction in that its constitution establishes the constructive vote of no confidence. But the

---

[156] Art. 154 para. 1.   [157] Art. 155. para. 2.

other constitutions also provide the governments with rather safe areas of independent political action.

The newly emerging institutions of constitutionalism are sometimes weakened by internal inconsistencies. As already mentioned earlier, the Hungarian constitution is prone to cause strife amongst the main organs over their respective powers which are not well demarcated. In all countries except in the Czech Republic this lack of balance applies mainly to the role of the president, be it that a strong legitimation is not matched by corresponding powers (Bulgaria), or that a relatively strong constitutional authority is not supported by a corresponding mode of election (Hungary), or that the president is largely excluded from playing an active role in the solution of political crises (Slovakia). These inconsistencies make the countries vulnerable to political instability because the constitution, rather than providing the instruments for the resolution of political crises, may become their source.

The Czech constitution appears least vulnerable to this danger because its scheme of powers appears well balanced. Yet its concern for institutional stability and its largely individualistic conception of civil society may jeopardize the stability of the political system in times of major economic and social crises. Indeed, other constitutions, like the Bulgarian, which are much more concerned with social integration may be better prepared to cope with a crisis despite their partial incoherence.

4

Building and consolidating democracies

1 Introduction

The creation of constitutions is a necessary, but not a sufficient condition of a consolidated democratic polity. As we argued in the first chapter, we consider the successful and complete institutionalization of agency the essential prerequisite of a consolidated and sustainable democratic polity. Obviously the lack of transformative interests which we identified as one of the main characteristics of the breakdowns of 1989 renders the formation of agency a major problem. Since the old regime did not breed a counter-elite standing for a coherent program for the new social order and the path to it, no uncontested actor was available who could claim the unequivocal mandate for political action. Without a clear answer as to who is entitled to shape the new institutions of democracy almost every issue is liable to embittered contestation.

In this chapter we deal with the politico-institutional conditions which enabled, facilitated, discouraged, or disabled the surfacing of agency in the field of political will-formation. In the countries under study democracy started with free elections, shifting political decision making from personal rulers to impersonal rules. In section 2 of the chapter we examine the electoral systems, more particularly the questions of whether the different modes of extrication shaped their character, what consequences they have for the number of parties (two parties or multi-partism), for the power relations between them (symmetric or asymmetric), and for the mode of party competition (moderate or polarized competition). Section 3 deals with the properties of political parties which have been pushed into the center of political action. The structure and the interaction of political parties are the most significant variables which contribute to the consolidation or failure of the political systems of democratic polities.

To be sure, our analysis of electoral and party systems will not tell the whole story about the consolidation of democracy. Three further elements which we could not include in our inquiry on the grounds of time and space should be noted briefly. First, political parties are not the only institutional devices of democratic interest articulation and aggregation. Otherwise the consolidation of the party system would be tantamount to the consolidation of the democratic system as a whole. Obviously this is not the case. In consolidated pluralist democracies a wide range of interests and value commitments are processed through functional channels and direct bargains with elected politicians and appointed state officials. They form an intermediate system of interest representation of social groups, also propelled and maintained by their own institutional logic of operation (Schmitter 1992). Studies in this field have convincingly demonstrated the weakness and inadequacy of the systems of interest representation in the post-communist societies of the CEE countries. The institutional emptiness provides strong incentives to reinforce passive expectation and anarchic defense behavior which is rampant in these societies and may become a major obstacle to successful transition (Hausner and Wojtyna 1993: 227; Ost 1993, 1994; Waller 1993).[1]

This leads to our second qualification. Regime changes do not only occur in the form of a sharp discontinuity at the macro-level of the regime, institution, and collective agency, but also at the more diffuse micro-level of the attitudes of the individuals. These changes concern the somewhat vague concept of political culture. The introduction of democracy in the CEE countries was an elite's project and preceded the integration of democratic values and culture among the masses. Popular democratic culture such as tolerance, trust in institutions, participation, and commitment to the democratic rules and norms emerge and are likely to become rooted in the attitudes of the ordinary people if they regard their experience of democracy as satisfying in terms of legitimate and efficient government. Given the fluidity of opinions and the difficulty in identifying changes with respect to values, it seemed appropriate to largely neglect this element.

Finally, we do not ignore the significance of the reform of the state administration for a successful transition to democracy. In particular the submission of the state apparatus to the rule of law, its disengagement

---

[1] As far as associations in the field of the labor market are concerned, a more detailed account will be given in chapter 6.

from broad areas of social life which it used to control under communism, and the introduction of the institution of local government are indispensable ingredients of the democratic character of the new regimes. Here we have to restrict ourselves to references to the elaborate research which has been conducted in this field by other scholars (Hesse 1993; Toonen 1993; Stalhlberg 1993; Regulska 1993; Coulson 1995).

2 The choice and consequences of the electoral systems

Choosing an electoral system has been one of the most intricate and important decisions to be made during the transition from communist rule. Rule making for electoral systems and decision making under electoral rules had to take place simultaneously. In addition, the first freely elected assemblies often functioned both as a legislature and as a constituent assembly (Bulgaria, former Czechoslovakia). Thus the choice of the electoral formula not only contributed to the composition of the parliament, but to the constitution-making process and to the legitimacy of the constitution itself.

The most important decisions to be made concerned the *electoral formula* itself (majoritarian, proportional, or mixed formulas) and issues closely related to it such as the choice between the election of personal candidates or the selection from closed party lists; the option for or against *electoral thresholds*; and the decision on the *assembly size*, i.e., the total number of seats available for electoral representation; and the *district magnitude* regarding the number of elected representatives per district and the location of the districts. These four main dimensions of any electoral system have consequences not only for the level of proportionality but also for the management of ethnic, cultural, religious, or linguistic conflicts.

First and foremost, electoral systems regulate the transformation of voting preferences into democratically legitimized political power, i.e., into a given distribution of governmental authority; in democracies, typically into a given number of parliamentary seats allocated between the competing political parties according to the number of votes received by the respective parties (Rae 1971: 14). Secondly, they are the midwives of political parties. They create political agency by shaping the structure of the party systems and they determine the demise or survival of political parties by providing them with various possibilities for gaining access to political power. Thirdly, they make an important contribution to the management of political, social, economic, and ethnic divisions. Different electoral systems use different inclusive or exclusive mechanisms regarding the allocation of parliamentary representation. Thus they affect the mode of political competition, making it either more consensual or conflictual. Fourthly, they structure the alternatives with which voters are confronted during elections. They either narrow the voters' choice or extend it to a wide range of different alternatives. They have "constraining" effects on voters' choice and "reductive" effects on the number of political parties (Sartori 1994: 32–3). Lastly, electoral systems also have consequences for governmental agency. They contribute to the degree of fragmentation of parliaments and thus influence the creation and durability of governments which depend on the enduring confidence of a parliamentary majority.

2.1 The origin and structure of the electoral systems

In Bulgaria and Hungary the electoral laws were shaped during the Round Table negotiations between the old *nomenklatura* and the opposition forces. In Czechoslovakia the electoral system was thoroughly imposed by the opposition.

In the first elections, the communists, who had managed to retain some political power and who had expected to sustain it after the first elections, typically opted in all countries under study for the majoritarian principle. There were at least three important reasons for this: (i) they had a better organizational basis than the opposition forces; (ii) they anticipated that members of the local *nomenklatura* would still have the ability to attract the mainly rural voters; and (iii) they hoped to present candidates at the national level who were better known publicly (Jasiewicz 1993: 141). In some cases they proved right but in other instances they were completely wrong.

In the *Bulgarian* tradition, the electoral formula "has usually been viewed as a key factor determining the prospects of competing parties and coalitions. In post-communist Bulgaria, the restoration of a multi-party parliament also revived the instability of electoral regulations, traditional to pre-war Bulgaria" (Kolarova and Dimitrov 1994: 50). This instrumental factor dominated the shaping and reshaping of the Bulgarian electoral laws.

The electoral law for the Grand National Assembly which simultaneously operated as a legislature and as a constituent assembly, was part of the second package formulated at the Round Table Talks signed on March 30, 1990 (Ashley 1990; Szajkowski 1991; Kolarova and Dimitrov 1996). It included major topics such as constitutional amendments regarding presidential powers, basic principles of the new party law, and the electoral law.

At the Round Table, the communists argued that only the election of a National Assembly, consisting of 250 seats and operating purely as a legislature, should take place before June 1990; also that the elections should be conducted using a mixed electoral formula focussing on majoritarian representation through which 175 seats in the National Assembly would be filled. The remaining 75 seats were to be distributed according to the proportional principle. They hoped that experience of earlier elections would give them an undue organizational advantage and that the winner-take-all rule would favor strongly their own better known candidates both at the national level and in the rural districts.

The opposition, which was united in the Union of Democratic Forces (UDF), favored a proportional electoral system. They expected that this model would safeguard the minority parties' representation in the Assembly. They also demanded that elections should not be held before September 1990 as they needed time to organize their electoral campaign.

A compromise was reached by political logrolling. The opposition agreed to early elections in June 1990, whilst the communists agreed to limit presidential powers. The compromise reached over the electoral law was a combination of both proposals. It required two rounds of voting to be held on June 10 and June 17, 1990 respectively. Two hundred of the 400 seats in the Grand National Assembly were balloted using the majoritarian principle, requiring more than 50 percent of all votes. Failing an absolute majority in the first round, the two best-supported candidates then had to enter into a second round on June 17, 1990, where a simple majority qualified them for the Constituent Assembly. The remaining 200 seats were allocated according to party lists requiring a single vote on June 10, 1990, using the d'Hondt formula and introducing a 4 percent threshold at the national level. Thus the Bulgarian electoral formula at these first elections proved to be one of the least proportional in CEE.

The constitution-making process stipulated that after the adoption of the Constitution new parliamentary elections should be held within three months of the self-dissolution of the Grand National Assembly.[2] The existing National Assembly was then in a position where it had rapidly to discuss and design the new electoral law between July and August of 1991. As a result, the majoritarian components of the electoral law of 1990 were skipped and a strong proportional system was introduced using the d'Hondt formula and maintaining the 4 percent threshold again. This change occurred because the position of the various political factions had changed markedly. The anti-communist coalition, the UDF, was confronted with increasing internal struggles

---

[2] Clause 7 (1) of the "Transitional and Concluding Provisions" of the newly adopted constitution of July 12, 1991.

and splits.[3] Thus for them the risk of losing the next election through a majoritarian or a mixed voting system seemed too high. For the BSP, the majoritarian component was risky too, as opinion polls demonstrated that the anti-communist UDF had improved its electoral position and now had a chance of winning the election. The Turkish MRF also campaigned for proportional representation because it saw in this the best guarantee of its minority position. Thus all the important political players believed that proportionality would best secure their interests in the second election and would assure them an adequate share of parliamentary seats.

In addition, a number of other issues had become important, in particular the voting rights of Bulgarian citizens abroad, the right of organizations not registered as parties to participate in the elections, the method of computing electoral results, and the color of the ballot sheets (Kolarova and Dimitrov 1994: 50–1). Discussions over these issues were contentious and reached their peak when President Zhelev vetoed the bill and the BSP subsequently were able to overrule his veto because the opposition boycotted parliamentary sessions.

The clause, never publicly discussed, which regulated the voting rights of citizens abroad and of those who had recently changed their place of residence within the country, discriminated particularly against the Turkish minority. Voting was possible only for those citizens who had the time and sufficient funds to travel to their place of residence in Bulgaria. Those most affected were the 30 percent, approximately, of ethnic Turks who had left Bulgaria since 1989. These restrictions were abolished both for the presidential elections and for the December 1994 parliamentary election (Kolarova and Dimitrov 1994: 52). The latter was conducted under the same proportional formula as the 1991 elections.

Former *Czechoslovakia* was the only country in which political power was no longer in the hands of the old communist elite and where the negotiations over the electoral law were therefore supervised by the opposition. The remarkable fact is that in the end the decision to adopt proportional voting was taken by the very group, Civic Forum – especially Havel and his close advisers – which had everything to gain from adopting majority voting and which, moreover, had the power to impose that system. One of Havel's close associates remarked that "this decision will be seen either as the glory or the weakness of the November revolution: we were winners that accepted a degree of self-limitation."

---

[3] The splinter groups from the UDF called themselves the UDF-Center and UDF-Liberals and both campaigned in the October 13, 1991 elections, but failed to meet the 4 percent threshold.

From the positive (as distinct from the normative) point of view, the episode offers an important counterexample to the proposition that parties invariably favor the electoral system that favor them (see chapter 3, section 1.2 above).[4]

Havel, at that time, was animated by two distinct desires. On the one hand, he did not want to exploit the dominant position of Civic Forum so that the movement would win all the seats in parliament. It was clear, however, that with majority voting Civic Forum would have swept the elections, as Solidarity had done for the elections to the Polish Senate in June 1989 when they got all deputies but one. By contrast, proportional elections would allow for the representation of other political tendencies too, including the communists. On the other hand, Havel was notoriously opposed to the party system. He wanted an electoral method that would allow for the selection of independent candidates. The method which does that par excellence is, of course, the majority system. Although systems exist – notably that of the "single transferable vote"[5] – which permit the simultaneous satisfaction of both Havel's desires, there is no evidence that any of them were contemplated at the time. In the proportional system that was eventually adopted the voters were allowed to modify the order in which the candidates were listed on the ballot, but nevertheless had to choose from the party list.

The former communists and their affiliates were not guaranteed success in elections conducted by majoritarian representation. A proportional electoral formula, on the other hand, would give them some chance of parliamentary representation and of a continued political existence. Thus, there was a convergence of preference of the democratic opposition and the incumbent rulers in propounding a proportional electoral system. In addition, the fact that proportional representation seemed to be a simple mechanism, was important because elections for the Federal Assembly and the two National Councils of the Republics were due to be held simultaneously.

The 150 seats in the House of the People were based on the ratio of the population in both of the former Republics (101 Czech and 49 Slovak seats) whilst there was an equal number of seats in the House of Nations (75 seats); together they constituted the Federal Assembly. Each party submitted two tickets, one for the upper and one for the lower House. The share of the vote of the parties in each of the 12 districts – eight in the Czech Republic and four in Slovakia – determined the number of seats available. The seats awarded to each district were not determined *ex*

---

[4] For two Polish counterexamples see Elster 1993: 207–8.
[5] For a survey see Hylland 1991.

ante but *ex post* according to the turn-out of the relative district. The seats were allocated by using the so-called Droop-Quota (for details see Pehe 1990; Wightman 1990). The National Councils of the two Republics were different in size, the Czech council consisted of 200 seats and the Slovak of 150. Elections for these seats were to be conducted using the same electoral formula.

In order to avoid the extreme party fragmentation of the inter-war period, the new law made a number of reforms to the pure party list system that had been used at that time. It stipulated that all political parties, movements, or coalitions of parties must consist of at least 10,000 members or, failing that, be in possession of a petition with sufficient signatures to guarantee them this level of support. Secondly, every party, movement, or coalition had to pass a threshold consisting of 5 percent of the vote either in the Czech or the Slovak Republics in elections to the Federal Assembly and to the Czech National Council. In the Slovak National Council the threshold was reduced to 3 percent. Overcoming this hurdle in one Republic would thus qualify them for representation in both parts of the Republic. Thirdly, voters were able to cast up to four preferential votes per party list. This idea, proposed by Civic Forum, provided that elections in the new Republic would favor individual candidates as opposed to the more anonymous lists of the political parties. For the 1992 elections, the Federal Assembly adopted an amended electoral law. Its main feature was the introduction of stricter and more variable thresholds than those of 1990: 5 percent for the parties, 7 percent for coalitions of two or more parties, and 10 percent for larger coalitions. The respective laws for the republican elections were different. While the Slovak National Council adopted the same features as the Federal Assembly, the Czech National Council introduced a 5 percent threshold for single parties, 7 percent for two party coalitions, and 9 percent for coalitions of three parties, whereas coalitions of four or more parties would have to overcome an 11 percent threshold (Juberias 1994: 13; Pehe 1992b).

Havel now promoted a change from a proportional to a majoritarian system, where voters could choose between individual and party affiliated single district candidates. His rationale was to improve relations between the elected and the electorate, anticipating that only those candidates who were better qualified to represent the feelings and interests of the electorate would win majorities (Havel 1992: 53–8). His proposal which came close to being "an authentic anti-party law" (Juberias 1994: 12) was – not surprisingly – rejected by the Federal Assembly.

The amendment of the electoral law reflected the increasing shifts and splits within the newly emerging party system. The breakaway factions from the Civic Forum Movement and Public Against Violence had dramatically increased the number of parties and political groups in parliament, in both the Federal Assembly and the respective National Councils. Introducing higher thresholds seemed justified in order to create fewer and stronger parties (or party coalitions) thereby improving the preconditions for better government. In the federal and national assemblies, politicians and parties had been far more exercised in endless debates over issues of principle and in enunciating personal aversions and hostilities than in achieving compromise in the interests of effective legislation. Raising the electoral thresholds also signaled a more pragmatic approach to politics and countered the former "anti-political politics" approach. But the raising of the threshold was not motivated only by the desire to limit the number of political parties represented at parliament and to reduce the growing confusion of an electorate that was being confronted with too many options (Juberias 1994: 11–15). The fact that the change was voted by the parties which, according to opinion polls, expected to gain seats in parliament suggests that party interest was also at work.

In *Slovakia*, the October 1994 election was conducted under the same electoral law as the 1992 elections to the National Council. Parliament did debate certain changes, but no bill proposing a change to the electoral formula gained a majority.

The *Hungarian* electoral law was part of an electoral package which included rules for the presidential and vice-presidential elections as well as the rules for the members of the local councils which had been negotiated at the National Round Table. It was passed by the old "Parliament" on October 20, 1989 (Körösényi 1990; Kukorelli 1991; Hibbing and Patterson 1992). The "triangle" Round Table agreed to amend an earlier draft from the Ministry of the Interior and delegated the task to Committee No. I/3 which began work on July 3, 1989 discussing and making amendments clause by clause.

At the National Round Table Talks on September 18, 1989 the following agreement was reached. The total number of representatives would be 374; 152 of whom would be elected in individual districts and 152 on territorial lists, based on 19 counties and Budapest City. The fraction votes[6] in both individual and territorial districts would be transferred to a national list comprising 70 seats in parliament. The

---

[6] So-called fraction votes are votes given to party lists in individual and district constituencies in the first round, but which did not result in parliamentary seats. Fraction votes of each party are summarized and distributed according to the d'Hondt formula.

conditions for setting up a party list were widely discussed in connection with questions of the preconditions for effective government and the establishment of a properly functioning parliament (Kukorelli 1991: 141). The Round Table agreed that a territorial list required the successful nomination of candidates in at least 25 percent of the individual districts; that a national list could only be set up by parties which were able to produce seven territorial lists.

At the beginning of the Round Table negotiations, the Hungarian Socialist Workers Party (HSWP) favored a one-vote, single-member district formula within a two-round ballot (300 parliamentary seats elected by single-member district votes and 50 seats on a national list; Kukorelli 1991: 140). The reason was to maintain the existing constituencies in which the communists had better-known representatives and dominated the whole infrastructure. In contrast, the opposition had less well-known local candidates due to its more urban character and its lack of mass movement support and to its lack of organizational infrastructure at the local levels. It seemed more likely that the HSWP would get a governing majority under a majoritarian system with only a minority of the votes. Moreover, the opposition was divided and had to devise an unanimous motion on the basis of the lowest common denominator. At its meeting on July 25, the movements and political parties of the Opposition Round Table reached an agreement which they all adhered to until the end: the votes for a party-list candidates and the votes for individual candidates would be equal in number, the former cast under the proportional principle and the latter under the majoritarian one, and both would respect the existing constituencies.

Alternatively[7] at the National Round Table favored a system allocating a third of the seats by party lists and two-thirds in individual districts. This made sense because the two-thirds individual district system gave social groups and other non-affiliated politicians a better chance of election. They were also opposed to the extremely party-orientated system of nomination. They claimed that the nomination of candidates would be easier if it were done by the individual voters themselves (Kukorelli 1991: 141). But the HSWP and the political parties of the Opposition Round Table both took the view that only organizations which met the requirements of the Party Law should be able to participate in the parliamentary elections.

The main question over the electoral law was whether or not the old parliament would accept the agreement reached by the National Round

---

[7] This mainly consisted of social movements, members of churches, and some former members of the official trade unions.

Table since it would mean ousting some of the members of parliament "elected" in 1985. Various parliamentary committees and groups had indeed worked on the electoral law, and it was accepted by parliament with one amendment. It dispensed with the equal distribution between majoritarian and proportional seats. The 386 parliamentary seats were now filled up by 176 candidates elected in single-member constituencies, 152 from regional party lists, and 58 from national party lists.

In the 176 single-member districts there were two rounds of voting. If the candidate gained an absolute majority, he or she would be elected. If no candidate achieved the requisite majority, the first three candidates and those who gained more than 15 percent of the vote could participate in the second election one week later, in which a relative majority was sufficient to secure election. The second ballot was reserved for regional party lists. Each region was allocated a certain number of seats in parliament, according to its size. Seats for each region were distributed under the proportional principle (using the Hagenbach–Bischoff method).

In order to ensure an effective government and a functioning parliament there were four "built-in thresholds" which reduced the number of political parties represented in parliament: (i) a 4 percent threshold for the regional and national party lists; (ii) anyone running in a single-member district (either a party member or an independent candidate) had to have at least 750 signatures of local residents; (iii) a party list could be nominated only if the party itself was able to nominate candidates in at least a quarter of the single-member districts in that region; and (iv) a national party list could be set up only if a party was able to put up at least seven regional lists.

For the August 1994 elections, the electoral law was slightly amended, raising the threshold from 4 percent to 5 percent. To change the electoral law, the Hungarian constitution requires a qualified two-thirds majority within parliament thus stipulating a grand coalition between the strongest parties. No party was willing to alter the electoral formula substantially, since they all expected to benefit from the strong majoritarian component. The smaller parties were too weak to instigate a change to a more proportional formula through which they would get higher representation. However, two of the ruling coalition parties, the HDF and the Independent Smallholders, developed significant splits which led to the formation of two new parties.[8] Some of the parties which had not been able to reach the 4 percent threshold in the 1990 elections now saw a real

[8] A former HDF member, Istvan Csurka, founded the Hungarian Justice and Life Party and former Smallholder's members that of the United Smallholders Party, both with support from some members of parliament.

chance to compete successfully in the 1994 elections. The major parties tried to keep them out of parliament by increasing the threshold. But, given the electoral risk of the newly created parties, it seems likely that many voters voted cautiously and re-elected parties which were familiar and already represented in parliament. Indeed, none of the "old" parliamentary parties were ousted from parliament nor was any new party admitted (Juberias 1994: 17).

2.2 The consequences of the electoral laws

The results of the 1990 *Bulgarian* elections came as a shock. Whilst in most of the former communist countries the first elections had proved to be referendums against the former communists, in Bulgaria, they were able to retain power even through electoral competition. The Bulgarian Socialist Party (BSP) received 47.1 percent of the vote and gained 52.75 percent of the parliamentary seats giving them a governing majority. The Union of Democratic Forces (UDF), gained only 36.2 percent of the vote which gave them 36.0 percent of the deputies represented in the Grand National Assembly. The Turkish minority party, the Movement for Rights and Freedom (MRF) came in third and got 5.75 percent of the seats in parliament while the Agrarians of the Bulgarian Agrarian National Union (BANU) got only 4 percent of the seats with 8.3 percent of the votes (see table 4.1a). In the first round of voting, the single-member districts brought the BSP twice as many seats as the UDF, while the seats distributed under the proportional principle gave the UDF 75 seats and the former communists 97 (Szajkowski 1991: 23, 27, table 1); in the second round of voting on June 17, 1990, seats for the remaining 81 single-member districts in which no candidate had gained an absolute majority were distributed according to the trend established during the first round (Szajkowski 1991: 23).

In short, the BSP was favored by the electoral system. Firstly, they benefitted from the brevity of the period which elapsed between the final agreement of the Round Table (March 30, 1990) and the first round of elections on June 10, 1990. This had left little time for the opposition to build up a nationwide organizational infrastructure. As a result, the BSP gained support predominantly in the rural areas, whereas the UDF was supported mainly in the cities. Secondly, the electoral system favored parties whose support was geographically concentrated rather than those with an equal distribution of electoral support throughout the country. This is why the 8.3 percent of the votes cast for the agrarian party BANU translated only into 4 percent of the seats: whereas the party benefitted from the proportional component of the electoral system, it did not gain any seats from the single-member districts. Thirdly, the BSP successfully played on the fears of the electorate. On the one hand, it campaigned for gradual change and promised to minimize economic crises such as inflation and unemployment, successfully translating the fear and uncertainty about the future into electoral support. On the other hand, it exploited the ethnic cleavage by playing upon historic fears of the "Turkish Yoke" (Troxel 1993). The unexpected electoral defeat made the UDF extremely bitter and pushed it to adopt a highly ideological and strongly anti-communist stance.

In accordance with the transitional constitutional text, after the adoption of the new constitution on July 12, 1991, the Grand National Assembly dissolved itself and new elections were scheduled. As an ordinary legislature rather than a constituent body, the new National Assembly would have only 240 seats. In the election on October 13, 1991, only three parties gained seats in the National Assembly, the other parties failing to pass the 4 percent threshold. Those who had failed to qualify and other parties who were disqualified on technical grounds constituted 25 percent of the overall vote (Engelbrekt 1991: 2). Whilst this level of unrepresented voters showed the strength of the electorate's disillusionment with the party politics of the government and opposition, the position of the Turkish MRF demonstrated the consistency of its predominantly ethnic constituency. The decreasing electoral turnout provides a further indication of the voters' disillusionment with politics. It dropped from 90.8 percent in 1990 to 83.9 percent in 1991 to only 75 percent in the 1994 elections.

In the 1991 elections, the UDF won 34.36 percent of the vote and got 110 seats (45.9 percent), the BSP got 33.14 percent and 106 seats (44.2 percent), and the MRF 7.55 percent and 24 seats (10.0 percent) (see table 4.1b). No party obtained an overall majority and the UDF was constrained to put together an informal coalition government which included the MRF.

After several unsuccessful votes of no confidence, deep economic crisis and political stalemate, the UDF-led government under Prime Minister Dimitrov was forced to resign through a vote of no confidence in December 1992. The new "government of experts," headed by Lyuben Berov, an economic historian and former adviser to President Zhelev, was unable to resolve the economic crisis and to impose a policy of privatization. The Berov cabinet which was not backed by a party of its own (or by a stable coalition) depended on support from such diverse quarters as the BSP, the MRF, and a parliamentary faction comprising former UDF deputies. Toward the middle of 1994, President Zhelev who first promoted the new "government of experts" publicly withdrew his support. He realized that the need to rely on the informal support of diverse political forces brought about political stalemate and slowed down all governmental initiatives.

As in the 1990 elections, the 1994 result came as a shock. Although many observers expected an electoral victory for the BSP, almost no one had considered the possibility of an absolute majority. Gaining 43.6 percent of the votes the BSP acquired 124 parliamentary seats which gave them a majority of eight seats. The UDF lost as dramatically (24.2 percent and 70 seats) as the Turkish MDF (5.4 percent and 15 seats). Two new parties entered the National Assembly, the Peoples Union (NS) (6.5 percent votes, 18 seats) and the Bulgarian Business Bloc (BBB) (4.7 percent and 13 seats)(see table 4.1c). Although the electoral formula was proportional, the combination of a high number of electoral districts (31), a relatively low assembly size (240), and the 4 percent threshold reduced the degree of proportionality and gave the formula a slight majoritarian slant.[9] It also systematically favored parties whose support was evenly spread across the country. In most of the (rural) districts, the BSP was able to organize strong support. Except for a few areas, such as the larger cities and the Turkish dominated districts, BSP was able to organize strong support in all the districts. The parties such as the Turkish MDF and – to a lesser degree – the UDF which only managed to successfully campaign in some districts, dominated by ethnic, religious, or cultural groups, were thus systematically disadvantaged.

In Bulgaria, the share of unrepresented voters increased dramatically from 3.6 percent in 1990 to 24.9 percent in 1991 decreasing to 16 percent in 1994. The newly introduced 4 percent threshold was blamed by most commentators for hindering the representation of smaller parties in parliament.

In *Hungary* the situation was very different. As in Bulgaria and the former Czechoslovakia, at the beginning of the electoral campaign a large number of organizations registered as political parties. But as a result of the "legal filters" built into the electoral law only six parties gained seats in parliament, whilst all the others failed to get representation (Kukorelli 1991: 146).

The "hybrid electoral system" (Hibbing and Patterson 1992: 432) made it possible for the HDF to command 42.8 percent of the seats in parliament with only 24.7 percent of the vote whilst the AFD[10] with 21.4

---

[9] This is a commonly shared perception amongst scholars of electoral systems; cf. Lijphart 1994: 10–4.

[10] The ADF (Alliance of Free Democrats) stands for rapid privatization, liberal political values, and human rights and freedoms; for details see chapter 3, section 1.

percent of the vote got only 23.6 percent of the parliamentary seats (see table 4.4a). When receiving relatively equal treatment through the proportional system, the HDF got 50 and the AFD 57 of the 210 seats distributed according to the proportional formula (for details see Hibbing and Patterson 1992: 438ff). The majoritarian elections in the 176 single member districts were very different. In both the first and the second round the HDF got 114 of a total of 176 possible candidates (64.8 percent), while the AFD got only 19 percent. This happened "not because it [the HDF] had popular individual candidates, not because it was strong in sparsely populated, low turnout areas, not because of its alliance with the Smallholders, and not because of the majority requirements of the electoral system; HDF success unfolded mainly because interelection vote shifts gave HDF an advantage over the AFD. This situation may have developed because voters jumped on the bandwagon after the HDF's first-round successes, or because voters simply liked what they saw of the HDF's interelection campaign" (Hibbing and Patterson 1992: 447).

The former communists, the Hungarian Socialist Party (HSP), strongly miscalculated. They only gained 33 seats in parliamant and were pushed into the status of a minority party. Under majoritarian rule, as preferred by them during the Round Table negotiations, they would have been kicked out of the parliamentary arena. Their political survival was only secured by the proportional element of the electoral system, put forth by the then opposition.[11]

The 1994 elections dramatically changed the political landscape within a stable party system. When compared with the 1990 elections, no new party entered parliament and none of the parties who had won seats in the 1990 election were eliminated.[12] This was a unique case throughout the CEE region. But within the unchanged party system the 1994 election revealed a dramatic shift in voter preference. The strongest party, the HDF, lost over 33 percent of its parliamentary seats, whereas the HSP increased its share by about 45 percent thus gaining an absolute majority with 54.1 percent of the seats.

The electoral system now strongly favored the HSP. Whereas they only gained 28.5 percent of the possible parliamentary seats from proportional voting in the district and national lists they gained 84.7 percent of the majoritarian vote. Contrary to the 1990 elections, the HSP deputies were

[11] In the majoritarian elections in the single-member districts the HSP only gained one district whilst through regional and national list they gained all the other seats.
[12] There was only one exception. One seat in a single member district was won by a candidate of the Liberal Bloc, a party which was still not yet represented in the Hungarian parliament.

now mainly elected in the single-member districts; in the second round of voting about 85 percent of the districts were won by HSP candidates. The AFD which came second in the majority vote only gained 9.7 percent of the available seats and all the other parties got 5.6 percent (see table 4.4b). Thus it was the majoritarian part of the electoral formula which made the landslide victory of the MSP possible and caused the relative demise of the other parties.

Until the 1994 elections, Hungary had seemed able to square the circle. On the one hand, the electoral system allowed for the representation of all the major political forces within parliament, excluding only a small margin; the share of unrepresented voters being 12.7 percent.[13] On the other hand, its majoritarian component permitted the creation of a strong, reasonably stable government. Hungary was the only country in the CEE countries which did not have a premature dissolution of parliament.

However, several profound problems with the Hungarian electoral formula emerged from the May 1994 elections. The overwhelming consequences of the majoritarian bias, which had allowed the HSP to gain a majority of parliamentary seats with a relatively small share – only 33 percent – of the voting majority,[14] clearly produced and still produces a high margin of "manufactured majority." It gives one or more parties a disproportionate advantage. Thus, the legitimacy of this majority is open to question whereas "earned majorities" (Rae 1971: 84–6) are always perceived as fair. The result was that the HSP attempted to broaden its political legitimacy by successfully constructing an electorally unnecessary but politically plausible coalition with the AFD.

The problem of the legitimacy of a "manufactured majority" is exacerbated when constitutional politics is involved. The coalition of the HSP and the ADF, with 72 percent of the seats, was (and still is) able to amend the constitution and pass constitutional laws. Soon after the 1994 elections, the HDF questioned the legitimacy of the new government, especially in connection with the amendment of the law on local government elections, which, as a constitutional law, requires a two-thirds majority. For the first time since the breakdown of the communist regime the opposition boycotted parliamentary sessions. In principle, the new coalition could impose the new constitution. Still working within the framework of the old amended constitution, one of the most important

---

[13] Only Poland and Albania have a lower percentage of unrepresented voters; see McGregor 1993: 13, table 2.

[14] The mathematical formula of the Hungarian electoral formula makes it impossible to gain a two-thirds majority in parliament (which is needed to change the constitution or to pass constitutional laws, such as changing electoral formulas, etc.) only by having a 50 percent majority vote.

tasks of the new parliament will be to draft and decide upon a new constitution.

In former *Czechoslovakia*, at the beginning of 1990, an increasing number of political parties emerged. As in Hungary, the "legal filters" of the electoral law reduced the number of parties. The 5 percent threshold for the Federal Assembly worked as an additional filter and again reduced the parties represented in the Federal Assembly to five in the Czech Republic and six in Slovakia. In the Czech National Council there were four parties, whilst there were seven in the Slovak National Council because of the lower 3 percent threshold.

At the elections in Czechoslovakia on June 8–9, 1990, Civic Forum won an absolute majority of Czech votes 53.13 percent for the House of the People and 49.96 percent for the House of the Nations. Public Against Violence won 32.54 percent and 37.28 percent of the Slovak vote (see tables 4.2a and 4.2b). When translated into seats it was clear that both parties had been able to obtain a decisive majority in both chambers with 87 seats in the House of the People and 83 in the House of the Nations (Wightman 1991: 323).

At the federal level, Civic Forum, Public Against Violence, and the Slovak Christian Democratic Movement formed a coalition government. There were three reasons for this. First, a broad coalition was regarded as desirable in order to cope with the difficulties of creating a market economy. Secondly, to enact constitutional amendments and other major legislation requires a three-fifth majority both in the Chamber of the People and in the Chamber of the Nations. In the latter, a three-fifth majority of both the Czech and the Slovak deputies was needed. Thirdly, the political leaders of the opposition parties wanted to establish good relations between the Federal Government and the Slovaks by including a Slovak party in the government coalition (Wightman 1991: 325).

At the beginning of the transformation process Czechoslovakia had a broadly based government, which succeeded in radically transforming the political, economic, and legal system of the country (for an overview see Pehe 1992a), but it failed to achieve the most important political goal: the framing and adopting of the federal and republican constitutions. The constitutional framework, the breaking of Civic Forum and Public Against Violence,[15] the disintegration of the political

---

[15] In spring 1991, Civic Forum split into the Civic Democratic Party, led by the Minister of Finance V. Klaus, the Civic Movement of the Minister of Foreign Affairs J. Dienstbier; a number of other elected deputies joined other political parties. Public Against Violence, facing an increase in nationalist sentiments in Slovakia split into the nationalist Movement for a Democratic Slovakia, led by V. Meciar, and the federally orientated Civic Democratic Union.

parties,[16] and the increasing national conflict between the Czechs and Slovaks led to a parliamentary situation in which "the entire decision-making process in Czechoslovakia appeared to be increasingly paralyzed, because the Federal Assembly was split along the Czechoslovak lines" (Pehe 1992a: 30).

The 1992 elections, held on June 5–6, changed the political map dramatically. In both Republics the formation of new coalition governments was relatively easy, but they were politically opposite. In the Slovak National Council, the HZDS[17] gained 74 of the 150 seats and was therefore short of an absolute majority. It quickly formed a coalition government with the Slovak National Party (SNP) (15 seats) which comprised eleven members of the HZDS, one member of the SNP, one non-party aligned General, who became Minister of the Interior; the coalition was headed by Prime Minister V. Meciar. In the Czech National Council the right-of-center parties had a majority of five seats, and formed a coalition government of the Civic Democratic Party (76 seats) and the Christian Democratic Union – made up by Czechoslovakia's People's Party (15 seats) and the Civic Democratic Alliance (14 seats) – lead by Prime Minister V. Klaus (see table 4.2d).

In contrast, the political outlook of the Federal Assembly promised to produce a permanent political and parliamentary deadlock. The parties willing to continue with the radical economic reforms (the right-of-center parties of V. Klaus' Civic Democratic Party, the (Czech) Christian Democratic Union/Peoples Party, and J. Carnugorsky's Christian Democratic Movement in Slovakia) held only 113 of the 300 seats in the Federal Assembly. The "leftist" and nationalist political parties occupied 147 seats in the Federal Assembly (Pehe 1992b: 26). The remaining seats were held by ethnic and nationalist parties (see table 4.2c).

No potential political coalition seemed able to construct a governing majority. While the leftist and Slovak nationalists had a majority in the House of the People, the right-of-center parties had a majority in the Czech chamber of the House of the Nations. Similarly, the Slovak nationalists had a clear majority in the Slovak body of the House of the Nations. "Yet any government without support of both Klaus and Meciar

---

[16] At the beginning of 1992 the number of parties and political movements in the Federal Assembly had grown from six to almost 20. The Social Democrats achieved representation in the Federal Assembly because a number of deputies from Civic Forum switched to the Social Democrats without facing re-election (Pehe 1992a: 24).

[17] The HZDS (Movement for a Democratic Slovakia), led by the populist V. Meciar, was a split off of the former Public Against Violence (for details see below, section 3.).

would have virtually no chance of survival" (Pehe 1992b: 27). In addition, no other plausible coalition would have the qualified majority needed for constitutional amendments to construct the federal framework of the future Czechoslovakia.

After the June elections both Klaus and Meciar tried to broker a political accord to produce a governmental coalition in the Federal Assembly. They reached an agreement which laid down the principles of the coalition and the guidelines for relations between the two parties (for details see Obrman 1992: 27–8). But the political will to adhere to this agreement was very weak and the main issue, the permanent constitutional crisis over the formation of the Federation, remained unsolved. As a result, the secession of the Slovak Republic seemed unavoidable and the decision to separate was taken in August 1992. After several failed attempts to create a framework for a federation, on November 25, 1992 the Federal Assembly passed a law dividing Czechoslovakia into two separate and sovereign states to take effect from January 1, 1993 (for details see chapter 3, section 1.3).

After national independence, both Republics were governed by the parties which had been elected to the National Councils in the June 1992 elections. In Slovakia, Meciar's HZDS found an informal coalition partner in the Slovak National Party (SNS). Meciar was able to consolidate, unopposed, his previously strong position by filling all the important posts with loyalists. In the absence of an elected president, and in accordance with the new constitution, he also assumed presidential powers. Internal disputes rocked Meciar's government due to his authoritarian style of resolving conflicts within government, so that during 1994 members of his own party, and a number of ministers and deputies defected from the HZDS as well as from the SNS, and formed their own parties or factions within parliament. After a spectacular presidential speech of President M. Kovac in parliament criticizing Meciar's government and his style of politics, he was deposed with a vote of no confidence in March 1994. As a consequence, new elections were scheduled for October 1, 1994.

The results of the October 1994 elections were surprising. Meciar returned as the prime minister for a second time, displaying his talent for political resurrection. The electoral campaign was organized with the help of Forza Italia, the party of the then Italian prime minister, Silvio Berlusconi, and the HZDS finished as the strongest party (61 seats), but still needed coalition partners to govern. The HZDS and the SNS – the former coalition partner – took only 70 seats. The opposition parties, which had very diverse programs, together gained 67 seats (see table 4.3). Both sides needed the political support of the far left ZRS. After refusing several times, the ZRS joined a new coalition with the HZDS/RSS and the SNS. The latter held four important ministerial posts in the new government which was sworn in on December 13, 1994.

2.3 Tentative conclusions

In the first elections in Bulgaria and Hungary, the mixed structure of the electoral systems was shaped by the logic of power sharing.[18] The communists retained some power which they sought to defend against the emerging opposition. The latter demonstrated its political strength by successfully mobilizing the masses. The forces were (relatively) balanced and both were able to push through some of their respective interests safeguarding them within institutional frameworks. In Bulgaria it led to a complete addition of the respective proposals, whereas in Hungary the intervention of the old "Parliament" prevented a similar outcome; it only marginally changed the Round Table agreement but gave it a more majoritarian slant.

While in former Czechoslovakia one might have expected the democratic opposition to plead for majoritarian voting, which they would have been in a position to impose, they practiced self-restrain and opted for a proportional system which converged with the interests of the communists. One additional factor may have contributed positively to the introduction of proportional representation, namely the idea of an historical identity, which referred back to the electoral laws of the democratic interwar period.

After the founding elections, the shaping of the electoral laws was dominated by the increasing factionalization and fragmentation of the various political groups.[19] To a greater or lesser degree, political agency was plagued by the formation of splinter groups, defections of members of parliament, and the emergence within parliament of parties which had failed to overcome the electoral threshold. In Hungary and in the Czech and Slovak Republics, stabilizing coalitions were formed against small parties. In Bulgaria the two big parties changed the electoral law to a proportional one in order to minimize their risks. In all cases, the distributional consequences of the electoral formulas were the main motives for change. Political fragmentation preceded the adoption of proportional representation, not vice versa. Thus, the major causes for political factionalism and fragmentation of parliaments were to be found

---

[18] The "logic of power-sharing" did not produce proportional formulas, as Lijphart (1992) suggests, but mixed systems.

[19] For a detailed overview see Kopecky 1995; Lomax 1995; Waller 1995.

outside the reductive effects of the electoral systems (Jasiewicz 1993: 145; see below section 3).

When analyzing the short-term effects of the electoral systems on the number of parliamentary parties, one is faced with an unexpected result. Up until the 1994 elections, Bulgaria, which had the most proportional system, produced the least number of political parties, whereas Hungary with its far less proportional system had the highest number, namely seven, with the Czech and Slovak Republics somewhere in between, with six and five.

In order to explain this, a modification of Sartori's treatment of the reductive effects of electoral systems on the number of political parties may be in order. According to Sartori (1994: 37–8) electoral systems are only effective as long as the party systems express "a natural system of channelment" (Sartori 1994: 37) for political, social, economic, and ethnic conflicts, and if voters identify with abstract party images and do not vote in accordance with volatile alignments. This statement is mostly used as a caveat against what Sartori calls "mere parties of notabilities" (1994: 38), but the situation of the CEE countries may be analogous: given programmatically diffuse parties, their weak organizational basis, an unsatisfactorily structured party system, and volatile voter alignments, electoral rules are unable to reduce the number of parties and to structure the party system.

The most common index for measuring party system fractionalization is the "effective number of parties" (Taagepera and Shugart 1989: 77–91) which can be calculated on the basis of either the share of the vote or parliamentary seats.[20] The latter index measures the degree of fractionalization in the party system. For Bulgaria in the 1990 and 1991 elections, it is 2.4, thus reflecting the coalitional importance of the Turkish MRF, for 1994 it is 2.75, reflecting the significance of the two new parliamentary parties. Hungary displays the highest value (3.8) and both the Czech and Slovak Republics come close to Hungary (each 3.4). After the 1994 elections, Slovakia increased to 4.41 and Hungary decreased to 3.0, reflecting the absolute majority of the HSP.

An additional feature of (proportional) electoral systems is the level of representativeness, which is an important indicator of the legitimacy of

[20] The effective number of relevant parties can be calculated as $N_s = \frac{\Lambda}{\Sigma^2}$ is the seat proportion of the ith party and the formula – in short – means that the "weight" of each party is squared and each "weight" is added up to an index, the Herfindahl–Hirschmann-index (HH). The inverse of the summed values (1/HH) displays the effective number of parliamentary parties. For a detailed discussion of the different indices for measuring the fragmentation of party systems see Lijphart 1994: 67–72.

the elected government. One rough method for measuring this is the level of unrepresented voters in parliament, meaning those voters who back political parties which fail to gain parliamentary seats. The most common method to reduce the level of representativeness is the use of electoral thresholds. One common feature of the CEE political party landscape is the large number of (often small) parties running in elections and – as a result of thresholds – a significant lack of representation. In the Czech Republic, Bulgaria, and Slovakia about one quarter of the active voters were not represented in parliament (respectively 26.3 percent, 25.1 percent, (1994: 16.1 percent) and 24.9 percent (1994: 12.8)); in Hungary in the two preceding elections the proportion was about 10 percent.

That Hungary has the least proportional electoral system corresponds with the fact that it is the most ethnically homogeneous country whereas the other countries have strong ethnic minorities: the Turkish minority in Bulgaria and, clearly, the national split in the former Czechoslovakia. The former republics and now the new states have additional ethnic minorities: a strong Hungarian minority in Slovakia, and, in the Czech Republic, a small German minority. An explanation by Stein Rokkan may perhaps be broadened here, that ethnically and religiously divided countries prefer a stronger proportional representation than ethnically homogeneous countries (Rokkan 1970: 175; Lijphart 1992a: 216–17). Our account of Bulgaria and of former Czechoslovakia clearly confirms this hypothesis.

One indicator for consolidated democracies is the existence of relatively stable electoral rules. In the short period between the first (semi-free) elections in Poland in 1989, and the most recent elections held in Bulgaria on December 18, 1994, the electoral formulas in many CEE countries have been (and still are) in a state of constant flux. The changes in Bulgaria (Albania, Romania, and Poland) have been relatively important, they have been minor in former Czechoslovakia, and insignificant in Hungary and Slovakia. The struggle over the rules of the political competition became an issue whenever the relative weight of the political forces changed. While electoral rules are the object of bargaining in all democratic systems, in no other part of the world, nor within such a short period of time were the rules of the electoral game changed so frequently (Juberias 1994: 27). Obviously attempts to circumvent fortuitous and undesirable outcomes decrease the legitimacy of democratic institutions and hint against consolidation. Yet, the volatility of electoral rules is only part of a longer story which deals with the structure of political agency, cleavage lines cutting across the parties, and their consequences for the mode of party competition. These questions will be dealt with in the following section of this chapter.

3 Political parties, cleavage structures, and party systems: the prospects for party competition

During transitions from authoritarian rule, democracy begins with (more or less) competitive elections. Competitive elections bring political parties to the forefront. But the CEE countries had a unique starting point. They could not start with either pre-existing or redemocratized political parties (except for the former communist parties) as some Western countries after World War II, where the pre-totalitarian or pre-authoritarian party structures provided the main starting point for the recreation of the new parties (e.g., Germany after 1945, Austria, Greece, and Italy). During short-lived authoritarian political regimes some parties may continue to exist or manage to retain a continuing membership or long-term loyal voter alignments; by contrast, the situation in the CEE countries was in the main a *tabula rasa*. Moreover, there was no external agency in exile waiting to return, prepared to take charge of the recreation of political parties on the basis of elaborated political and ideological programs. With the exception of the former communist parties, the main parties and the party systems emerged throughout the turmoils of 1989 and beyond. Not surprisingly, they reflect the peculiarities of the democratic beginning in post-communist societies.

Most analysts expect that having passed through a period of reconstruction the parties will embody all the elements of Western political parties. Another hypothesis reads that the distinctive initial structure of the CEE parties and the party systems of the transition period of 1990 will become frozen in much the same manner as in the West.[21] This in turn would obviously stimulate questions such as: is a distinctive type of party and a corresponding party system emerging during the post-communist transition periods? Which are the cleavage lines along which the parties are differentiating themselves in the attempt to attract voters? To which constituencies with which social basis are they appealing? What are the different strategies that the respective types of parties are developing in order to mobilize support within an unstructured electoral market?

From the experience of Latin American and Southern European transitions to democracy it appears that the institutionalization of party systems and the consolidation of democracy are intimately linked (Pridham (ed.), 1990; Diamond and Linz 1989: 20–4). In modern

---

[21] Concerning Western political parties, it is a well-known thesis of Lipset and Rokkan that the party systems of the late 1960s reflect, with a few but significant exceptions, the cleavage structures of the beginning of the century. Thus, party systems seem to become frozen (see Lipset and Rokkan 1967: 50–6).

democracies, government is government by parties. Thus the structure of the parties and the character of their electoral competition are likely to have major effects on the stability of the democratic institutions. In what follows we will first identify the types of parties which developed during the transition from communist rule. Thereafter, we will describe the properties of the party systems and the modes of interaction between them.

3.1 The peculiarities of political parties and the cleavage structures in post-communist societies

Political parties in CEE countries are transitional and transitory phenomena. They are *transitional* because they were brought into being by the transition process itself and did not themselves cause the transition. They were mainly by-products of the decaying regimes and they did not emerge from within the old communist societies with any coherent program, articulated ideology, clear-cut blueprints for change, or strong organizational basis. They are *transitory* because their original positioning on the political map was in response to the problems of transition, so that they can be expected to disappear or undergo radical changes once a new equilibrium emerges.

At the outset, one distinctive feature of CEE countries was the strong *anti-party approach* of their democratic oppositions based on the concept of "anti-politics.".In reaction against the party of the former communists, the newly emerged political agents exhibited a pronounced organizational bias toward loosely organized movements, forums, or networks of friends. The idea of a forum-party became the model for most of the countries, as the Hungarian Democratic Forum, Civic Forum in the Czech Republic and Public Against Violence in Slovakia, and the Union of Democratic Forces in Bulgaria. Central to the idea of anti-political politics, conceptualized by V. Havel, G. Konrad, A. Michnik, and other dissidents, was its concern for an autonomous civil society, which would be independent from the state rather than connected to it with political parties as mediators.

Seven years after the demise of communist rule, this type of oppositional proto-party and political movement has survived in Bulgaria and in Hungary. In the Czech and Slovak Republics Civic Forum and Public against Violence, respectively, have disappeared from the political stage. In Hungary, schism within the opposition prevailed *before* the first elections thus giving the emerging parties somewhat more stability afterwards. In any case, the various new political parties are – as in other countries – much more characterized by their different political styles, images, and the dominant personalities than by political programs and issues (Körösényi 1991: 121). In the Czech and Slovak cases the oppositional parties underwent the necessary process of diversification *after* the 1990 elections (Wightman 1995a: 243). Only in Bulgaria did the initial bi-polar structure of the Round Table negotiations between the communists and the unified opposition survive. The Union of Democratic Forces (UDF) was forced to unify itself in reaction to the exceptionally powerful Bulgarian Socialist Party (BSP) which succeeded in winning the first (and the third of December 1994) free elections.

With the exception of Bulgaria the new type of anti-party dominated the political map after the first elections; pre-communist parties had no great significance in structuring the party system. It was essentially a new beginning and not a redemocratization through a revival of the past (Körösényi 1991).

In *Bulgaria*, the Bulgarian Agrarian National Union (BANU) was a revival from the pre-communist era.[22] It was the most important agrarian party which gained 8 percent of the vote in the June 1990 elections. The Petkov Agrarian Union and the Bulgarian Social Democratic Party played an important role within the unified democratic opposition, the Union of Democratic Forces (UDF). They saw themselves as the successors of the pre-war parties (Karasimeonov 1995: 159; Szajkowski 1992: 3). In former Czechoslovakia, the Slovak National Party, the People's Party, and the Christian Democratic Party could also be related back to the inter-war period. In Hungary, only the Smallholders Party (SHP),[23] the Christian Democratic Peoples Party (CDPP), and the Social Democratic Party (SDP) were historical parties (Körösényi 1991: 175). Together they gained about 20 percent of the votes; only the Social Democratic Party failed to achieve the 4 percent threshold.

The Agrarian and/or Christian parties are perhaps best situated to reorganize themselves and establish an identity as historical parties. To some extent they represent the rural-agrarian interests and values. Although their constituencies have changed rapidly they may still be able to call upon agrarian and religious values which have outlived communist rule and may revive constituencies which communist policies failed to eradicate. By contrast, secularized historical parties with constituencies rooted in class or occupational status have been less successful (Wightman 1995b: 241–2). This is evidenced by the obvious failure of the

---

[22] During communist rule, it also existed as a satellite of the communist party.

[23] Although the Smallholders Party was less important in structuring the Hungarian party system, it was politically relevant in pushing through "natural restitution" in the coalition with the HDF after the first free elections in 1990.

social democratic parties. Even those parties which in the pre-communist period had been able to hold a successful electoral following were unable to shape the post-communist period.

Of the *former powerholders* only the Bulgarian communists – having renamed themselves the Bulgarian Socialist Party (BSP) – have remained relatively stable. Despite a 50 percent decline in its one million membership it has managed to preserve its political unity, organizational strength, party-owned communication media, most of its former property, and has until now retained a hard core of voters (Karasimeonov 1995: 164–5). In Hungary, the reform wing of the communist party broke with the past founding a new party, the Hungarian Socialist Party (HSP), which required a brand new membership. The hardliners merely changed their old party name to the Hungarian Socialist Worker's Party (HSWP) and became insignificant after the first elections. Only in the former Czechoslovakia did the communists hold on to their traditional name right up to the end of 1993, having run in the 1990 elections as the communist party of Czechoslovakia with astonishing success (they gained about 13 percent of the vote in both republics).

The pressing need to hold free elections left little time for building organizations, programs, and ideologies. From the outset, political parties were financed by the state; hence an organized membership was not essential for financing electoral campaigns and the activities of parliamentary caucuses. Political parties became the vehicle for personal political careers. New parties were often formed by members of parliaments pursuing personal or ideological conflicts, or career objectives. In Hungary, for example, in the 1990 elections seven parties gained seats in parliament whereas by the end of 1993 eighteen parties, factions, or party formations had seats (Bihary 1994: 41). In the former Czechoslovak Federal Assembly, the number of parties increased from the original six to almost 20. Internally created parties, which emerge from within legislative assemblies, are liable to have weak or non-existent external organizational resources, and also tenuous links to the economic and/or social cleavages in society. Given the specific circumstances of the CEE transitions, short-term rewards seemed an easier goal to attain for the newly created parties than long-term investments in organizational infrastructure and programmatic coherence.

It was easier to play the electoral game than to pay much attention to the strength of the party as an organization. Political leaders saw that their parties could attract electoral support through mainly television dominated electoral campaigns. Indeed, without a strong organizational base at the national, regional, and local levels, only the media enabled them to mobilize voters and campaign in elections. The organizational weakness of their parties and their dependency on the media may have caused the "media wars"[24] which have swamped post-communist societies in the last few years.

Politicians and parties were faced with an almost entirely open electoral market. As only a few voters entered the electoral market with pre-existing partisan loyalties there was a *wholly new electorate* to tap (Mair 1991: 134).[25] In addition, the volatility of the electorate was fostered by the lack of a differentiated civil society and of a corresponding set of organizations which could create and sustain collective identities based on interests (Evans and Whitefield 1993: 543–7). Only ethnic minorities provided clear-cut constituencies where voting along ethnic lines was a means of reinforcing ethnic identity. Obviously this applies to Bulgaria where the Movement for Rights and Freedoms is *the* party of the Turkish minority and to Slovakia where the Hungarian minority by and large vote for the Hungarian Christian Democratic Movement/Coexistence.

Moreover, short-term investments in the electoral game are likely to prevail over long-term investments in the party if the stakes are as high as in the CEE countries (Mair 1991: 133–4). Political power and the state bureaucracy are up for grabs; conflicts over restitution or reprivatization of former property divide societies; and bitter battles are fought over retribution/lustration against the former incumbents.

In the absence of established, autonomous forms of association and weak social differentiation, the political parties in the CEE could not emerge along pre-existing socio-economic cleavage lines. Party formation took place mainly over the heads of society on the basis of polarizing cultural and ideological antagonisms constructed within the political elites which borrowed a great deal from the current ideological resources of the last two centuries.

In *Hungary* the major differences between the most important political parties, the HDF and the opposition AFD/AYD can be explained by the "traditional and mutual prejudices of the urban and populist wings of the Hungarian intellectuals . . . . The subcultural hostility between the two elite groups strengthened their ideological differences, and determined the left–right scale" (Körösényi 1991: 172). The HDF represents the populist, rural wing, and lays claim to what an analyst of the region has

---

[24] For Hungary see Hankiss 1993; for Slovakia see Bútorová and Bútora 1995; for Bulgaria see Gotovska-Popova and Engelbrekt 1993.

[25] To be sure, when introducing universal suffrage in Western Europe, waves of newly enfranchised and newly available voters flooded into the electoral market. Distinct to CEE, they flooded into structured electoral markets and often with pre-existing identities and preferences. Democratization in Eastern Europe provided an almost entirely new electorate (see Mair 1991: 134).

called a "substantive" as opposed to a "procedural" interpretation of democracy (Körösényi 1991). The same applies to the two coalition partners of the Democratic Forum, the Christian Democratic Peoples' Party and the Independent Smallholders' Party. The latter also pushed on the issues of compensation and reprivatization for the expropriated agrarians. On the other hand, the AFD (and AYD) uphold a largely "procedural" conception of democracy, relying on the historic demands for the political emancipation of the lower classes and claiming universal and secret suffrage, the right of assembly, trade union rights, and individual rights (cf. Körösényi 1991: 170–2). Both parties were created by these two small groups of intellectuals and after the founding elections became the most important parties in Hungary.

One striking (but not suprising) feature of CEE party politics is the absence of the socio-economic gap in the traditional class conflict between workers and owners. As a result, in Hungary, there was no working class or Social Democratic party among the six parliamentary parties. No party has a clear working-class constituency (Körösényi 1992: 347). The influence of the traditional left, the social democratic parties (or socialist or labor parties), was very weak. After the 1994 elections, the HSP became the strongest party and now seems fully committed to being a Western style social democratic party. But even so the capitalist/manager versus worker cleavage finds no real representation and expression in the party system. They are only represented as being of purely "theoretical interest" and not as the well-defined interest of a particular social group (Staniszkis 1991: 229). Although all the parliamentary parties were plagued by internal disputes and splits, overall they remained relatively stable (see Lomax 1995). None of the parties disappeared from the political scene and all were returned to parliament after the second election. But the balance of power had changed drastically.

The situation in former *Czechoslovakia* was very different. In the founding elections of 1990 the opposition, the Czech Civic Forum and the Slovak Public Against Violence, commonly won an overwhelming victory at the federal level. However, viewed separately, both "parties" experienced quite different results within "their" respective Republics. While the Czech Civic Forum won a strong majority of about 50 percent of the vote in the Czech lands, the Slovak party attracted only about 30 percent of the vote in the Slovakian part of Czechoslovakia. The remaining votes were much more evenly distributed amongst the other political contenders than in the Czech lands. Public Against Violence campaigned with a federal and libertarian program, running against other successful parties which displayed strong clerical, national, and religious tendencies. This applied mainly to the Christian Democratic Movement and the Slovak National Party which gained about 20 percent and 13 percent of the vote respectively in the first election (see Juberias 1992; Wightman 1995a).

Soon after the first elections (June 1990), the splits in both the movements brought about a complete change in the whole Czechoslovakian party system. The Slovak party system, especially Public Against Violence, was racked with divisions mainly over the nature of the federal set-up and the balance of power between the federal government and the National Councils of the constituent republics. The constitutional cleavage finally entailed the break-up of Public Against Violence in early 1991 and of the Christian Democratic Movement at the beginning of 1992.

The divisions within the Czech Civic Forum concerned the future character of this loosely organized movement and the politics of privatization which it envisaged. After his election as Civic Forum's first chairman, V. Klaus, the former federal Finance Minister, challenged the "anti-politics" views of the other members and former dissidents, emphasizing the need for a strong and traditionally organized political party which would support his course of economic reforms effectively. Today, Klaus' Civic Democratic Party seems to be one of the most stable and well-organized political parties in the region (Wightman 1995b: 248).

After the split of the Civic Forum, Klaus' party became a dominant element of the Czech Republic's party system. The party promoted rapid and quick privatization, strong market allocation, was critical of the political criteria of distribution, and pursued a libertarian and international orientation. Similarly, the split of Public Against Violence led to the creation of the strongest party in Slovakia, the Movement for a Democratic Slovakia (HZDS). Headed by V. Meciar already before the "velvet divorce," it promoted the claim to self-determination for the Slovaks within a sovereign Slovakian state, a slower process of privatization, a more cautious approach to marketization in order to mitigate the social hardships of economic transformation, and state involvement in crucial economic sectors. It also stood for strong Christian values, supported demands for Slovakian cultural development, and propagandized a communitarian concept of democracy. Other important Slovak parties, such as the Christian Democratic Movement (KDH) and the Slovak National Party (SNS), steadily increased their nationalist/ethnic aspirations. Only the Party of the Democratic Left was, in the main, organized along the traditional left–right scale, defending the social security values of the workers.

After the break up of the federation, the party structures in the Czech Republic remained relatively stable. The 1992 elections rendered Klaus' Civic Democratic Party, which ran in electoral alliance with the Christian

Democratic Party, the dominant force in the government coalition, which included two other parties, the Civic Democratic Alliance and the Christian Democratic Union/Czech Peoples' Party. The parliamentary opposition consists of the left bloc, the renamed former communist party of Bohemia and Moravia which, unlike most of the former communist or socialist parties, refused to adopt a social democratic line and continues to propagate communist values. It also includes the extreme right-wing party, the Association for the Republic, which is a new parliamentary party and is as hostile to any kind of democracy as the Left Bloc. Both are typical anti-system parties. Another newcomer to the Czech National Council has been the Czech Social Democracy Party which is committed to traditional social democratic values (see table 4.3).

On the whole there was no need for the Czech parties to revise their ideology and programs after the break-up of the federation. The situation was different in Slovakia where no political force had formulated a coherent program for the politics of post-independence (cf. Bútorová and Bútora 1995). Moreover, the national issue had been solved with unexpected speed. Nationalist mobilization is a high-stake game with quick results. In contrast, the building of institutions for a new nation state is a protracted, complicated, and time-consuming process.[26]

The SNS which came second in the 1992 elections, had a monothematic program for national independence and needed to broaden its focus in order to relocate itself within the party spectrum. During the spring of 1993, a liberal wing emerged from within the party demanding privatization and a market economy, and criticizing the HZDS' privatization program which tended to espouse the economic interests of the HZDS and to favor the old industrial lobby. It tried to occupy the rightist and market-oriented territory left vacant after the 1992 electoral defeat of the Democratic and Civic Democratic parties (Bútorová and Bútora 1995: 126). Only the Party of the Democratic Left remained relatively stable because it managed to stick to its social policies and to its concept of cautious privatization in a period of increasing uncertainty after national independence. The HZDS itself was rocked by internal disputes and splits (for a detailed account see Bútorová and Bútora 1995: 122–5).

In *Bulgaria*, the party structure mainly developed around either rapid privatization, marketization, and aggressive anti-communism or slow privatization and redistribution, the former being represented by the

---

[26] It seems more accurate to treat the Czech Republik as the successor state incorporating all the historically and actually important ingredients whilst Slovakia is the typical case for secession, followed by the complicated process of nationstate building.

different political forces unified in the UDF and the latter by the reform communists of the BSP. Like many other parties in the CEE countries, most of these were electoral coalitions. The number of coalitions increased from one in 1990 to seven in the 1991 elections. The BSP stood as an "Election Alliance of the BSP" instead of a single party as it had done in 1990 (Szajkowski 1992: 10–11). The only party with a homogeneous constituency is the MRF, the party which calls for the democratic rights and freedoms of the Turkish and Muslim minorities; its electorate consists mainly of ethnic Turks for whom voting for the MRF reinforces their ethnic identity. It stands for redistribution and slow privatization since its constituency is seriously disadvantaged by economic reforms.[27]

In the countries which we examined the cleavage lines of party differentiation are functioning mainly at the level of the political elites. Moreover, ideological conflicts which divide the different political parties are at the same time also divisions within the parties themselves. All parties in the CEE countries, the communists being no exception, are strongly fractionalized internally, having to a greater or lesser degree their respective liberals, nationalists, religious-conservatives, social democrats, populists, and sometimes anti-democratic radicalists.[28] As a consequence, any change in the internal affairs of one party immediately influences the internal discussions and actions of all the other parties. If we examine the Hungarian political parties, which appear some of the most stable in the region:

> it is realistic to presume that any of them could move in any direction . . . . This means, first of all, that almost all major ideological platforms and political ideologies could find leading personalities even in the event of any given party taking a radically new direction. . . . all six parties contained strong political personalities who did not have any significant position in the given party, but who would be able to direct the party in an entirely new direction at any time. (Kéri and Levendel 1995: 136)

There are strong indications that none of the parties in the countries under study are anchored in the divisions in society; rather, they are "floating" over society (Agh 1992b: 23) and in a constant state of flux. This is matched by the constant wavering of voters in their party preferences, which are related neither to class/social status nor to the various elements of the new economic order (Simon and Bruszt 1992: 195–200). Instead, voter preferences depend mainly on secondary social

---

[27] The ethnic Turks are predominantly agricultural workers in the tobacco industry.
[28] A detailed account of factionalism within the political parties of Hungary, the Czech Republik, and Bulgaria is provided respectively by Lomax 1995; Kopecky 1995; and Waller 1995.

attributes such as age, residence, and educational status. [29] Given the low level of institutionalization of political parties and of electoral markets with a high level of electoral availability, the *interactions* of the parties may become a key variable for the stability of the whole political system.

3.2 The mode of party competition: polarized or moderate pluralism?

All party systems in the countries under study are multi-party systems.[30] After the 1990 elections, Bulgaria began with a two-and-a-half party system in which the reform communists of the BSP and the UDF were the two main parties. Both needed the smaller MDF to build up a coalition with a governing majority. From late 1992 onwards, the fragmentation of the UDF increased the number of parliamentary parties and tipped the balance in favor of a multi-party system (as distinct from a two-party system); the 1994 elections resulted in five parliamentary parties with the BSP as the dominant party.

Hungary may also be classified as having a multi-party system with a dominant party as was the case for the Czech and Slovak Republics after the 1992 elections. In the Czech case the dominant party was the ODS of Prime Minister V. Klaus and in Slovakia the HZDS of Prime Minister V. Meciar. The concept of a multi-party system with a dominant party highlights the relative strength of the respective parties[31] and the causal relations between a multi-party system and cabinet stability: the greater the number of parliamentary parties and the more the relative weights of the parties decrease, the more unstable the governments will become (Blondel 1968: 198–200).[32] Yet, the existence of a dominant party as such is no guarantee of governmental stability. Although Bulgaria and Slovakia display a multi-party system with a dominant party, the permanent succession of governments, prime ministers, ministers, and state officials are the ingredients for the current state of governmental instability. We hypothesize that at least the dominant party in a multi-party system must

---

[29] On voting behavior and the volatility of voting preferences for Hungary, see Kéri and Levendel 1995; Bruszt and Simon 1992; for the Czech Republic, see Kostelecky 1995.

[30] Note that the parties are not measured on the basis of the average of their electoral success but are measured in terms of parliamentary seats.

[31] The typical case for a multi-party system without a dominant party is still Poland.

[32] To be sure, institutional structures intervene. The stability of a government also depends on whether there is a simple or a constructive vote of no confidence in the prime minister and his/her cabinet.

BUILDING AND CONSOLIDATING DEMOCRACIES

be rooted in particular social milieus, have stable constituencies and achieve a certain degree of institutionalizion in order to produce stable governments. Moreover, the mode of party competition within the respective multi-party systems is another important causal element. Here we refer mainly to Sartori's distinction between *moderate and polarized pluralism* (Sartori 1976: 131 ff., 173 ff.).

The various party systems of the countries being compared here may be located somewhere between moderate and polarized pluralism. They do not have the characteristics of a polarized party system[33] as was the case for example in the Weimar Republic and the Fourth French Republic, nor do they resemble the moderate party systems,[34] of say, post-war Germany or Spain after Franco. But generally, they all have a strong tendency toward a centrifugal drive and to becoming polarized, thus making the consolidation of democracy more difficult.

In most of these countries we observe a bi-polar party structure, which means a duality of alternating coalitions among a plurality of parties. Bi-polar constellations are often, although not always, an attribute of moderate pluralism.[35]

In *Hungary*, after the 1990 elections, the bi-polar system consisted of the conservative and nationalist Christian right-wing parties of the governing coalition (HDF, SHP, CDPP) and the other consisted of the liberal parties (ADF, AYF); the left-wing parties (mainly the BSP) had only marginal representation in parliament (Körösenyi 1992: 349).

The two poles consisted of explicit or implicit political coalitions and in principle every party has been able to form a coalition with every party[36] thus reducing the gap between the poles. Because of the smaller ideological distance, party competition oscillates around a politically defined center. The ever-increasing hostility between the HDF and the AFD/AYD which arose after the 1990 elections created a greater centrifugal drive thereby shifting the position slightly toward a polarized pluralism, which increased the instability of the party system (Körösényi 1992: 353). Sharp political, ideological, and constitutional conflicts

---

[33] The most common definition of polarized pluralism is provided by Sartori 1976: 131–45; 342–51.

[34] For a seminal definition and discussion of moderate pluralism see again Sartori 1976: 173–85; 342–51.

[35] As long as the ideological distance between the parties of the two poles is not wide, party competition is concentrated on the median voter and displays moderate pluralism.

[36] In the so-called "April-Pact" in 1990 the two strongest and at the same time, opposing parties, the HDF and the AFD, agreed on major constitutional changes (the parliamentary election of the president, the introduction of the constructive vote of no confidence, etc.); see Agh 1992a; Majoros 1990.

between the ruling coalition and the oppositional parties increased during the electoral campaign at the end of 1993 and the beginning of 1994. However, this did not undermine the ground rules of coalition building.

After the 1994 elections, in which the HSP gained an absolute majority of parliamentary seats, the party system changed to a tri-polar structure. One pole, the HSP, with its social democratic approach representing the left wing of the party system; the second comprising the liberal parties (AFD, AYD), and at the third pole, the national conservatives in the shape of the former ruling parties, led by the HDF. A new development emerged in the mode of party competition with the establishment of a coalition between the left-wing HSP and the liberal ADF. Whereas the former conservative coalition had been ideologically relatively homogeneous, in the shape of the nationalist-conservative parties, the new coalition spans two different ideological camps. It signals a more moderate level of party competition between the liberal and the social-democratic positions, but at the same time shows a tendency to increase the distance to the national-conservatives pole. But the Hungarian party leaders have often insisted upon the centrist quality of their respective parties, manifesting a "pursuit of the center ground" (Kéri and Levendel 1995: 142). In fact, the ideological gulf between the parties is not as wide as in the party systems of the other CEE countries under study.

Polarization may arise when party competition shifts to the constitutional level. The new coalition, which was promoted by the disproportionate electoral formula after the 1994 elections, is now able to push through not only constitutional laws but also to amend the constitution by a two-thirds majority in parliament. In principle, the socialist–liberal coalition can unilaterally impose the new Hungarian constitution, which is expected to be drafted and passed during the new parliamentary period. Hungarian politics is now confronted with the possibility of a "supercoalition", which will be able to act as "constitutional dictator," reducing all opposition to insignificance (Arato, 1994a: 29). The impetus for party competition is largely dependent on the consensual or conflictual approach of the ruling coalition.

In former *Czechoslovakia*, the bi-polarity was expressed not by a *two-party* system but by two *party systems*, each of them concentrated in one of the two republics. There were only a few parties which were organized as federal parties and only one, strangely enough the Communist Party of Czechoslovakia, which gained parliamentary seats. Even the parties which stood for the federal build-up of the state were organized at the level of the republics. In addition, the federal and republican elections were held simultaneously. Hence the incentive to create federal parties which bridged the ethnic/nationalist divide at the level of the republics were very weak, especially in Slovakia. Indeed the failure of the Republics to provide federal actors, federal agendas, federal identities, and a federal legitimation of the democratic state resulted in increasing ethnic/nationalist tensions. The sequencing of the "founding election" and the structure of the party system facilitated the disintegration of the federation and the increase in national/ethnic conflict (Olson 1993; Wightman 1995a; Linz and Stepan 1992).[37]

It is paradoxical that given the increasing nationalist tensions between the Czechs and Slovaks the second elections in 1992 followed the same pattern. Once again, none of the significant political parties were organized at the federal level. Thus, the voters in each of the two republics were seperately faced with two different party systems operating separately in the two republics. Moreover, in each of them the respective dominating party stood for diametrically contrary political goals in the issues of federation and statehood. Social and economic matters, mainly the speed and scope of privatization, were reformulated and overlapped with the nationalist/ethnic divide. The growing success of Meciar's HZDS populist and nationalist mobilization forced the other parties to reformulate their ideological positions and redefine their political strategies over the nationalist cleavage (Juberias 1992: 162–4). As a result, the electoral campaign in Slovakia displayed all the elements of nationalist outbidding.

In *Slovakia* the campaign for the elections on September 30/October 1, 1994, in the second year of Slovakia's existence, entailed a growing fragmentation and an extreme polarization of the party system (for details cf. Malová 1993a, 1993b; Bútorová and Bútora 1995). Roughly following Sartori, we speak of fragmentation if more than five parties are represented in parliament and interact in the sphere of government (Sartori 1976: 126 f.). First, a group of deputies left the HZDS who had led a minority government since March 1993 (with the exception of a short period at the end of 1993 when it formed an official coalition with the SNS). In February 1994, the SNS split into two factions, one of which supported the coalition with the HZDS. Fragmentation continued mainly amongst the opposition but nevertheless gave them a relative majority in the Slovak National Council. On March 11, 1994 they united to oust

---

[37] Linz and Stepan (1992) focus on the cases of the Soviet Union and Yugoslavia and not so much on the Czechoslovakian case. But the situation is very similar. Compared with Spain, after the death of Franco the "founding elections" were organized at an all-union level and the parties organized themselves as all-union parties with all-union agendas. After that initial structuring of the polity the federal government successfully dealt with the regional issues of the Basques and Catalans (Linz and Stepan 1992).

Prime Minister Meciar by a (non-constructive) vote of no-confidence. The new government majority agreed upon holding new elections in the fall of 1994. During this six month period the new Prime Minister, Moravcik, headed a government which was supported by the whole of the Anti-Meciar political spectrum, demonstrating an unexpected degree of cooperation throughout the period. Understandably, the Moravcik government avoided strongly contentious decisions, such as the reduction in budgetary expenditure; but it handled quite successfully other less controversial issues.

After his victory in the fall 1994 elections, Meciar revenged himself on those whom he blamed for having ousted him out of office in March 1994: President Kovac, the previous government, the political parties which issued the vote of no confidence, and sections of the media. His political style was highly confrontational and has been described as "liquidation syndrome *vis-à-vis* the opposition" (Bútorová and Bútora 1995: 121). In the period of the construction of the new nation it was comparatively easy to label the opposition and the critics of the ruling regime as "anti-Slovaks" who were damaging the new state abroad or acting in the interests of hostile foreign forces. Moreover, in this period the focus of political conflict shifted from policies to the rules of the game. On several occasions Meciar's HZDS attempted to change the structure of the political regime, for instance advocating a German-style chancellor system, trying to establish a presidential system, or proposing a bill on the State Defence Council which would have allowed Meciar, with relative ease, to declare a state of emergency and to act without parliamentary approval and control (Malova 1993a: 5). Meciar's shock at being ousted from power twice meant that the HZDS no longer shared the basic commitment to the rules of the political regime which it had shaped itself in 1992. This undermined the legitimacy of the newly built institutions of democracy and justified the promotion of an authoritarian regime. Since the stakes in the period of nation-building following secession were high, there was a strong incentive to push party competition into a polarized mode.

In the *Czech Republic* a multi-party system developed comprising eight parliamentary parties with the ODS of V. Klaus as the dominant party (with about 30 percent of the vote). At first glance the Czech party system fits perfectly the main features of *polarized pluralism* which Sartori identified (cf. Sartori 1976: 131–45). It contains, first, *anti-system parties* of both the left and the right wing, namely the still unreformed communist party and the extremist Republican party, which try to undermine the legitimacy of the democratic institutions they oppose; second, these two together form the *bilateral opposition*, which is mutually exclusive; third, there is an *occupied center*, which consists of Klaus' Civic Democratic Party and its coalition partners, which discourage political competition around the center position; fourth, a *high ideological distance* exists between the poles of the party spectrum moving from radical/ nationalist via neo-liberalism and social-democratic ideologies to an only slightly modified communism. Contrary to Sartori's proposition which suggests a polarized pluralism, i.e., a centrifugal drive of party competition where these conditions obtain, in fact politics in the Czech Republic is far more pragmatic than the ideological patterning of the political rhetoric suggests. The center parties tend to lower the ideological temperature by reducing the distance between parties, so that the anti-system parties are gradually included within the institutionalized rules of the game.

Bulgaria's party system is strongly shaped by bi-polarity with the reform-communists of the BSP at one pole and the democratic forces organized in the UDF at the other (Szajkowski 1992: 8). The Turkish minority party (MRF), located somewhere in between, acts as a possible coalition partner for both poles. However, here both poles of the party system embody different ideologies, cultural patterns, and contradicting economic and social policy objectives; the ideological gap between the parties is unbridgeable and the temperature of the political struggles is very high. The UDF, notably under its former leader F. Dimitrov, was driven by a strong anti-communism which made any rapprochement between the two poles impossible. In contrast to moderate pluralism and despite the mediating role of the MRF, there is a great ideological distance and intensity between the two poles. Thus the change from government to opposition is not a pragmatic switch from one policy to another but between principal and mutually exclusive ideologies. The political buffer between them is the MRF which, however, as a party of the Turkish minority is unable to attract a broader range of median voters. It has an exceptionally immovable core of predominantly ethnic voters for whom voting for the MDF reinforces their ethnic identity.

The centrifugal drive of the party system was reaffirmed in the 1994 elections. The BSP gained an absolute majority of the seats with only 43 percent of the votes. The initial bi-polar structure of the RTT was retained and both the BSP and the UDF were successful in preventing the emergence of strong new parties, although not of new modestly successful parties altogether (see table 4.1c).

The popular election of the Bulgarian president reinforced bi-polarity. As the 1992 election demonstrated, only a candidate affiliated to one of the two blocs had a chance of being elected. It is indeed likely that the next presidential election at the beginning of 1996 will sharpen the polarization of the bi-polar Bulgarian party system still further (Krastev 1994: 9).

3.3   Conclusion

All party systems under comparison differ, but all, however, exhibit elements of fragmentation and ideological polarization. Both fragmentation and ideological polarization signal political and institutional instability and prevent the CEE countries from reaching an institutionalized party system, i.e., a consolidated state of moderate pluralism with its stable, pragmatic, and structured system for channelment. Whilst the purely numerical criterion for fragmented party pluralism does not provide extremely eccentric data for our countries under study the following qualitative particularities justify a slightly skeptical assessment of their levels of institutionalization:

(i)   The *lack of internal coherence* makes personalities more important than the actual party they represent. Party leaders are far more committed to short-term political power plays and the goal to acquire executive and other governmental positions than to strengthen their party's profile through long-term programmatic ideas and political projects. Being vulnerable to the idiosyncrasies and the rise and fall of their concrete political leaders political parties are badly equipped to play a constructive role in the consolidation of a democratic polity.

(ii)   With the exception of the former communist parties (and possibly the Czech ODS of V. Klaus) the parties in the CEE countries possess *weak organizational capacities*. We hypothesize that this is largely due to their character as what we want to call "factional catch-all parties". With this we mean the following: in entrenched Western democracies the dominant parties have undergone a three-stage development from cadre parties, to democratic "parties of social integration" (S. Neumann), encapsulating segments of the society and inculcate identities, to so-called catch-all parties, which gradually broaden their programmatic "supplies" in order to compete for a larger share in the electoral market (Mair 1990). The "factional catch-all party" started the other way round. Lacking tight organizational channels to society it is unable to structure the electoral market.[38] The lack of rootedness in the basic social structures of the society is one reason for what has been called "overparliamentarization" of politics (Agh 1993: 6), i.e., the over concentration of the organizational and personal capacities of the parties in parliament.

---

[38] An important exception, clearly, are some former communist parties, mainly the Bulgarian Socialist Party, whereas, e.g., the HSP was not able to stabilize and maintain a hard-core segment of voters during the transitional period.

This is at the same time a cause and an effect of the parties' weak ability to build partisan institutions at the grass-roots level.

(iii) Due to the parties' programmatic and organizational weaknesses they do not have the necessary *institutional autonomy* to tolerate other organized agencies and other autonomous spheres of politics. The ongoing instability and poor performance of political parties and governments has been a major impediment to a proper institutionalization of an elaborate system of interest mediation and of independent intermediary bodies (Hausner and Wojtyna 1993).

(iv) The parties are unable to create stable and *organizationally based identities* which can structure the volatile and open electoral markets. As yet they have been unable to close the electoral markets. As long as the electorate is diffuse, erratic, and highly individualized, the stabilization of the party system, the capacity for continuity during the changes of the political environment, and hence the consolidation of democracy, will prove difficult (Mair 1991).

Thus, the current state of development of the parties and the party system contains many risks of enduring instability largely due to the unfavorable character of the predominant social conflicts which complicate the evolvement of a stable and moderately pluralist party system. Drawing on a similar contrast of Hirschman (1995)[39] (and adding a further dimension), we distinguish between distributional, constitutional, and categorical conflicts. Distributional conflicts relate to divisible goods, i.e., they are about "more or less." They are easily accessible to bargaining procedures and to compromise in terms of "just" sharing. Constitutional conflicts pertain largely to the basic norms and fundamental institutions of democracy, including the rules about the competition for political power; as our account of the constitution-making processes in chapter 3 shows, constitutional conflicts are the domain of both bargaining and impartial arguing. They are the domain of ideological struggle. The most essential prerequisite is the existence of a diversity of pre-constitutional actors who are able and willing to assume the roles which a democratic constitution assigns to them and who therefore are able to cope with conflicts about the constitution in the spirit of constitutionalism. Finally, categorical conflicts are conflicts about the very fundament of social coherence, cooperation, and solidarity, namely about social belonging and identity. Categorical conflicts are not about "more or less," but about "either-or." Ethnic and religious conflicts are well-known examples of categorical conflicts. They tend to be extremely confrontational,

---

[39] See a more detailed account of this distinction in chapter 7.1.

"uncivilized", i.e., undomesticated by rules, and frequently they lead to the verge of civil war if not to civil war itself.

It is safe to assume that the prospects of political stability are most favorable where distributional conflicts predominate. The more market-ization proceeds and social differentiation is fostered, and the more the countries are ethnically homogeneous, the more party competition will refer to conflicts about bargainable interests; hence, it can be expected to be moderate. The obvious candidates for such development are Hungary and the Czech Republic. By contrast, in Bulgaria the process of political agency formation is still underway at the same time ethnic division plays a certain role in the political game; hence party competition is more polarized. Where ethnic divisions play a role and where the difficulties of political agency are still burdened with the additional problem of nationstate-building, then political polarization and uncivilized forms of political competition and struggle prevail. This is the case in Slovakia.

Appendix

Bulgaria

Table 4.1a. *General elections: 1st Round: June 10, 1990; 2nd Round: June 17, 1990*

Parties	% of votes	S.M.D. 1st Round	S.M.D. 2nd Round	nat. List (and %)	Total seats
Bulgarian Socialist Party (BSP)	45.5	75	39	97	211 (52.7)
Union of Democratic Forces (UDF)	36.5	32	37	75	144 (36.0)
Movement for Rights and Freedoms (MRF)	7.7	9	2	12	23 (5.7)
Bulgarian Agrarian National Union (BANU)	5.8	–		16	16 (4.0)
Fatherland Union	0.5	–	2	–	2 (0.5)
Fatherland Party of Labor	0.4	–	1	–	1 (0.25)
Social Democratic Party	0.0	–	1	–	1 (0.25)
Independents	0.0	–	2	–	2 (0.5)
Non-represented voters	3.6		–	–	–
TOTAL	100.0	116	84	200	400 (100.0)

Source: Ashley 1990.

Table 4.1b. *Election results: October 13, 1991*

Parties		Votes in %	Seats	Seats in %
Union of Democratic Forces (UDF-Movement)	–	34.7	110	45.8
Bulgarian Socialist Party (BSP)		33.1	106	44.2
Movement for Rights and Freedoms (MRF)	–	7.6	24	10.0
Bulgarian Agrarian National Union (BANU-United)		4.0	0	0
Bulgarian Agrarian National Union (BANU-Nikola Petkov)		3.4	0	0
Union of Democratic Forces (UDF-Center		3.2	0	0
Union of Democratic Forces (UDF-Liberals)		3.8	0	0
'Kindom of Bulgaria' Confederation		1.8	0	0
Bulgarian Business Bloc		1.3	0	0
Bulgarian National Radical Party		1.1	0	0
Non-represented parties		24.9	–	–
TOTAL		100.00	240	100.0

Source: Karasimeonov 1995: 166.

Table 4.1c. *Election results, December 18, 1994*

Parties		Votes in %	Seats	Seats in %
Bulgarian Socialist Party (BSP)		43.6	124	51.7
Union of Democratic Forces (UDF-Movement)	–	24.2	70	29.2
Peoples Union (NS)		6.5	18	7.5
Movement for Rights and Freedoms (MRF)	–	5.4	15	6.2
Bulgarian Business Bloc (BBB)		4.7	13	5.4
Democratic Alternative		3.8	0	0
Non-represented parties		16.0	–	–
TOTAL		100.00	240	100.0

Source: Official Statistics of the Ministry of Interior.

Czechoslovakia

Table 4.2. *General elections: June 8–9, 1990*

	% votes	Seats
House of the People		
Czech Republic		
Civic Forum (OF)	53.1	68
Communist Party of Czechoslovakia (KSCS)	13.5	15
Christian and Democratic Union (KDU)	8.7	9
Society for Moravia and Silesia (HSD-SMS)	7.9	9
Others	16.8	–
TOTAL	100.0	101
Slovak Republic		
The Public Against Violence (VPN)	32.5	19
Christian Democratic Movement (KDH)	19.0	11
Communist Party of Czechoslovakia (KSCS)	13.8	8
Slovak National Party (SNS)	11.0	6
Coexistence	8.6	5
Others	15.1	–
TOTAL	100.0	49
House of the Nations		
Czech Republic		
Civic Forum (OF)	50.0	50
Communist Party of Czechoslovakia (KSCM)	13.8	12
Christian and Democratic Union (KDU)	8.7	6
Society for Moravia and Silesia (HSD-SMS)	9.1	7
Others	18.4	–
TOTAL	100.0	75
Slovak Republic		
The Public Against Violence (VPN)	37.3	33
Christian Democratic Movement (KDH)	16.7	14
Communist Party of Czechoslovakia (KSCS)	13.4	12
Slovak National Party (SNS)	11.4	9
Coexistence	8.5	7
Others	12.7	–
TOTAL	100.0	75

	% votes	Seats
Czech and Slovak National Councils		
Czech National Council		
Civic Forum (OF)	49.5	127
Communist Party of Czechoslovakia (KSCM)	13.3	32
Society for Moravia and Silesia (HSD-SMS)	10.0	22
Christian and Democratic Union (KDU)	8.4	19
Others	18.8	–
TOTAL	100.0	200
Slovak National Council		
The Public Against Violence (VPN)	29.3	48
Christian Democratic Movement (KDH)	19.2	31
Slovak National Party (SNS)	13.9	22
Communist Party of Slovakia (KSS)	13.3	22
Coexistence	8.7	14
Democratic Party (DS)	4.4	7
Green Party (SZ)	3.5	6
Others	7.7	–
TOTAL	100.0	150

Source: Szajkowski 1991: 62/63

Table 4.3. *General elections, June 5–6, 1992*

Party	House of the People		House of Nations		National Council	
	%	seats	%	seats	%	seats
Election results in the Czech Republic						
Civic Democratic/Christian Democratic						
Party (ODS-KDS)	33.9	48	33.4	37	29.7	76
Left Bloc (LB)	14.3	19	14.5	15	14.1	35
Czechoslovak Social Democracy (CSSD)	7.7	10	6.8	6	6.5	16
Republican Party (SPR-RSC)	6.5	8	6.4	6	6.0	14
Christian Democratic Union (KDU)	6.0	7	6.1	6	6.3	15
Liberal Social Union (LSU)	5.8	7	6.1	5	6.2	16
Civic Democratic Alliance (ODA)	0	0	0	0	6.0	14
Association for Moravia and Silesia	0	0	0	0	5.9	14
Election results in the Slovak Republic						
Movement for a Democratic						
Slovakia (HZDS)	33.5	24	33.8	33	37.3	74
Party of the Demoratic Left (SDL)	14.4	10	14.1	13	14.7	29
Slovak National Party (SNS)	9.4	6	9.3	9	7.9	15
Christian Democratic Movement (KDH)	9.0	6	8.8	8	8.9	18
Coexistence/Hungarian Christian						
Democratic Movement	0	0	0	0	7.4	14
Coexistence/Hungarian Christian						
Democratic Movement/Hungarian						
People's Party	7.4	5	7.4	7	0	–
Social Democratic Party of Slovakia						
(SDSS)	0	0	6.1	5	0	–

Source: Pehe 1992b: 29.

Hungary

Table 4.4a. *General elections: 1st round: March 25, 1990; 2nd round: April 08, 1990*

Party	% of votes 1st round	Seats S.M.D.	Seats reg.list	Seats nat.list	Total seats (and %)
Hungarian Democratic Forum (HDF)	24.7	115	40	10	165 (42.8)
Alliance of Free Democrats (AFD)	21.7	34	34	23	91 (23.6)
Independent Smallholders' Party (ISP)	11.7	11	16	17	44 (11.4)
Hungarian Socialist Party (HSP)	10.9	1	14	18	33 (8.5)
Alliance of Young Democrats (Fidesz)	8.9	1	8	12	21 (5.4)
Christian Democratic Peoples' Party (CDPP)	6.5	3	8	10	21 (5.4)
Hungarian Socialist Workers' Party (HSWP)	3.7	0	0	0	0 (0.0)
Hungarian Social Democratic Party (HSDP)	3.5	0	0	0	0 (0.0)
Agrarian Alliance (AA)	3.1	0	0	0	0 (0.0)
Entrepreneurs' Party (VP)	1.9	0	0	0	0 (0.0)
Patriotic Electoral Coalition (HVK)	1.9	0	0	0	1 (0.2)
Hungarian Peoples' Party (HPP)	0.8	0	0	0	0 (0.0)
Hungarian Green Party	0.4	0	0	0	0 (0.0)
Independent	0.0	6	0	0	6 (1.6)
Joint Deputies[*]	0.0	4	0	0	4 (1.0)
Total seats filled					386 (100.0)

Notes: Turnout: 1st Round: 63.1 %
2nd Round: 45.5 %
[*] Deputies representing more than one party (two joint AFD/Fidesz, one joint AFD/Fidesz/CDPP, and one joint Agrarian candidate.
Parties in italics passed the 4 percent barrier and were allocated regional and national seats.
Source: Juberias 1994: 32; Hibbing and Patterson 1990.

Table 4.4b. *General elections: 1st round: May 8, 1994; 2nd round: May 29, 1994*
Share of votes for country party lists and final distribution of seats in the National Assembly

Party	% of votes 1st round	Seats S.M.D.	Seats reg.list	Seats nat.list	Total seats (and %)
Hungarian Socialist Party (HSP)	33.0	150	53	6	209 (54.1)
Alliance of Free Democrats (AFD)	19.8	17	28	25	70 (18.1)
Hungarian Democratic Forum (HDF)	11.7	3	18	16	37 (9.5)
Independent Smallholders' and C. Party (ISP)	8.8	1	14	11	26 (6.7)
Christian Democratic Peoples' Party (CDPP)	7.1	3	5	14	22 (5.7)
Alliance of Young Democrats (Fidesz)	7.0	0	7	13	20 (5.1)
Workers' Party	3.2	0	0	0	0 (0.0)
Republican Party	2.5	0	0	0	0 (0.0)
Agrarian Alliance	2.1	1	0	0	1 (0.2)
Hungarian Justice and Life Party	1.5	0	0	0	0 (0.0)
Liberal Bloc	0.6	1	0	0	1 (0.2)
All nonrepresented parties	10.0	–	–	–	–
Total seats filled					386 (100.0)

Notes: Turnout: 1st Round: 68.9%
2nd Round: 55.1%
Parties in italics passed the 5 percent barrier and were allocated regional and national seats.
Source: Oltay *1994*; Juberias *1994*: 32.

Slovakia

Table 4.5. *General elections: September 30/October 1, 1994*

Party	Votes	in %	Seats	in %
Movement for a Democratic Slovakia (HZDS)	1,005,488	35.0	61	40.7
Party of the Democratic Left (SDL)	299,496	10.4	18	12.0
Hungarian Bloc	292,939	10.2	17	11.3
Christian Democrats	289,987	10.1	17	11.3
Democratic Alliance	264,444	8.6	15	10.0
Slovak Workers' Party	211,321	7.3	13	8.7
Slovak National Party (SNS)	155,359	5.4	9	6.0
Unrepresented Voters	–	13.0	0	–
TOTAL	2,875,458	100.0	150	100.0

Source: Official Statistics of the Ministry of Interior.

Czech Republik

Table 4.6. *General Elections: June 2, 1996*

Party	Votes (in %)	Seats
Civic Democratic Party (ODS)	29.62	68
Czech Sozial Democrats (CSSD)	26.44	61
Communist Party of Bohemia and Moravia (KSCM)	10.33	22
Christian Democratic Union/Czech Popular Party (KDU-CSL)	8.08	18
Republican Party/Alliance for the Republic (SPR-RSC)	8.01	18
Civic Democratic Alliance (ODA)	6.39	13
Other Parties	11.16	— —

Source: Pravo, June 3, 1996.

5

Building capitalism in Eastern Europe

1 Introduction

Under communism, the economic and the political sphere were tightly coupled. With the nomenklatura, a single elite existed which governed both the polity and the economy. State ownership and state planning, along with the unfettered power of the ruling elite, provided for nearly complete and highly discretionary political control of the economy. The transition to capitalism is precisely about the softening of this tight coupling and the institutionalization of a relatively autonomous economic system. As for the economy, the drawing of clear boundaries between the political and the economic system corresponds to what we have dubbed "horizontal consolidation." In addition, the consolidation of the new economic order presupposes a sufficient degree of internal institutional structure, that is, the existence of a set of well-defined and generally recognized rules that specify property rights and facilitate exchange by reducing transaction costs. This is the "vertical" dimension of consolidation.

Consequently, one might distinguish between two central elements of East European economic reform. On the one hand, there are those measures that aim at redefining the relationship between the state and the economy, both by limiting the state's role in the economy and by replacing the old hands-on mode of state interference with a more indirect, rule-based, and framework-oriented approach. This group of reforms comprise the privatization of state-owned enterprises, the abolition of central planning and the liberalization of economic activities, as well as the trimming of state expenditure.

The retreat of the state from the economy, however, is but a necessary condition for the emergence of a consolidated capitalist economy. As well-functioning markets grow up "from below" but slowly, the carving out of markets must be supplemented by the furnishing of markets. What is needed is, first of all, the adoption of an appropriate legal-regulatory framework. This touches upon both the constitution and a plethora of specific regulations, including property, contract, company, competition, and bankruptcy law.[1] In addition, the furnishing of markets also comprises financial, informational, and organisational support for the emergence of market actors, as well as the removal of non-institutional obstacles to marketization – for example, the cancellation of enterprise debt or the demonopolization of state-owned enterprises.

It is in both dimensions that East European economic reforms differ from other episodes of large-scale economic reform, such as post-war economic reconstruction or economic reforms in the Southern cone. In Eastern Europe, both markets and private enterprises were virtually non-existent for about 40 years. Moreover, most East European countries experienced their industrialization under communism, so that the national economies were not only damaged or distorted, but in fact created by central planning (Yavlinsky 1994: 4). Therefore, East European economic reforms are not about removing a thin layer of regulations from distorted yet basically existing markets or about privatizating a handful of state-owned enterprises, but about creating the very fundamentals of capitalism. In none of the afore-mentioned other cases of economic reform, state ownership and state regulation were as comprehensive as under communism. Nor had a capitalist economy to be built from scratch. Instead, reformers could take the existence of a certain institutional infrastructure, of certain actors, and of a minimum acquaintance with the operation of markets for granted. As a consequence, reforms after 1945 and in the Southern cone have primarily been about releasing market forces, less about building markets.

This chapter will survey the progress of economic reform in the four countries under analysis. Its structure follows the above-mentioned distinctions. The two main sections review the reforms which have been undertaken. The first section looks at the state's retreat from the economy, the second one at the furnishing of the new markets. They are preluded by a brief account of the constraints and dilemmas of the economic reform process. The chapter concludes with an assessment of the particular form of capitalism that has emerged in Eastern Europe and the prospects for the reforming countries.

---

[1] For useful compilations of the legal framework of a capitalist economy, see EBRD 1994: 69–77; Gray *et al.* 1993: 1–22.

In line with the general design of the book, the chapter's focus is on the institutionalization of capitalism and the problems and paradoxes of state-led destatization. As a consequence, the macro-economic aspects of the transformation which rank prominently in the economic literature will be somewhat neglected.

2 The state and the economic reform: constraints, dilemmas, paradoxes

2.1 The long arm of the past

East European economic reforms have implied a fundamental institutional overhaul. In spite of this need for building the new institutions from scratch, however, the post-communist economies have not been "virgin territory" (Frydman and Rapaczynski 1994: 176). Instead of having a clean blackboard to write on, reformers have faced a number of "Leninist Legacies" (Jowitt 1992a). These non-institutional legacies have resulted in a number of constraints which have severely complicated the transition to capitalism.

(i) The sectoral structures of the communist economies were highly distorted (Heitger *et al.* 1992: 38–42; Winiecki 1988: 73–98). The primary and, in particular, the secondary sectors were significantly larger than in capitalist countries with a similar level of income. In contrast, the service sectors lagged behind. Over industrialization was especially pronounced in Bulgaria and Czechoslovakia. Among the three countries, the sectoral structure of the Hungarian economy came closest to the capitalist pattern. As a consequence of these distorted sectoral structures, the transition to capitalism has not only been about changing ownership and creating markets, but has implied a sweeping reallocation of capital and labor, too.

(ii) Forty years of communism have left their imprint on individuals' habits, attitudes, and behavior. Survey results consistently hint at the prevalence of certain mental residues ranging from high risk aversion and the inclination toward grab-and-run behavior to negative egalitarianism (see, e.g., Mason 1992). According to most surveys, related attitudes have been particularly ingrained in Bulgaria and relatively weak in the Czech Republic. The lack of the corresponding "software" has thus complicated the introduction of capitalist institutions. "Incongruent" attitudes have been a source of political resistance to reforms, as well as an obstacle to the "proper" functioning of the newly established institutions.

(iii) Communist industrial structures were characterized by the dominance of large enterprises and rather high degrees of concentration (Ehrlich 1985). Succumbing to the idea of economies of scale and for mere administrative convenience, communist leaders promoted the merging of existing enterprises and the formation of industrial giants. This tendency was aggravated by the firms' interests in better control of scarce supplies by vertical integration. From a comparative perspective, concentration has been particularly high in Bulgaria and Czechoslovakia. In Czechoslovakia, for example, the average number of workers in each firm in 1989 was 3,000 as against approximately 300 in the West (Estrin and Takla 1993: 46). In Hungary, concentration was lower, though still far higher than in Western market economies.

This particular industrial structure has bedeviled economic reform, too. It has been a further reason for why the transition to capitalism has been associated with massive changes in the economic structure. Moreover, a high degree of concentration has rendered the welfare effects of price liberalization and privatization less obvious by infringing upon competition. Finally, the small number of enterprises and the high degree of vertical integration have implied rather strong ties between suppliers and customers. Such ties have made for a high "systemic risk." Failure of an individual enterprise has provoked the danger of a chain reaction. The resulting fragility of the enterprise sector has complicated both institutional reforms and the conduct of macroeconomic policy.

(iv) Under communism, credits were allocated according to planning prerogatives and irrespective of enterprises' creditworthiness. Therefore, many enterprises entered post-communism with debt obligations that lack any economic rationale. Correspondingly, the new commercial banks which were spin offs from the old monobanks started their operations with credit portfolios characterized by a high percentage of highly concentrated unrecoverable claims. The bad debt overhang was higher in Bulgaria and Czechoslovakia than in Hungary. On the one hand, enterprise indebtedness exceeded the Hungarian level. On the other hand, credit allocation in Bulgaria and Czechoslovakia was particularly distorted.

Like the communist industrial structure, the bad debts have increased the economic vulnerability of both enterprises and banks, thereby further raising the "systemic risk." Those enterprises that have been saddled with massive debt service obligations have been highly sensitive to deterioration in performance. Likewise, the large share of bad loans in the bank portfolios have aggravated the fragility of the financial sector. Again, communist legacies have increased the danger of chain reactions. The banks' exposure has also impeded bank control of enterprises, as the fragile bank portfolios have favored "creditor passivity." Finally, the debt overhang has also troubled privatization by inducing potential buyers, the state and creditors to haggle over the distribution of debt write-offs.

(v) Most East European countries inherited a huge monetary overhang from communism. Given price controls and the endemic shortage, monetary expansion under communism partly resulted in involuntary money holdings and repressed inflation (Nuti 1985). The monetary overhang at the outset of the transformation was higher in Bulgaria than in Czechoslovakia and Hungary. Whilst Bulgarian monetary policy had been loosened in the 1980s, the Czechoslovak government had maintained a tight macro-economic policy. In Hungary, part of the monetary overhang had already been eaten away in the aftermath of the pre-1989 price reforms. The macro-economic stock disequilibria associated with the monetary overhang have complicated price reform. They have made the liberalization of prices riskier by boosting the price hike to be expected and by thus amplifying the danger of persistent inflation.

(vi) Unlike Czechoslovakia, Bulgaria and Hungary accumulated a huge foreign debt in the second half of the 1980s (Bönker 1994: 41). Hungary even became the country with the world's highest foreign debt per capita in 1989. The resulting problems of internal and external transfer have complicated the conduct of macro-economic policy. Debt service has put a heavy burden on public budgets, thus bedeviling fiscal consolidation. The large foreign debt has also rendered the use of exchange rate policy as a stabilization device more difficult, as the need for achieving current account surpluses has suggested the maintenance of a "competitive" exchange rate.

2.2 The orthodox paradox

The need for building a capitalist economy from scratch, along with the pervasive legacies of the past, have rendered economic reform complicated. The ubiquitous "orthodox paradox" (Kahler 1990) has emerged. As it is well-known from other episodes of privatization and marketization from all over the world, destatization can only be accomplished by the state and thus presupposes state interventions and a "strong state."[2] As a consequence, destatization is fraught with massive problems of credible commitment (Weingast 1993): reformers must make sure that state interventions are undertaken in order to end all state interventions and are thus of a once-and-for-all nature.

For a couple of reasons, the "orthodox paradox" has featured

[2] This is the economic equivalent to the above-mentioned paradox that democracy cannot be created by democratic means.

particularly prominently in Eastern Europe. Both the need for and the dangers of state intervention have been pronounced, especially as the implementation of the state's retreat from the economy and the furnishing of the market have demanded such massive state interventions. Likewise, the absence of a "dormant" capitalist economy waiting to be revived has made an orderly retreat of the state necessary. Reformers have faced the danger of too early a withdrawal of the state actually endangering the proper institutionalization of a capitalist economy by giving rise to institutional voids. For all these reasons, the need for state interventions, as well as the associated danger of "state desertion" (Abel and Bonin 1993), have been rather strong.

At the same time, however, the danger of overshooting state interventions has loomed similarly large. The strong tradition of state interventionism in the region which goes beyond the communist era has aggravated the danger of the state repeating all its past mistakes. Moreover, the limited autonomy of the post-communist states has infringed upon the credibility of the announced gradual retreat from the economy. It is partly against this background that advocates of laissez-faire have emphasized the need for a sharp break with the past and have warned against the mirage of "fine-tuning."

Reformers have thus faced a basic dilemma. On the one hand, there has been a clear case for massive state interventions and a gradual retreat of the state. On the other hand, these very state interventions have been fraught with massive credibility problems. This dilemma loomed behind the debate on "big bang" versus "gradualism" which has framed both the academic and political discourse on economic reform in Eastern Europe (Brada 1993; Murrell 1992; Roland 1994). Whilst "gradualists" have pointed to the problems of too early and too hasty a retreat of the state, "radicals" have stressed the credibility problems of a gradual withdrawal of the state. Unfortunately, this debate has often suffered from a rather sterile juxtaposition of "radical" versus "gradual" strategies of economic reform. The belaboring of dichotomies has tended to hide the underlying dilemmas of the structure. Yet it is precisely those dilemmas which have given rise to the muddy strategies, the oscillations between strategies, and the massive differences between areas of reforms that can be observed in Eastern Europe.

3 Bringing the state back out

Given the omnipresence of the communist state, the state's retreat from the economy has been a multi-dimensional process. The main dimensions of the state's withdrawal from the economy have included the liberalization of the market entry, the liberalization of prices, the slashing of state expenditure, the liberalization of capital markets and the inauguration of an independent central bank, the liberalization of wages and the introduction of collective bargaining, and, finally, the privatization of state-owned assets.

3.1 The liberalization of market entry

The liberalization of market entry was among the first reform steps in all countries (Bönker 1993: 48f.). Free entry was widely regarded as a central pillar of a capitalist economy and as a means to instill competition and to improve the supply of goods. In Bulgaria and Hungary, market entry had already been partly liberalized within the framework of the economic reforms of the 1980s, so that the post-1989 governments could confine themselves to eliminating the remaining legal restrictions. In Hungary, these changes culminated in the passage of the Law on Private Enterprise in January 1990 which guaranteed free market entry in a comprehensive way. In Czechoslovakia, where no entry reforms had taken place before the "velvet revolution," the Law on Private Entrepreneurship, as adopted in April 1990, established the right to free entry and repealed the old licensing system. These reforms were complemented by parallel constitutional amendments that expanded the domain of private property (Bönker 1993: 31–4). In the course of the reform process, the right to free entry was further protected by provisions in the new constitution and by court decisions.

The CEE countries also saw far-reaching liberalization of foreign trade which aimed at importing competition and a "correct" price structure (Bönker 1993: 49f.). In Bulgaria and Czechoslovakia, the 1991 Reform Programs were associated with comprehensive trade liberalization that brought the old system of obligatory trade licenses and nearly all quantititative import restrictions to an end. In contrast, Hungary, again, experienced a more gradual trade liberalization. With the share of convertible currency imports subject to licensing requirements already down to about 60 percent in 1989, Hungarian trade liberalization pursued a gradualist path. In all countries, the initial trade liberalization was smoothed by the imposition of temporary import surcharges and undervalued exchange rates. In the course of the transition, however, a certain backtracking has occurred (Gács 1994; Messerlin 1995). Tariffs and non-tariff barriers have been significantly increased. Trade policy has been used to cushion domestic producers and to attract foreign direct investment. The Czech Republic has been the main exception to this "drift toward more protection" (Messerlin 1995: 41). Benefitting from the relative "smoothness" of the transition and the persistent under-valuation of the Czech currency, the Czech government has maintained one of the most liberal trade regimes in Europe.

3.2 The liberalization of prices

At the outset of the transformation, controversies over the pace of price liberalization featured prominently. Adherents to a more gradual approach warned against the inflationary potential and the unacceptable distributional consequences of freeing prices. They argued that the liberalization of prices should be made conditional upon progress with demonopolization and the introduction of competition into the economy. These ideas gained a certain currency in 1990. After initial flirtations with a gradual liberalization of prices, however, East European governments ultimately opted for the radical liberalization of prices (Bönker 1993: 47f.). Hungary has been the only country where gradual price liberalization took place. Here, however, the liberalization of prices had already been initiated under the old regime. When the Antall government came to power in 1990, the share of administered consumer prices was thus already down to 20–5 percent. In Bulgaria and Czecho-slovakia, which started reforms from a system of nearly complete price control, the bulk of prices was liberalized at one stroke at the beginning of 1991 following some minor price reforms in 1990. In both cases, price decontrol was an essential element of the stabilization programs that were adopted in close collaboration with the IMF. By the end of the 1991, regulated prices applied to less than 15 percent in all three countries.

The decision for bold price liberalizations was driven by several motives. Governments were eager to get rid of the responsibility for the determination of prices. Any more gradual price reform would have put governments in charge of regularly selling price increases to the public. Given the distorted price structures, the maintenance of price controls, too, would have provoked high efficiency losses (Boycko 1991; Murphy *et al.* 1992). The liberalization of prices also was to bring about the elimination of shortages, thus creating immediately visible benefits for a population which was fed up with queues and shortages.[3] In contrast, any gradual price liberalization would necessarily have induced hoarding and speculation. A case in point is the Bulgarian experience in 1990, when the

---

[3] "Indeed, no numbers can convey the experience; for people who for decades 'hunted' the streets carrying 'just-in-case' bags (*anuzka*) for whatever might 'appear,' who joined lines because lines meant that 'they must have thrown something,' the spectacle of stores filled with products one could acquire just by paying a price was a wonder" (Przeworski 1993: 155).

Table 5.1. *Inflation rates (consumer prices, annual average), 1989–1995*

	1989	1990	1991	1992	1993	1994	1995[P]
Bulgaria	6.4	26.3	333.5	82.0	73.0	96.3	68
Czechoslovakia	2.3	10.8	–	–	–	–	–
Czech Republic	–	–	56.7	11.1	20.8	10.0	10
Slovak Republic	–	–	61.2	10.1	23.1	13.4	11
Hungary	17.0	28.9	35.0	23.0	22.5	18.8	29

Note: [P] projection.
Source: EBRD 1995: app.11.1.

Lukanov government tinkered with gradual price liberalization and, as a consequence, food and petrol had to be rationed. Price level adjustment was also broadly considered to be the best way to eliminate the accumulated monetary overhang which was initially regarded as a main obstacle to stabilization and economic reform. Conceivable alternatives, most notably monetary reform, were rejected both for economic and political reasons.

In Bulgaria and Czechoslovakia, the liberalization of prices, along with the large parallel devaluations, involved severe price shocks. Monthly inflation rates initially ballooned beyond expectations. In the first month after price liberalization, price levels soared by 105.2 percent in Bulgaria and 25.8 percent in Czechoslovakia. Part of the price increase was due to monopolistic price setting. As for Czechoslovakia, for example, it has been estimated that the lack of competition accounted for more than 40 percent of the total 1991 increase in the price level (Drabek *et al.* 1994: 168). Whilst Czechoslovakia managed to bring inflation down to a moderate level and soon became the East European country with the lowest rate of inflation, inflation in Bulgaria has shown a high degree of inertia (Table 5.1). The price hike was accompanied by a sharp drop in real wages (Tables 5.2 and 5.3). In 1991, real wages fell by a quarter or so in Czechoslovakia and by about two-fifths in Bulgaria. Due to the higher-than-expected price increase, the actual decline in real wages in both countries substantially exceeded the decreases which were "agreed upon" with the trade unions. In contrast, the gradual price liberalization in Hungary corresponded with a less volatile development of both prices and real wages.

After the bold initial liberalizations, price reform has followed different routes. In Czechoslovakia and Hungary, price controls have been further relaxed in the course of the transition. In spite of the tremendous and

Table 5.2. *Average gross monthly wages (real), annual change in %, 1990–1994*

	1990	1991	1992	1993	1994*
Bulgaria[a]	5.3	−39.0	5.7	−8.7	−23.9
Czech Republic[b]	−5.7	−24.5	9.8	3.7	6.5
Slovak Republic[c]	−5.9	−25.1	8.7	−3.6	3.0
Hungary[d]	−3.7	−7.0	−1.4	−3.9	7.0

Notes: *preliminary.
[a] Excluding private sector. Net wages, from 1992 estimate for gross wages.
[b] In 1991 wages in enterprises with more than 100 employees; from 1992 enterprises with more than 25 employees.
[c] In 1990 excluding farm cooperatives.
[d] Net wages. In 1992 and 1993 wages in enterprises with more than 20 employees; from 1994 enterprises with more than 10 employees.
Source: WIIW 1995: Tables.VI/1.1, 1.3, 1.4, 1.8.

Table 5.3. *Average gross monthly wages (real), 1989–1994 (1989=100)*

	1990	1991	1992	1993	1994*
Bulgaria[a]	105.3	64.2	67.9	62.0	47.2
Czech Republic[b]	94.3	71.2	78.1	81.0	86.2
Slovak Republic[c]	94.1	70.5	76.6	73.8	73.0
Hungary[d]	96.3	89.6	88.3	84.8	90.7

Notes: *preliminary.
[a] Excluding private sector. Net wages, from 1992 estimate for gross wages.
[b] In 1991 wages in enterprises with more than 100 employees; from 1992 enterprises with more than 25 employees.
[c] In 1990 excluding farm cooperatives.
[c] In 1992 and 1993 wages in enterprises with more than 20 employees; from 1994 enterprises with more than 10 employees.
Source: See Table 5.2., own calculations.

higher-than-expected costs of liberalizing prices, governments have not compromised upon price reform. From a comparative perspective, the completion of price liberalization has progressed slower in the Czech Republic than in Hungary and Slovakia. The Czech government has spread the adjustment of energy prices and rents over time in order to secure the political acceptance of reforms. Unlike the other countries,

Bulgaria has seen a partial reintroduction of price controls since 1992 (EBRD 1995: 37). In mid 1995, the share of genuinely free prices was down to about 54 percent. The reimposition of price controls has partly been a reaction to public outcry over "excessive" prices and profits. Moreover, price controls for foodstuffs have been used as a social policy device.

3.3 Slashing state expenditure

The liberalization of prices has been closely related to the elimination of subsidies. Budgetary subsidies have been drastically reduced and are by now close to the OECD level (Schaffer 1995). Between 1989 and 1993, the share of subsidies in GDP dropped from 15.5 to 4.8 percent in Bulgaria, from 12.1 to 4.8 percent in Hungary, and from 25 to 4.4 percent (Czech Republic) and 4.8 percent (Slovakia) in the former Czechoslovakia (IMF 1994: 82f., table 15). As in the case of price liberalization, Hungarian gradualism has contrasted with a more discontinuous pattern in Bulgaria and Czechoslovakia. Whilst subsidies in Hungary have continuously fallen since 1987, Bulgaria and Czechoslovakia saw a drastic shake-out of subsidies in 1991 within the framework of the adopted stabilization programs (OECD 1991: 70f.; OECD 1992: 15). In both countries, the share of subsidies in GDP fell by about 10 percentage points in that single year.

However, the hardening of enterprises' budget constraints and the imposition of financial discipline has remained incomplete (Kornai 1993). In all countries, budgetary subsidies have partly been replaced with different kinds of "hidden" and "indirect" subsidies. Among the most prominent devices have been the toleration of tax arrears and "soft" lending by state-owned banks (Fan and Schaffer 1994: 156; Schaffer 1995: 125–41). Accumulated tax arrears have now reached an order of several percent of GDP, and there is plenty of evidence for the covert use of the banking sector for subsidizing loss-making enterprises.

For a number of reasons, curbing budgetary subsidies has proved to be easier than terminating "implicit" subsidies: the IMF's eye on the budget and the higher visibility of budgetary subsidies have strengthened the government's position in the bargaining over budgetary subsidies. Phasing out budget subsidies has been less demanding in political and administrative terms than engaging in the collection of back taxes. Governments have been confronted with the same problems as other creditors, such as swamped courts and the non-existence of assets which would have covered tax payments. Like other creditors, they have faced incentives to make concessions in the hope of gathering at least some of the outstanding taxes. Moreover, governments themselves have often

Table 5.4. *General government expenditure, 1989–1995 (% of GDP)*

	1989	1990	1991	1992	1993	1994	1995[P]
Bulgaria[a]	58.4	65.9	45.6	45.4	50.8	43.8	na
Czechoslovakia	64.5	60.1	54.2	52.8	–	–	–
Czech Republic	–	–	–	–	48.5	49.0	na
Slovak Republic	–	–	–	–	49.1	40.7	na
Hungary[b]	61.0	57.5	58.3	63.4	60.5	na	na

Notes: [P] projection.
[a] Cash basis. Includes the state, municipalities, social security, and extra-budgetary funds.
[b] Includes the state, municipalities, and extra-budgetary funds.
Source: EBRD 1995: app.11.1.

deliberately gone off-budget in order to keep recorded budget deficits low and to conceal the costs of subsidization.

In most East European countries, the massive cuts in budgetary subsidies have paved the way for a substantial reduction of state expenditure (see table 5.4). In the former Czechoslovakia, state expenditure, as a percentage of GDP, fell from 64.5 percent in 1989 to 49 percent in the Czech Republic and 40 percent in Slovakia in 1994. Bulgaria has even witnessed a decline from 58.4 to 43.8 percent. Hungary has been the only country where state expenditure has more or less remained at its 1989 level. Save for Czechoslovakia and the Czech Republic, however, expenditure cuts, drastic as they were, have not been sufficient to prevent the emergence of large fiscal deficits (see table 5.5). Due to the deep transformational recession, the difficulties in building a new tax system, and massive tax evasion, revenues have fallen faster than expenditures (Campbell 1995; IMF 1995; Rosati 1994a). In turn, the resulting budget deficits have infringed upon the state's retreat from the economy: the state has absorbed a large part of private savings, thus risking the crowding out of private investors. In Hungary, for example, the government share in total credit reached a level of 55 percent in 1993 (Dittus 1994: 350f., table 1). Moreover, the looming fiscal problems have also prevented further tax cuts and have favored hasty and discretionary changes in taxation which have increased investors' uncertainty.

A couple of factors account for the intercountry differences in fiscal consolidation. Unlike Czechoslovakia, Bulgaria, and Hungary have suffered from a huge stock of external and internal debt.[4] The need for

---

[4] To stress the country's outstanding fiscal performance, the Czech government

Table 5.5. *Budget deficits/surpluses, 1989–1995 (% of GDP)*

	1989	1990	1991	1992	1993	1994	1995[P]
Bulgaria[a]	−1.4	−12.8	−14.7	−15.0	−15.7	−7.0	na
Czechoslovakia	−2.8	0.1	−2.0	−3.3	–	–	–
Czech Republic	–	–	–	–	1.4	1.0	0
Slovak Republic	–	–	–	–	−6.7	−3.7	−3.0
Hungary[b]	−1.4	0.5	−2.2	−5.6	−6.4	-8.2	na

Notes: [P] projection.
[a] Includes the state, municipalities, social security, and extra-budgetary funds.
[b] Includes the state, municipalities, and extra-budgetary funds.
Source: EBRD 1995: app.11.1.

servicing the debt has put a heavy burden on the budget. In Bulgaria and Hungary, interest payments amounted respectively to 10 and 5 percent of GDP in 1993.[5] In contrast, the respective figures for the Czech and Slovak Republics were but 1.9 and 3.3 percent (IMF 1994: 82f., table 15). The importance of debt service obligations is further highlighted by a comparison of overall and primary balances.[6] Hungary ran positive primary balances from 1990 to 1992. It took until 1993 before the primary balance plunged into red. Likewise, Bulgaria achieved primary surpluses in 1990 and 1992. Thus, differences in debt service obligations account for a large part of the intercountry variance in fiscal performance.

A second determinant has been intercountry differences in social expenditure. Unlike the Czech Republic, Hungary, Bulgaria, and Slovakia have seen significant increases in the social expenditure ratio. Between 1989 and 1993, the share of social security benefits in GDP rose from 10.4 to 15.8 percent in Bulgaria, from 14.4 to 18.2 percent in Hungary, and from 13.6 to 16.7 percent in Slovakia,[7] while remaining stable in the Czech Republic (IMF 1994: 82f., table 15). This increase in the social

even tinkered with the introduction of a balanced-budget amendment in 1994. In another symbolic move, the Czech government repaid the country's outstanding debt to the IMF two years ahead of schedule in 1994.
[5] Bulgaria and Hungary have been among those CEE countries facing the danger of being caught in a debt trap. In Hungary, for example, the share of interest payments in GDP nearly doubled in the period from 1993 to 1995. In 1995, interest payments on state debt already absorbed 30 percent of budget revenues and 9 percent of GDP (OECD 1995b: 129).
[6] The primary balance is the fiscal balance less interest payments.
[7] 1989 figures are for Czechoslovakia.

expenditure ratio has been a main reason for the pervasive fiscal problems in most CEE countries (Barbone and Marchetti 1995; Sachs 1995).[8]

Finally, differences in the performance of profit taxes have mattered. The decline in revenue from profit taxes has been strongest in Bulgaria and more pronounced in Hungary than in the former Czechoslovakia (IMF 1995: 107–12). In the period from 1989 to 1993, revenues from profit taxes, as a percent of GDP, fell from 23.2 percent to 5.6 percent in Bulgaria, from 8.1 to 2.2 percent in Hungary, from 11 to 6.5 percent in Slovakia, and from 11 to 7.5 percent in the Czech Republic (IMF 1994: 80f., table 14).[9] These differences have largely been related to differences in enterprise profitability. Moreover, Bulgaria has suffered from the exceptionally large share of profit taxes in total taxes at the outset of reform which has made overall revenues highly sensitive to the deterioration of enterprise performance (Bogetic and Hillman 1994). There is also some evidence for significant differences in the capacity to enforce taxation. In Bulgaria, the relatively strong autonomy of state-owned enterprises and the weak tax administration have severely undermined this capacity. In contrast, tax authorities in Hungary and in the former Czechoslovakia have been in a stronger position.

3.4 From the central allocation of credits to capital markets cum monetary policy

In all CEE countries, the state's retreat from the allocation of credits has followed a uniform sequence (Rostowski 1993). It started with the creation of a two-tier banking system by splitting up the traditional Soviet-type monobank into a central bank and a number of state-owned commercial banks. The breaking up of the monobank system was followed by the liberalization of banking activities and entry into banking. The third step which is still on the agenda, has been the privatization of state-owned commercial banks.

The introduction of a two-tier banking system dates back to the old regime. In Hungary, central and commercial banking have been separated ever since January 1, 1987. In Bulgaria, the fission of the monobank system was first decreed in 1987, yet only partly implemented before the end of 1990. In Czechoslovakia, the creation of two-tier banking took place after the "velvet revolution," but had already been prepared under

---

[8] However, it is not so clear that social spending in the CEE countries has been overly generous, as argued by Sachs (1995). Although high relative to per-capita income, social expenditure ratios may be considered not that excessive given the massive social problems in the transition countries (Cichon and Hagemejer 1995).

[9] Again, 1989 figures for the Czech and Slovak Republics are for Czechoslovakia.

the old regime. The basic idea behind these reforms was to soften the state's grip on the allocation of financial flows and to introduce some commercial realism into enterprise financing.

The introduction of a two-tier banking system did not mean the simultaneous inauguration of central bank independence.[10] Until new central bank laws were adopted in 1991, central banks remained subject to government prerogatives. Between 1989 and 1991, only the National Bank of Hungary enjoyed a certain autonomy. The new central bank laws then put the relationship between governments and central banks on a new legal footing by calling for independent central banks. The laws have largely been patterned on the West German provisions and have provided for a relatively high degree of legal independence.[11] In spite of the common source of inspiration, provisions have differed in detail. Generally speaking, the National Bank of Hungary has been less independent than the other central banks.[12] Whilst the tasks of the Bulgarian, Czech, and Slovak central banks are narrowly defined as safeguarding currency stability, the Hungarian law explicitly obliges the Hungarian central bank to support the government's economic program. Unlike the other central banks, the National Bank of Hungary is not allowed to determine exchange rate policy on its own. Finally, the Hungarian law provides for the greatest political leverage on leadership selection.

The central banks' position has suffered from the underdevelopment of capital markets, the fragility of the financial sector, and high budget deficits. Because of this fragility, central banks have been forced to abstain from too strong a tightening of monetary policy. Huge budget deficits, along with underdeveloped capital markets, have compelled central banks to finance large parts of the state budget deficits. Save for the Czech Republic, the rather strict legal constraints on deficit financing by the central bank[13] were violated in all countries. This particularly applies to Bulgaria where central bank loans to the government, as determined in the annual Budget Laws, have again and again exceeded

[10] The following paragraphs partly draw on unpublished material from a conference on central banks in Eastern Europe and the NIS which was hosted by the Center for the Study of Constitutionalism in Eastern Europe and held in Chicago on April 21–3, 1994.

[11] For dimensions and indices of legal central bank independence as used in the burgeoning empirical literature on the impact of central bank independence on economic performance, see Cukierman 1992: 371–82.

[12] The provisions in the Law on the National Bank of Hungary have also fallen behind earlier drafts. Critical observers have moreover argued that the law's provisions even curtail the central bank's independence as against the practice in 1989 and 1990 (Várhegyi 1993: 151f.).

[13] For the legal provisions, see Coratelli 1993: app. III.

the legal maxima. In Slovakia, the Meciar government breached the Central Bank Act in 1993 by massively overdrawing its operating account at the National Bank of Slovakia.[14] In Hungary, market financing of the huge budget deficits caused no problems until mid 1993. In December 1993, however, the legal ceilings on central bank financing had to be raised from 4 percent of projected revenue (some 50 bn Ft. at that time) to 80 bn Ft. in order to cover the budget deficit. Except for the Czech Republic, the attempt to gain credibility by tight central bank laws has thus somewhat backfired. In Bulgaria, Hungary, and the Slovak Republic, the violation of legal provisions has clearly infringed upon central banks' reputations.

The adoption of the new central bank laws gave the then governing parties the opportunity to influence future monetary policy by selecting the first generation of bank governors. Decision makers thus faced a choice between investing in central bank credibility by appointing independent candidates, on the one hand, and minimizing the political risks of independence by installing political favorites, on the other. In Hungary, the balance clearly tipped in favor of the second option. The Antall government used the passage of the new central bank law as a pretext for the dismissal of G. Suranyi, the bank's well respected, but politically inconvenient former governor, and replaced him with P. A. Bod, a close associate of the prime minister. Bulgaria might be treated as the other extreme. Here, parliament decided for T. Vulchev, a respected and independent economist, who was one of the architects of the 1991 economic reforms. J. Tosovsky, the Governor of Czechoslovakia's central bank who also became the Governor of the Czech National Bank after the dissolution of Czechoslovakia, may be located somewhere in between. More controversial was the appointment of V. Masár, a former state secretary at the Slovak Ministry of Finance, who was made Governor of the Slovak National Bank in July 1993 after an interregnum of more than six months.

In all countries, certain frictions between governments and central banks have surfaced. Not surprisingly, these frictions have been particularly pronounced in those countries that have witnessed changes in political majorities. However, the new central banks have by and large resisted political pressure. Political pressure upon the central bank has been most pronounced in Hungary. Here, the Horn government followed in the steps of its predecessor by causing Bod to resign in December 1994. In order to succeed, it even considered amending the Central Bank Act.

---

[14] Ironically, these operations would have conformed to the original Czechoslovak central bank law (OECD 1994a: 108).

Bod was ultimately replaced with Suranyi in order to appease the public and the international financial community.[15]

The hiving off of state-owned commercial banks from the monobank did not imply the immediate liberalization of banking activities either. There has also existed a fairly broad consensus that capital markets should be liberalized, but gradually. Alarmed by Latin American experience, governments and economic advisers alike have feared that too early a liberalization might provoke financial crashes and infringe upon macro-economic stabilization (McKinnon 1991). Hence, a number of controls have been phased out step by step. This applies to the liberalization of interest rates which was not completed before January 1991 in Bulgaria and Hungary and April 1992 in Czechoslovakia. In addition, monetary policy has also heavily relied on credit ceilings. In Bulgaria, they continued to be the single most important instrument of monetary policy by the end of 1994. In Czechoslovakia, credit ceilings were imposed on large commercial banks until October 1992. The Slovak National Bank was forced to reintroduce them in early 1993 in the wake of the economic turbulences after the dissolution of Czechoslovakia. Only the Hungarian and Czech central banks have so far been in a position to rely on more market-conform indirect instruments of monetary policy, such as open market policy.

This cautious liberalization of capital markets has not prevented the occurrence of fraud and bank crashes. This has led to a certain retightening of banking regulation in the course of the transition. In the Czech Republic, market entry was temporarily restricted at the beginning of 1994 in order to promote the consolidation of the banking sector and the participation of foreign investors in domestic banks. In all countries, the banking system is now undergoing a massive consolidation process, as many of the newly founded banks have not been viable.

In spite of a surge in new private banks, the nascent capital markets are still dominated by those commercial banks which were originally carved out of the old monobank and which are still largely state owned. Although their market shares have been falling, these banks have continued to account for the bulk of assets, deposits, and loans.[16] According to EBRD estimates (1995: 161, table 10.2) the share of the top five banks in total banking assets in mid 1995 still reached 63 percent in

[15] The Slovak Moravcik government also dismissed one of the two Deputy Governors of the Slovak National Bank. However, the removal of M. Tkac had not been motivated by controversies over SNB policies, but by charges of collaboration with the communist secret police.

[16] Market shares of some of the old banks have partly infringed upon the existing legislation. The Czech National Bank has simply ignored a clause within the Czech Banking Law that has put certain ceilings on the banks' market shares.

Hungary, 65 percent in the Czech Republic, and 79 percent in Slovakia.[17] The new banks, including the foreign ones, have largely confined their activities to certain market niches. As a consequence, competition within the banking sector has remained limited.

The privatization of state-owned banks has got ahead fastest in the former Czechoslovakia. Save for the Slovak Savings Bank, all state-owned banks were included in the first wave of voucher privatization. However, voucher privatization covered only 45–51 percent of shares, so that the state has remained the single most important shareholder. Only one bank, Zivnostenká Banka, was fully privatized. In Hungary, the 1991 Banking Law has obliged the government to reduce its shares in banks to a maximum of 25 percent until the end of 1996. Yet only the Foreign Trade Bank had actually been privatized until the end of 1995. Government shares in the other big commercial banks have fallen since 1987. However, most of the divested shares have gone to state-owned enterprises and other public institutions. The privatization of the two biggest commercial banks – Credit and Commercial Bank and Hungarian Credit Bank – will probably not be accomplished before 1997–8. In Bulgaria, the privatization of the banking sector has been complicated by the fragmentation of the banking system. The Bulgarian National Bank was originally broken into 70 larger and about seventy smaller commercial banks in order to increase competition among banks. Yet the bulk of these banks proved to be unviable. As a consequence, a Bank Consolidation Company was established in early 1992 which has been in charge of merging and, subsequently, privatizing the state-owned commercial banks. The last of seven mergers was completed in October 1994. At the end of 1994, bank privatization started with the floating of minority holdings in some smaller banks.

State ownership of banks has given governments some scope for influencing banks' lending policies. This influence has been exercised both indirectly, that is via the power to fill major management and supervisory board positions, and directly. The banks' dependence upon the takeover of bad loans by the government has made them rather prone to government influence. For these reasons, the governments' leverage on bank lending has remained high. This has been a major reason for why banks have continued to hand out or to guarantee credits to drifting enterprises or have financed large parts of the fiscal deficits.

3.5 The liberalization of wage bargaining

All countries have seen the institutionalization of collective bargaining.

---

[17] Unfortunately, no comparable data are available for Bulgaria.

Guarantees of free collective bargaining and the right to strike were among the first constitutional reforms. In line with Western practice, the new or amended Labor Codes now basically confine the state's role in the determination of wages, employment standards, and working conditions to the adoption of minimum standards.[18] At the same time, however, all countries have temporarily relied upon tax-based incomes policies. The state's withdrawal from wage regulation has been a gradual and incomplete one.

Governments have faced a difficult choice (Coricelli and Lane 1993; Jackman and Rutkowski 1994: 142–6). On the one hand, wage controls have carried an interventionist smack and have tended to impede structural change by infringing upon the desired broadening of wage differentials and by favoring the extension of non-wage benefits. Moreover, wage controls have loaded part of the responsibility for the determination of real wages onto the government. This has increased the government's burden to justify its policies and has simultaneously complicated the consolidation of collective bargaining. On the other hand, wage controls have been widely regarded as a necessary device for checking inflation and real wages. Given the persistence of weak ownership in state-owned enterprises, governments have moreover feared that a premature liberalization of wages might favor a decapitalization of enterprises and thereby reduce enterprise values and prospective privatization proceeds.

In line with recommendations by the international financial institutions and the bulk of economic advisers, the new governments finally opted against an immediate liberalization of wages and embarked upon tax-based incomes policies. In Bulgaria and Czechoslovakia, wage controls were an essential element of the stabilization programs launched in the beginning of 1991. In order to minimize the welfare losses associated with wage regulations, wage guidelines have largely been confined to state-owned enterprises[19] and have taken the form of wage bill ceilings thus providing some incentives for labor shedding. Given the above-mentioned problems of tax-based incomes policies, as well as the growing discontent of unions and employers' associations with wage controls, government policy towards wages has been prone to policy changes.

In Hungary, wage controls have not played the same role as in the

[18] As the new or amended constitutions provide for a right to work (see chapter 3, section 2.2.3), however, governments have retained some nominal responsibility for ensuring full employment.
[19] This has been achieved either by leaving private enterprises per se untaxed (Bulgaria) or by exempting small enterprises from taxation (Czechoslovakia until the end of 1992, Czech Republic, Hungary).

other countries. Due to the different pre-reform history, there was no need for a tough stabilization package equivalent to the 1991 ones in Bulgaria and Czechoslovakia. Nevertheless, wage guidelines have been formulated by the National Council for the Reconciliation of Interests.[20] These guidelines have been rather generous. By and large, wage growth has been close to the recommended maxima. Initially, wage guidelines were backed by excess wage taxation. Yet excess wage taxation which was already relatively "soft" in 1991, was not enforced during 1992 and was officially repealed at the end of that year. The Horn government initially planned to reimpose wage controls within the framework of a broader social pact. In fact, neither the pact nor the wage controls have so far materialized. Instead, the government has tried to check wage growth by putting ceilings on wages within public administration, by exercising ownership rights in state-owned enterprises, and by moral suasion (OECD 1995b: 54–7).

In Czechoslovakia, a tax-based incomes policy was part of the tripartite General Agreement in January 1991. Following controversies with the unions and some uncertainty over the continuation of wage regulation, excess wage taxation was unilaterally reintroduced by the government for the second half of 1992, but expired with the dissolution of Czechoslovakia (Buchtíková and Flek 1994). In the Czech Republic, wage controls were reimposed by the government in mid 1993 after increasing wage pressure and maintained until July 1995. This time, ceilings were set more generously and did not prevent real wages from running well ahead of GDP and productivity growth (OECD 1994a: 79–81). Unlike in the Czech Republic, the first Meciar government did not reimpose wage controls, even if the 1993 Budget Law authorized it to do so.

In Bulgaria, wage controls have been maintained ever since the start of reforms. The development of wage controls has mirrored the general history of tripartism in the country (Rock 1994). The 1991 stabilization program heavily relied on wages as a nominal anchor (Bogetic and Fox 1993). Wage adjustment and excess wage taxation were part of tripartite agreements. Under the Dimitrov government, wage guidelines and wage taxation were unilaterally imposed by the government. The Berov government again tried to negotiate wage guidelines. However, the enforcement of wage controls has significantly loosened over time (EBRD 1995: 37). In 1993, only about 10 percent of the excess wage tax revenues were in fact collected (Jackman and Rutkowski 1994: 145).

The Czech case points at the potential merits of wage regulation. Wage controls have held real wages down and have dampened inflationary

---

[20] For the history and the functions of this body, see chapter 6, section 3.

pressures. By containing labor costs, they have helped to stabilize employment. Wage controls have also been conducive to the emergence of a wage gap between the public and the private sector. In the Czech Republic, unlike in Hungary, average wages in the private sector have exceeded average public sector wages (Aghion and Blanchard 1994: 35, table 5). This has stimulated turnover from the public to the private sector.

In Czechoslovakia and, subsequently, in the Czech Republic, adoption and maintenance of wage controls were closely related to the strict anti-inflation outlook of the government. Wage controls have been embedded in a consistent program of economic stabilization. Moreover, they have not prevented real wages from gradually recovering since 1992. Unlike in the other countries, real wages did not experience a further fall in 1993.[21] This particular time path of real wages – a sharp decline in real wages in 1990/91, followed by a slow, but steady rise – has been conducive to the acceptance of wage controls.

In the other countries, the earlier retreat from wage regulation has clearly aggravated inflationary pressures. Governments did not share the anti-inflationary zeal and the technocratic self-assurance of their Czechoslovak and, later, Czech counterpart. They soon gave in to opposition against wage controls from trade unions and employers' associations. Structures of trade unions and collective bargaining have played a role, too. In Czechoslovakia, the weakness of the unions and the relatively centralized system of collective bargaining have favored wage restraint. In contrast, conditions in Bulgaria and Hungary have been less favorable. Bulgarian unions have been more influential than their Czechoslovak colleagues. At the same time, their strategic capacities have suffered from the rivalries between Podkrepa and CITUB, the two main unions. Moreover, collective bargaining in Bulgaria has become highly decentralized, thus rendering any central wage policy difficult. In Hungary, the fragmentation of the unions has likewise infringed upon the commitment to wage restraint. Finally, the lack of a visible recovery of real wages in these countries has undermined the acceptance of wage restraint and wage controls.

3.6 Privatization

The privatization of state-owned enterprises has turned out to be a rather protracted process. Save for the Czech Republic, about a half or more of all enterprises targeted for privatization were still state-owned at

---

[21] For the development of real wages, see, again, tables 5.2 and 5.3.

the end of 1994.[22] In Slovakia, privatization virtually came to a halt under the first Meciar government and has been troubled by political instability ever since. In Hungary, privatization also slowed down under the Antall government. In Bulgaria, privatization has yet to take off. Given this slow pace of privatization, the rise of the private sector has thus largely been due to new start ups.

Moreover, what has been called privatization has often been but a partial one, resulting in forms of "recombinant property" which defy any simple dichotomy of public versus private property (Stark 1993, 1994). Small-scale privatization has largely meant the lease and not the outright sale of property (Earle *et al.* 1994). In addition, the state has retained substantial stakes in "privatized" enterprises. In Czechoslovakia, for example, the shares of less than 20 percent of the 1,491 enterprises at offer in the first round of voucher privatization were sold completely (Svejnar and Singer 1994: 46). Finally, complex patterns of cross-ownership have emerged within the enterprise sector, as many private or privatized enterprises are partly owned by state-owned enterprises. The most prominent example are the Czech investment funds. Seven of the nine largest funds which now own the bulk of shares in privatized enterprises were established by the large state-controlled banks.

Property reform clearly represents the area of economic reform where intercountry differences in strategies and performance have featured most prominently in political and scholarly discussions. However, these differences have regularly been exaggerated. Privatization strategies have been multifaceted in all countries. In fact, governments have relied on and experimented with different methods of privatization (Bönker 1993: 37–46; Frydman *et al.* 1993).

In Hungary, the stage for the privatization of state-owned enterprises was already set with the adoption of the famous Company and Transformation Laws in 1988/9 (Brusis 1994; Major 1994). The enactment of both laws caused a wave of "spontaneous privatizations." Public outcry over dubious transactions led to the creation of the State Property Agency in March 1990 and to a certain recentralization of the privatization process. The State Property Agency launched a number of privatization programs. In mid 1992, the Antall government somewhat changed its course. It reacted to the growing discontent with the slow pace of privatization and the predominance of foreign buyers by drawing up

---

[22] It should be noted that privatization figures are among the most intransparent statistics. In Hungary, for example, the State Property Agency has assumed any enterprise with at least 20 percent private ownership as being privatized. As a consequence of these statistical problems, estimates of the number and the share of privatized enterprises in the CEE countries have widely differed.

schemes for subsidized credits. The centerpiece of these schemes, the "Small Investor Shareholder Program," which was finally launched in October 1993 came close to a mass privatization program. A further part of the credit schemes were specifically addressed to employees. The incoming Horn government stopped the "Small Investor Shareholder Program" and announced its preferences for cash sales of enterprises. However, privatization had a slow start. A new Privatization Law did not pass parliament before mid 1995. In February 1995, the resignation of F. Bartha, Hungary's privatisation commissioner, in the wake of controversies over the privatization of Hungar Hotels raised uncertainty over the future course of Hungarian privatization. Though privatization has gained momentum since, the government will not be able to fullfil its ambitious original plans.

Czechoslovakia has been famous for its program of voucher privatization. The first wave which included 1,491 enterprises was launched in May 1992 and completed by mid 1993. In the Czech Republic, a second wave of voucher privatization was initiated in late 1993 and completed in November 1994. This time, shares in 861 firms were floated. 185 of these had already been partially privatized in the first wave. Though voucher privatization has certainly represented the centerpiece of privatization in the former Czechoslovakia and, subsequently, in the Czech Republic, it has not been the whole story. Privatization has been multifaceted and has relied on a couple of different methods (Kotrba and Svejnar 1994). Besides voucher privatization, Czechoslovakia has also seen a particularly effective scheme of small-scale privatization via auctioning. Unlike Hungary, Czechoslovakia embarked upon a program of natural restitution. Finally, a number of enterprises have also been directly sold to foreign investors. One characteristic feature of Czechoslovak privatization has been the rejection of any preferential treatment for employees.

Unlike in the Czech Republic, the Slovak Meciar government took a sceptical stance toward mass privatization and emphasized its preference for standard privatization methods. In practice, privatization more or less stagnated until February 1994. However, 45 firms worth several bn koruny were sold to supporters of MDS and SNP in a covert and intransparent manner during the interregnum between February 14 and March 11, 1994 when the Meciar government lost its parliamentary support, but did not finally fall. The new Moravcik government pledged to speed up privatization. A second wave of voucher privatization with about 310 enterprises involved was launched, but could not be completed before the elections in October 1994. This program was suspended by Meciar within 24 hours of taking office. It took until June 1995 before the new government came up with a Privatization Program which, again,

called for the sale of state-owned enterprises and envisaged the transformation of vouchers into five-year state bonds to be served out of
privatization revenues.

Bulgaria was the last CEE country to pass a privatization law. It has
been among the countries which have made the smallest inroad into
privatization. Due to the frequent changes in government and controversies within the different governments, a privatization law was not adopted
before April 1992. The incoming Berov government stressed the need for
accelerating privatization. A first privatization program, largely based
upon the sale of assets, was launched in December 1992. By mid 1994,
however, only one in 16 large-scale enterprises had been privatized. After
a long period of governmental infighting, the Berov government finally
came up with a mass privatization program which envisaged the privatization of 340 enterprises in June 1994. The new BSP-led government that
was sworn in in early 1995 has basically stuck to mass privatization.
However, implementation has progressed but slowly.

These qualifications notwithstanding, the Czech Republic and Hungary
have represented two polar approaches toward the privatization of state-
owned enterprises and the retreat of the state in general.[23] In spite of the
"Small Investor Shareholder Program," Hungary has remained the most
prominent example of a case-by-case approach to privatization. In
contrast, Czechoslovakia and, later, the Czech Republic have pioneered
mass privatization with their schemes of voucher privatization.

Privatization in Hungary has aimed at an orderly retreat of the state.
The Hungarian approach has put emphasis on the creation of "real
owners." Governments have attempted to link privatization to the
injection of capital and the inauguration of effective ownership structures.
This has led to a number of successful privatizations. At the same time,
however, the reliance on the sale of assets has given rise to a couple of
problems. Domestic savings, although larger than expected, have not
been sufficient for financing the acquisition of state owned assets. This
has limited the demand for privatization. Due to these absorption
problems, Hungarian privatization has also resulted in a high degree of
foreign ownership. Between 1990 and mid 1992, more than 70 percent of
the privatized property was acquired by foreigners (Major 1994: 117).[24]
This massive foreign involvement has infringed upon the legitimacy of

---

[23] For the general merits and problems of these opposite approaches, see, for
example, Blanchard and Layard 1992; Frydman and Rapaczynski 1994; Kornai
1992a.

[24] Due to the advanced state of economic reform and the privatization strategy
pursued, Hungary has been the frontrunner in attracting foreign direct
investment in the region (Bönker 1994: 42f.; Meyer 1995). The second largest

the whole privatization process. The insistence on sales has also gone hand in hand with the adoption of rather rigid bargaining strategies by the State Property Agency. In its quest for revenues, the State Property Agency has regularly taken a rather tough stance, often ignoring the discrepancy between book and market values as well as the deterioration of asset values in the course of the transformation. In the case of foreign investors, the State Property Agency has moreover been confronted with accusations of squandering Hungarian assets at bargain prices. As a consequence, the high asking prices and the other transaction costs related to the sale have deterred many potential investors.

In contrast, the Czech approach has emphasized the speed of privatization. The underlying idea has been to divest state assets as soon as possible. Mass privatization has allowed to overcome the absorption problems which have fraught the case-by-case approach and has made economic reforms popular. Voucher privatization has already passed a number of potential hurdles. Most of the dire scenarios which were forecast by many critiques have not yet materialized. Neither serious liquidity problems on the side of the investment funds nor a stock market crash have occurred. Due to the more or less spontaneous emergence of investment funds, voucher privatization has also neither resulted in a highly dispersed ownership structure nor in Russian-style insider control. In retrospect, the Czechoslovak decision to distribute shares in enterprises – instead of shares in intermediaries, as recommended by the most prominent academic advocates of mass privatization – has thus turned out to be a clever move: *ex ante*, it has reduced distributive quarrels and has lessened the managers' opposition against mass privatization (Frydman and Rapaczynski 1994: 5). *Ex post*, the spontaneous formation of investment funds which acquired the lion's share of the new stocks has prevented the emergence of an ownership structure too dispersed for efficient corporate control.

In spite of the rise of the investment funds, the rapid shedding of state-owned assets has nevertheless been achieved "at the expense of ownership and governance quality" (EBRD 1994: 49). In case of some funds, too large portfolios have impeded the announced exercise of active corporate control. The fact that the major investment funds are owned by banks has given rise to a conflict of interest between the need for restructuring and the banks' desire to avoid bankruptcies. Finally, corporate control by investment funds has been hindered by the remaining influence of the state (Brom and Orenstein 1994).

recipient has been the Czech Republic. In contrast, foreign direct investment inflows to Slovakia and, even more so, Bulgaria, have been but paltry.

The differences in the adopted privatization strategies have been related to a number of factors (Bartlett 1992; Brusis 1993; Stark 1992). Again, the budgetary situation has mattered. Privatization had originally been perceived as an attractive source of state revenue. It thus comes as no surprise that the cash-strapped governments of Bulgaria and Hungary initially opted for the sale of assets. In Hungary, privatization proceeds had been explicitly earmarked for servicing the foreign debt. In contrast, the Czechoslovak government could more easily afford to forgo potential revenues by giving away state assets. In the same vein, the increasing popularity of mass privatization throughout the region has partly resulted from the growing awareness that net privatization proceeds are significantly lower than originally thought.

The choice of privatization strategies has moreover been related to the different pre-histories of economic reform. In Bulgaria and Hungary, the economic reforms which were undertaken before 1989 implied a certain decentralization and gave managers and workers a greater say in enterprise management. This led to the creation of implicit property rights which could not be ignored by reformers. It is for that reason, that preferential treatment for managers and employers played a greater role in Bulgarian and Hungarian than in Czechoslovak privatization. In addition, the existence of these implicit property rights also favored the adoption of a case-by-case approach towards privatization, as such an approach gives incumbents a greater leverage on the privatization process. In contrast, no such impediments to mass privatization prevailed in Czechoslovakia.

Finally, there has been another, more direct element of path dependency in the choice of privatization strategies: In Hungary, privatization was already on its way in 1989. In this situation, the adoption of a mass privatization scheme would have put the completion of the ongoing privatizations at risk. Again, this problem did not exist in Czechoslovakia. Here, the virtual absence of economic reforms before 1989 nourished concerns about ultimately staying behind which were conducive to the adoption of big – and unorthodox – leaps.

3.7   Conclusion

The comparative analysis of reforms has shown that the state's retreat from the economy has been a protracted process. Although no outright restatization has occurred, the withdrawal of the state has proven to be more complicated than originally expected by most observers. In some cases, the withdrawal of the state has progressed but slowly. This applies to the privatization of state-owned enterprises, to the termination of enterprise subsidization, or to the curbing of fiscal deficits. In other cases, the retreat of the state has partly been reversed in the course of the transition. The analysis has identified a number of instances where the initial liberalization of economic activities has not been sustained and controls have been reimposed. Cases in point are the drift toward protection in Bulgaria, Hungary, and Slovakia, the reintroduction of price controls in Bulgaria, or the reimposition of wage controls in Czechoslovakia in mid 1992. Thus, the retreat of the state from the economy has been both a slow and a non-linear process.

The retreat from the retreat partly reflects a creeping policy drift. In a number of instances, governments have accommodated reform fatigue by slowing down or reversing reforms. Cases in point are the re-erection of trade barriers or the reintroduction of price controls. However, this is not the whole story. Neither the slow withdrawal of the state nor the reimposition of state controls can simply be reduced to mere manifestations of a vanishing reform commitment. There is some evidence for the dangers of a "premature" liberalization of economic activities, in particular of labor and capital markets. Seen from this angle, the retreat from the retreat has partly represented a genuine learning process. In particular, the East European experience clearly hints at the merits of maintaining wage and credit controls in the first stage of the transformation.

Our analysis has also pointed at the existence of substantial inter-country differences in policies and performance. In Czechoslovakia and, later on, in the Czech Republic, the bold initial price and trade liberalization, as well as mass privatization, have somehow contrasted with the cautious liberalization of capital and labor markets and the delayed completion of price reforms. The Czech Republic has also been the country with the lowest policy drift. Under Meciar, post-independence Slovakia has clearly departed from the former Czechoslovak course. Compared with the Czech Republic, the retreat of the state has been partly reversed, partly slowed down. In Hungary, the retreat of the state has followed a more gradual pattern. Policy drift has been rather high. Governments have not managed to contain state expenditure and deficits, to accelerate privatization, or to prevent the reintroduction of trade barriers. Nor have they been strong enough to maintain wage controls. Finally, we have Bulgaria. Here, the retreat of the state has progressed most slowly. At the same time, the bold initial liberalization of prices and trade has partly been reversed.

4 The furnishing of capitalism

The furnishing of the new markets has included legal-institutional reforms and more direct interventions in the inherited economic structures. Whilst the adoption of a Western-style legal framework has been uncontroversial, the second group of measures has stirred fierce debates. Governments have been reluctant to promote marketization and restructuring by directly shaping economic structures.

4.1 The adoption of a legal framework

The retreat of the state from the economy has been highly intertwined with the legal furnishing of markets. Governments have tried to harmonize both elements of economic reform in order to avoid the emergence of legal-institutional voids. In spite of certain commonalities, however, the particular national reform paths have, again, differed. The reforming countries have drawn on different legal sources for building the legal infrastructure of markets. Moreover, the pace of reform has significantly differed.

Hungary enjoyed the most favorable starting conditions. It had never experienced such a strong an exorcism of pre-communist law as Bulgaria or Czechoslovakia. Moreover, the pre-1989 economic reforms had been associated with the adoption of a company, competition, bankruptcy, and tax law that was rather close to Western standards. At the end of 1989, Hungary thus had a clear headstart. As a consequence, it has been the frontrunner of legal-institutional reform. The legal furnishing of markets has progressed fastest in Hungary. Hungary has been the first country to pass most of the new laws. By and large, Hungarian legislation has also been among the most elaborate and sophisticated in the region. Due to the pre-1989 reforms, the retreat of the state and the legal furnishing of markets have proceeded in parallel.

In Czechoslovakia, starting conditions were significantly worse than in Hungary. The communist departure from pre-communist law had gone farther than in Hungary and no significant reforms had been undertaken in the 1980s. Nevertheless, Czechoslovak legal-institutional reform moved on rather fast. When the country dissolved at the end of 1992, the major elements of the legal framework of capitalism were already in effect. Unlike in Hungary, the state's withdrawal from the economy initially preceded the furnishing of markets. When prices and trade were liberalized in January 1991, the existing legal framework for the emerging markets was still highly fragmentary.

Bulgaria has made the slowest progress with legal reform. Here, the political instability has massively infringed upon reforms, so that the existing legal infrastructure still suffers from a number of gaps. Initially, governments confined themselves to tinkering with the famous Decree 56, a reform law which had been passed in January 1989. Thus, the legal-institutional framework at the time of price and trade liberalization in January 1991 was even more rudimentary than in Czechoslovakia. From a comparative perspective, most Bulgarian laws were passed rather late.[25] Finally, the professional quality of the adopted laws has been worse than in the other countries.

4.1.1 THE SEQUENCE OF LEGAL REFORM The legal furnishing of markets has followed a similar sequence in all countries which has largely been dictated by legal and economic "requirements." The first wave of reforms comprised basic reforms of property, contact, company, and competition law. The reform of property law started with amendments to the old constitutions which eliminated the communist property hierarchy and enshrined guarantees of private property. These changes were supplemented by the gradual amendment of property-related provisions in other laws. In Bulgaria, the Property Act was overhauled in 1990. In Czechoslovakia and Hungary, the Civil Codes' most important provisions on property were amended in 1991 and 1992. However, these provisions had already lost any actual normative force when they were amended.

In spite of all moves away from the traditional unity of civil law, the communist countries had never fully broken with the civil law tradition (Westen 1993). As for contract law, governments could thus build upon the communist Civil Codes. Yet reform paths differed (Brunner 1992: 43f.; Gray et al. 1993: 35f., 55f., 80–2). In Hungary, where the unity of civil law had largely been retained, the 1959 Civil Code was further unburdened from communist remnants and became the general frame-work for both non-commercial and commercial transactions. In Bulgaria, the provisions for individuals were initially likewise extended to all transactions. However, the Bulgarian Civil Code, the Law on Obligations and Contracts, with its distinction between contracts among individuals and contracts among socialized enterprises remained unaltered until 1993. In 1993, a second book with provisions for commercial transactions was added to the 1991 Commercial Code. In Czechoslovakia, where pre-communist civil law had been abrogated more completely under com-munism than in the other countries and where a separate Business Code for transactions within the socialist sector had existed, the reform of contract law took a different course. In April 1990, the purview of the –

---

[25] Again, this contrasts with the early enactment of a new constitution.

amended – Business Code was extended to all commercial transactions. In November 1991, the Business Code was replaced with the new Commercial Code (Glos 1992). The adoption of the new Commercial Code went hand in hand with the amendment of the Civil Code.

The reform of company law could draw on existing provisions, too. In Bulgaria and Hungary, the foundations of Western-style company law had already been laid under communism. In Hungary, the Law on Economic Associations which was adopted in 1988 has seen some minor amendments, but has basically been retained. In Bulgaria, Decree 56 initially continued to serve as a framework for the organization of business activities. Yet it was replaced with a new Commercial Code in May 1991. In Czechoslovakia, where no reforms of company law had been undertaken under the old regime, the liberalization of market entry in April 1990 was accompanied by the adoption of a preliminary corporate law. Whilst the Law on Joint-Stock Companies established the legal framework for joint-stock companies, a couple of amendments to the old Business Code made the other standard types of companies legitimate. This preliminary framework of company law was superseded by the new Commercial Code.

Competition law was reformed parallel to contract and commercial law. In this case, only Hungary could rely on legislation stemming from the communist period. The 1984 Competition Act which had already been close to Western provisions (Vörös 1986), was overhauled in November 1990. In Bulgaria and Czechoslovakia, temporary provisions against the abuse of monopoly positions were adopted in 1990. Fully-fledged Competition Laws were promulgated in January 1991 in Czechoslovakia and in May 1991 in Bulgaria. However, it took some time before the new Competition Offices effectively took up their work. In the first months after the liberalization of prices at the beginning of 1991, there were thus no Competition Offices which could have effectively sanctioned the abuse of market power.

Unlike contract, company, and competition law, bankruptcy law was enacted relatively late. Again, Hungary was the forerunner. Following a number of minor amendments to the 1986 Bankuptcy Law, a fundamentally revised law was adopted in September 1991 and went into effect on January 1, 1992 (Hegedus 1994). Czechoslovakia saw the passage of a bankruptcy law in June 1991. However, this law was never really enacted. Both the Czech and the Slovak Republic decided for substantially revised versions of the Czechoslovak law which eventually went into effect in mid 1993 (Paulus et al. 1993). In Bulgaria, Decree 56 contained some rudimentary bankruptcy provisions. A full-scale bankruptcy law did not come into force before August 1994 (Goleva 1995). The late enactment of bankruptcy laws was closely related to the slow retreat of the state from the subsidization of loss-making enterprises. Governments have been reluctant to let unviable enterprises go bust. For that reason, it also comes as no surprise that the new bankruptcy laws contain a plethora of provisions which extend enterprises' breathing space, encourage reorganisation, and allow for discretionary state involvement.

In all countries, legal reform has moved on from the basic and more general to the more specific issues. The basic reform of contract, company, and competition law was followed by the adoption of legislation for particular markets and market actors, such as regulations on capital and labor markets.

Banking Laws went into effect in December 1991 in Hungary, in February 1992 in Czechoslovakia,[26] and in March 1992 in Bulgaria. In Hungary, the furnishing of capital markets had already begun with the Law No.VI/90 on Securities and the Stock Exchange. In Czechoslovakia, the respective legislations were passed in April 1992. In Bulgaria, legislation on securities and the stock exchange had not been approved by the end of 1994.

The reform of labor laws began with the adoption of special provisions on collective bargaining which made the newly introduced constitutional guarantees of collective bargaining and the right to strike operational. In Hungary, a strike law had already been approved in March 1989. In Bulgaria, a first law on Collective Labor Disputes was promulgated in March 1990. In Czechoslovakia, a law on Collective Bargaining was passed in December 1990. The passage of these provisions was an important precondition for the state's retreat from the determination of wages. In contrast, the rest of the labor laws have been reformed but slowly. In the former Czechoslovakia, the 1965 Labor Code was amended several times, most notably in May 1991 and early 1994. However, these revisions were of a predominantly "negative" nature, that is they primarily aimed at eliminating remnants of communist labor laws and not at designing new ones. In Hungary and Bulgaria, substantially revised Labor Codes were promulgated in the course of 1992. These new Codes brought labor laws closer to the general civil laws. They also put collective bargaining on a new legal footing.

4.1.2 THE SOURCES AND THE SPIRIT OF THE LEGAL REFORMS In all countries, the "first generation" of laws have been subject to frequent

---

[26] In Czechoslovakia, however, a rudimentary Banking and Saving Banking Law had already been adopted in December 1989 when a two-tier banking system was introduced.

and often quite substantial changes. For a start, many original laws were rudimentary and put together in a hurry. In addition, the flood of amendments has been an unavoidable by-product of the comprehensive character of East European legal reform. Legislation has taken place in a highly unstable legal environment. Because of the links and cross references between the different bodies of law, changes on one front have necessarily implied revisions on others (EBRD 1994: 47). Many provisions have thus inevitably remained transitory. Finally, the massive amendment activities have been associated with the unprecedented nature of the East European transformation in general. As the adoption of many provisions "proven" in the West has not led to the desired and expected results, law making has become a gigantic trial and error process.

However, the flood of amendments has clearly been ambiguous. Inevitable as it may have been, it has also complicated the consolidation of the new legal framework. It is not only that the frequent legal changes have increased legal uncertainty. They have also favored the maintenance of the traditional strategic use of law. Given the massive amendment activities, many people have continued to regard the law not as a given framework, but primarily as an object of political manipulation. Likewise, the frequent amendments have nurtured the expectation that non-compliance with the law might not lead to sanctioning, but instead trigger an adjustment of the law.

In designing their new legal frameworks, the East European countries have relied on different sources. For a number of reasons, they could not simply restore pre-communist law. Due to the brief periods of national independence, pre-communist law had suffered from a certain lack of consolidation (Korkisch 1958: 201–5). Moreover, it had contained a number of highly interventionist provisions and would have clearly been insufficient for governing a modern capitalist economy (Heitger *et al.* 1992: 134–6). Nor have the reforming countries confined themselves to the import of Western ready-mades, as recommended by some economists. Instead, they have tried to draw on different sources in order to account for specific local circumstances and to make use of the unique chance of designing a legal system more or less from scratch. As a consequence, the emerging borrowing patterns have been rather complex and characterized by combinations of a number of historical and foreign inspirations (Bönker 1994: 37–9).

Pre-communist law was not restored, either in the long-term or as a temporary substitute for repealed communist provisions in any of the countries. The only country where such a return to the past was seriously considered has been Bulgaria where the restoration of pre-war Commercial and Bankruptcy Laws was discussed (Gray *et al.* 1993: 36). However, this is not to deny that pre-communist law has mattered in all countries. Elements of it have lingered on and have helped to smooth the legal transition. Pre-communist law has been an important source of inspiration, too. Traces of the old regulations can be identified in the Czechoslovak Commercial Code, in the Bulgarian Bankruptcy Law, or in the Hungarian Law on Economic Associations, to take but three prominent examples. Moreover, pre-communist law has influenced the approach to foreign models, as reformers have tended to "shop around" in countries with shared legal histories.

The European Union has represented a main external "focal point." This orientation toward the EU has been closely related to the CEE countries' desire to join the EU. Hungary officially applied for membership in spring 1994. Bulgaria and the Czech Republic followed in late 1995 and January 1996 respectively. The Association Agreements with the EU have called for an assimilation of the East European countries' legal framework. This particularly applies to competition law and the protection of intellectual property. The Association Agreements explicitly obliged the East European signatories to bring their competition law (except for the provisions on state aids) in line with EU provisions before the end of 1994 and to adjust their law on the protection of intellectual property by the beginning of 1997. Though the Association Agreements do not contain other specific time limits for the assimilation of law, the East European countries have been keen to adjust their law in order not to give the EU a pretext for slowing down the enlargement of the Community.[27]

All countries have institutionalized their endeavor for EU compatibility. In Hungary, for example, the law-making bodies have been obliged to consider EU law and to outline the relations between EU law when considering any draft bill since March 1990. Following the conclusion of the Europe Agreement, an Interministerial Commission in charge of coordinating integration-related policies was installed in April 1992 (Vida 1994). The Hungarian parliament set up a European Affairs Scrutiny Committee with a similar agenda and in 1994, compatibility with EU law was made a legal requirement. Similar steps have been undertaken in the other countries. The EU has assisted by sending experts and providing information.

In practice, the adoption of the rules of the *acquis communautaire* has turned out to be a protracted process. Many laws which were promulgated early in the process, proved to be not fully compatible with EU law

---

[27] A recent EU White Paper has specified the needed legal adjustment, but has not provided for a time schedule (CEC 1995).

(CEC 1995). A good case in point is competition law (Hoekman and Mavroidis 1995; de la Laurencie 1993). Although basically modeled upon the EU's approach, the new competition laws suffered from a couple of incompatibilities. Among other things, they provided for too great a leeway for "public interest" defences. The Bulgarian and Czechoslovak laws were fraught with unclear distinctions between horizontal and vertical restraints upon competition. In both cases, the initial laws did not fully specify to what extent provisions against the abuse of market power were also to apply to agreements between firms at different levels in the production chain. Part of these incompatibilities were already eliminated; others will have to be corrected either by amendment of the national law or by an EU-oriented interpretation of the law by the courts.

Among the EU countries, the Federal Republic of Germany has served as the single most important external model. This applies to Hungary in particular. As parts of the former Habsburg monarchy, Hungary and Czechoslovakia had shared the German–Austrian legal tradition. In Bulgaria, the German Law had historically exercised a strong influence, too (Pfaff 1993). Germany has also been the largest trading partner of the CEE countries and one of the biggest investors in the region. Along with Austria and Sweden, Germany has moreover been regarded as the incarnation of a "social" market economy, and all surveys suggest that it is this model of capitalism with its implicit promise of a reconciliation of economic strength and social welfare which has been preferred by a large majority of the East European population.

Again, however, borrowing patterns have been complex. The reforming countries have not simply copied the German system. This is clearly illustrated by the furnishing of capital and labor markets. The appropriate structure of both factor markets has been amongst the most controversial issues. Here, proponents of different models of capitalism have clashed most directly. As for capital markets, controversies among adherents to a Japanese–German model of intermediary-based insider control and advocates of an Anglo-Saxon model of market-based outsider control have featured prominently (Corbett and Mayer 1991; Grosfeld 1994; Stiglitz 1992). Whereas the former have argued for a strong role of the banks in corporate control and financial intermediation, the latter have favored corporate control via stock markets and a stronger separation of banks and enterprises. Likewise, there has been a fierce controversy over the merits of corporatism in industrial relations (Freeman 1994). In both areas, the German influence can be felt, but has been far from pervasive.

As for capital markets, only Bulgaria and Czechoslovakia have established a system of universal banking along German lines (Thorne 1993:

968). The Bulgarian and Czechoslovak Banking Laws set certain ceilings on banks' shares in non-financial enterprises, but basically allow for universal banking. Especially the Czechoslovak law closely follows the German *Kreditwesengesetz* (Ziebe 1992). In contrast, the Hungarian law provides for a separation between commercial and investment banking and limits bank involvement in corporate decision making. In practice, however, it gives commercial banks the opportunity to engage in securities trading and investment fund management by setting up subsidiaries (Várhegyi 1993: 160).

In Bulgaria and Czechoslovakia, certain tensions over the decision for universal banking, the eagerness in quickly establishing a stock market, and the adopted privatization strategies have emerged. Once more, these tensions clearly point at the limits of the German influence in the CEE countries. In all countries, governments have been keen to establish stock markets. Despite the subordinate role stock markets play within the framework of the German–Japanese model, they have been somehow treated as synonyms for capitalism. In Czechoslovakia, moreover, the reform of the financial system was initially not harmonized with the pursued privatization strategy (Corbett and Mayer 1991). Voucher privatization was originally clearly inspired by an Anglo-Saxon model of "popular capitalism" and stock market control. Due to the emergence of bank-controlled investment funds, however, mass privatization has ultimately given rise to one of the most pronounced insider systems in the region.

In the case of labor markets, the evidence is also ambiguous (Moerel 1994; Thirkell *et al.* 1994). Though the East European countries have clearly leaned toward a corporatist model of industrial relations, they have only partly emulated particular German institutions. All countries have introduced and maintained some form of institutionalized tripartism. In Hungary and the former Czechoslovakia, the structure of wage bargaining with its industry-wide settlements has been similar to the German model. At the same time, however, only Bulgaria and Hungary have so far launched a dual system of interest representation along German lines. In both countries, works councils have made for a second tier of interest representation besides the unions. Unlike in Germany, however, both the Bulgarian and the Hungarian government originally considered making the works councils bargaining agents for collective agreements. In the former Czechoslovakia, legislation does not provide for such a second tier of interest representation. In May 1990, the repeal of the State Enterprise Act of 1988 brought the abolition of the elected enterprise councils. The amended Labor Code did not call for the creation of works councils. Nor does the Czech and Slovak legislation that has been adopted after the split of Czechoslovakia.

4.2 The state and economic restructuring

By and large, post-communist governments have refrained from direct interventions into the inherited economic structures. Instead, they have confined themselves to promoting economic restructuring through market forces. This reluctance for intervention has stemmed from a number of causes: initially, governments clearly underestimated the importance of communist legacies and optimistically assumed that the economy would grow out of the inherited stock problems. They have suffered from a lack of financial and administrative capacities. Finally, the distrust in the state and the fear of sending the wrong signals have loomed large. For all these reasons, governments' ultimate attempts to remove obstacles to marketization stemming from the inherited non-institutional constraints have tended to remain half-hearted. This applies to the demonopolization of enterprises, the tackling of the bad loan problem, and the involvement in enterprise restructuring. As a consequence, a number of measures which might have favored economic restructuring have not been undertaken.

4.2.1 THE FAILED DEMONOPOLIZATION The issue of demonopolization featured prominently in the early stages of the transition. In many early policy documents, breaking up the existing monopolies was regarded as the only feasible option to instill competition into the economy and was thus treated as an essential precondition for price liberalization and privatization.

In fact, however, there has not been much administrative demonopolization. In all countries, a first wave of break-ups occurred in early 1990. In Czechoslovakia, for example, the number of state-owned enterprises in most industries doubled or tripled between the end of 1989 and mid 1990. In construction, the number increased from two to 49 between January and April 1990 (Charap and Zemplinerová 1993: 3f.). These break-ups were largely initiated "from below," that is by plant managers striving for greater independence. The first wave of demonopolization was part of a broader process of spontaneous privatization. It was soon stopped by the national governments who faced a public outcry over dubious transactions and they feared that they might lose control over the privatization process. In Hungary, this discontent led to the creation of the State Property Agency in March 1990.

Instead of splitting up state-owned enterprises, governments then largely confined themselves to stimulating competition by removing barriers to entry, facilitating start-ups, bringing in foreign competition, and institutionalizing competition policy. However, these measures have turned out to be insufficient to bring concentration ratios down to Western levels and to prevent collusion and the abuse of dominant market positions. Nevertheless, governments have abstained from initiating any further break-ups before privatization and have instead tried to split enterprises in the course of the privatization process. Linking demonopolization and privatization, however, has posed a dilemma, as the governments' aim to increase competition has conflicted with their revenue interests. In a number of cases, the balance has tipped in favor of the revenue motive. Though privatization has brought a certain deconcentration, it has thus left a number of dominant market positions untouched.

4.2.2 THE DELAYED TAKEOVER OF BAD LOANS Governments have also been reluctant to tackle the overhang of bad loans in the portfolios of the big banks which has turned out to be one of the major obstacles to the disentangling of the dense ties between enterprises and banks. By favoring creditor passivity, the high stock of low-performing loans has infringed upon the hardening of budget constraints and economic restructuring. Initially, the soaring bank and enterprise profits and the absence of Western-style accounting rules somehow concealed the dimensions of the existing stock problem. Moreover, inaction has been favored by governments' budgetary concerns and their fears that the takeover of loans might provoke moral hazard problems.

Against this background, governments initially confined themselves to supporting the creation of risk reserves by tolerating large interest rate spreads. Czechoslovakia was the first country to embark upon more active measures. In March 1991, the Consolidation Bank was established. As its first big transaction, it took over the bulk of the so-called TOZ credits, a special category of credits granted before 1989, from the banks. The banks' balance sheets were cleared of CSK 110 bn or almost 20 percent of total bank credits at that time. Simultaneously, the government injected CSK 50 bn of state bonds in the banking system. These measures which were adopted grudgingly were later supplemented by further debt-for-debt swaps and capital injections (Capek 1994; Vojtisek 1993). After the dissolution of Czechoslovakia, the Czech government has been more active in further tackling the problem of bad debts than its Slovak counterparts.

In Hungary, the adoption of measures took longer (Nyers and Lutz 1993). In mid 1991, the Hungarian government guaranteed about half of the inherited pre-1987 bad debt. According to estimates, this guarantee covered about half of the non-performing loans on the banks' books. At the end of 1992, a comprehensive Bank Consolidation Scheme was drawn up which ultimately led to the takeover of loans worth 102 bn Ft (Mizsei 1994: 141f.; OECD 1993: 141–4). However, this scheme was fraught with a number of problems.[28] As the conditions for swapping debt for government bonds were highly unfavorable for the banks, the scheme did not lead to a lasting improvement of the banks' financial situation. Therefore, a further recapitalization was undertaken in 1993 (OECD 1995b: 107–11).

In Bulgaria, the government took over enterprise debt in an order of magnitude of 9 bn Lv in 1991 and 1992 (Dobrinsky 1994). These measures were primarily fashioned as financial assistance to troubled enterprises and designed in a rather arbitrary way. As a consequence, this bailout in fact aggravated the bad loan problem by provoking massive moral hazard problems. It took until December 1993 before the National Assembly adopted a large-scale recapitalization scheme.

In all countries, the adopted measures came too late and were insufficient to prevent a snowballing of bad loans. The share of bad loans in the banks' portfolios actually increased in the course of the transformation. Estimates for 1993 put it at about 20 percent in Hungary and the Czech Republic, about 25 percent in Slovakia, and about 30 percent in Bulgaria. From a comparative perspective, the Czech Republic and, after some delays, Hungary have been most successful in overcoming the bad debts problem. Although still fraught with huge problems, the Czech and Hungarian banking systems have been in a better shape than the Slovak and Bulgarian. As a consequence, Czech and Hungarian banks have been in a better position to exercise corporate control and to induce enterprise restructuring.

4.2.3   THE NEGLECT OF INDUSTRIAL POLICY   Initially, governments have practised a permissive approach towards state-owned enterprises. They have given managers large leeway and have exercised control in an *ad hoc* fashion. For a long time, "privatization before restructuring" was a shibboleth in all countries. In many cases, the resulting lack of direction favored enterprise drift and pre-privatization agony. Yet the slow pace of privatization, the further deterioration of the values of state-owned enterprises, and the larger-than-expected output decline have given rise to calls for a more active approach toward the restructuring of state-owned enterprises.

---

[28] Mizsei (1994: 142) thus calls it "the worst economic policy action of the Antall government."

Hungary was the first country to embark upon an explicit industrial policy (OECD 1995a). In 1991 and 1992, two ambitious policy documents were adopted. In late 1992, a program of crisis management and restructuring for 13 large industrial enterprises was approved. Costs of the program were estimated at 8 bn Ft. In another move, a holding company in charge of administering the government's ownership in about 163 enterprises, in which the government intended to retain full or partial ownership, was established in June 1992. In both cases, however, restructuring efforts suffered from a lack of financial and administrative resources and a rather "soft" approach toward the included enterprises. The Hungarian State Holding Company was remerged with the State Property Agency after the 1994 elections.

In the other countries, industrial policy has remained in an even more rudimentary state. The Czech Republic saw a certain strengthening of the Ministry of Industry and Trade. Yet coordination problems among the Ministry, the National Property Fund, and the Consolidation Bank, as the main state agencies in charge of exercising state ownership, have lingered on (OECD 1994b: 97–113). In Slovakia, the call for an industrial policy has been louder (OECD 1994a: 116–18, 1994b: 115–35). The "Strategy of Economic Revival" which was promulgated by the Meciar government in November 1992 and further elaborated in April 1993 stressed the need for industrial restructuring under state guidance. However, unclear objectives and budgetary difficulties have delayed its implementation. The original plan of the Ministry of Economy to establish a special fund to finance its development objectives had to be shelved in July 1993 due to a lack of funds. In Bulgaria, a similar gap between announcements and actual measures has prevailed.

This neglect of industrial policy has often been criticized (Amsden *et al.* 1994; Miller 1995). Critics have referred to the East Asian countries or post-war France as illustrations for the merits of industrial policy. However, it seems doubtful whether Asian-style industrial policy would have been a feasible option for the CEE countries (Bönker 1994: 38). Given the very weakness of the post-communist states, in particular their lack of autonomy *vis-à-vis* the state enterprise sector, the conduct of a credible selective industrial policy has been a highly difficult endeavor. Moreover, East Asian industrial policy has been about building up a competitive industry and not about restructuring an oversized industrial sector.

5 The long road to functioning markets

It is fair to say that the economic transformation has proven to be more troublesome than initially expected both by the East European

Table 5.6. *GDP (real) annual change in percent, 1989 – 1995*

	1989	1990	1991	1992	1993	1994	1995[P]
Bulgaria	0.5	−9.1	−11.7	−7.3	−2.4	1.4	2.5
Czechoslovakia	1.4	−0.4	–	–	–	–	–
Czech Republic	–	–	−14.2	−6.4	−0.9	2.6	4.0
Slovak Republic	–	–	−14.5	−7.0	−4.1	4.8	5.0
Hungary	0.7	−3.5	−11.9	−3.0	−0.9	2.0	3.0

Note: [P] projection.
Source: EBRD 1995: app.11.1.

Tabble 5.7. *GDP (real), 1989–1994 (1989=100)*

	1990	1991	1992	1993	1994	1995[P]
Bulgaria	90.9	80.3	74.4	72.6	73.6	75.5
Czech Republic	99.6[a]	85.5	79.4	79.3	81.3	84.6
Slovak Republic	99.6[a]	85.2	79.2	76.0	79.6	83.6
Hungary	96.5	85.0	82.5	81.7	83.4	85.9

Notes: [P] projection.
[a] Czechoslovakia
Source: See table 5.6., own calculations.

population and by outside observers. Economic performance has been worse than even notorious pessimists initially prognosticated. The single most important manifestation of these unexpected complications has been the massive decline in output after 1989 (see tables 5.6 and 5.7). Even if the official figures clearly overrate the slump in GDP, the reforming East European countries have experienced an output decline without historical precedence since the Great Depression of the 1930s. Between 1989 and 1993, when GDP more or less bottomed out in all countries, the recorded cumulative decline amounted to between 20 and 30 percent. In the post-war era, such two-digit output declines have been confined to small mono-exporting countries (Blejer and Gelb 1993: 4f.). Last decades' economic reforms in Latin America, for example, have been associated with much smaller output losses than the ones in Central and Eastern Europe.

The output decline can be treated as an across-the-board indicator of the difficulties of institution-building in the CEE countries. As the universal character of output decline suggests and the burgeoning literature on the causes of the "transformational recession" (Kornai) confirms (Blejer and Gelb 1993; Kornai 1994; Rosati 1994b; Schmieding 1993; Williamson 1993), the drop in GDP can only partly be explained by contingent factors, such as policy mistakes, or by exogeneous events, such as the demise of CMEA and the "Soviet trade shock." Instead, the output decline first of all points at the difficulties in replacing the coordination mechanisms of the communist economic system with new ones. The disintegration of the old formal and informal modes of coordinating economic activities has left a kind of void, as the emergence and consolidation of market coordination and the adjustment to the new institutions have taken time (Kornai 1994: 47–9).

This very nature of the transformation crisis can be highlighted by two thought experiments. Summers (1993) has proposed thinking about the effects of a sudden breakdown of about two thirds of all telephones in the West.[29] In a similar vein, Schmieding (1993: 236) has proposed imagining "the coordination problems that would befall a Western market economy if all firms discovered one morning that their entire staff for sales, advertising, finance and legal matters had gone off on a three-year holiday to Mars – together with all the lawyers, judges, bankers and public administrators."

5.1 A stylized description of East European capitalism

In Eastern Europe, an original form of capitalism has emerged from the ruins of communism (Stark 1993). It has come closer to Latin American capitalism than to the West European and Anglo-American types of capitalism upon which the new institutions were originally patterned. The main attributes of this East European blend of capitalism have been the large share of "uncivil" economic activities and a particular economic "dualism."

Economic reform has been accompanied by the rise of an "uncivil economy" (Rose 1992). Symptoms have ranged from pervasive tax evasion to trader tourism and the rise in corruption and organized crime. Whereever you are in Central and Eastern Europe, there is talk about the mafia. Estimates now put the "shadow economy" at 20 to 30 percent of

---

[29] "Suppose that suddenly two-thirds of our telephones stopped working. Economists would observe that telephone services were a small part of GDP and struggle to attribute the resulting loss of output. Would demand shocks be responsible – because of inability to place orders? Or supply shocks – because firms do not talk to their suppliers? Eventually sanity would prevail and we would see the problem for what it is – a temporary absence of effective coordination mechanisms" (Summers 1993).

GDP, that is a level significantly higher than in most OECD countries and matched only by the Mediterranean countries. Parts of this "shadow economy" have stemmed from the old "second economy," (Sik 1992). Contrary to expectations, many "second economy" entrepreneurs have not transformed their activities into regular businesses and have never left the "twilight." Most newly established private businesses are in some ways "multicolored." Moreover, even big state-owned enterprises have frequently been engaged in massive tax evasion.

Such "uncivil" practices can be interpreted as rational, defensive reactions to the deterioration of material conditions and the weakness of the state. Declining real wages and increasing unemployment have somehow pushed the people to look for alternative ways of getting by, whilst the poor state of the tax administration has lowered the risk of being caught. At the same time, however, such "uncivil" behavior has also been nourished by the lingering on of behavioral patterns which were moulded under communism. Accustomed to distrusting and to cheating the state and to make opportunistic use of the law, many people have continued to do so after the change in regime.

A second – related – characteristic of the post-communist economies has been a particular "dualization" of the economy. The first sector has been the nascent private one. This sector has primarily consisted of small enterprises, many of them in trade and services, and has been characterized by the dominance of spot transactions, grab-and-run behavior, and reckless business practices. Enterprises have suffered from undercapitalization and a lack of long-term financing. Trading activities have dominated investment activities. It has been this sector where the bulk of bankruptcies have occurred.

The ruthless, short-term behavior which has so far remained typical of this sector, has had different sources, too. The high uncertainty over future developments has put a premium on short-termism. The weakness of the state and the lack of law enforcement have greatly eased the disregard for the law. Again, however, mental residues have mattered. Under communism, the existing – legal, semi-legal, and illegal – markets were sellers' markets. Due to the endemic shortage, sellers could demand high prices and did not need to think about quality or marketing. Many entrepreneurs have thus entered the market with unrealistic ideas about "normal" profits. In addition, the precarious status of private economic activities under communism had nourished short termism. Confronted with an unbound government, most participants in the private sector had refrained from investments and longer-term engagements.

The second sector has been populated by large state-owned enterprises, the big banks, and many partly or completely privatized enterprises.

Other important players have been central and local governments. This sector of the economy has been characterized by rather dense ties and a high degree of immobility. A generalized perception of mutual vulnerability has favored cautious moves and passive behavior. Creditors, for example, have hesitated to initiate bankruptcy proceedings. Similarly, customers have been reluctant to switch suppliers. The underlying ties have taken different forms. Part of them date back to the communist era. This applies to personal connections, as well as to supply and credit chains. Other ties have emerged since the end of 1989. In all countries, the bulk of low-performing debt, including inter-enterprise credit, was accumulated after the start of the transformation. Likewise, property reform has increased cross-ownership among enterprises. As the Czech case illustrates (Brom and Orenstein 1994; McDermott 1994), the mere change in ownership title has not necessarily resulted in the disentanglement of the inherited ties.

Both sectors of the economy have been highly intertwined. In many cases, the private sector has been built upon assets which have been transferred – more or less legally – from the state sector. Many managers of state-owned enterprises have set up private firms, run either by themselves, relatives, or partners, or have collaborated with private firms. There are many examples of private firms having bought goods from state-owned enterprises at artificially low prices. Such cases of plundering state-owned enterprises have been legion throughout Central and Eastern Europe.[30] On the other hand, the private sector has suffered from the state sector's drag on resources. As state-owned enterprises have attracted large shares in state expenditure and bank credit, private enterprises have often been crowded out.

At the same time, both sectors have been fraught with precisely the opposite problems. Roughly speaking, ties have been too "weak" within the new private and too "strong" within the old state sector. In the private sector, the lack of trust" (Dasgupta 1988; Hardin 1991) or "social capital" (Putnam 1993) has induced grab-and-run behavior and has been

---

[30] A good example is the case of the Czech truck maker Tatra Koprivnice. "According to a recently released report by the Czechoslovak Management Centre, the scheme began in 1990, just after Tatra was loosened from state control. One of the first things Tatra did was to cut its ties to Mokotov, the old state monopoly in charge of motor equipment exports. In its place, Tatra managers set up as many as 100 private exporting firms, run by the managers themselves, their family members or former Motokov employees. Tatra sold its cars at a loss to the exporting firm, which then sold them at huge profits to the company's foreign trading partners" ("The Enemy Within," *Business Central Europe*, February 1995, 48).

detrimental to the adoption of a longer-run calculus. This has infringed upon the consolidation and the expansion of the private sector. The lack of social ties has led entrepreneurs to abstain from investment projects and from mutually advantageous long-term contracts. Just the other way round, the dense ties within the state-dominated sector have infringed upon competition and restructuring by favoring passive behavior.

In sum, East European capitalism has clearly suffered from a lack of consolidation. In the horizontal dimension, the retreat of the state has been incomplete. The public sector has remained large. Though budget constraints have been hardened, governments have continued to subsidize loss-making enterprises and to use state-owned enterprises for political purposes. In the vertical dimension, deficiencies have prevailed, too. Though the basic legal framework has been laid in all countries, actors are still struggling to accept their new roles and to conform to the formal and informal rules of capitalism.

5.2   The state of restructuring

This lack of consolidation has infringed upon the restructuring of the East European economies. This is not to deny that they have undergone massive structural changes. In all countries, private sectors have expanded. The EBRD (1995: 11, table 2.1, see also 28, table 1) has put mid-1995 private sector shares in GDP at 45 percent in Bulgaria, 60 percent in Hungary and Slovakia, and 75 percent in the Czech Republic. Sectoral structures have been substantially transformed, too. In all countries, the industrial sector was hit most strongly by the output decline. The economic recovery has largely been driven by the flourishing service sector. As a consequence, the shares of the industry and the service sector in GDP and employment have changed. These sectoral shifts have been associated with a massive labor shedding. Throughout the region, employment precipitated. Save for the Czech Republic, unemployment rates jumped to two-digit levels.[31] Moreover, the transforming economies have also experienced a dramatic reorientation of foreign trade (see the data in WIIW 1995: chapter 7). Between 1990 and 1994, the share of developed market economies in East European exports rose from 26.3 to 46.7 percent in Bulgaria[32], from 43.7 to 59.9 percent in the Czech Republic, and from 54 to 72.1 percent in Hungary. In Slovakia, exports to the West have also risen strongly.[33]

---

[31] For a detailed analysis of employment patterns, see chapter 6.
[32] The first figure is for 1991.
[33] As WIIW data for the period from 1990 to 1992 exclude "trade" within the

In spite of these changes, however, restructuring is still in its beginnings (EBRD 1995). As investment figures show (WIIW 1995: tables II/1.1, 1.3, 1.4, 1.8), neither the shift in the sectoral composition of the economy nor the expansion of exports to the West have been associated with a lasting modernization of production. Investment has as yet only recovered in Hungary and the Czech Republic. The Czech Republic was the first country where the investment decline was arrested. After a 32.5 percent fall in 1991, gross fixed investment grew by 16.6 percent in 1992, by 8 percent in 1993, and 4 percent in 1994. In Hungary, a less extreme decline in investment came to a halt in 1993. In 1994, growth of gross fixed investment amounted to 10.4 percent. In contrast, investment in Bulgaria and Slovakia experienced a further decline in 1993 and 1994.

The slow pace of restructuring is also indicated by the small number of liquidated state-owned enterprises. In Bulgaria and the former Czechoslovakia, bankruptcy provisions became effective rather late. Even after the enactment of the Czech Bankruptcy Law, enterprises included in voucher privatization were exempt from bankruptcy files. Governments have intervened in order to prevent liquidations. Moreover, bankruptcy proceedings suffered from packed courts and continuing creditor passivity. In the Czech Republic, a mere 37 state-owned enterprises had thus actually gone bankrupt by November 1994 (*Business Central Europe*, March 1995, 64).

In Hungary, the Bankruptcy Law went into effect in January 1992. Due to the law's – later abolished – unique "Harakiri" clause which required enterprises to declare themselves bankrupt once liabilities were more than 90 days overdue, the enactment of the law led to a surge in bankruptcy filings. Its effect on restructuring was ambiguous (Mizsei 1994; OECD 1993: 83–7; 1995b: 96–101): On the one hand, it triggered liquidations and reorganization endeavors. On the other hand, many of the reorganization plans which were wound up were of a rather dubious nature. Moreover, the increased uncertainty over enterprises' future which was aggravated by the slow processing of claims by the legal system left debtors and creditors alike in a state of limbo which infringed upon restructuring.

There is also a growing number of enterprise case studies which point at a slow pace of restructuring (Brada *et al.* 1994; Carlin *et al.* 1994; Fan and Schaffer 1994: 154–63). A significant share of state-owned enterprises have remained passive. Instead of undertaking substantial organizational

former Czechoslovakia, the persistently high exports to the Czech Republic have contributed to a decline in the reported share of exports to the West. In the Czech case, exports to Slovakia have not played that large a role.

and behavioral changes, they have confined themselves to labor shedding and real wage cuts. Other enterprises have more actively responded to the changing environment, but have engaged in activities and organizational innovations which are not necessarily conducive to the transition to a market economy. Enterprise drift has been favored by weak state ownership and the uncertainty over privatization. Pre-privatization agony has featured prominently in all countries.

From a comparative perspective, the restructuring of the state enterprise sector has been most advanced in Hungary and the Czech Republic and more advanced in Slovakia than in Bulgaria. Empirical evidence suggests that enterprise restructuring has been deepest in firms with concentrated outside ownership (EBRD 1995: 128–38). Consequently, Hungary has made the largest inroads into restructuring. The sale of state-owned enterprises which has characterized Hungarian privatization has brought in capital and know-how. In contrast, the weaker outsider-control in mass-privatized enterprises, the maintenance of wage controls, and the "soft" bankruptcy provisions have somehow delayed restructuring in the Czech Republic. In Slovakia and, even more so, Bulgaria, the less-advanced state of privatization and economic reform has infringed upon enterprise restructuring.

5.3   Comparative performance

The interesting question, then, is to what extent the variant of capitalism that has emerged in Eastern Europe will linger on. While optimists would take the current problems as mere temporary frictions, pessimists would point at the reinforcing potential of the observable behavioral patterns and the resulting danger that the reforming countries will get locked into inferior equilibria. Given the above-mentioned characteristics of the post-communist economies, future prospects of the CEE countries depend on the building of "trust" in the "new" economic sector and the disentangling of the ties within the "old" one. The main preconditions for a consolidation of the new private sectors have been a proper legal-institutional framework, political stability, and a certain continuity in economic policy. Breaking up the dense ties among the old state-owned enterprises and banks implies the retreat of the state from the subsidization of non-viable enterprises, the cleaning of the enterprises' and the banks' portfolios, and, ultimately, the privatization of state-owned enterprises. Against this background, the economic prospects of the countries under analysis have differed. Roughly speaking, they are best for the Czech Republic and Hungary and better for Slovakia than for Bulgaria.

Prospects have been most dreaded in the Bulgarian case. Here, the interplay of bad starting conditions and enduring political instability has severely infringed upon progress with reforms. Communism had left Bulgaria with a large stock of foreign debt and severe macro-economic problems. In the course of the transition, the resulting problems have been further aggravated by the unfavorable political situation. The repeated changes in government have been inimical to policy continuity. The Popov and the Berow governments have been "expert" governments without a proper political basis. Therefore, both the legitimacy and the administrative capacity of the Bulgarian governments have been rather low. Thus, it comes as no surprise that both the retreat of the state and the furnishing of the market have moved on but slowly. With privatization and other reforms being still in a rudimentary state, the private sector has remained small.

Slovakia's recent macro-economic performance has confounded many sceptics. In 1994 and 1995, inflation rates were close to the Czech level. GDP growth was even higher than in the Czech Republic. However, these impressive figures are not reflected in the restructuring. While macro-economic policy has remained relatively sound, structural reform has slowed down since the dissolution of Czechoslovakia. The retreat of the state has come to a halt. The Meciar government has delayed privatization and has extended state interference. By filling management positions with political favorites and by selling enterprises to political cronies at concessionary prices, it has "re-politicized" the economy and has strengthened the ties within the old state sector. At the same time, the pervasive political instability and the hands-on approach of the Meciar government have been inimical to the consolidation of the private sector.

Hungary has remained the frontrunner of institutional reform and economic restructuring. However, these achievements have been overshadowed by the unresolved macro-economic problems and the prevailing reform fatigue (OECD 1995b). The twin deficits in the budget and the current account have called for unpopular austerity measures. Reform fatigue has gone hand in hand with a substantial policy drift. The retreat of the state has been slowed down, while the uncertainty over the course of economic policy has impeded the growth and consolidation of the private sector.

In the Czech Republic, medium-term economic prospects look brightest. Thanks to the high overall political stability and the determination of its leadership, the Czech Republic has been the CEE country with the lowest policy drift. A well-balanced policy mix, made possible by favorable starting conditions, has allowed reformers to ensure the political acceptance of reforms. Though restructuring, if compared to Hungary, has somehow been delayed, it has not lost momentum yet.

6

Social policy transformation

1 Introduction

The welfare state is an area of public policy where only few basic changes have occurred in recent years. While almost all political and economic institutions of the communist regime were fundamentally challenged during the first five years of transition, social protection systems were largely maintained. Neither has the old welfare state been radically dismantled, as announced and repeatedly demanded by prominent economic liberals in the wake of the peaceful revolutions. Nor have post-communist social reformers succeeded in transforming it into some variant of "the strong" West European welfare state, as initially intended. Compared with those areas of societal transformation considered in the previous chapters, welfare state institutions, on the whole, have remained notably stable. New institutions were only created, so as to respond to emerging unemployment and mounting poverty.

The present chapter aims to outline the state of reform in the countries under study. It takes a largely descriptive account and analyzes the steps that have actually been taken in Bulgaria, the Czech Republic, Hungary, and Slovakia over the period 1989 to mid 1995 to reform the old welfare regimes. Their main characteristics are briefly described in *section 2*. *Section 3* looks at main policy areas and sketches the institutional changes that have occurred so far. The presentation is confined to identifying main trends and qualitative variations. Moreover, the outline cannot claim to be either complete or fully up-to-date because the national social protection systems have been constantly under revision in the period considered. Statistical information is displayed only marginally, for

reliable data that allow for cross-national and/or longitudinal compari-
sion of East European welfare state development are still hardly available.
Section 4 goes beyond the national policy level and deals with issues of
decentralization and interest coordination in CEE welfare states. It asks
for new agents in the social sector (employers and trade unions, service
providers and local governments) and briefly discusses their role in
governing social protection. If not indicated otherwise, the empirical
findings and assessments presented in both section 3 and 4 are based
upon a study of legislative material, press items, and more than 50
interviews carried out with policy makers and consultants in the four
countries between March and September 1994. *Section 5* finally sum-
marizes the evidence.

2   The old welfare regime and the reform ambitions after 1989

Under the old regime, social policy was not considered as a separate
policy area with its specific institutions and actors. It was an integral
component of the production process necessary to generate a productive
and loyal work force. Social policy was primarily seen as producing (and
reproducing) the labor force in accordance with its "needs," as defined by
the party-state. Thus, the locus of welfare provision was the state-directed
enterprise. Firms formerly provided crèches, holiday homes, housing,
health services, training, and other welfare facilities for their staff. In
addition, most cash benefits came with the job. Continuous and lifelong
participation in the production process was the proviso of collectivist
protection. Those who did not work (for whatever reason) had no access
to basic transfers and services allocated at the workplace. This tight
coupling of production and social policy, as captured in the formula of
the "unity of economic and social policy," set the state-socialist welfare
regime apart from all "worlds of welfare capitalism" (Esping-Andersen).

In market economies, a functional differentiation is made between the
business firm and the welfare state as well as between the interests of
employees (or trade unions and works councils) and employers. The
welfare state is designed as an institutional *supplement* to the labor market
which compensates for "social risks" *ex post*, in case the persons
concerned cannot be expected to (fully) meet their needs by their own
efforts.[1] In capitalist welfare regimes, social policy is to enhance productivity and efficiency in a much more indirect way than in central planning
systems. Social programs provide incentives to strive for gainful employ-

---

[1] The different "logics" governing state-socialist and capitalist welfare states have
been spelled out in greater detail in Offe 1993.

ment. Some of them, such as vocational training and promotion of regional mobility, may directly lead to productivity gains. Moreover, welfare programs help to maintain "social peace" which appears a basic requirement for steady economic growth. However, there is no perfect correspondence between employers' and workers' interests as in an imagined "classless" society. Obviously, capitalist welfare states do not follow the logic of a "unity of economic and social policy" which governed communist social policies.

Formerly, the social protection systems were broad and universal, but guaranteed only a relatively low standard of living. The coverage ratio of the core social programs (pension, sickness, medical care, and family support schemes) was close to 100 percent. However, benefits and services were often very low in real terms (as in the case of pensions) or of poor quality (as in the case of health services) (cf. Deacon 1992: 3–5). None of the welfare "rights" was legally enforceable in the sense that unconditional entitlements were conferred on those having fulfilled the relevant conditions (having participated in the labor market for a couple of years, lacking other means of subsistence, etc.). Form, content, and level of benefits were ultimately determined by the party-state and, thus, were rather "gifts" than "rights" in nature (Ferge 1992: 207).

These programs operated under the conditions of a full employment economy, that is a labor market regime which minimized citizens' dependence on the welfare state, while providing a broad revenue base. Full employment was considered a major "achievement" of socialism. The ambitious claim was even laid down in communist constitutions which affirmed a "right to work" for each citizen. It was the state's duty to provide jobs, and the "worker-citizens" were obliged to accept them. This accomplishment was paid for in terms of vast inefficiencies of production and often resulted in "unemployment on the job" (cf. Kornai 1992: chapter 10). Moreover, social insurance benefits were supplemented by extensive subsidies on staple consumer items (such as foodstuff, housing, energy, transport, and drugs) and by a developed system of fringe benefits, mostly benefits in kind.

The public social programs were largely financed by earmarked contributions of enterprises (payroll taxes), but funds were not separated from the general state budget and benefits not linked to previous contributions. The contribution of the market or the non-profit sector to the provision of social welfare was close to zero. State protection also presided over family care to enable women to participate in the labor market and, further, to ensure political control over the socialization of children. The family and the neighborhood economy only served as stopgaps to alleviate the deficiencies of collectivist protection.

After the demise of communism, a profound reform of existing social
protection systems was considered an indispensable element of societal
transformation. The majority of the political forces envisaged major
departures from the status quo. The economic liberals' reform program
was to radically reduce state social protection and give emphasis to
private security-enhancing arrangements instead. They argued that the
old social protection systems imposed too heavy a financial burden on
the economy in general and the state budget in particular. Moreover, they
viewed radical social reforms as a necessary step to break the "culture of
dependency" cultivated over the long period of communist rule. They
wanted to introduce, as Vaclav Klaus used to say, a "market economy
without an adjective": an economic regime that would not be encum-
bered with much social policy and would not smack of state *dirigisme* and
paternalism. Therefore, economic liberals demanded that overall social
expenditures should be curtailed, major welfare responsibilities be shifted
to the private sector, and government support be strongly "targeted".

The main alternative approach that became increasingly popular in the
region – in particular among social policy experts working in the
respective administrative branches or involved in social policy research
and advising the government – was a radical "Europeanization" of the
social protection systems. Rather than giving up the idea of a strong
welfare state, the ambitious plan was to introduce West European
institutional arrangements and social security standards as soon as
possible. The German-Austrian "social insurance model" or "social
market economy" approach enjoyed great popularity and was regarded as
the best model to meet concerns for both "economic efficiency" and
"social justice."[2] Reform proposals that have been worked out in
accordance with this approach included the following structural shifts in
the welfare state in the medium run:

(a) *A new public–private mix in benefit provision.* Contrary to the old
regime, social insurance was thought to be only one, though still the
main source of income support. Public programs should be supplemented by private welfare arrangements. Yet social insurance should
continue to play the dominant role for virtually everyone, with
benefits satisfying the criterion of "social adequacy."

---

[2] Note that all CEE countries have historical affinities to this model (see above,
chapter 2). It is not only the "golden West," but also their own "golden past"
which has served as a point of reference (Offe 1993). Remarkably, the
Scandinavian model only played a minor role in post-communist social policy
discourse. It was taken into consideration mainly in the Baltic States. Only in
Hungary was the Scandinavian approach included in the policy debate by
academics, such as Zsuzsa Ferge and Júlia Szalai.

(b) *A reduction in the redistributive effects of state intervention.* As in Germany, social insurance should help people to preserve their social status in the case of lost earnings and not aim at reducing income inequalities which were (increasingly) generated in the market. Hence, the preference for strongly earnings-related benefit formulas.

(c) *As in West European political economies, a clear distinction between insurance benefits and non-insurance-type schemes.* Social insurance was seen as cushioning those "standard risks" individuals were regularly exposed to in market economies; citizens could therefore be obliged to adequately provide for these in advance (such as sickness, invalidity, old age, unemployment). Other state support schemes (family benefits, housing subsidies, aid for the chronical handicapped, social assistance, etc.) were seen as instruments of interpersonal redistribution designed to meet particular needs and, thus, should be targeted.

(d) *The introduction of off-budget financing of social security and cost sharing between employers and employees.* This was to regain transparency and strengthen cost awareness and accountability among policy makers, program administrators, and beneficiaries. More generally, the driving force of reforms was to limit the heavy burden which social policies imposed on the economy in general and the state budget in particular.

(e) *A reduction in enterprises' social policy functions.* It was intended to largely insulate the welfare state from the sphere of production. Key social benefits should no longer be channelled through the enterprise. In particular, the bulk of social assets and facilities owned by state enterprises should be transferred to local agents. This was to reduce the enterprises' non-wage labor costs and make the benefits available to all citizens.

(f) *Finally, a change in the old command mode of social policy-making.* To account for a plurality of interests, post-communist elites wished to introduce intermediate bodies of interest coordination and associational self-regulation. Only the general issues of benefit regulation should remain in the realm of the government and/or parliament, while newly emerging collective actors were supposed to take on responsibility for routine scheme management.

These plans were demanding and implied a major overhaul of existing institutions. What is more, they had to be translated into public policies under conditions of fiscal crisis, increasing social needs, and political instability. Emerging unemployment and the decline in real wages called for immediate reactions. Post-communist governments were also facing popular expectations which ran high. Notwithstanding all the deficencies just mentioned, the arrangement of social protection and job security generally belonged to the more attractive aspects of the old regimes. What people expected after the demise of communism (and had been promised) was an eventual improvement of their living conditions, not a deterioration compared with the overall level of security and protection the old regime had guaranteed.

3   Reform policies since 1989: institutional continuities and changes in the realm of social policy

At the outset of the reform process, CEE countries could not rely on any extant institutional policy system to address the problem of unemployment. Under communist rule, unemployment had been a taboo subject and largely "hidden" policy issue. The same is true of the problem of poverty which had been officially ignored as well. Job security, transfers, and subsidies had been supposed to allow for a reasonable living; those who had failed to lead an "ordinary" way of life had lived on the margin of society. In 1989, adequate income support systems for the rising number of poor were virtually non-existent. In both areas, albeit more in the former than in the latter, post-communist governments were facing an "institutional no-man's-land." They had to *start from scratch* and set up an appropriate institutional framework, so as to tackle the "new" social problems. Regarding pensions, health care, sick pay, and family support, social policy makers were in a different situation. They had inherited from the old regime a package of social programs, as sketched in the beginning, which was in need of profound reform. They were compelled to *rebuild* the existing institutional arrangements and adapt them to the environmental conditions of a market economy. The following is an outline of what has been done in these three areas of social reform so far.

3.1   Coping with unemployment

Since the beginning of transition, CEE countries have experienced dramatic changes in the labor market. Instead of full employment and job security, *the* foundation of the old welfare regime, there has been massive labor shedding, and high levels of unemployment have been built up. Both registration data and survey-based measures of joblessness indicate the incidence of *mass unemployment* (Boeri 1994a: 16f.). The unemployment rate remained low in 1990 in all four countries, but far exceeded the symbolic threshold of 10 percent in the following years. The major exception is the Czech Republic where the unemployment rate has

Table 6.1. *Registered unemployment as a percentage of the labor force (1990–1994, end of year)*

Country	1990	1991	1992	1993	1994
Bulgaria	1.5	11.1	15.3	16.4	12.8
Czech Rep.	0.8	4.1	2.6	3.5	3.2
Hungary	2.5	8.0	12.3	12.1	10.4
Slovakia	1.5	11.8	10.4	14.4	14.8

Source: EBRD 1995: App. 11.1.

remained strikingly low. At the end of 1994, the total number of registered unemployed in the labor force was still only 3.2 percent in the Czech Republic, while amounting to 12.8 percent in Bulgaria, to 14.8 percent in Slovakia, and to 10.4 percent in Hungary (see table 6.1).

High levels of unemployment may well become a persistent feature of labor markets in transition countries. As Boeri (1994a; 1994b) has revealed, "transitional unemployment" appears to take the form of a *stagnant pool.* In spite of massive labor shedding, the average monthly rates of flow into unemployment were very low, by Western standards, in the Czech Republic, Slovakia, and Hungary (although not in Bulgaria) Unemployment has been rising nevertheless, because exit rates from unemployment have so far been extremely low in CEE countries (except for the Czech Republic). Most workers directly moved from the state sector to the emerging private sector without an intervening spell of unemployment or left the labor force altogether. As the private sector has hardly recruited from the unemployment pool, it has been very difficult for the unemployed to find a new job. The result has been a rapid increase in the incidence of *long-term unemployment.* Data available from labor force surveys indicate that over 40 percent of the jobless had been unemployed for a year or more in Hungary and Slovakia at the end of 1994. In Bulgaria, the proportion of the long-term unemployed amounted to as much as 60 percent, by contrast with the Czech Republic where still only a quarter of the unemployed had been out of work for at least a year in late 1994 (CEC 1995: 9f.).

In all CEE countries, except for Hungary, more women were registered as unemployed than men in the period considered. A further marked feature of unemployment throughout the region is the rapid growth of youth unemployment. The jobless rate among the young was much higher than the average rate for the workforce as a whole. The risk of becoming jobless was also higher for unskilled than for skilled workers.

Minority groups, especially the less skilled Gypsy population living in rural areas far from the capital, were suffering disproportionately from employment adjustment (CEC 1993: 5–8). Finally, there were marked regional disparities in the incidence of unemployment. Apart from the importance of on-the-job search mentioned above, it is the increasing mismatch between the regional distribution of unemployment and vacancies that accounts for the low outflows from unemployment in transition countries (Boeri 1994a: 9–11; Scarpetta and Wörgötter 1995).

In all of the countries surveyed, governments have immediately adopted a series of measures to tackle the emerging problem of unemployment. Generally, the policies adopted to combat unemployment can be divided into four groups: (a) policies which aim to minimize workforce reductions and stabilize employment in the state sector; (b) measures designed to reduce labor supply; (c) income support measures intended to alleviate the financial consequences of unemployment (unemployment benefits); (d) active labor market policies which either try to modify the supply side (training and retraining programs) or labor demand (job creation and public works programs) in order to get the jobless quickly re-employed. Everywhere, post-communist governments have tried to combine these types of measures. However, priorities have been set differently and the program designs have varied from country to country.

3.1.1 AVOIDING LAYOFFS At early stages of economic restructuring, enterprises contrived to minimize workforce reductions. Management and unions agreed to adjust hours worked rather than to implement large-scale layoffs. They arranged reductions in the number of shifts in response to falling demand. They also introduced short-time work and periods of unpaid leave in order to keep as many workers as possible in some form of employment. Needed staff reductions were achieved mainly via attrition and recruitment freeze (Boeri 1994b: 20). Governments have helped to spread employment adjustment over time by impeding collective dismissals and subsidizing short-term job maintenance arrangements. They also refrained from an indiscriminate imposition of hard budget constraints on state enterprises at the beginning (Jackman and Rutkowski 1994: 146–50). In the absence of large-scale layoffs, labor hoarding actually increased in all transition countries until 1991 (Góra 1993: 75).

Employment reduction in the state sector has been less dramatic in the Czech case than in the other countries. Several factors helped to stabilize state employment and keep unemployment low. One of them was a wage control policy.[3] Real compensation costs (including non-wage labor

---

[3] See above, chapter 5, section 3.5.

costs) have been kept comparatively low in the Czech lands over the first years of transition (Godfrey 1994: 4f.). Another instrument for preventing massive labor shedding was the exchange rate policy. In 1990, the Czechoslovak koruna was strongly depreciated by more than 100 percent. This fall in the exchange rate which preceded trade liberalization helped to protect the export sector from international competition in the first years. Moreover, the Czechoslovak government took various measures to prevent the bankruptcy of state-owned enterprises during privatization. The most obvious measure was the repeated postponement of bankruptcy legislation which did not come into effect before April 1993.[4] At least in the Czech part of the country, these policies proved very effective (cf. also Orenstein 1994a). However, the Slovak economy was more hit by output decline and job destruction in the state sector than the Czech. In addition, the private employment growth was weaker than in the Czech lands. Both factors seem to be important in explaining differences in the Slovak and the Czech unemployment rates (Svejnar et al. 1995; OECD 1994: 13).

In Bulgaria, the state sector contracted sharply in 1991 and 1992, while the private economy did not grow fast enough to offset the decline in state employment. For fiscal reasons, the governments were forced to cut subsidies to enterprises, and firms were not able to protect employment on a large scale anymore. Bulgaria appears to have already passed through the stage of massive labor shedding, but little has been achieved with regard to micro-economic reforms, and the prospects for economic recovery look still gloomy (Blanchard et al. 1994: 61, 65; Bobeva 1994: 1–8).[5]

In Hungary, the fall in employment relative to output decline was large as well, though lagging behind output changes. The private sector did not fully absorb the job losses in the public sector, but induced itself a considerable number of layoffs. So far Hungary is the only country among the four countries where firm liquidations on a large scale have as yet occurred, though the employment implications associated with these processes are difficult to assess (cf. Commander et al. 1994: 6–12).

3.1.2 REDUCING LABOR SUPPLY Starting from a high level by West European standards, *labor force participation* has sharply declined in CEE countries. The drop in activity rates was most pronounced in Bulgaria. Nearly 10 percent of the working-age population actually disappeared from the active labor force in the first three years of societal transformation. The development in the other cases was slightly less marked. The inactive population increased by 6.5 percentage points in the Czech

[4] See above, chapter 5, section 4.1.1. [5] See above, chapter 5, section 4.3.3.

Republic, by 8.5 points in Slovakia, and by 5.5 points in Hungary between 1989 and 1992 (CEC 1993: 16).

It is hard to disentangle the factors that actually account for this development. On the one hand, changes in activity rates over the transition have been induced by policy changes. On the other hand, data reflect people's "spontanous reactions" to the problem of inadequate job creation that has arisen. Participation rates, especially among men, have been reduced by squeezing workers above or close to the standard retirement age out of the labor force. Some of those who disappeared from the register might have been mothers with small children who opted to take child-care leave to escape unemployment. They saw small chances of being reemployed and were discouraged from further job-search. Indeed, the decrease in participation was higher for women than for men in the four countries, most significantly in the Czech and Slovak Republics (CEC 1993: 16). The Czechoslovak government had explicitly extended the period of paid child-care leave from two to three years in mid 1990 to reduce labor supply.[6] Contractual work in foreign countries appears an additional factor. In particular in regions which border on Germany and Austria, the number of citizens who started to work in foreign countries went up. In Bulgaria, net emigration apparently played a role. In addition, some of those who disappeared from the register were presumably working in the private sector not yet fully recorded by the official statistics or were engaged in the "black" economy.

Social policy makers in transition countries were facing a sharp trade-off between pension reform and employment policies: under the old regime, the standard retirement age had been low by Western standards (55 for women and 60 for men or even lower), but many pensioners could not afford to fully withdraw from regular work due to the low level of their pensions. Since 1989, on the one hand an increase in the retirement age has been on the agenda. In order to render the pension systems financially viable and to guarantee a minimum standard of living for the elderly, it is required to gradually increase the age at which the elderly receive full benefit. On the other hand, policy makers want to increase exits from the labor force at almost any cost.

Considering the deteriorating situation in the labor market, governments have traded off the former for the latter so far. They have rejected any increase in the standard retirement age, but encouraged *early retirement*. Over the period 1990–1992, many older workers agreed to end their employment contract and make use of early retirement offers or

---

[6] In early 1995, paid child-care leave was further extended up to age four in the Czech Republic (Rys 1995: 11).

disability pensions (Boeri 1994b: 21). Among the four countries, early retirement has been most extensively used in the Czech Republic to cut back on employment of older workers. At the end of 1993, the number of people who received early pensions as a percentage of the labor force was twice as high in the Czech lands than in Hungary and Bulgaria and three times as high as in Slovakia.[7] In all countries however, it is now considered necessary to shift priorities more toward pension reform and no longer promote early exits at any cost. The Czech government moved in that direction in early 1993 by rendering early retirement less attractive. Only a person who is unemployed and whose unemployment benefit has expired may now retire up to two years earlier. Claimants have to accept pension deductions, until they reach the regular retirement age. In Bulgaria, the early retirement scheme was completely suspended in early 1992 because of its limited effectiveness and cost concerns. Budget constraints limited the possibilities to further promote "soft" measures of workforce reduction. Besides, claimants often did not give up employment, but continued to work under "civil contract" or illegally.[8] Bulgaria turns out to be the only country among the four countries where the number of officially working pensioners has not significantly declined since 1989. The majority of pensioners are still forced to look for regular work to supplement their pensions (MLSW 1994: 11).

3.1.3 UNEMPLOYMENT BENEFIT SCHEMES Income support schemes for the unemployed were introduced right at the beginning of the transition process. Notably, all of the countries strived to set up *insurance-type schemes*: Benefits should replace wages, payments should not be subject to a means test, and the scheme should be funded by

[7] Calculation based on data provided by the Labor Ministries. In the Czech lands, there were about 100,000 beneficiaries of early retirement at that point in time (2.8 percent of the labor force) and in Slovakia about 20,000 persons (0.9 percent of the labor force). The Hungarian early retirement program set up in 1988 has not proved to be very attractive for employers and county labor offices to "softly" cope with redundancies (less than 7,000 participant). They have rather attempted to shift the financial burden to the pension insurance that offers a so-called "preliminary pension" for jobless people close to retirement age (roughly 40,000 beneficiaries; in total 1.3 percent of the labor force). Bulgaria had about 44,000 recipients in 1992 (1.2 percent of the labor force).

[8] In Bulgaria, irregular forms of employment have been widespread since 1989, in particular in the private sector and among pensioners. Until the end of 1993, employers could avoid paying social insurance contributions, if they hired people for short periods of time under so-called "civil contracts" not regulated by the Labor Code. Pensioners could avoid deductions in their pensions this way. This loophole in the law has meanwhile been closed, but there is reason to expect the "informalization" of the economy to grow nevertheless (cf. Chavdarova 1994).

earmarked contributions deducted from wages.[9] Political actors strongly rejected the idea of introducing just a flat-rate scheme, as proposed by experts from the IMF and the World Bank. A flat-rate benefit at or above the minimum wage, some advisors argued, would be more targeted on the poorer strata than an earnings-graded scheme, as equal benefits replace a larger percentage of lower than higher incomes. If coupled with earnings-related contributions, the flat-rate scheme would have a distinct redistributive effect. It would also be much easier to implement and operate than an insurance-type scheme (cf., e.g., Holzmann 1991: 7; Boeri 1994a: 18).

For East European social policy makers, however, an insurance-type scheme appeared a much more attractive model: first, the concept of unemployment insurance was realized everywhere in the West and these arrangements were apparently working quite well. Considering that there was no time for experimentation, political actors in the East were inclined to copy well-tried, "successful" institutional patterns of Western welfare states. Second, they put the new risk of unemployment into the same category as sickness and old-age to be cushioned by income replacement benefits. Flat-rate payments were considered a deviation from this "philosophy" and had the smack of a statist emergency measure. Third, it was especially the high-wage sectors (heavy industry, mining) where massive labor shedding was expected to occur immediately. Yet workers with higher salaries were to receive less under a flat-rate scheme compared with an earnings-related system. Governments were reluctant to demand additional sacrifices from these groups and feared the unions' resistance. Finally, the problem of long-term unemployment was not the primary concern at the beginning and the difficulties of administering an insurance-type scheme in the transition economies were underestimated.

Initially, all countries surveyed established rather generous income support schemes. Yet political actors soon started to tighten eligibility criteria, to reduce the replacement rate (ratio of benefit to previous earnings) and the duration of payments, to define upper and lower limits to benefit levels, to increase the contribution rates, etc. The rapid spread of unemployment and growing fiscal constraints both which had been underestimated when the schemes were designed were one reason for these curtailments. The "classical" dilemma of supporting the unemployed has quickly appeared: the employment decline affects outlays and funding of the systems at the same time. The moment expenditure on the schemes increases (because more people claim benefits), revenue declines

---

[9] For a detailed description of the new schemes, see CEC 1995; Scarpetta and Reutersward 1994.

(because the jobless no longer contribute). The problem of tax evasion[10] exacerbates those fiscal imbalances. Another reason for cutting benefits was as an incentive to search for jobs. Soon after 1989, the perception of the problem of unemployment changed. At the outset, the unemployed were commonly regarded as the "victims" of restructuring who were to be cushioned. But then the public debate shifted to benefit "misuse," "cheating," "laziness," etc. Less social protection, or so it was argued, would encourage the unemployed to take the initiative and strive for reintegration into the labor market.

Today, all schemes provide only modest income support for the unemployed. Average unemployment benefits are close to or even below minimum wages and subsistence minima. Yet as the average wage level is still rather low, average benefits come very close to the wages that job-seekers are facing on the market. The problem of defining "reasonable" benefit levels is most complicated regarding the low paid. For many unskilled workers unemployment benefits are presently too low to avoid deprivation, but too high to encourage the acceptance of employment (cf. Scarpetta and Reutersward 1994: 270; Köllö 1994: 25f.). After eligibility for unemployment benefit ceases, the unemployed can apply for social assistance. Social assistance benefits are conditional on a means-test and, as a rule, much lower than insurance benefits (see below, section 2.2).[11]

Further, all schemes now operate *de facto* as *flat-rate systems* (Boeri 1994a: 16–18).[12] One reason for this is the introduction of tight upper limits which has strongly narrowed the range of actual payments. Since mid 1992, unemployment benefits are supposed to range between 90 and 140 percent of the minimum wage in Bulgaria. In the Czech and Slovak Republics, a minimum level of benefit is no longer guaranteed. The upper bond was set at 150 percent of the minimum wage (resp. 180 percent during retraining) in the beginning of 1992. In Hungary, the minimum benefit now equals 96 percent of the minimum wage (resp. 100 percent of the previous wage for those with salaries below that benchmark). The maximum was set at 200 percent of the minimum wage (resp. 167

---

[10] See above, chapter 5, sections 3.3, 4.3.1.

[11] However, it should be born in mind, when comparing benefit levels, that what matters in the end is the incidence of various transfers and taxation. The unemployment benefit as such may be low, if compared with wages, but may turn out fairly high for some, if topped up by child allowances, additional earnings, tax advantages, etc.

[12] For the time being, Poland is the only CEE country where the government gave up its initial commitment to the insurance principle and opted for a flat-rate approach in early 1992. However, the reintroduction of an insurance-type scheme is still under discussion.

percent after three months) starting from 1993. These amendments have effected a marked redistribution in favor of the low-paid. Add to this unemployment benefits (above the minima) are not indexed for inflation in any of the four countries. This is to say that with increasing duration of unemployment the "real" replacement rates turn out to be much lower than the initial ratios stipulated by law (Scarpetta and Reutersward 1994: 271f., 290). The levelling of actual payments around minima becomes even more evident when the fact is considered that workers with lower income are overrepresented in the unemployment pool. Micklewright and Nagy (1994), e.g., have figured out that the vast majority of beneficiaries in Hungary in March 1992 had previously received wages around the minimum wage.

The coverage of the schemes has sharply declined over the period 1990–1993. According to data provided by the Labor Ministries, the proportion of registered unemployed receiving benefits has fallen from more than 70 to less than 40 percent in Slovakia, to roughly 50 percent in Hungary and the Czech lands, in Bulgaria from slightly over 50 to less than 40 percent during the first four years of transition. This is due to both the incidence of long-term unemployment and changes in benefit regulation. There is a rising number of persons who have exceeded maximum duration of payments and have only slim chances of building up entitlements again through employment in the labor market. Policies of retrenchment affecting access to benefits and duration of payments have added to the drop in the share of unemployed receiving benefits.

In the Czech case, lower inflows to and higher outflows from unemployment also seem to reflect a stricter approach to benefit provision compared with the other countries. Already by 1991, the administration had adopted tight regulations concerning any additional income a person might receive while claiming unemployment benefit and stopped registering job-seekers who had reached retirement age.[13] The Slovak administration was more benevolent at the beginning than its Czech counterpart, thus encouraging workers to quit their jobs voluntarily, but then copied the eligibility rules effective in Bohemia and Moravia. In Bulgaria, the law allows income to be doubled during the unemployment spell through employment under "civil contract." Moreover, there is evidence that the labor offices are still not well enough equipped to check "abuse" of benefits effectively. The Hungarian Employment Act also allows the combination of benefits with earnings from

---

[13] It has been estimated that the official unemployment rate would have been between one and two percentage points higher in 1992, if all those people had not disappeared from the statistics (OECD 1994a: 15f.).

jobs offered by the labor centers (up to the minimum wage). The reason
for such "generosity" is, of course, to prevent poverty among the
unemployed. The Hungarian employment administration, too, is said to
be rather lax when deciding on the claimants' eligibility to benefits (cf.,
e.g., Frey 1994: 46f.).

3.1.4 ACTIVE LABOR MARKET POLICIES All countries under study
have established a network of public employment services and introduced
a diverse series of measures to foster the reintegration of displaced
workers into the labor market, such as training and retraining programs,
job creation schemes, self-employment subsidies, public works, and
programs targeted to sub-groups of the unemployed (the youth, women,
long-term unemployed, Gypsies, people living in "crisis regions"). All
these "active" measures are well known from OECD countries, as are
many of the problems associated with their introduction. Nearly everywhere, financial and administrative constraints have as yet seriously
limited the actual implementation of these instruments. Nevertheless,
many of the programs set up right at the beginning of the transition
process have been significantly improved and extended. Both as to the
scale of reintegration efforts and the *composition* of the program packages,
differences between the countries are noticeable.

Over the period 1990–1993, different expenditure patterns have
emerged in Eastern Europe. First and foremost, the intercountry variations reflect disparities in the dynamics of unemployment: The increase
in total labor market expenditures as a percentage of GDP was mainly
due to the rise in unemployment in the four countries rather than to an
increase in support per unemployed person. Only the Czech government
could increase both effective spending per head as well as the share of the
active component in labor market expenditures because unemployment
inflows remained low (Scarpetta and Reutersward 1994: 256f.). The other
extreme is Bulgaria where expenditures for active policies developed pro-
cyclically. With unemployment rising steeply, spending for income
support went up to 90 percent of the employment budget and, thus,
crowded out funds available for active measures.[14] However, the main

[14] This is because the unemployed have a right to income support, while support
for employment promotion is only optional. The crowding out effect is likely to
occur, if active and passive measures are financed out of the same budget, as in
most CEE countries. Only in Hungary, two separate funds have been established:
The "Employment Fund" (supported by state budget transfers) is to finance
active measures, while the "Solidarity Fund" (employers' and employees'
contributions as well as state budget transfers, if necessary) was set up to cover
income support for the unemployed. Here, the Labor Ministry fears another

problem in employment promotion in Bulgaria was not a lack of financial
resources, but the absence of a clear concept of labor market policy, a
blockage of administrative reforms, and the unfavorable economic conditions.[15] In 1992 and 1993, a considerable amount of the small means
available for employment promotion remained unused in the Fund; the
surplus was used to finance pension outlays.

In the Czech Republic, a large share of money goes to the promotion
of self-employment and job-creation in the private sector as well as public
works. In 1992, about 2.8 percent of the labor force was on average
involved in some kind of *job subsidy program* (Scarpetta and Reutersward
1994: 284). The large-scale implementation of these programs appears
another factor that accounts for the low unemployment rate in the Czech
lands. Moreover, the Czech employment offices are comparatively well
equipped to fulfill their tasks of registration, guidance, and placement.
On average, the caseload per member of staff is extremely low by East
European standards and the personnel are very successful in getting new
vacancies (Scarpetta and Reutersward 1994: 283). So far, little attention
has been paid to the cost-effectiveness of the various programs.

In Slovakia, the legal framework for employment policies at present
differs only slightly from the one established in the Czech lands. Core
programs were set up prior to 1993, although with some delay compared
with the rapid pace of reform in Prague, and no important changes
occurred in this area in the first year after the "velvet divorce." As for the
type of active measures, emphasis is laid on subsidized employment (as in
the Czech case), but also on retraining (as in Hungary). A large share of
the Slovak labor force participated in various types of active programs in
1992 (job creation about 3.1 percent, retraining 1.0 percent; Scarpetta
and Reutersward 1994: 284). The efforts of the Slovak employment
administration to increase employment takeup have been impeded by the
fact that there were large numbers of disadvantaged people. Most
importantly, it is the Gypsy population living in East Slovakia that is hard
to integrate into the labor market. The same holds true for the large
ethnic minorities in Hungary and Bulgaria.

In Hungary, the most important type of measure to date is *training*

<hr>

problem. Owing to the separation of the funds, it is difficult to shift the surplus
in the Solidarity Fund which is expected to occur with the number of
beneficiaries decreasing, to the Employment Fund. For the tripartite committee
who has to decide about the utilization of the money generally prefers a
reduction of contribution rates.

[15] The effect of the subsidized credit scheme, e.g., has been seriously limited so far
by the fact that interest rates are very high in Bulgaria. If market rates amount to
about 70 percent, a 10 percent reduction offered by the state is almost negligible.

and retraining, whereas subsidized employment plays only a minor role compared with the Czech and Slovak Republics. Hungary is the country in the sample that had already experienced some changes in employment policy by the mid 1980s.[16] Several programs had been set up to avoid open unemployment, yet they had not been significant as to numbers of participants. Contrary to expectations, these policy legacies did not speed up the pace of labor market institution building in post-communist Hungary relative to her neighbors. For one thing, the experience gained from these policies was limited and was not enough to reduce uncertainty among policy makers. For another, policy legacies invited incrementalism. At the outset of transition, Hungarian reformers had good arguments at hand for not changing past policies completely, but to further expand, modify, and refine what was already in place. This is contrary to the Czech case where reformers had to start from scratch and, thus, had no reason to believe in sluggish institutional reform.

Bulgaria is exceptional in that labor market policies are still based on individual decrees representing not more than *ad-hoc* solutions to occurring problems. These decrees have not been integrated into a comprehensive policy strategy so far. Several versions of an Employment Bill have been worked out, but none of them has as yet been passed through parliament (cf. ILO-CEET 1994: 127, 131; MLSW 1994). Various ambitious programs have been abandoned for budgetary reasons since 1992. Bulgarian employment offices[17] are still understaffed and not sufficiently well equipped to fulfill their tasks. In comparison with the other three countries, the number of participants entering active programs is extremely low (only about 0.7 percent of the labor force in 1992; Scarpetta and Reutersward 1994: 284).

In sum, the comparative policy review suggests that a combination of structural factors and government policies have helped to keep unemployment low in the Czech Republic during the first five years of transition:[18] employment reductions in the state sector have been successfully stretched over time; a great number of workers have been pushed out of the labor force; the unemployment benefit scheme has been very restrictive since 1992 which has led to significant dropouts from the register; in addition, a series of active labor market policies were implemented effectively at the very beginning of transition. Each of these

---

[16] See above, chapter 2, section 2.2.

[17] Both in Bulgaria and Hungary, the right to offer an employment service has been liberalized. Since 1991, job placement is no longer a state monopoly. The actual role of private employment services has as yet proved very limited.

[18] See, e.g., Svejnar *et al.* 1995; Orenstein 1994a; Boeri 1994b; OECD 1994a on this point.

factors has presumably lowered the official unemployment rate by one or two percentage points.

Furthermore, some structural factors deserve mention which have doubtless contributed to the Czech employment "miracle." One of the Czech Republic's structural advantages has been the position of Prague as "the major" tourist attraction in the region. Both the boom in the tourist sector and the expansion of services for foreign businesses have helped to keep unemployment at zero there. Another advantage has been the geographical proximity to Germany and Austria. Cross-border employment has relieved the local labor markets in the border regions much more than in the other cases. Since the break up of the Federation, the population is also more ethnically homogenous than in the other three cases. Especially, the Gypsy population is smaller and the unemployment rate among them is lower than, e.g., in Slovakia. And, finally, one must recall that the effective implementation of the programs listed above (e.g., early retirement, parental leave, job subsidies) was significantly eased by the fact that the government had more financial and administrative resources at its disposal than its counterparts in the neighboring countries at the outset of transition.[19]

3.2   Protecting the poor

There is ample evidence that the standard of living deterioriated and *poverty* spread enormously in the first years of transition. This holds true for all four countries studied, but most of all for Bulgaria. In 1993, approximately a quarter of all Bulgarian households were living in poverty, if the poverty line is taken as only 27 percent of the 1989 average wage which constitutes the lowest officially calculated poverty threshold. The poverty rate even rises to nearly 60 percent, if a wider poverty definition is used.[20] In the other three cases, the incidence of poverty has been clearly contained to much more bearable dimensions so far (see table 6.2). Data on the number of people receiving social assistance regularly confirm this picture. Bulgaria experienced a nearly 30-fold increase in the number of permanent recipients of social assistance between 1990 and 1992, while between 1989 and 1990 the figure had

---

[19] See above, chapter 2, section 2.
[20] Under the old regime, "subsistence minima" and "social minima" were regularly calculated for various prototypical families, but were not used as a base for setting minimum wages and social benefits. The "subsistence minimum" typically oscillated between 25 and 35 percent and the "social minimum" between 35 and 50 percent of the national average wage (Cornia 1994: 297; see also Sipos 1992: 3–6).

Table 6.2. *Estimates of the percentage of people living in poverty (1989–1993)*

Country	Poverty line[a]	Percentages				
		1989	1990	1991	1992	1993
Bulgaria	45	–	13.8	52.1	55.5	59.4
	27	–	2.0	12.7	21.8	25.3
Czech	35	4.2	8.6	29.8	26.7	–
Republic	21	0.2	0.2	0.2	1.4	–
Hungary	40	10.1	–	15.6	–	22.5
	24	1.1	–	2.3	–	4.0
Slovakia	40	4.1	4.9	30.2	27.8	31.3
	24	0.1	0.1	3.1	3.0	5.1

Note: [a] expressed as a percentage of the 1989 average wage; first figure represents a wider poverty definition, second figure is set at 60 percent of the first benchmark to indicate extreme poverty
Source: UNICEF 1995: 8.

stabilized. Hungary saw a more moderate increase in the number of welfare recipients between 1989 and 1992, whereas in the Czech and Slovak Republics this section of the population remained small (UNICEF 1993: 83). This development can be attributed mainly to a sharp contraction in real average earnings. Price liberalization supported by strict wage controls have led to a steep decline in real wages in the four countries over the past four years.[21] On average, people earned less in real terms in 1993 than in 1989 and a considerable number of them lost their jobs in the regular economy. While poverty was highest among pensioners in the past, it spread particularly among large and single-parent families between 1989 and 1993 as well as among the long-term unemployed and the "working poor" (UNICEF 1993: 5–14; UNICEF 1995: 9f.; ILO-CEET 1994: 156–9).

Post-communist governments have immediately started to address the problem of mounting poverty. Three major policy responses may be identified: (a) Governments set out to fill the institutional vacuum and establish social "safety nets" as a last resort for the poor. (b) They tried to protect workers and their dependents against impoverishment by fixing minimum wages as a basic floor for the wage structure and as an anchor

[21] See above, chapter 5, section 3.2 with tables 3.5 and 5.2.

for the other income support schemes. (c) They also felt compelled to preserve (or to reintroduce) elements of the old welfare regimes, such as price subsidies or company social funds, for the time being in order to reduce the social costs of transformation especially for the poorer strata.

3.2.1 SOCIAL ASSISTANCE REFORM Seeing the rising number of people slipping into poverty, social reformers have set up means-tested benefits as a last resort. Under communist rule, social assistance in cash or in kind had been provided mainly for the destitute handicapped and frail elderly. These programs had not been designed to support people solely lacking an adequate income. Nor did the citizens formerly have a right to social assistance. Access to assistance and the level of support had not been legally guaranteed. Rather, the determination of eligibility and the setting of payments had been a matter of discretion left to the local administration.

These patchy schemes have been profoundly reshaped and extended. The most comprehensive reform has so far been accomplished in Prague where the government effectively implemented a national living minimum. The Living Minimum Act passed in November 1991 set a nationwide poverty line and guaranteed government support to everyone living below this benchmark. The law also obliges the government to adjust the living minimum if prices have increased by more than 10 percentage points. In both republics, the living minimum has become the upper bound of social assistance benefits. Social assistance in cash and/or in kind is provided up to the national living minimum (other social transfers deducted) if the claimants demonstrate that no other income is available, that they are engaged in job-search, etc. According to data provided by the Czech Labor Ministry, the living minimum of a four-person household, for example, amounted to roughly 1.2 times the average wage in 1993 which appears to be a quite favorable relation. However, as wages are still very low, the minimum standards created are, in fact, quite minimal.

In Slovakia, benefits were adjusted in line with inflation half a year later than in the Czech Republic (only in October 1993), but the benchmark was about the same by the end of 1993. Both the Czech and the Slovak governments were considering introducing new Social Assistance Laws in the course of 1995, so as to finally systematize benefit provision and clarify financial responsibilities.

Considerable progress has also been achieved in Bulgaria in this area. To support economic reforms a new social assistance scheme was adopted in March 1991. The incidence of poverty was no longer ignored, though the government at that time avoided defining a nationwide poverty line, being concerned that this would create non-feasible claims to the social protection system. This so-called "second safety net" has been amended several times since 1991 (ILO-CEET 1994: 177f., 189). Similar to the Czech and Slovak schemes, benefit levels vary according to age and household size. Overall, payments are very low because the benefit adjustments did not keep pace with inflation. Nevertheless, the efforts made in Bulgaria to protect the poor are noteworthy, if compared with other areas of social security.[22] Social assistance reform in that country was supported by the World Bank and other external actors. They showed a special concern for the situation of the poor while advocating benefit curtailments for everyone else.

The Hungarian government made clarification of financial responsibilities the first target of social assistance reform (cf. OECD 1995: chapter 6). Between 1989 and 1991, local governments were given the responsibility for providing income support and social care to those in need. However, progress in benefit reform was rather slow. The Antall government had committed itself to working out a new social assistance scheme during 1991, but the reform was pending for a long time. The Social Welfare Bill finally passed in early 1993 was to systematize eligibility criteria and to introduce new kinds of benefits aimed at protecting large families, pensioners, and the long-term unemployed from marginalization. The latter, for example, are now entitled to a means-tested benefit as long as they continue job-search. The benefit, however, is set at a very low level (about 50 percent of the minimum wage; Köllö 1994: 8).

3.2.2 MINIMUM WAGES Minimum wage policy was another device for reducing poverty. After 1989, all governments, together with the unions, introduced or maintained national minimum wages as a basic floor for the wage structure. With employment becoming contingent upon labor contracts, it was considered necessary to protect workers against unacceptably low wages. While tax-based incomes policy was adopted to induce wage restraint and, thus, contain wage-push inflation, minimum wage fixing aimed at maintaining a minimum standard of living for the low paid. In addition, minimum wages increasingly served as a reference wage for calculating social benefits, in particular for defining the lower and upper bounds to benefit provision. If the minimum wage was regularly adjusted, transfer levels would be kept in line with wage growth.

In practice, however, minimum wage policies did not fulfill these expectations. In the four countries surveyed, minimum wages have only

---

[22] See below, section 3.3.

infrequently been adjusted to inflation and have declined much more than average wages over the period 1990–1993. While minimum wages represented up to 70 percent of national average wages at the outset of transition, the ratio declined to between 30 and 40 percent until the end of 1993. This pattern of minimum wage erosion emerged in all four countries, regardless of whether inflation was high or not. In fact, as Vaughan-Whitehead (1993) indicates, post-communist governments have used the minimum wage as an instrument for controlling labor costs and limiting public expenditures. Because the minimum wage served as an anchor of the social protection system and public sector wages were tied to the minimum wage as well, any increase had enormous financial implications. Governments tried their best to keep that benchmark at a constant level, the price of this policy being a creeping erosion of social protection standards during the early years of transition.[23]

3.2.3 PRICE SUBSIDIES AND FRINGE BENEFITS Under the old regime, the purchasing power of wages had been increased by extensive subsidies on basic consumer goods. As a removal of these subsidies was likely to have a severe impact on the welfare of the poor, political actors had a good case for excluding staple consumer items from price liberalization, at least temporarily. Nevertheless, in none of the four countries under study was this strategy extensively used.[24] Food products were largely included in the first wave of price liberalization.[25] Yet price controls remained in force for a few critical items, such as fuel, transport, housing, and drugs in the first years after 1989. The Czech Republic has maintained a fairly strong system of rent control since the beginning of transition which is expected to be phased out in the coming years. Moreover, some essential goods were initially excluded from VAT policies, so as to alleviate the social costs for the poor (cf. UNICEF 1993: 48; Bobeva 1994: 4; Reiner and Strong 1995: 204).

Non-wage benefits distributed at the workplace continued to play a crucial role in improving workers' welfare after 1989. This was especially true for Bulgaria and former Czechoslovakia where the governments introduced strict wage fund controls together with price liberalization. To by-pass wage fund limits, managers and unions often agreed to increase

[23] The Polish story reads slightly differently. In contrast to the other countries, Poland improved the purchasing power of the minimum wage (from 19 percent in 1989 to roughly 40 percent of the average wage in 1993). This was possible because the calculation of unemployment benefits was disconnected from the minimum wage (Vaughan-Whitehead 1993: 7f.).

[24] See above, chapter 5, section 3.2.

[25] In Romania, by contrast, food prices were not decontrolled before mid 1993.

fringe benefits paid out of the company social funds instead of money wages. Up to now, those funds continue to exist in many enterprises thoughout the region. The empirical evidence on the scope of enterprise-level benefit provision and the types of benefits offered, however, is very scanty still. Hungarian survey data indicate that the importance of fringe benefits in relation to wages has not declined economy wide. In particular, "key employees" with a strong labor market position have been able to keep their privileges during the early years of transition (Fajth and Lakatos 1995).

In Slovakia, the legal duty to set up social funds was repealed at the end of 1992, so as to decrease the wage bill of inefficient state enterprises which had to be subsidized from the general state budget. From 1993, it was a matter of collective bargaining whether the funds existed or not. Yet the unions soon pressed the government heavily to reintroduce social funds. Considering that the public system of social guarantees was weakening, the unions argued that social funds were still necessary to improve employees' social conditions. While the 1993 Meciar government in principle supported the "philosophy" of social funds, the incoming Moravic government was very much against it at first, arguing that firms should be largely relieved from social policy functions. However, shortly before the 1994 general elections, the Social Funds Act was passed. As of September 1, 1994, it is again mandatory for Slovak firms to set up social funds and to contribute between 0.6 and 1.0 percent of the net wage bill (depending on the firms' profitability) to these funds; state enterprises enjoyed a four months' grace. The use of the money is confined to social policy purposes (for recreation facilities, transport costs, lunch tickets, social aid for employees in difficult living conditions, etc.). If enterprises exceed the upper bound stipulated by law, they will have to pay punitive taxes. The unions regarded this step as an "outright victory," though they were not happy with the low sum of money raised.

3.3 Social security reform

While governments have immediately responded to unemployment and poverty, the envisaged reform of the social security system has turned out to be a protracted process virtually everywhere. Since the beginning of transition, hundreds of bills, decrees, and regulations have been devised to compensate for the failures of the exisiting welfare systems. However, most of those measures adopted were emergency solutions, aiming to ensure the basic functioning of the existing arrangements rather than to radically alter the programs in place. Contrary to initial proclamations, most post-communist governments decided to largely adhere to pre-1989 programs for the time being and try to consolidate them over the long term. Reform goals have become much less ambitious and, compared with other policy areas, the pace of reform has been decidedly slow. In fact, only a few structural modifications in financing and benefit provision have been enacted so far in the Czech Republic, Hungary, and Slovakia; in Bulgaria social security reforms were still on the drawing board as at the beginning of 1995. The following outline focuses on three issues which capture the core aspects of the debate: (a) reform of financing, (b) pension reform, and (c) changes in the family benefit schemes.[26]

3.3.1 FINANCING OF SOCIAL SECURITY Only Hungary and Slovakia have accomplished the shift towards the off-budget financing of social security to date. The Hungarian Social Insurance Fund was established as an independent body to finance the core programs of the welfare state as early as in 1989. In March 1990, a reform of financial responsibilities was adopted. The Social Insurance Fund was assigned the task of covering expenditures on health care, pensions, and sick pay while family allowances were to be paid from the central budget from then on. The institutional autonomy of this body was achieved in May 1993, when the general elections to the pension and health care insurance boards were held. The General Assembly of the Pension Insurance has 60 members, two-thirds of whom represent insurees' and one-third employers' interests; in the case of the National Health Insurance, insurees and employers are represented by 30 persons each. These two bodies now have a major say in pension and health care reform, yet final budget decisions have remained the responsibility of parliament. In contrast, the Hungarian government has been less successful in limiting the payroll tax burden. Contribution rates which were traditionally divided between employees and employers have been repeatedly increased and reached an extraordinarily high level[27] in 1993 (see table 6.3). Nevertheless, the funds have to be regularly supported by transfers from the central budget.

---

[26] The progress made in health care reform will be explored in greater detail in the section 4.2 of this chapter.

[27] Note that, for the time being, low wages partly offset the high payroll tax burden. Notwithstanding the high social insurance contributions, total labor costs are still much lower in CEE countries than in the Western part of Europe, and even lower than in the low-wage countries of the European Union, such as Portugal, or in East Asia (Salowsky 1993). Adequate measures of cost competitiveness, however, are still difficult to construct for Eastern Europe, given the problems of assessing labor productivity. For an intra-regional comparison see OECD 1993a.

Tab. 6.3. *Social insurance contributions*[a] *as a percentage of payroll/wages (1990/1993)*

Country	1990			Early 1993		
	Employer	Employee	Total	Employer	Employee	Total
Bulgaria	30.5	0	30.5	42.0[b]	0	42.0
Czech Rep.	50.0[c]	0	50.0[c]	36.0[d]	13.5[d]	49.5[d]
Hungary	43.0[e]	10.0[e]	53.0[e]	51.0[f]	12.0[f]	63.0[f]
Slovakia	50.0[c]	0	50.0[c]	38.0[f]	12.0[f]	50.0[f]

Notes: [a] Includes pension, short-term benefits, family benefits, and unemployment compensation; health care paid out of general tax revenue, if not indicated otherwise.
[b] Average payroll burden.
[c] Figures are for Czechoslovakia as of 1991; unemployment benefits paid out of general tax revenue.
[d] Includes health insurance.
[e] Includes health insurance; unemployment and family benefits paid out of general tax revenue.
[f] Includes health insurance; family benefits paid out of general tax revenue.

In the wake of the tax reform which took effect in both successor states of Czechoslovakia in 1993, social security financing was divided between the employer and the individual worker. The reform reduced the companies' financial burden and shifted a large part of the financial responsibilities on to the employees (see table 6.3). In Slovakia, the shift toward contribution-based financing was supplemented by efforts to set up an autonomous National Insurance Company in charge of the pension, health care, and sickness funds. The institution is governed by a tripartite board of representatives nominated by the Slovak parliament. However, the initial problems of the off-budget financing were tremendous, in particular, as the state started to cut down regular transfers to the funds. Today, the funds continue to record huge deficits, and the fiscal process has not become more transparent (cf. Kvapilová 1993: 177; Krizan *et al.* 1995).

In contrast, the Czech government has retained state control over the social insurance funds. The reason is quite obvious. In the past years, contribution revenues repeatedly exceeded expenditures, especially in the case of the Employment Fund. Thus the state could use the surplus for other (social policy) purposes without consulting anyone else.[28] This has been a very controversial point among the coalition partners. Recently, Prime Minister Klaus and his Civic Democratic Party have been forced to comply with the establishment of a special pension fund, albeit as part of the state budget and not as a separate body (Rys 1995: 11).

In Bulgaria, too, governments have not been inclined to give up control over payroll tax revenues, given the growing financial imbalances in their own budgets. In 1992, payroll tax rates were massively increased (see table 6.3). This led to a temporary surplus in the funds, which served the government as a pretext to withdraw from its financial liabilities taken earlier (ILO-CEET 1994: 160f.). Since 1993, the budget situation has deteriorated severely. One reason seems to be the lack of "financial discipline" among the ministries involved which continuously exceeded their budgets. Most importantly, however, did the deficiencies in the Bulgarian contribution collection system account for the overall deficits – a problem which is said to be much worse than in the other three countries. The Ministry of Finance estimated that about 75–80 percent of the self-employed and 25–30 percent of the enterprises did not pay social insurance contributions in 1993. In view of this situation, Bulgarian governments have repeatedly postponed the plan to separate the funds from the general budget and to grant these institutions any financial and organizational autonomy. To divide insurance contributions between employees and employers has been considered also, but at the time this report was written – at the beginning of 1996 – the issue had still not been settled.

3.3.2 CHANGING ENTITLEMENTS: PENSION REFORM Pension reform has proceeded particularly slowly throughout the region. Everywhere, major reform bills were still pending or not yet fully drafted during the period considered. So far, the Czech government has engineered the most far-reaching reforms in this core area of the welfare state, though even in this case reforms have not been pursued vigorously.

At the very beginning, social policy experts in Prague developed a comprehensive strategy for social security reform. In 1990, an expert group was formed to identify key issues of social reform and work out principles for a novel design of the entire system. The *idée directrice* for rebuilding the state-socialist welfare regime was derived, first, from the country's inter-war social policy tradition. Further, the institutional patterns of Western welfare states were evaluated and copied (cf. Tomes

---

[28] The government only slightly reduced employers' and workers' contributions to the Employment Fund by 0.25 percentage points at the beginning of 1994.

1991; Miller 1992; Potucek 1993). Initially, principal agents in the Federal Labor Ministry were much in favor of a "solidaristic" variant of pension insurance, with a national basic pension program plus an earnings-related additional scheme. After the government reshuffle in 1992, however, the ministry was instructed to revise its initial proposal. Prime Minister Klaus' new social policy guidelines were to limit the overall level of state protection and give more room for private welfare provision.

The first reform realized was the bill on complementary pensions passed in early 1994. The Klaus government rejected the idea of introducing an occupational pension regime and opted for an individual approach instead, encouraging citizens to contribute to private pension funds. The law roughly regulates the statutes of the funds and stipulates that the state will subsidize each participant's contributions directly (rather than granting tax allowances). The second initiative which aimed to reform the existing basic pension program was pending until very recently. In particular, the new design of the pension formula (a strong reduction of the replacement rate in line with the neo-liberal reform agenda) and an envisaged increase in the standard retirement age over a period of 12 years met strong parliamentary resistance. As it happened, the bill passed in parliament with a bare majority in mid 1995. In short, the Czech government actually managed to scale back one of the core social programs inherited from the past regime.

Hungary has been lacking a scenario for coordinated social reform comparable with the Czech program over the period 1989 to 1994. As outlined above, responsibilities in financing have been redefined step by step, but no comprehensive strategy has been developed to reorganize benefit provision. In October 1991, the parliament passed a general resolution to set up a three-tier pension system with a universal minimum pension, an earnings-graded additional scheme, and optional private pension arrangements. Efforts to reform the existing pension system have failed, however. To be sure, the level of benefits has been repeatedly adjusted to the rising cost of living. Yet basic features of the Hungarian pension system, such as the pension formula or the standard retirement age, have not been altered.[29]

So far, only the third element of the 1991 concept has been realized. After two years of discussion and redrafting work, the Hungarian parliament passed a bill on private pension and health care funds in

---

[29] In February 1993, the Hungarian parliament decided to gradually raise the retirement age for women, beginning in 1995, while a decision affecting the retirement age of men was postponed. Shortly before the 1994 general elections, the government suspended the project on the grounds that it should be made more tolerable for the elder cohorts affected.

November 1993. The law offers tax privileges to companies and employees that launch so-called "voluntary mutual benefit funds" to provide pensions, medical services, or short-term cash benefits. Hungary thus chose a different road in private pension policy than the Czech Republic. The Hungarian government did not place confidence in the insurance industry and opted for an occupational pension regime. The Klaus government preferred an individual approach to private pensions[30] and rejected the idea of introducing company-based schemes.

Post-communist Bulgaria appears no less oriented towards "the West" than the other countries. The draft White Paper on Social Insurance Reform has been prepared in close collaboration with experts from EU countries and the United States and aims to imitate "well-tried" institutional patterns of Western welfare states. However, political actors have been reluctant actually to alter the status quo. The same may be said of Slovakia. Generally, the Slovak governments followed the original Federal plans for social reform after 1993. However, few changes have been brought about that affect the entitlements of large parts of the population. As in Bulgaria and Hungary, pension reform is still in its infancy. Only the introduction of a complementary pension scheme has recently been considered.[31]

3.3.3 TARGETING OF BENEFITS: FAMILY SUPPORT In the countries under study, there was also a serious debate on whether and how to streamline the other existing social programs. Generous family benefit schemes were a core part of communist legacies. They had provided, amongst other things, high monthly allowances per child, with payments rising with the number of children and eligibility tied to employment, but with no reference to income. These transfers had hitherto been a necessary supplement to low wages and, hence, an important instrument in combating poverty (cf. Sipos 1994; Milanovic 1994a). Moreover, the

---

[30] The scheme has become an important instrument of capital formation. The Czech Republic's 41 private pension funds have one million participants and expect assets of US$ 100 million by the end of 1995. Hungary's 39 funds have less than 200,000 participants and expect assets of US$ 30 million by that time (de Fougerolles 1995: 7).

[31] Experts from the World Bank and the IMF express growing concern about the sluggishness of pension reform in CEE countries. A way out of the impasse, they argue, is suggested by the Chilean model of pension reform. That is, to shift, at least partly, from a pay-as-you-go to a funded financing system, while changing the basic features of the pension system. Resistance against reform would become smaller, it is argued, and the capital accumulated would promote economic recovery in the transition countries (cf., with different emphasis, Holzmann 1994; Barr 1994: 208–20; Sachs 1995; de Fougerolles 1995).

allowances had been intended to promote births, yet they did not prove very effective in this respect. Since 1989, two policy changes have been discussed to improve the "targeting" of the program: either to set income limits directly or to include the allowance in income tax.[32] Both devices were considered a simplified means-test, less costly and stigmatizing than comprehensive means-testing on which access to social assistance was depending.

Both the Czech and the Slovak Republics have recently made the family support scheme more restrictive and systematically reshaped the provision of benefits. Already by 1993, the family allowance and the related compensation for price increases were cut back for higher-income households in Slovakia, whereas in the Czech lands only the compensatory allowance became means-tested at first. In the following months, the Czech Labor Ministry worked out a draft bill on how to integrate all kinds of social allowances granted to families into one coherent transfer system. The reform bill was passed by parliament in May 1995. The so-called "state social support system" now constitutes the second "floor" of the Czech welfare state, supplementing social insurance and the social assistance branch. The child allowance and other transfers are only paid to families whose income does not exceed a certain limit, i.e., all benefits have been means-tested since. Unlike social assistance, however, the national living minimum represents just a reference point for the various formulas (not the upper bound of benefit provision), and only the income situation of the applicant is considered (no assets-test). For the time being, the income limits are set at a fairly high level (in relation to wages) which excludes only a small segment of the population from benefit provision.[33] Thus the major achievement of the bill has been the systematization of transfers and the installation of a mechanism for trimming benefits in the future: the income-test. Slovakia has followed a similar plan and during 1994 worked out the draft principles of a new "state social support system."

In Bulgaria, the scheme as such has not been basically challenged since 1989. Benefits have not become means-tested as yet. The governments have also refrained from scaling back the parental leave arrangement, but have used it as an instrument for reducing the labor supply, as in the

[32] On the concept of "targeting" and its drawbacks, see, with different emphasis, Jarvis and Micklewright 1992; ILO 1993; Sipos 1994; Andorka et al. 1994.

[33] Noticeably, the Labor Ministry stressed the "political" rather than the financial implications of the reform during the parliamentary debate. Even if we can not expect to save much money by this step, means-testing is necessary, Czech reformers argued, to "change the people's mind" and cure them of their "claim-attitudes" acquired over the long period of communist rule.

other countries. Due to high inflation, however, the child allowance has sharply lost its real value, only partly offset by compensatory payments (UNICEF 1993: 64).

In Hungary, family allowance was turned into an universal scheme in April 1990 by the outgoing communist government in the wake of the tax reforms introduced in the late eighties. The allowance was extended to all children in the family. Further, support is no longer conditional on a satisfactory employment record (Jarvis and Micklewright 1992: 3–6). The Antall government, with the Ministry of Social Welfare headed by a Christian Democrat, has resisted constant pressure from external advisors to give up universalism in order to contain costs. The proposal to include family benefits in the personal income tax base, thus reducing the value of transfers to higher-income households, has been rejected on several grounds. Taxation was not a good targeting mechanism, it was held. Benefits still played an important role in supplementing low wages or insurance income, so the argument went on, and universalism was to meet the objectives of horizontal equity (i.e., equalizing costs of living between households with and without children). Moreover, generous family benefits were seen as a marked feature of the Hungarian welfare state and no one wishes to be blamed for abandoning it.

Yet the thrust of policy has changed since the socialist–liberal cabinet headed by Gyula Horn took over in mid 1994. Facing severe budgetary pressures, the government has made the family benefit scheme a target of reform, so as to limit social expenditures. The government's austerity package of March 1995 included substantial cuts in family benefits. Unsurprisingly, the plan was highly unpopular and led to the resignation of the Minister of Social Welfare. In July 1995, the Hungarian Constitutional Court quashed the bill. The judges argued that the cutback was not reasonable without giving young couples the opportunity to reconsider their family planning.[34] To date, it is uncertain whether the reform will actually be implemented.

3.4 Political obstacles to reform

The general pattern we can observe is that political actors in CEE countries have been reluctant to basically challenge the social security system inherited during the early years of societal transformation. Despite strong reformist ambitions at the outset of transition, a great many programs have seen only minor adjustments. Even in the Czech case, where social reform has been pursued most comprehensively so far,

[34] See above, chapter 3, section 2.2.3.

major bills have long been pending and, with the exception of health care reform treated below, changes to entitlements to secure a basic standard of living have been implemented very cautiously (cf. also Cichon 1995a; Rys 1995).

The reasons for the slow pace of social reforms are manifold. First of all, it doubtless took reformers some time to study foreign models and develop distinct reform plans. They had to acquaint themselves with social policy techniques and modes of social protection governance applied in the West before they could formulate reform plans for their own countries. Initially, the idea of sequencing may also have played a role. Except for the sub-fields of unemployment compensation and social assistance, a significant reform of social security was clearly not the first priority of post-communist governments when taking power. Major social reforms could be launched, so the initial schedule went, after the most pressing tasks of stabilization and restructuring had been accomplished.

The main reason for the "sluggishness" of welfare state reform seems to be that welfare state reform is a highly unpopular and politically risky undertaking, given the fiscal strains post-communist governments are facing. In mature welfare states, in the East as in the West, changes in core programs affect the entitlements of large segments of the population.[35] None of the transition countries has the financial resources to cure the failures of the old welfare regime by merely topping up what is already in place. Rather, social policy transformation will impose losses on various groups, making some income groups, occupations, or cohorts worse-off in relative or absolute terms compared with the situation under the old regime. In short, there is a zero-sum game in which governments have to pursue reforms very cautiously, if they want to be re-elected.[36]

In addition, one must recall the striking weakness of the post-communist state.[37] To launch reforms, political actors have to be

---

[35] See, in particular, Pierson (1994, 1995) who has outlined the distinctive qualities of retrenchment politics in Western welfare states.

[36] However, the parallel between interest group politics in the West and the East should not be exaggerated. Jeffrey Sachs (1995) has recently argued this point. He claims that social reforms have not yet progressed far because of the electoral considerations of populist politicians. Left-wing parties have succeeded in winning the recent elections almost everywhere precisely because they promised the electorate the maintenance of an extensive system of social guarantees. Yet Sachs fails to fully acknowledge the actual needs arising from the process of economic restructuring. See the replies by Cichon (1995b) and Kabaj and Kowalik (1995) to Sachs's article; see also the study by Cichon and Hagemejer (1995).

[37] See chapter 1.

"strong" enough to carry out their policy intentions. "Strength" means, first of all, that post-communist coalition governments must have the ability to reconcile conflicting interests and actually come to a decision. On the contrary, political instability invites political actors to adopt short-term, "trial-and-error" policies. Unfortunately, it is the latter scenario that has become the reality in most post-communist societies. Adding to political instability, post-communist governments do not usually possess sufficient financial and administrative resources to implement policies. Moreover, governments still lack strong, reliable societal partners, organized interests outside the realm of the parliamentary system, which could be used to overcome resistance, launch reforms, and assume welfare responsibilities. Only the Czech reformers have enjoyed more favorable conditions which enabled them to implement a number of far-reaching and probably irreversible changes in the welfare state.

4   Management of social protection: from state command to interest coordination

This section shifts the focus from the national policy level to issues of governance in post-communist welfare states. Under the old regime, as spelled out above, everything rested on the party apparatus to decide. It was not planned that autonomous collective actors articulated welfare needs "from below," to say nothing of an arrangement of associational self-regulation to substitute for direct state control. The trade unions, the mass youth organizations, or the economic chambers (surprisingly, the latter had existed in Bulgaria and in Hungary in the eighties) had formerly no independent political voice, but were supposed to realize, at the workplace mainly, that what was determined above as the "common goal." This command style of governance could no longer persist after 1989. Post-communist elites wished to introduce what Cichon and Samuel (1995) called a "second level of social proctection governance" bridging legal provisions and administrative practice. To account for a plurality of interests, political actors made efforts to set up *intermediate bodies* of interest representation, institutions for continous consultation, coordination, and supervision of the system's performance. Old affiliations, informal practices, and bargaining routines had to be reshaped and newly emerging corporate actors were in need of support to learn their roles. The following remarks deal with three aspects of social protection management in transition countries: (a) the establishment of national tripartite bodies of consultation, (b) mechanisms of interest-coordination in the health care sector, and (c) the governing of social protection at the local level.

4.1   Tripartism

All of the four countries created tripartite institutions at the very beginning to ensure social peace and ease the implementation of economic reforms (cf. Cichon and Samuel 1995: 73–95).[38] Employers' organizations, the third party besides the government and the unions, however, were no key player in tripartite negotiations at the beginning. Inviting them to participate nevertheless was to introduce a distinction unknown before, the distinction between "private interests" and the "common good," and to help them find their roles. Business associations were step by step bestowed with rights and recognition to allow the state to retreat from the economic sphere (cf. Wiesenthal and Stykow 1994: 4f.). First of all, tripartite consultations and agreements meant a compromise between the government and the trade unions: wage restraint and strike-stops were exchanged for collective bargaining rights and official recognition; "trade unions moderate their substantive demands in exchange for status rewards" (Orenstein 1994b: 6).

The Czechoslovak Council of Economic and Social Accord was formed in autumn 1990, with each side represented by seven delegates. Similar bodies were established in both republics. The tripartite was the brainchild of the social democratic wing of the Calfa government that wished to initiate a social dialogue, inspired by the Austrian, Scandinavian, and Portuguese corporatist accord (Haller et al. 1993: 40f.). The "social partners" have convened regularly since to discuss issues of wage policy, social policy, and labor relations. Despite his strong anti-union stance, Prime Minister Klaus has so far accepted the corporatist structure to keep the unions off the streets. The government has allowed the (formerly communist) unions to keep their property, has given them a formally strong legal framework for collective bargaining, and has permitted them to serve as consultants in social policy making, but making no substantive concessions on any matter of importance (Orenstein 1994b). The General Agreements signed every year were not binding documents, neither legally nor according to the understanding of the parties. The General Agreement for 1991 still contained precise commitments by the government on minimum wage indexation and other social policy issues, but the government soon failed to deliver her side of the bargain and avoided underwriting more than vague statements of intent in the following years. In the General Agreement for 1994 the parties even gave up the practice of specifying the policy goals in terms of recommended indices on the

---

[38] Note that this is no univeral pattern in Eastern Europe. Poland and Romania have only recently embarked on tripartism.

grounds that benchmarks were insignificant anyhow. Moreover, the government has announced that it will reduce its role in the tripartite altogether (Myant 1993a: 69–71; Orenstein 1994b: 19).

The unions' direct impact on economic and social policy making has been very limited in Czechoslovakia respectively the Czech Republic. The trade unions neither prevent the massive erosion of the minimum wage, nor did they succeed in eliminating wage regulation or having their ideas on pension reform accepted. However, the critical point was that, despite Klaus' neo-liberal rhetorics, they did not have much to enter a protest against. From the beginning of transition, the government flanked economic reforms with a comprehensive set of social democratic policies designed to keep unemployment low and create basic minimum standards (Orenstein 1994a). By contrast, the Slovak unions' direct impact on decision making has increased since the break up. Political instability has invited them to play a more prominent political role and to defend "workers' interests" more agressively. The unions' "victory" with the Social Fund Act mentioned above is a case in point (cf. also Myant 1993; Rutland 1992/3: 118–28).

Hungary has developed a similar framework of corporatist accord, as the neighboring countries did. The National Council for the Reconciliation of Interests was formed in late 1988 as a forum to discuss issues of wage liberalization, inspired by central wage bargaining practiced in Sweden and Belgium. In August 1990, the Council was revitalized and all trade union confederations and employers' organizations were invited to join the forum.[39] Soon after, the institution stood its test, when the social partners managed to settle the taxi driver strike (Ladó 1994: 52f.; Kurtán 1993: 272). The Council for the Reconciliation of Interests is supposed to be a consultative body on all major questions of economic and social policy. The Labor Code of 1992 explicitly acknowledges the role of the tripartite in minimum wage setting and managing labor relations. Further, the government delegated authority to two subcommittees, the Labor Market Board and the National Training Council. They were

---

[39] Employees were represented at first by seven trade union confederations and employers by nine organizations. One trade union center "disappeared" from the conference table in 1991 because it did not accept the new procedural rules the other unions had agreed on. Noticeably, as yet, employers have maintained absolute silence on procedural rules to give no one a chance to question their bargaining legitimacy. Each side has only one vote – a rule adopted to promote intra-class consensus building. Today, participants hold that the tripartite preserves the existing intra-class fragmentation rather than helps to overcome it. None of the organizations represented at the round table has so far been prepared to give up its seat and unite with one of its rivals.

mandated in 1991 to fully decide how to spend the money available for employment policy.

Although the Hungarian leadership has been more in favor of including the social partners in public policy making than the Czech government, consolidation of tripartism has not yet been fully achieved. Competences and procedural rules have repeatedly been a major source of conflict between the three sides, albeit mutual understanding and recognition has significantly increased, since the "trade union war" over the distribution of property and the fall 1992 social conflict were settled (Ladó 1994: 27–32, 53f.; Greskovits 1994). With the Horn government taking office in mid 1994 and advocating a "new social dialogue," the prospects for consolidation improved (cf. also Herczog 1994; Brusis 1994). However, the government's austerity measures of March 1995[40] caused relations with the trade unions to deteriorate substantially.

In Bulgaria, tripartism emerged as a response to political crisis and industrial unrest that followed the events of 1989. In the early months of 1990, the main trade union confederation CITUB urged the Lukanov government to sign an agreement on collective bargaining issues and wage indexation and to enter into continual cooperation. Later, Podkrepa, the competing trade union, changed its position and acceded to the agreement. In 1991, the Tripartite Commission for Coordination of Interests became a standing body and, promoted by the IMF, two General Agreements were reached covering the whole range of economic and social issues. The newly elected UDF government gave social partnership a low priority and wished to reduce the unions' strong influence on public policy making. Efforts at specifying the role and the working rules of the tripartite failed and the commission was finally dissolved in September 1992. The successor government under Berov aimed to revive social accord and give tripartism a stable legal foundation. With the revision of the Labor Code coming into effect on January 1, 1993, standing Councils of Social Partnership were institutionalized at national, branch, and regional levels to regulate issues of wage policy, taxation, labor relations, privatization, and social policies. From 1993, six organizations have been represented at the round table: CITUB and Podkrepa plus four employers' organizations which succeeded in being recognized as national representatives by the Council of Ministers (ILO-CEET 1994: 77–120). However, tensions between the unions and the government soon grew again, and social dialogue has repeatedly been interrupted in the course of 1994.

The rise and fall of Bulgarian tripartism reflects political instability and

---

[40] See above, section 3.3.

economic crisis. All Bulgarian governments had only weak parliamentary support and only limited benefits to offer the electorate. They were highly dependent on trade union support and had no other choice than to include the main confederations in public policy making, so as to ensure social peace. The unions could claim to represent the interests of large segments of the population and managed to maintain a base of mobilized support after 1989 (thus being in a strong bargaining position as against the various governments) even though inter-union rivalry was continuing (Thirkell *et al.* 1993: 110). Considering the ongoing political stalemate and with living conditions worsening, the unions repeatedly took a broad stance on their role in policy making and attempted to use the tripartite to compensate for the slow pace of parliamentary activity (cf. also Waller 1993). As a consequence, the role of the Bulgarian tripartite has remained heavily contested so far. Nevertheless, the institution has played an important role in alleviating social tensions and has provided a framework for unions and employers' associations to learn new roles.

None of the four countries has so far clearly defined the future role of tripartism in public policy making. Initially, tripartism was meant to be a temporary arrangement to cope with the problems of societal transformation. In many countries, social partnership now seems to have become a permanent institution. Political elites in Hungary, Slovakia, and Bulgaria intend to uphold and/or further develop the corporatist framework of decision making. Only the Czech leadership appears no longer willing to continue on the road of social accord.

4.2 Management of health care

All four countries have developed plans for the future shape of their health care systems. Everywhere, reform proposals envisage turning the "public service model" inherited from the old regime into a kind of social insurance arrangement. This implies a comprehensive restructuring of the management of health care provision. Under communist rule, the state had been the owner of virtually all health care units, health care providers had been public employees, and financial resources had come out of general tax revenue. A social insurance regime differs from that arrangement in that the state is divorced from the financing and provision of medical services. Independent (statutory and private) health care funds shall now be in charge of the money provided by the insured and negotiate with health care providers about the allocation of financial resources. In the past, there had been a bi-polar relationship between the state (as financial intermediary and provider) and the population (as tax payers and recipients) (Cichon 1991: 313). To move to a social insurance arrangement means to establish a triangular relationship of routine scheme management between the health insurance(s), provider units, and the insurees. The government is supposed to have merely a "stewardship role" (Preker and Feachem 1994: 314) which includes quality control and overall cost containment. Reform plans provide that general issues of benefit regulation will remain in the realm of the government and/or parliament.

It proves a momentous task to set up such a framework of inter-associational communication and bargaining to substitute for direct state control in the health care sector. First of all, there is the issue of separating the funds from the state budget already touched upon above.[41] The shift to "off-budget" financing was thought of as a device to mobilize additional resources for the health sector. However, contributions were rarely sufficient to cover expenditures and the state had to continue subsidizing the ever-increasing expenditures (cf. Preker and Feachem 1994: 306).

Both in Hungary and Slovakia, one statutory, semi-autonomous health insurance body has been created. Only the Czech Republic abolished state monopoly in the health insurance market in the course of 1993. Yet enrolment has remained mandatory. In late 1995, there were 27 health insurance companies serving different population groups, but operating under the same legislative framework. These companies were competing for "attractive" members (young people, high wage earners), depite a system of revenue redistribution introduced to avoid adverse selection (Vyborná 1994: 10–13; Filer et al. 1995). However, many of the newly founded companies have strongly miscalculated their premiums; some are even said to be on the brink of insolvency. In view of this situation, a number of hospitals no longer accept their insurance cards and refuse to treat policy holders who cannot pay cash in advance.[42]

In Bulgaria, health care reform is still pending. The adjustments made have not basically challenged the existing "public service model" to date. From 1991, the Minstry of Health prepared several draft laws for reintroducing a national health insurance system in collaboration with an expert group established for that purpose. The recent proposal envisages a decentralized structure, with several politically independent health

---

[41] See above, sections 3.3.1 and 3.3.2.
[42] An additional incentive problem is caused by the institutional separation of the sickness funds (providing income support in case of sick leave) and the health insurance funds (covering medical services) maintained after 1989. Often, physicians agree to prolong the period of paid sick leave, if this is to avoid costly (inpatient) treatment which the health insurance companies would have to cover (Veprek et al. 1994: 25f.).

insurance bodies to cover basic medical services (cf. ILO-CEET 1994: 187–9; Schoukens 1994: 132).

Further, details of the provider payment systems must be worked out. Governments introduced performance-based reimbursement regimes for health care providers under contract with the health insurance companies, so as to improve the quality and cost-effectiveness of medical services. However, they had great difficulties in assessing the incentive effects of payment systems on providers' behavior and, thus, the financial implications of the reform. This all the more, as many Western countries also have problems in building an appropriate incentive environment in the health care sector. Hence, there is no ideal model for Eastern Europe to follow.

In 1992, the Czech Republic replaced official salaries by fee-for-service payments, i.e. a system in which medical suppliers are paid for each service they render. However, this system was introduced without a sufficient regulatory mechanism of price fixing or budget limiting. These "technical mistakes" (Vyborná 1994) have exacerbated the problem of cost containment. Within a few months, the annual budget of the health insurance funds was completely exhausted (cf. Filer et al. 1995; Preker and Feachem 1994: 299, 306). Slovakia adopted a new system of provider payments as of January 1, 1993. Here, too, the new method was badly prepared and not backed up by effective control mechanisms.[43] The law had to be frequently revised, and further revisions are on the agenda. Unsurprisingly, policy makers began to view the introduction of market forces into the health sector as an expensive enterprise and one to be pursued more cautiously.

Hungary tried to combine different financing methods for the different sub-sectors of the health care system. As in Great Britain, "family doctors" (general practitioners) receive capitation payments (a fixed sum per patient irrespective of the amount of treatment); outpatient specialists are reimbursed on the basis of the German "point system" (payments depend on the number of examinations performed, with the value of the points being determined in a process of negotiated price fixing); the financing method for hospitals is similar to the American "Diagnosis Related Group system" (the sum hospitals receive per patient is related to

[43] According to Krizan et al. (1995: 105), the list of medical procedures and point values attached to them was "a confused translation of the German original source." Moreover, they go on to argue, the German original "was elaborated in quite a different milieu (specific forms of medical care, the network of facilities, technical equipment, the rate of pay for an individual's labor, types of medical procedures, social and economic situation in general) and it could not be applied to the Health Service in Slovakia."

the condition with which the person is diagnosed). Health care experts doubt whether these methods add to a coherent financing structure and whether they will bring about the same results in the "underfinanced" Hungarian health care system as in the West (cf., e.g., Orosz 1994).

Finally, there is the issue of interest group formation on the providers' side. Self-regulation of the health care professions is still rarely effective in CEE countries (cf. Preker and Feachem 1994: 311). True, physicians' associations, trade unions of the hospital staff, interest groups of the pharmaceutic industry, etc. have soon (re)-emerged after 1989. However, these interest associations have so far shown little responsibility for enforcing professional standards and basic norms of conduct to which their membership feels bound (cf. Schoukens 1994: 135). The handling of the issue of "tipping" is a case in point. It is still common practice in all CEE countries to bribe doctors and medical personnel in order to be adequately treated. Doctors seem to be reluctant, for the time being, to give up the practice of receiving (and demanding) "gratitude money" as a means of supplementing their income and to impose respective rules of conduct on themselves. For instance, "when the Hungarian Medical Association was reestablished in September 1991, it was announced that the association would combat corruption, but the body's final statutes did not include any clause to this effect" (Pataki 1992: 62). Unless professional self-regulation is working, it will be difficult to adopt a decentralized model of health care management, e.g., the German-style method of negotiated price fixing which has become very popular among post-communist social policy makers.

4.3 Local social policies: revival of the "third sector"

Local government reform legislation has established a broad sphere of discretionary local powers and has strengthened the role of local author-ities in social policies. As mentioned above, the new social assistance schemes are run by the municipalities and have had an increasing role to play in protecting the poor since 1989. The Employment Laws assume local labor offices and local governments will take joint action to alleviate the tensions in local labor markets. Today, municipalities are in charge of public housing, urban development, and all kinds of community-based services. Eventually, they will become owners of hospitals and outpatient centers and will take over social policy assets from the firms, such as kindergardens, day nurseries, and recreation facilities. In Bulgaria, decen-tralization of welfare functions has proceeded the least, among the countries under study. Decision making has remained strongly centra-lized so far, whereas in the other cases, in particular in Hungary, local social policies have become increasingly important. The problem of resource endowment proves the major bottleneck of local social policies. Many welfare tasks have – *de jure* or *de facto* – been shifted from the central state to local units, but the municipalities still lack sufficient financial as well as professional resources to perform the tasks assigned to them appropriately (cf. Hesse 1993: 236–9). Reform legislation has granted the local units some share of central funds and new local taxes have been introduced. Moreover, municipalities attempted to increase their revenue base through fees for community-based services. Yet resources are seldom, if ever enough to maintain the earlier structure of social care, to say nothing of urgent investments needed to improve the quality of services. Consequently, many companies have hesitated over shedding the bulk of their social assets prior to privatization. Management and unions have resisted firms fully abandoning their social policy functions over the first years of transition, seeing that equivalent community structures were lacking (cf. Carlin *et al.* 1994: 42; Schaffer 1995).

Adding to the financial problems, poor administrative capacities have limited the implementation of new social programs at the local level. To set up a network of employment services, staff was transferred from existing administrative institutions to the new bodies. Generally, the staff were inexperienced with the new legislative framework and offices were not sufficiently equipped in the first years of transition. The same holds true for the old social administration departments. Due to low pay and poor social prestige, as against the private sector, the personnel is commonly low-skilled; its selection is in the main supply led. As Hesse (1993: 245) briefly put it: "the public service does not hire the staff it needs, but the staff it can get." Moreover, the present personnel is used to a rigid top-to-bottom approach of social protection governance and had little opportunity to initiate changes from below (Crawford and Thompson 1994: 334). In addition, it is fragmentation at the local level that seriously hampers the efficiency of public administration, especially in Hungary, the Czech Republic, and Slovakia (cf. Wollmann 1994). In view of these problems, many post-communist reformers still have reservations about decentralizing the governance of social protection.

To extend and improve the network of social service provision, social policy makers initially placed great hopes on voluntary or non-profit organizations. "Self-help" and "welfare pluralism" were proposed as an alternative to paternalistic state protection (cf., e.g., Kuron 1993). Indeed, the so-called "third sector," comprising large charity organizations with predominantly professional staff as well as very small self-help groups, has rapidly grown since 1989 in the four countries, especially in Hungary

(Laczko 1993). At the start, the most successful agencies seem to be organizations associated with the church. The new initiatives help to ease the social tensions of the transition period today. They provide free lunches, distribute clothing and medical equipment donated from abroad, organize home care for the elderly, provide shelters for the homeless, or simply act as pressure groups in the welfare field, thus supplementing the patchy public safety net. However, the initial consideration that the state can quickly withdraw from its social policy commitments because of the growing third sector appears entirely unrealistic.

First, it turns out that the development of the non-profit sector rests essentially on state support (direct government funding and/or favorable tax policies). In Hungary, for instance, local authorities are permitted to contract out social services to voluntary agencies. These agencies may claim the same amount of subsidies that is given to state-run institutions. Further, favorable tax policies have been decisive for the "spontaneous" growth of the third sector in that country. In Hungary, "such policies have been so liberal that they led many for-profit organizations to create fondations as a means of avoiding taxation" (Laczko 1994: 50). By contrast, the Czech government refrained from including state subsidies in the tax scheme. What is more, the bill on non-profit organizations was still pending at the end of 1994. As a result, the process of privatization of health care facilities, for example, has so far taken place without participation of non-profit agencies (cf. Veprek *et al.* 1994: 36; Filer *et al.* 1995: 409).

Furthermore, only small numbers of the population in CEE countries have as yet been prepared to do (unpaid or partly remunerated) voluntary work. In the first years of transition, people had to cope with the conditions of turbulent and painful transformation primarily. They could hardly afford to "work for peanuts" in the voluntary sector. The Hungarian experience is telling here. In March 1990, the Hungarian government introduced a so-called "care allowance," so as to strengthen informal care work. The allowance amounts to the minimum wage at maximum and can be paid to persons who give up (full-time) employ-ment, but at the same time do not receive other social transfers (pensions, parental allowance, or the like).[44] In addition, the time spent on care work is included in the service period considered for the calculation of pension entitlements. Relatively few persons have as yet applied for that allowance due to the low amount of the benefit and the tight eligibility rules (Széman 1994: 234f.). On the other hand, owing to

[44] A similar provision was introduced in the Czech Republic in 1993 (Kasalová 1994: 224).

mass unemployment and worsening of living conditions, low-paid voluntary work may well become increasingly attractive. A considerable number of the long-term unemployed restrained from registration at the employment offices in Hungary, after their entitlement to unemployment benefits had expired and opted for token-fee care work instead. The "salary" paid to the caregivers is equivalent to 75 percent of the means-tested unemployment aid (Széman 1994: 237).

Finally, one has to take into account the functional limitations affecting the activities of non-profit organizations and the social selectivity of their work. Non-profit associations and self-help groups do not emerge spontaneously in all places and are not open to every citizen. The potential benefits of the third sector are not universally available, but can be appropriated only by sections of the population: those who live within the associations' social catchment area, share their values, in case of self-help groups, possess certain social capabilities, and so on. The readiness and chances to engage in formally organized associations and informal self-help networks and make use of their services vary according to age, gender, social class, etc., as the experience of OECD countries suggests. Given these functional limitations, it is unrealistic to assume that the third sector could fill the gaps if the state reduces its welfare responsibilities. Moreover, there is a strong need for local governments to coordinate the proliferating non-profit and for-profit activities and ensure the quality of services provided.

5 Comparative assessment: state of reform and performance

On balance, post-communist welfare states have shown a remarkable degree of durability so far. Most changes of note in the old regime occurred in the field of labor market policies and social assistance, while governments hesitated in basically challenging many of the other core social programs in the early years of transition. However, the preceding analysis has also identified a number of important differences between the four countries both in the overall state of reform and in the priorities set.

By mid 1995, the Czech Republic's reform record seems to be the most successful. The pension scheme has been scaled back, health care reform has been put on track, financial responsibilities have been partly reorganized, and family benefits have become means tested. Even in the Czech case, however, several major reform projects have been pending for a long time. Moreover, the government did not pursue a radical strategy of residualization. Rather, Czech policies had a strong social democratic component which has helped to ensure social peace so far. Hungary and

Slovakia have also experienced some institutional changes. In both cases, the emphasis has been on organizational issues (i.e., on the creation of independent social insurance funds), while benefit reform is still pending. In Hungary, welfare state reforms were started earlier than in the Czech Republic and generally carried out in a less technocratic, more incremen-talistic way. Slovakia has clearly profitted from the fact that some reform steps were already taken before the "velvet divorce." Since 1993, govern-ments have roughly followed the original Federal plans for social reform. Yet it is becoming increasingly difficult for reformers to carry out policies with any medium-term dimension, given the unstable political context. Social reforms are clearly least advanced in Bulgaria. In that country, the process of social policy transformation was gravely hampered by frequent changes of government. When taking over, governments announced that they would completely overhaul the social security system, but then lacked the capacity to bring about and implement the respective laws. The adjustments made were mainly driven by short-term financial considerations and a concern for securing the basic functioning of the system. Generally, action on poverty relief had to take precedence over any structural reforms of the social security system.

The preceding *tour de force* across several areas of social policy has also unearthed a number of differences in program designs, e.g., in the composition of active labor market programs or in the reimbursement systems chosen for medical providers, in the design of private pension regimes or in the role assigned to tripartite institutions. Such kinds of intercountry variations largely reflect the normative orientations and strategic considerations of the political actors who have been involved in the process of policy formation (the prime minister, ministers and their administrators, advisers and lobbyists). When designing the new laws, none of the countries simply followed one particular Western model, nor did external actors directly impose particular policies from abroad. Rather, policy makers in the four countries attempted to imitate and combine a variety of institutional patterns of Western welfare states and to adapt them to actual country-specific conditions. Noticeably, little policy learning has taken place among the transition countries themselves so far. Nevertheless, even if post-communist welfare states have not come under the knife of reformers in the early years of transition, we have to acknowledge the fact that many welfare indicators have strongly worsened in the region since 1989. Thus, the case for institutional continuity should not be mistaken for a proposition about the social adequacy and financial viability of the existing programs. Everywhere, the social costs of transition turned out to be considerable and much higher than expected. Unemployment has increased markedly, most prices have been liberalized, and enterprises are reducing, albeit slowly, their social benefit provision. The welfare state institutions, however, were not designed to meet these tremendous demands and challenges. Today, the newly introduced unemployment benefit system reach no more than half of those on the register. The reshaped social assistance schemes provide very low benefits and reach only a limited number of the poor. Only the efforts made to preserve the living standards of pensioners have been relatively successful virtually everywhere.[45] As investments in the health sector have been negligible for two decades or more, health facilities, especially hospital buildings, are generally in a derelict state. Revenue shortfalls, the spread of corruption, but also the "technical mistakes" of the early reform initiatives, have exacerbated the crisis of the health care sector.

Nevertheless, there still remain crucial differences between the situation in Latin America and the social conditions in CEE countries. Most importantly, the poor have not represented a distinct underclass in post-communist societies up to now. As Milanovic (1994b: 4) has stressed, the gap between the poverty threshold and the income of the average poor is still quite narrow. Moreover, the educational and skill levels of the majority of the poor are quite high, and most of them have access to durable goods and dwellings. This suggests, as Milanovic goes on to argue, that if economic recovery is soon resumed and trickles down, a large number of the poor may escape poverty relatively easily. If income growth comes too late and/or only higher-income groups enjoy the benefits of economic revival, the picture of poverty may worsen dramatically, even in the more advanced transition countries of Central Europe where the decline in employment and income has recently come to a halt.

---

[45] Unfortunately, comprehensive cross national data on this point have not been available. For a brief survey of various performance indicators, see Cichon 1995a: 7f.; UNICEF 1995.

7

Consolidation and the cleavages of ideology and identity

The question that is to be addressed in this chapter is this: What kinds of actors, cleavages, and conflicts that are specific to the CEE post-communist transition play either a favorable or unfavorable role in the process of institutional consolidation? Consolidation means, first of all, a condition in which conflict is limited and contained within a framework of enforced and recognized rules. Instead of exclusion and violence carried out between enemies, consolidation is a condition in which mutual recognition, civilized conflict, and compromise between opponents prevails. Consolidation means that a recognized "form" is available to reconcile or make livable any "substance" of conflict. Actors refrain from – or are effectively discouraged from – challenging the rules according to which conflict is to be carried out, and agents within recognized institutional domains are endowed with rights and resources that allow them to practice their autonomy. As argued in more detail toward the end of chapter 1, consolidation is equivalent to the routinization of conflict and the pluralization of domains. To put it in negative terms: If consolidation is accomplished, no one appeals to "sacred causes" or substantive "higher reasons" that are held to be more valid than existing rules; and no one trespasses demarcation lines that define societal domains.

1   Categorical conflicts and class conflicts

We start with two assumptions. First, the societal conflicts that typically occur within post-communist societies are of a nature *other than class conflicts*. To be sure, the state socialist formation must not be confused with a "classless" society. But the practice of class conflict was repressed under state socialism, both regarding distributional struggles and struggles of the control of the production process. No collective actors were permitted to carry out and settle their conflicts of interest. The state, being a "workers' state," did not provide an arena for socio-economic conflict. It also imposed living conditions upon the mass of the population that were fairly uniform for the vast majority of the population, as far as consumption, housing, health, education, and even monetary income were concerned – with the exception, of course, of the living conditions of the higher ranks of state and party officials. Structuration along class lines was also missing in the immediate aftermath of the breakdown of the old regime. To be sure (as Kitschelt *et al.* 1995 emphasize), there were "positional" voting patterns in the first free elections, but these reflected individual properties of voters rather than associationally constituted sectors of society. For a new "mode of production" that could have generated a pattern of collective interest and action was not yet in place. People had no cue as to what their place within the emerging relations of production and distribution was likely to be, and which party would best serve their individual and collective interests. We can thus speak, concerning both the condition prior to the breakdown and the situation immediately following it, of a highly amorphous socio-economic pattern of interests and conflict and an atomized social structure in which answers to two key questions are hard to come by. These questions, made all the more urgent by the massive uncertainties of the incipient economic transformation, are: (a) Who are "our friends" or trustworthy allies who share with us similar interests? and (b) who are "our enemies" against whom "we" are to defend "our" common interest? It has been suggested that the amorphous nature of socio-economic bases of associability can partly even be held responsible for the prevalence and strength of ethnic cleavages in CEE: "In the painful revival of civil society . . . ethnic associations can be revived much more quickly and effectively than any others" (Gellner 1991: 133).

Incidentally, the amorphous nature of socioeconomic conflict lines in post-communist CEE provides the strongest argument for expecting very different trajectories and outcomes in this region as compared with the Latin American and Southern European cases of transition to democracy, with the latter exhibiting very clear-cut socioeconomic cleavages which evolved under their respective old regimes. The only (limited) exception to the rule that cleavages (and the potential for conflict implicit in them) do not emerge from the societal pattern of division of labor is perhaps the cleavage of the countryside vs. the city, which consequently played a significant role in organizational and electoral outcomes in CEE, as indicated by the rapid and ubiquitous emergence of agrarian parties after 1989.[1]

Instead of the largely absent, or rather nascent and poorly articulated collective actors representing class, or socio-economic interests, the political dynamic of the transition to liberal-democracy-*cum*-market-capitalism in Eastern Europe is largely determined through two kinds of cleavages that are at any rate much less significant in earlier transitions, particularly the Latin American ones. These cleavages are: (1) those of a political-*ideological* kind that divide the population into those who have been loyal or acquiescent under the old regime, including its elites and activists and those who identify themselves as its (more or less recent) opponents or victims, and (2) those cleavages of an *identity*-based kind that divide the population into members of the titular nation and religious, linguistic, and ethnic majorities of various kinds. As to the first of these cleavages, the ideological one, it needs to be remembered that the old elite and its constituency did not only have effective control over the respective country's political and economic resources, but also, if to widely varying degrees, had not effectively lost all of the legitimation and support extended to it by large sectors of the population, particularly as it has not been defeated by an oppositional or revolutionary movement. As to the second cleavage, the region of CEE exhibits a number of specificities, to be discussed below, which also sets the post-communist wave of transitions far apart from preceding waves.

Our second assumption on which our discussion of cleavages is based is axiomatic rather than founded on empirical observation, as is the first. It claims that *socio-economic* cleavages are more compatible with, or more easily processed through, the institutional machinery of liberal democratic capitalism than is either of its two alternatives, namely *political* cleavages (pertaining to conflicting preferences for or affiliation with regime types) and *cultural* cleavages (based upon ethnic, linguistic, or religious identities). As a consequence, the type of societal conflict that prevails will determine the potential for democratic consolidation. Why should this be the case? The answer, we submit, has to do with the differential suitability of different kinds of cleavages for compromise.[2] Socio-economic conflicts are about the distribution of income and the control over productive resources. While this type of conflict is often intense, stable solutions in the form of *quantitative* compromise are, as a matter of principle, easy to achieve through demands, threats, bargaining,

---

[1] Agrarian parties were typically allowed a largely nominal political role of their own within state-socialist "national front" governments.
[2] See also above chapter 4 section 3.3.

and concessions that are being made in terms of income, social security, or co-determination. Socio-economic cleavages allow for "splitting the difference," politico-ideological ones as well as ethno-cultural ones do not. As long as the substance of conflict is framed in terms of *interests* (rather than principles of *reason* or, for that matter, *passions*), parties can meet *halfway* – and they are more likely to do so the more they come to realize that they mutually *depend upon each other* within the framework of an interclass cooperative game. Divisibility of difference and perceived mutual dependence are conducive to limited conflict and the ready recognition of rules of the game.

1.1 Interests, ideologies, and identities

Conflicts between ideological proponents of different kinds of *political regimes* are less easily settled than socio-economic conflicts of interests through the use of compromise. One reason is that parties to this kind of conflict do *not* see themselves as depending upon each other: Each of them deems itself better off if the opponent were non-existent. Yet a number of techniques are known and proven that allow for the peaceful accommodation of conflicting ideological policy proposals and political philosophies. For instance, universal admission to political competition and collectively binding decision making through contested elections are methods through which conflict is not "resolved," but suspended – unless, that is, the political ideologies differ as to the appropriate ground rules of political competition. Similarly, "gag rules," the decentralization of decision making within federal structures, or the indefinite postponement of decisions often creates a space of coexistence of fundamentally opposed conceptions of the desirable political order.

Even less suitable for compromise or the suspension of conflict than politico-ideological conflicts are identity-based conflicts of an ethnic, linguistic or religious nature. In the worst cases of such conflicts, the parties involved consider each other as mutually *threatening*. Not only could they do without each other, but they can *only* live, in the extreme case, with the absence of the "other" from a given territory. There is no way in which strongly held and adhered to identities could easily "mix." "Meeting halfway" is a promising way out of most economic and many political conflicts, but not so in the case of linguistic, religious, and ethnic conflict. This is all the more the case if such conflict is fueled not only by myths, memories, and anticipations representing the values of one's own culture, but also by the hostilities, threats, and humiliations that the culture has been exposed to in the past (and is likely, according to this frame, to be confronted with in the future) from other neighboring cultures. As it is in the nature of history that it can neither be "changed" retroactively nor easily "forgotten," the problem of consolidation, i.e., the problem of coming to agree on and reliably comply with common binding rules is much thornier in the case of identity-based hostile passions than with conflicting socio-economic interests or politico-ideological cleavages.

We thus propose an analytical "reconcilability scale" of *interests*, *ideologies*, and *identities*. Along this scale, the perceived mutual dependency of the parties involved in conflict decreases; fair rules of competition and compatibility are harder to devise and more easily challenged; "meeting halfway" becomes an increasingly difficult and eventually positively non-sensical and outright despicable notion; the time frame becomes more extended, as interests are quickly satisfied and allow for rapid change, ideologies are most often fixed on a medium-term time horizon, but identities are usually associated with a sense of "eternity" that reaches back into the mist of some imagined past and extends with chiliastic ambitions into the indefinite future. Finally, there is one more dimension according to which the three differ. As we move from interest to ideology to identity and compare the substantive scope of conflicts, we see that more and more "integral" visions of what both sides desire are involved. Interests are focused upon some specific resource that one side has and the other does not have, but desires. Political ideologies involve designs and values that affect many spheres and aspects of the public life of the community. And ethnic, nationalist, and religious identities are again the most extreme in that they typically contain prescriptions for literally every aspect of social and personal life, encompassingly declared as "our way of life", with all its economic, political, esthetic, religious, educational, linguistic, etc. components.

Needless to say, this scale and the various dimensions that it analytically ties together allow for (and are in need of) a much more fine-grained graduation of different cases and types of conflicting interests, ideologies, and identities. Also, we must allow for the possibility that interests will just, as it were, "stand for" or are "dressed up" as ideologies or identities, and that conflicts of the two latter kinds can be resolved by someone "bribing" the opponents into peaceful cooperation by satisfying their interests. All these further complexities and possible refinements cannot be pursued here any further, as only the idea of a differential reconcilability of the three types of conflict was to be introduced here.

1.2 Accomodating cleavages of ethnic identities

Taking now the empirical generalization (concerning the weakness of patterned and organized socio-economic conflict of interest) and the analytical proposition (concerning the differential reconcilability of the three categories of conflict) together, we arrive at the rather sobering diagnosis that the type of conflict that is most *easily accommodated* and resolved is at the same time the *least pronounced* and least well structured (although to varying extents) within societies undergoing the process of post-communist transformation. To make things worse, also the reverse is true: those cleavages that are *least well suited* for conflict resolutions within liberal-democratic (or any other known and proven) procedures are in fact dominating the scene. These conflicts divide societies along (a) lines of ethnic belonging and loyalty and (b) along lines of political loyalty to and association with the "old" versus the new regime (Kolarova 1992). Let us consider these divisions in turn, as well as the methods and relative success of coping with them in our four countries. Again, the discussion is guided by the null-hypothesis that the characteristic presence in CEE of strong ideological and identity-based (in contrast to amorphous and rudimentary socio-economic) cleavages will operate as a powerful obstacle to the accomplishment of what we have established (in chapter 1) as the criteria of consolidation, namely vertical and horizontal differentiation. The legacy of strong ideological conflict, as well as the presence of strong ethnic and nationalist commitments and hostilities, renders it particularly difficult to agree on rules that become, once adopted, effectively binding to all, or to institute well-protected and demarcated spheres of autonomous action within civil society.

There are a number of observations that can be generalized about the role of ethnicity and ethnic politics in CEE.

First, the very notion of nationhood in CEE is not Western, "republican," and based upon the common citizenship within the "*demos*," but *ethnic*, cultural, and "Herderian," based upon the distinctive and exclusive identity of the "ethnos." Membership of the nation is based on *jus sanguinis*, not *jus soli*, and belonging to the nation is not primarily a matter of "willing" but of "being."

Second, it is commonly considered and emphasized as part of the national culture and identity in all of our four countries that the nation has been *victimized by imperial powers* – be it by the Ottoman Empire in the case of Bulgaria, the Soviet Union in the case of Hungary and Czechoslovakia, or Nazi Germany in all of these cases. From its beginnings prior to World War I, nationalist movements in CEE were separatist, aiming at the liberation of the nation from the control of imperial powers and the formation of smaller political communities, rather than unificatory (as in Germany and Italy).

Third, and partly as a historical result of such victimization by the Great Powers (epitomized by the Paris treaties imposed upon them after

World War I and the Yalta agreement after World War II), there are strong public sentiments of the nation being *deprived* of some of its legitimate territory, its population, and/or national sovereignty.

Fourth, the geopolitical arrangements resulting from the two post-war settlements have rendered the problem of *minorities* a lasting and often acute issue, with the respective minorities being either *internal* minorities with strong loyalties to a neighboring nation (Turks in Bulgaria, Hungarians in Slovakia – in both cases about 10 percent of the population) or, reciprocally, *external* minorities for whose protection and representation the titular nation claims some degree of responsibility (e.g., Hungary for Hungarians in Slovakia or Romania). As a rule, the presence of these minorities in their respective "inherited" territories and regions of the country is a fact based on a history of many generations (rather than recent immigration with a regionally dispersed pattern of settlement) – a history that has resulted in a "patchwork" distribution of *settled* ethnic communities that precludes any clear-cut territorial-separatist solution to (potential) ethnic conflict. Moreover, the neat distinction that Kymlicka (1995) has drawn between "polyethnic" situations (in which groups strive for cultural expression and self-realization) and "multinational" ones (in which groups desire their independent political incorporation or even secession) does not apply to CEE. As virtually every significant internal minority of any country of the region is at the same time (seen and suspected as) an external minority of a neighboring state (with the Romany being the most important exception to that rule), cultural minority rights (as would befit a polyethnic situation) are not easily granted as, given the alleged "lessons" of "history," such concessions might be turned, with the help of the neighboring "patron state," into dangerous irredentist claims and separatist moves. Thus majorities tend to justify practices of cultural oppression by pointing to the presumed dangers of escalation that would be triggered by granting cultural group rights.

Fifth, and in sharp distinction to subnational ethnic mobilization as it is known from West European cases (such as those of the Basques or the Tyrolians) and their demands for incorporation on the basis of cultural autonomy and regional or federal self-government, ethnic mobilization in CEE is – and has been under communist rule – a matter of *majorities* (namely titular nations trying to control "alien" and presumably potentially disloyal minorities within their population), while political mobilization among minorities was typically not ethnic, but anti-communist in its initial political impetus.

Finally, if surprisingly to some observers, the CEE experience after 1989 provides a vivid and compelling illustration of the rule that: (a)

ethnic-nationalist mobilization *thrives* on the newly won political resources (such as the right to form parties, free elections, and freedom of
the media) of liberal democracy (Alter 1995: 29), while (b) such mobilization, through its concomitant spread of fear, distrust, exclusion, and
repression, is in turn a powerful menace to the *maintenance* of liberal
democracy and its basic principle of equal and "single status" citizenship,
and hence to democratic consolidation in general. In short: Democracy is
good for ethnic mobilization, but not so *vice versa*.

2 Ethnic and other "identity-based" cleavages

Let us now see how and to what extent these challenges of ethnic division
and hostility have been coped with in the four countries under consideration, and how much of the substance of these conflicts has so far defied
its institutional regulation.

2.1 Bulgaria

Slightly less than 10 percent of the Bulgarian population are self-identified
ethnic Turks, mostly settling in two regions of the country. They differ
from the Bulgarian majority in ethnic, linguistic, cultural, as well as
religious respects. The history of their relations with the titular nation is
one of tension, repression, expulsion, and ethnic division of labor, with
the forced mass-emigration of an estimated 300,000 Turks to Turkey in
response to a repressive assimilationist "Bulgarization" policy of the
communist regime in 1984–85 and the mass exodus of Turks in the early
summer of 1989 being a fresh memory. Minority opposition to these
repressive policies, as well as the economically adverse consequences of
the mass exodus, have significantly contributed to the demise of the
communist Zhivkov regime in 1989 (a parallel to Hungarian minority
conflicts as a trigger to the breakdown of the old regime in Romania, cf.
Troebst 1990; Bates 1994). One specificity of the Bulgarian–Turkish case
is that the internal minority does not only share the ethnic identity of a
neighboring state (which is the standard case in the region), but that this
neighboring state is also the successor of the former Ottoman imperial
oppressor[3] that had ruled the country for 500 years and, as seen from the

---

[3] The liberation of the nation from the "Turkish yoke" is being celebrated on the
new national holiday of March 3. The fact that the internal minority is seen as the
external minority of the former oppressor is a feature that can also be observed in
Slovakia and (with qualifications, see below) in the Czech Republic. The most
dramatic consequences of this particular configuration have manifested
themselves, of course, with the Russian minority in the Baltic countries.

perspective of the Warsaw Pact military alliance, a key member of the hostile alliance of NATO. This has added – and continues to add – a connotation of external military security issues to the internal ethnic minority problem.

Apart from the problems of the Turkish minority, there are two additional minority problems surfacing in post-communist Bulgaria. One is the internal religious minority of an estimated 70,000 Pomaks, i.e., ethnic Bulgarians of Islamic religious faith. The other is the existence of an external minority within Macedonia and Serbia of Bulgarian language, a fact that also raises external security problems. It is worth noting that the demarcation lines between ethnicity, language, and religion do not coincide within the population of Bulgaria. For instance, within the second largest ethnic minority of (self-identified) Gypsies (close to 300,000), about three-fifths indicate a Christian and two-fifth an Islamic religious affiliation (Dimitrov 1995b: 177).

The ethnic Turks are represented within the Bulgarian polity by the Movement for Rights and Freedoms (MRF)[4] with a solid ethnic electoral base of 6 to 7 percent of the vote. The political role and even legal existence of this party, however, is rendered precarious by article 11, section 4 of the Bulgarian Constitution which, in the spirit of forging an ethnic community based on the *majority* rights of the titular nation, declares ethnic parties illegal. It was only due to a last minute decision of the Constitutional Court that the MFR was allowed, against the letter of article 3 of the newly adopted "Bill on Parties," to participate in the elections to the Constituent Assembly of June 10, 1990.[5] Apart from their precarious legal status, the MRF is politically isolated – in spite of the fact that it controls the swing vote between the two major parties, the Union of Democratic Forces (UDF) and the Bulgarian Socialist Party (BSP). The MRF cannot form a stable governing alliance with the BSP because of some *de facto* allegiance of the latter with the anti-Turkish policies of the old regime. On the other hand, the UDF cannot afford the MRF as a partner because that would spoil its "national" credentials that are decisive for their electoral success (Dimitrov 1995b: 196). As a consequence of both its legal precariousness and political isolation, the MRF is increasingly torn between a conception of the Turkish

[4] Symptomatically, the movement was denied the right to adopt the name "Movement for Rights and Freedoms of the Turks and Muslims in Bulgaria" through a court decision in 1990 (Kolarova 1992: 10).

[5] Similarly, it was only under the immediate pressure of the Council of Europe and its declared unwillingness to admit Bulgaria as a member that the Constitutional Court legalized the MRF by its decision of April 20, 1992, see also chapter 3, section 2.3.

minority as an external national minority of Turkey (with the implication of the *Turkish* state being the proper agency of representation and protection of the Bulgarian Turks) and, alternatively, an image of the minority as an ethnic group within the Bulgarian republic.

Further uncertainties about the status of the Turkish (and Pomak) minorities are generated by a theory, widely held by ethnic Bulgarian elites and the mass public, that amounts to an outright denial of the historical legitimacy of the identity of the Turkish/Islamic minorities. This theory claims that the alleged "Turks" are actually Bulgarians whose ancestors have been forced by Ottoman rulers to adopt the Islamic faith and Turkish language/identity and whose present-day descendants are just mislead into believing that they are ethnically different. This theory, of course, provides ample legitimation for a politics of re-assimilation aiming at the correction of the "Turkish" minority's deplorable error concerning its own identity; but it also provides the potential for the re-activation of minority militancy inspired by the perceived need to protect the Turkish community from assimilationist pressures and human rights violations.

The overall situation of ethnic conflict in Bulgaria must be considered as provisionally contained, mostly through a politics of undeclared concessions, opportunistic moves, and tacit agreements between the major political actors (Kolarova 1992). But it is by no means consolidated within the framework of stable and consented institutional arrangements and guaranteed rights. The absence of consolidation would be indicated by a situation in which, out of fear of violent clashes between ethnic groups, policies cannot be pursued (e.g., stable coalition governments formed on the basis of elected majorities) that the constitution does permit or mandate; even worse, policies *are* being pursued (e.g., the denial of civic rights without the victims having a recourse to the court system) that the constitution does *not* permit. In either of these cases, there is a breach of the political order in response to what was called in the Spanish case *poderes facticos* – mere factual powers strong enough to unhinge established rights and orderly procedures. Military, religious, and economic connotations of the ethnic divide have all the potential for unsettling a fragile equilibrium that has been maintained in the past, and can only be maintained in the future, through strong doses of internationally provided surveillance and incentives.

2.2 Slovakia

Slovakia is the most ethno-nationalist polity in our sample. The cause of Slovak majority identity and sovereignty was first the driving motive for the dissolution of the federation with the Czech part of the country, effective in January 1993, and then for the increasingly hostile relationship with the Hungarian minority (which not only had opposed the separation from the Czech lands in 1993, but was also seen as a remainder and reminder of the imperial rule and ruthless Magyarization policies by Hungary that lasted for 900 years until 1918). With the populist-nationalist government under the charismatic demagogue Meciar firmly reinstalled through the general elections of Fall 1994, and with the two coalitions parties of the ruling Movement for a Democratic Slovakia (HZDS) being positioned, respectively, on the far right (Slovak National Party) and the far left (Union of Slovak Workers), majority nationalism and the defense of the nation against its alleged enemies has become the unifying agenda of the governing forces. This commitment is also highlighted by the letter and spirit of the new Slovak constitution which, according to its preamble, is authored not by "We, the citizens of the Slovak Republic" (as in its draft version), but by "We, the Slovak People" (Rhodes 1995: 359). It is also the most radical among the generally rather "communitarian" interpretations that the new CEE constitutions extend to the concept of citizenship (Preuss 1995) in that it goes beyond the Bulgarian constitution (which, oddly enough, states in its Art. 36 that the use of the Bulgarian language is "an obligation" of every Bulgarian citizen) by saying, in its Art. 34, that minorities have "the right to learn the official language" – thus creating the mildly absurd suggestion that such a right could possibly be withheld from anybody and that the nation of Slovak speakers were generous to share its sacred symbolic capital with non-nationals!

Nor has this strong emphasis on protecting the substance of ethnic nationhood remained a matter of declaration of principles. The practical steps into which it has been translated include the dismissal of Hungarians from government positions; the Slovakization requirement for Hungarian names for official registries that was temporarily effective; the proposed declaration of a prominent Hungarian who had expressed critical views of Slovak government policies as *persona non grata*; and, above all, the delay in the ratification of a basic treaty with Hungary, which was provisionally signed by the two prime ministers under intensive pressures from European institutions in March 1995, through the governing coalition of the Slovak parliament.

The key term around which Slovak domestic and international politics appears to revolve is that of "protection": protection of religion and culture from Western liberalism, protection of the language through the limitation of linguistic minority rights, protection of the Slovak minority within those southern regions where ethnic Hungarians form a majority, protection of the honor and international reputation of the nation from the alleged efforts of critical journalists to stain it, protection of the state's property from being exposed to an overly rapid process of privatization, protection of Slovak producers from international (in particular Czech) competitors, protection of the national energy resources (among them the Gobcikovo hydroelectric dam project) from Hungarian and other international obstruction, and, not least, protection of the coherence of the ruling coalition and its leader through a regime of personal favors extended to friends and ruthless punitive action extended to foes (cf. Rosenberger 1993; Bútora and Bútorová 1993). As a consequence, numerous domestic opposition politicians as well as international observers and political leaders have expressed intense concerns that the Slovak politics of identity may threaten to destroy the rights and procedures on which a liberal democratic political order is built.

2.3 Czech Republic

The Czech Republic is unique in the region in many respects – not least for the fact that it is the only country that neither has a significant internal minority connected through ties of loyalty to any neighbor (which excludes the strong Romany minority[6]) nor a significant external minority whose members settle "across the border." The internal ethnic problems of bi-national Czechoslovakia was resolved when, effective from January 1993, the Czech and Slovak parts of the country formed fully separate states. The only ethnic problem – as opposed to the largely regionalist problem concerning the extent to which Moravians and others should be granted the powers of regional self-government (Rhodes 1995: 352–56) – of the Czech Republic derives from the fact that it *used* to have

---

[6] The number of Gypsies residing within the Czech Republic is estimated at 200,000, with the usual doubts applying to such quantitative assessments of strongly dis-privileged minorities. Apart from massive cultural, political, and also legal discrimination, the situation of Czech Gypsies has dramatically worsened after the adoption of the Czech citizenship law of December 29, 1992. This law makes the granting of citizenship (and social transfers reserved for citizens) contingent upon (a) two years of residence in Czech territory and (b) a clean criminal record for the last five years. As either or both of these condition cannot be met by many Gypsies, many of whom are post-war immigrants from what is now Slovakia and hence have still been officially registered as "Slovak," there is now a sizeable population of non-citizens within the Czech Republic. The poor level of social and cultural integration of Gypsies is highlighted by the fact that to the question whether "even among the Gypsies, many decent people are to be found," not more than 53 percent of the Czechs surveyed gave an affirmative answer (Brenner 1995: 97; Edgington 1994).

a strong and significant internal minority of ethnic Germans – the Sudeten. The vast majority of the Sudeten was expropriated and expelled from the country on the basis of the Benes decrees of 1945. These decrees, in turn, were based on the summary presumption of all German residents having been part of (and hence collectively guilty of) Nazi crimes and must be summarily punished through expropriation and expulsion. Today, there is just a tiny minority of Germans residing within the Czech Republic, numbering 53,000 persons and hardly visible as a minority in terms of culture and politics (Brenner 1995). Yet the German ethnic minority problem, while seemingly being a matter of the past, still ranks very high on the present domestic political agenda, as well as burdening the bilateral and transnational relations involving Germany and the Czech Republic – relations that appear more strained in 1996 than those between Germany and any of its other neighbors in the region.

This issue (together with its setting within a fascinating interaction of reason, passions and interests, of the past, the present, and the future, of national and international problems, and of state and non-state collective actors) cannot be fully explored here. Considerations such as the following shape the dynamics of the issue. From the Czech point of view, there are presently unsurmountable difficulties to recognize in binding ways that the Benes decrees were null and void from the beginning, as they have lacked any basis in national or international law that would legitimize the momentous consequences inflicted by these decrees on the German minority. The reasons that stand in the way of such recognition are obvious: the hurt feelings of a nation humiliated and occupied by the murderous regime of Nazi Germany; the fears of governing elites that such hurt feelings, if further hurt by an official recognition of the nullity of the decrees, might lead to a mobilization of far right and far left political forces who jointly would be able to upset the balance of political forces as it emerged after 1989; and the economic concerns that an admission of the illegality of the decrees would automatically lead to a huge wave of German restitution claims[7] and a virtual German takeover of much of the Czech economy – a danger that is already seen by some to be implied in the new openness of the border between the two states. For all these fears and passions, a dispassionate formal-legal assessment of the decrees and the admission of their invalidity is an act that must appear close to suicidal to any segment of the governing elite of the Czech Republic. On the other hand, the German government, apart from being exposed to some pressure coming from the Sudeten associations, does

---

[7] As to the amount of such potential claims, the truly breathtaking figure of DM 265 bn has been cited (Bren 1994).

not consider itself to be in a legal position to renounce restitution claims on behalf of those having been dispossessed of their property, because that would make the government itself liable to such claims. The German government has also tied the issue of reparation payments to Czech victims of occupation and war to a resolution of the Sudeten issue.

Taken together, these political and economic considerations amount to a seemingly insuperable obstacle to casting the highly explosive substance of conflict into any procedural form of conflict resolution and reconciliation. In spite of the fact that not only the justice, but also the wisdom of the post-war Czechoslovak state to rid itself of no less than a quarter of its population (and, by implication, of its multi-cultural qualities) have been intensely questioned by Czech intellectual and other elites throughout the post-war era (Adams 1995), the current Czech leadership is literally in a bind dictated by the facts of the domestic configuration of political power. Although the Czech Constitutional Court in its decision of March 8, 1995 has declared President Benes' decree on the "confiscation of hostile property" (which, in its view, implied that it was not directed against a national group, i.e., the Sudeten Germans, as such) "legal and legitimate" and hence an integral part of the present Czech legal order, the matter remains politically and morally unsettled. What remains, is officially suggested silence on the issue, a quasi-official ban of the very word "expulsion" from public use, and various dilatory moves that political elites have undertaken in order to buy time – a quintessential case of an identity-based conflict in the, so far futile, search of an uncontested procedure for its reconciliation.

2.4 Hungary

Although numerous, the ethnic minorities in Hungary are small and comparatively well integrated into the Hungarian society and polity. To the extent ethnic problems exist in Hungary, they are largely a matter of the protection that Hungarian governments wish to extend to the cultural autonomy of (up to 5 million) Hungarians living abroad. The vast majority of Hungary's external minorities live in Rumania, Slovakia, Serbia, and the Ukraine. International treaties on the legal status of these Hungarian minorities have been negotiated and (partly, as of late 1995) ratified by the Hungarian parliament, but not so by the parliaments of the nations in which these minorities live, most significantly Slovakia and Rumania. As far as the consolidation of the Hungarian polity is concerned, it seems safe to assume that no negative effects are to be expected from these unresolved questions of the status of external minorities, and that, moreover, the positive and negative sanctioning power of the Council of Europe and other European transnational organization will be sufficient to prevent any violent international territorial conflict to emerge. Thus Hungary is the only country in our sample in which identity conflicts do not stand in the way of consolidation.

3 Politico-ideological cleavages

3.1 Bulgaria

The post-war history of Bulgaria is different from all the other CEE countries in that the communist regime of this country is the only one that has never been involved in a conflict with Soviet political, military, and ideological hegemony. What is missing in the history of the country is both any notorious domestic regime crisis (of the type being crushed by Warsaw Pact "fraternal assistance" in Budapest and elsewhere) *and* any "elite deviance," as it occurred in the field of economic policy in Hungary since the early seventies or in Romanian foreign policy. Bulgarians, it seems, were atypically faithful to their communist leadership, and the leadership in its turn unusually faithful to the policies of the Soviet imperial center – so much so that for some time even the formal incorporation of the country into the Soviet Union was entertained as a plan by the party leadership.[8] In fact, the regime change of November 1989 is widely seen, both by outside observers as from within Bulgaria, as having largely been an intra-party "factional coup" carried out by members of the communist party in an attempt to preserve the political leadership of the party (Melone 1994: 259).

As a consequence of the fact that the communist leadership was evidently firmly rooted in large segments of Bulgarian society, the Bulgarian Socialist party remained strong in the founding elections of June 1990, as it drew the overwhelming support from the elderly, the less educated, and the populations of small towns, and villages (Tzvetkov 1992: 34). The renamed communists thrived and continue to thrive on the promise of protecting those most vulnerable to the consequences of the economic decline that followed the breakdown of the old regime, and these target populations have developed an evidently robust preference for dealing with "the devil you know," which is unsurprising given the

---

[8] This dual loyalty may be attributed, among other things, to the vividly remembered fact that it has been, back in 1877, the military initiative of Tzarist Russia that helped the nation to liberate itself from what still today is routinely referred to in Bulgaria as the "Turkish yoke."

vast material, administrative, and manpower resources that remained under the control of the successor party. In addition to protectionist and clientelistic advances, part of the politically successful appeal of the BSP has also been a strong emphasis on majority-ethnicity, i.e., on protecting the Bulgarian titular nation from some perceived "Turkish threat." The party also benefits from the fact that it controls, in addition to key administrative positions, those in the top management of the reluctantly privatized state industries – a mode of transferring property titles for which the term "nomenklatura privatization" has gained currency. As a consequence, political and economic elite continuity in Bulgaria is probably greater than in any other post-communist country of the region, as being a party cadre was not a liability, but rather an important asset that turned out to be convertible into power and privilege after 1989.

The relative strength[9] of the BSP can also be attributed to the weakness of the non-communist parties, most of them still allied within the loose and ideologically highly heterogeneous league of parties Union of Democratic Forces (UDF) that has so far not been able to extricate itself from the bind of a predominantly negative, i.e., anti-communist programmatic orientation. The question of friend and foe continues to be answered in categories inherited from the old regime. It can be said that the Bulgarian case of post-communist political modernization is, among the countries in our sample, clearly that which runs most markedly behind schedule – if the schedule is assumed to be one of the rapid pluralization of a party system that was only initially dominated by the communism/anti-communism ideological cleavages but then rapidly splits up into a "modern" party system that is to be mapped along the familiar left–right and liberal–conservative axes. In Bulgaria, that initial cleavage seems to be frozen, as the major axis of political conflict is, as late as 1995, still the divide between the BSP (holding the majority in government) and the UDF alliance, with the same ideological conflict dividing the BSP controlled government and the presidency supported by the anti-communist forces. In the same ideological polarity is cast the debate over whether decommunization or rather "recommunization" is taking place, the policies of higher education, of restitution, etc. Virtually every political issue is coded in terms of the conflict between the "old" and the "new" forces, leaving little space for differentiation and competition

---

[9] This strength has symptomatically not suffered from the fact that the first socialist prime minister after 1990, Petur Mladenov, had to resign over a statement by which he advocated the violent crushing of the November 1989 demonstrations by military means.

among the latter. The lasting dominance of this often embittered decommunization issue (together with the temporarily dormant ethnicity issue), in the heat of which the bindingness of procedural rules (such as the division of powers between the presidency and the parliament) are likely to evaporate, can be explained in terms of the dismal economic situation of the country which does not allow for an autonomous pursuit of economic interests to unfold. "The fact that the space for economic maneuver is small may help explain the displacement of political debate to questions of 'decommunization' and the claims of nationalism" (Baylis 1994: 325).

In Bulgaria – as similarly also in Slovakia – a style of political argument and political conflict prevails that differs sharply from what citizens and elites are accustomed to in consolidated democracies. Its ingredients are a passionate, expressive and often alarmist tone of political debate; the resort of elites to "non-conventional" forms of political action, such as walkout from sessions of parliament, signature campaigns, sensitive memorial celebrations meant to provoke political enemies, mass petitions, calls for referenda, and purely symbolic parliamentary acts;[10] the widespread use of suspicions and accusations of conspiracy and corruption by elite members against other elite members and parties, with the subsequent relatively frequent turnover of the personnel of key government agencies through dismissal (e.g., for "technical and moral incompetence") or resignation. Rival elites groups often seem to be at war with each other, as well as with those segments of the media they do not control. The logic of political conflict is virtually the same as that known from the old regime: the clash of some "correct line" with the line of "traitors" or conspiring "enemies." They also tend to exploit the tensions that are built into any system of divided powers to the utmost. A sequence that was repeated several times on important pieces of legislation in the course of the year 1995 is this: the government submits a draft law to parliament; parliament passes the law over constitutional objections of the opposition; the bill is then submitted to the president for signature; the president vetoes the bill for alleged procedural or substantive deficiencies; parliament votes again and overrules the presidential veto; the president submits it to the Constitutional Court, which declares the law unconstitutional; whereupon the governing party declares the Court its political enemy and the president publicly warns of the danger

[10] A case in point is the majority of the Slovak parliament (National Council) taking a vote of no confidence against the president on May 5, 1995. This vote, even had it been supported unanimously, would have remained evidently and entirely inconsequential, as voting the president in and out of office does not belong to the constitutional responsibilities of the Council.

of "re-communization." This logic of confrontation, escalation, and relentless exploitation of positional advantages is often not visibly mitigated by the willingness to engage in assurance games, enter into bargaining, or to accept rules as effectively binding.

3.2 Slovakia

If residues of the state socialist order play a role in Slovakia, they do so more on the mass level than on the elite level. To be sure, the Slovak prime minister is a former communist. There are even strong indications that he has served as an agent of the secret police StB (Abrahám 1995: 96). His nationalist-populist party HZDS depends for the parliamentary majority it controls on the post-communist Union of Slovak Workers (ZRS). Also, the rule of the communist party was more firmly rooted in Slovakia than in the Czech lands, as there were fewer purges during the period of "normalization" after 1968 in the former, where also prominent former communists remained active in politics. The communist regime has never been challenged in the Slovak part of the CSSR to any extent as was the case in the Czech part of the country, particularly in Prague. The 1968 vision of "socialism with a human face" was entirely a Czech, not a Slovak phenomenon. Whatever the ultimate motivation (or, for that matter, unintended dynamics) of the "velvet divorce" in December 1992 may have been, there is no doubt that part of this dynamics was the "rising Slovak opposition to rapid and deep reforms" and the desire to establish a political "basis for subsequently avoiding them" (Higley and Pakulski 1995: 425). According to one more specific interpretation of the motives behind the 1992 independence campaign staged by Meciar is that he and his supporters sought to escape the reach of the lustration law (Abrahám 1995: 95).

On the other hand, an explicit state socialist rhetoric is rarely resorted to by the government, which seems to have largely replaced it with a nationalist-protectionist one. This rhetoric has won the coalition significant electoral support (of an aggregate 47.6 percent) in the 1994 election. It is this broad *mass* support that needs to be accounted for. According to Bútora and Bútorová (1993), the mass support for statist, collectivist, and authoritarian policies can be accounted for in terms of the mental residues that the state socialist past has left behind. People have become used to protection and want it to last, particularly in predictably hard times. They have acquired under the old regime attitudes of "learned helplessness" and "social infantilism" (Bútora and Bútorová 1993). Another author describes the *leitmotifs* of domestic politics as a sense of betrayal, fatalism, and ignorance (Abrahám 1995). Protection can only be provided by a strong state, and objections against authoritarian forms of rule have little base in the political culture and history of the country. State socialism, according to this reading, survives not so much on the level of state and party as on the level of the micro-structures of the insulated and alienated life world of the population that is frightened by the winds of change. If anything, its antipathy to statist authoritarianism is significantly milder compared with that of the Czech Republic. Reforms are seen at least as much as threatening as they are seen as promising. Isolation from the West and the constantly invoked topic of being victimized by the Czechs (and before that, the Hungarians) provide the fertile soil for demands that privatization must proceed differently (meaning: more slowly and to a more limited extent) in Slovakia than it did in the Czech Republic, with the resulting economic order being envisaged as one that is "neither socialist nor capitalist," as Meciar has put it as late as 1993.

These dispositions inherent in the Slovak post-communist political culture have been successfully exploited by the charismatic, highly confrontational, and impulsive leader Meciar and his far left and far right coalition partners, in contrast to which the opposition parties (Social Democrats, the liberal Democratic Union (DU), and the conservative Christian Democrats (KDH)) seem virtually marginalized, i.e., without a chance of forming a majority alliance among themselves or with any of the parties of the governing bloc. With its ruthless pursuit of monopolistic control the governing coalition has been not only against its political opponents, but also against the supposedly "countervailing" powers and spheres of agency that the constitution provides for (such as the presidency, the media, the judiciary, the education system and the privatization agency "National Property Fund"); the power struggle is in constant danger of turning into a struggle *over* the form and the constitutional foundations of the regime itself. As the top judiciary of both the Supreme Court and the Constitutional Court, including the Prosecutor General, has been turned into loyal tools of the governing bloc, "very little protects either the Constitution or the democratic structure from the attacks of the victorious politician" (Abrahám 1993: 91). The cleavages that shape political life in Slovakia are entirely "historical"; they divide, in a unique amalgamation of ideological and identity-based issues, one camp that entertains favorable references to both the state socialist regime *and* the fascist Slovak Tiso-Republic (1938–44), and one minority camp in which *all* the conventional political forces of a liberal democracy are confined. In such a configuration of forces, any appeal to power-constraining rules and liberties is branded as divisive and "anti-Slovak" by the ruling bloc (Bútora and Bútorová, 1993:

717). Invoking constitutionally codified rules (such as the division of powers between the prime minister and the president) is considered a virtual betrayal, and politically punished accordingly. More than any other country in our sample, Slovakia approximates what in the typology suggested by Higley and Pakulski (1995: 416) is termed "takeovers by ultra-nationalist regimes through coups or plebiscitary victories, with regimes becoming state-corporatist in form and quasi-fascist in operation."

3.3 Czech Republic

The Czech Republic is the only country in our sample (and in the region as a whole) that has maintained an un-renamed communist party. At the same time, and arguably for the same set of reasons, it is the country that has cut itself loose most energetically from the ideological residues and legacies of communism. Party communism, far from being a hegemonic popular force under the old regime, has left behind a de-politicized and alienated civil society that emerged entirely unprepared, if we disregard for the moment its tiny dissident elites, from the sudden and unexpected *tabula rasa* situation of late 1989. The famous lustration law of 1991 (cf. Offe 1994: chapter 8) was designed to make a vast number of party cadres ineligible for appointment to higher positions in virtually all institutional sectors for five years, without the benefit of individualized court proceedings and other rule-of-law guarantees. The rigorism with which the Czech government has eradicated and punished former communist functionaries is unparalleled in any other post-communist country (with the possible exception of the GDR); it has been strongly criticized as an act of witch-hunting leading to a negative criterion for elite recruitment, with the decisive qualification of a person for a position often residing in the fact that she/he has *not* been part of or linked to the party's nomenklatura (von Beyme 1993: 411).

3.4 Hungary

Of all CEE communist parties, the Hungarian one was the earliest to enter into a process of economic and political reforms. Not only was the political elite of Hungary highly professional and reformist as early as 1989; it was also disposed toward cooperation with the country's counter-elite (Andorka 1993). As a consequence of this early and daring elite reformism, the ruling party became not only an influential partner in the Round Table Talks of 1989–90, but also was able to transform itself and to win, as a basically reformed social democratic party, decisive electoral support and the mandate to lead a left-liberal coalition government of Gyula Horn in 1994. But as early as 1990, the "political programs of the six parties represented in parliament show no important differences" (Andorka 1993: 369). One of the unique features of the Hungarian transition, the origin of which dates back to the brutal crushing of the popular revolt in 1956 and the intense memories of these events, is the fact that the major (if not particularly deep) political divide after 1989 is not that between communist and non-communist political forces, but between the (effectively marginalized) communist hardliners and all the proponents of transformation, among them a number of prominent "communists". Hence neither the call for wholesale purges nor the conservative effort to resist and escape purges has been a major topic on the agenda of Hungarian transition politics. It is only with the rather exceptional Hungarian experience of a consistent centripetal self-transformation of the old party elite in mind that one can postulate a lawlike emergence of competent and professional post-communist political elites (cf. Agh 1995: 435).

4 Conclusion

The argument advanced in this chapter is that, among the three families of cleavages spelled out at the beginning, the identity-based and ideological ones constitute significant obstacles to consolidation. Inversely, the materials presented in the previous chapters also strongly suggest that institutionalized conflict over economic control and the distribution of income and security will strongly contribute to favorable effects upon consolidation, as (non-ideological forms of) "class conflict" has a much greater potential for reconcilability and as class conflict tends to supersede and neutralize the two other families of cleavages the longer it is being practised. We would thus expect (and, in fact, conclude from materials analyzed in earlier chapters) that the successful completion of privatization, the installation of a private property regime with its legal framework, the building of encompassing and comparatively non-ideological associations representing primarily workers and employers, but also small business, professionals, and the agrarian sector is conducive to consolidation and inversely related to the intensity of ideological and identity-based cleavages. In fact, the incidence of strikes that are considered as legitimate, the presence of non-political associations of workers, employers, and investors, and the elaboration of a property rights regime are all more advanced and less contested in the two countries in which consolidation is least put in jeopardy by the prevalence of identity and ideological cleavages concerning the very form of the regime.

As far as the role of identity-based and ideological conflict is concerned, as well as their negative impact upon what we have defined as "consolidation" in chapter 1, our four countries are clearly to be subdivided in two groups: Czech Republic and Hungary are the "easy" cases, and Slovakia and Bulgaria the "difficult" and precarious ones. What are the commonalities and differences between these two groups? Five of such inter-group differences can be identified.

(1) Per-capita GNP is considerably higher in the favorable than in the unfavorable group of cases. This relatively advanced economic situation correlates with the predominant type of conflict, which tends to be much more of a distributional and class politics sort in the Czech Republic and Hungary than in Bulgaria and Slovakia. The causal interpretation of this correlation can plausibly operate in either direction. One of them would suggest that economic prosperity leads to an emphasis upon the distributional type of conflict; the other states that it is a necessary condition of economic growth that identity-based and ideological conflicts are largely bracketed, with the main emphasis being on distributional ones, which allow for a binding procedural framework of conflict resolution to be widely accepted as valid, which in turn allows for a steady flow of investment.

(2) The two favorable countries are those without a significant minority population being present in the state's territory. The two poorly consolidated countries do have such minorities. Moreover, these minorities are relics of a past during which the respective countries, Slovakia and Bulgaria, were oppressed and marginalized components of an empire dominated by the nation of the present minority for almost 500 and 900 years, respectively. The significance that is presently attributed to this past is what makes the emphasis placed upon the identity of the (majority, or titular) nation so salient and hence exacerbates the ethnic cleavage. The long arm of the past shapes present divisions and lines of conflict.

(3) The two favorable countries have the experience of relatively stable democracies in the inter-war period, as well as significant accomplishments of industrialization prior to World War II. It may make a difference that this period was ended, in the case of the Czech lands, through an internationally sponsored decision that allowed the Czech part of the country to fall victim to Nazi occupation, whereas the Slovak part of the country was elevated to the status of becoming a nominally independent Republic under the auspices of Nazi Germany.

(4) The two favorable countries have, in their less distant past (namely in 1956 and 1968, respectively) undergone the deeply shocking experience of Warsaw Pact troops crushing popular uprisings and reformist movements and restoring the Soviet-designed order by the use of tanks. It was the irreversible and cumulative loss of legitimacy and credibility of state socialism and its monopolistic party that allowed this party to maintain a mere facade of legitimacy in the Czech Republic (and forced it on to a course of reform and self-revision in Hungary), but which prevented the ideology of state socialism to play any divisive role in the two countries' politics after 1989. In contrast, Bulgaria and Slovakia are the two countries that have arguably been those in which state socialism was most firmly rooted, and in which dissident and opposition forces arose the latest and were weakest. To put it somewhat simplistically: While, in the more consolidated countries, the hegemony of state socialism was, as a matter of fact, defeated *prior* to its actual demise, the cleavage that it imposed upon society and the more than residual legitimacy accorded to it is still to be overcome long *after* its formal demise in the other two countries.

(5) Finally, the two groups of countries show some remarkable similarities and differences. As to Bulgaria and Slovakia, the components of a party system that we are used to and would normally expect in a capitalist democracy, i.e., an assortment of social democratic, liberal, Christian, conservative and perhaps green-libertarian political parties, are all present but at the same time locked into a shared structural minority position. The tactical alliance (such as the UDF) they feel compelled to form within this position of shared marginality hinders the articulation of policy ideas and their assimilation within civil society, and therefore the unfolding of competition. Here, political control and electoral success remains in the hands of a quasi-monopolistic successor-party (BG) or in those of the coalition put together by Meciar in Slovakia, with any coalition bridge being built across this master divide appearing next to impossible in either case. In contrast, the politics of competition, coalition, and opposition have unfolded in Hungary and the Czech Republic, with questions of the old vs. the new regime having largely all but evaporated from the domestic politics of these two countries.

As to the question of rank-ordering the countries *within* our two groups, there remains by necessity a space for interpretive discretion. If consolidation means, as suggested before, that the rules governing the accommodation of conflict are treated as "given" by conflicting agents, and if it also means the presence of clearly demarcated domains of action that are both independent from each other and interconnected through "horizontal" communication, then Hungary seems to rank somewhat higher on the scale than the Czech Republic. Nuances between the two could be claimed to exist with reference, on the one hand, to the unusually robust role that Hungary's Constitutional Court has played in constraining governmental or parliamentary ambitions, and, on the other, to the spirit of the "lustration" purges and the confrontational ideological rhetoric that is still occasionally being employed in Czech domestic as well as international politics. The latter case is illustrated by the failure of the Czech government to both recognize and use the rules and tools of international law for a negotiated settlement of the Sudeten issue prior to the elections scheduled for May 1996.

As to rank-ordering in the second group of countries, the following aspects suggest a somewhat higher ranking of Bulgaria compared with Slovakia, notwithstanding our earlier statement that, with respect to political modernization, Bulgaria runs most markedly behind schedule. Ethnic and religious conflict seems to be largely contained within conciliatory agreements that have been worked out with the Turkish minority and its political party, the MRF. The tactics of the BSP government are less confrontational, charismatic, and populist than those of Meciar's HZDS government. Bulgaria's Constitutional Court has played a much more activist and independent role than its counterpart in Slovakia. And president Zhelev's position is better entrenched and less vulnerable than that of president Kovac. While the BSP government is clearly inspired by strong ideological commitments which has led it repeatedly to attempted violations of the constitutionally established "horizontal" differentiation, it has not waged the relentless nationalist war of words and deeds against political opponents and constitutional organs that has been the mark of Slovakia's Meciar government elected in 1994.

8

Conclusion: the unfinished project

1 Criteria and prerequisites of consolidation

Five years after the collapse of the communist rule all countries under
study have undergone considerable changes. Each of them experienced
two peaceful national elections which entailed non-violent change or
confirmation, respectively, of the governments; they have established
parliaments, a competitive pluralist party system, administrative agencies
under the control of the government, and independent courts. Private
banks and the stock exchange are operating, basic institutions of social
security provide their services; in none of them do we find major
political forces which advocate the return to the old order, and none of
them must be identified as a hybrid in which the new order is still
heavily contaminated with elements of the old regime (Schmitter 1994).
Yet, our analysis of the four countries under study provides a less
straightforward answer to the question of whether the goal of the
transition process – consolidated democratic institutions and the essential elements of a capitalist market economy – has been successfully
accomplished by all of them. The gauge by which we measure success is
the concept of consolidation as expounded in the first chapter,[1] impli-
cating such basic (though hard to individualize) pre-constitutional
ingredients as a balance of conflict and consent, of particularism and

---

[1] Cf. for more or less divergent concepts of consolidation O'Donell 1992; v. Beyme
1994; Haggard and Kaufmann 1994.

common good orientation, and of self-interested competitiveness and trust.[2]

Many observers of the transformation processes in CEE (including some of the authors of this book at the start of the project) were quite pessimistic about the ability and the chances of the post-communist societies to meet this standard and to establish a sustainable development democracy-*cum*-market economy (Elster 1990; Offe 1991). They anticipated the bleak prospect of a vicious circle which they feared might appear in either of two variants: according to one version the unrestrained use of democratic freedoms would undermine any national program of economic recovery because the citizens would use their newly acquired voting power to remove out of office every government that dared to impose on them economic and social hardships; governments would anticipate this reaction and abstain from profound reforms, which would prevent economic recovery, increase public debts, spur inflation, eventually give rise to profound disappointment of the masses in the results of the transformation, undermine the construction of democratic institutions altogether and finally breed the quest for some kind of authoritarian restoration. Pursuant an alternative scenario, the unrestrained use of state power to impose economic reform of the "shock therapy" kind on society irrespective of the social costs would necessarily provoke active or passive resistance of society against the reform and at the same time cause a considerable number of people to live in poverty and even in misery. In the last instance this would not only destroy the basic elements of democratic solidarity, but would also undermine the emergence of the plurality of social institutions through which individuals participate in the active shaping of society and realize their sense of responsibility for the common good. This in turn would strengthen the tendencies toward social atomization and political authoritarianism and prevent society from developing into a democratic polity. Finally, in the most extreme cases the overall weakness of political and economic institutions and the lack of trust in them and the new elites could generate a degree of collective frustration that could only be appeased through a nationalist construction of collective identity and the concomitant fabrication of national enemies.

The results of our research show that fortunately neither of these hypotheses has come true in their extremely pessimistic versions. In particular, the assumptions about the mutual blockade of economic and

---

[2] The significance of mutual trust both among citizens and toward basic social and political institutions is analyzed by Richard Rose 1994; Samuel P. Huntington 1968, and the empirical approach of R. Markowski 1994.

political reform have proven to be far too bleak – at least as they concern the CEE countries outside the territories of the former Soviet Union. With the benefit of hindsight we can observe, that the cumulation of two of the three reform tasks which we identified – economic and political reform – have had a triggering and encouraging effect in all four countries under study in that immediately after the breakdown of the old regime both the new elites and the masses had a clear sense that radical and painful changes were necessary for a new beginning.[3] Admittedly, this tolerance of economic decline and frequently social misery did only persist uncompromisingly in the Czech Republic, and even there it subsided clearly in 1996 (when the Klaus coalition lost its absolute majority in the elections of June 1996, while the Social Democratic Party which appealed largely to the losers of the reform quadrupled its votes, thus coming close to the strength of Klaus' conservative-liberal ODS which, however, remains the strongest single political party of the Czech Republic); but also in Bulgaria, Hungary, and Slovakia where the governments had to yield to widespread popular feelings of frustration, economic reforms were slowed down, but never entirely stalled. As we shall argue in the final section of this chapter, the institutional channels for a democratic abolition of the economic reform and for democracy altogether are more difficult to use than many skeptics anticipated.

This is not to say that the transition processes of all countries under study display in all areas which we examined – the constitutions, the political institutions, the economies, and the welfare systems – outcomes which we could readily consider to be consolidated, much less as fully satisfying in terms of consolidation. The more or less smooth "technical" or "positivist" operation of the newly established economic and political institutions as such is a necessary, but not a sufficient condition of consolidation. Here a reminder of what we said earlier[4] about the lack of transformative interests typical of the transition from communism to a democratic society seems appropriate. While in all post-communist societies the transformation process has quickly engendered the constitutional and legal forms of the *representation* of interests, those very interests are at best in the making and still more or less in their incipient formation. Domains of agency are reasonably sharply demarcated, but no agents on the scene willing or capable to perform the respective roles and functions within those demarcation lines. Thus, the new elites, having

---

[3] Cf. the analysis about the interrelations between economic and political reform Bönker 1995.
[4] Chapter 1, section 3; chapter 2, section 3.

full control over the symbolic forms of interest representation (Ionin 1994), are still in search of the interests which they could represent. The creation of social agency which we regard as the primary purpose and indicator of consolidation can be described as the completion of a process in which the newly available symbolic forms of social representation – be they political, cultural, or legal – are "filled" with the social interests for whose articulation and representation these forms have been created in the first place.[5] Consolidation is endangered where, as we analyzed in more detail,[6] "categorical" conflicts over identity prevail over interest conflicts along socio-economic class lines. Obviously the origination of a reform constituency would be the most important precondition for the making of collective social agents which are not just playing with the symbolic forms but are able to organize and satisfy the real problems of society.

In the following section (2) we give a brief account of the results of the transition processes in the four countries under study in each of the fields of our investigation. In the final section (3) we will try to give some explanations for the differences which we found.

2 Evaluation of the outcomes of the transition process in the four countries under study

2.1 Bulgaria

Given the historical and sociological background of Bulgaria, it is surprising that the country was (together with Rumania) the fastest constitution-maker in that region and enacted no later than in July 1991 a completely new constitution. Yet while we may assume that among the political elites the idea of constitutionalism is in very high esteem, its practice is to a large extent still quite poor. Protracted struggles over the independence of the judiciary between the then majority of the parliament (BSP plus Movement for Rights and Freedoms) and judicial bodies revealed, to say the least, a lack of sensitivity of the majority for the

---

[5] Ionin 1994, reports about a group of students who in 1991 in the center of Moscow formed a picketing line demanding the release of "all political prisoners." Asked by a radio reporter whether there were any political prisoners in the Soviet Union their spokesman admitted that they did not know for sure, but that the Soviet Union's history renders this possibility quite probable, and that therefore their slogan was justified. He added that due to the people's lack of reaction to their demonstration they were thinking about carrying it on next day with other slogans and demands.

[6] Chapter 7, section 1; see also chapter 4, section 3.3.

independence of the judicial bodies.[7] On the other hand, the anti-communist SDS showed a limited understanding of the constitutional function of the parliament when they – incidentally, not for the first time[8] – boycotted it for several weeks and at the same time blamed the majority for acting unconstitutionally because it lacked the necessary quorum.[9] These turbulences in the sphere of the parliament are not safely checked by the Constitutional Court whose role is still unclear. It has been observed that it has acted "more as a moderator than an active participant" (Kolarova 1993). This means, that it has not yet gained a position of uncontested superiority over the actors of the political game,[10] although it has clearly proven its independence in highly controversial cases (Kolarova 1993: 50). Yet, the institutional integrity of the Court is not beyond question in all political camps. Regular changes in the Court's composition made it appear in the political majority's eyes as "anti-BSP," which inspired a BSP MP to introduce a draft law which envisaged cutting the salaries of the justices and the abolition of their right to retire after the termination of their mandate. A more serious attack on the independence of the judiciary was the BSP-sponsored budget law which allowed the Council of minsters to restrict the budget of the Judicial Council (the self-government body of the judiciary). The law was declared unconstitutional by the Constitutional Court;[11] yet it is not likely that the Court was able to nullify the bent which inspired this undertaking in the first place.

Despite the political turmoils the economy of the country performed quite well in 1994. Although the World Bank delayed the payments of credits during the time of the resignation of the Berov government and the formation of a new government after the elections of December 1994 the industrial output went up by about 4.5 percent against 1993, the

---

[7] EECR Summer/Fall 1994 (= Vol. III/3 and 4), pp. 5 ff.; Engelbrekt 1995, 19–22. The draft law, parts of which were finally declared unconstitutional by the Constitutional Court allowed, among other things, the removal of justices in case of "behaviour that destroys the prestige of the judiciary." It stipulated requirements for senior positions in the judiciary which could only be fulfilled by formerly high-ranking communists, and it aimed at the immediate removal of the then prosecutor general and the chairman of the Supreme Court who had been appointed by the preceding government.

[8] See chapter 4.

[9] EECR Summer/Fall 1994 (=Vol. III/3, 4), pp. 5 f.

[10] Thus, the government and the BSP-dominated majority in the parliament defied the decision of the Constitutional Court about the unconstitutionality of the removal of incumbent judges from the Supreme Judicial Council and elected new members, see EECR Summer/Fall 1994 (Vol. III/3 and 4), p. 6.

[11] EECR Fall 1995 (Vol. IV/4), pp. 7 ff.

balance of payments reached a $277–million surplus against a $322–million deficit of the last year, and imports into the EU increased (Engelbrekt 1995:20). However, these momentary data are no conclusive evidence for economic recovery under consolidated conditions of a market economy. Most crucial is the lack of a reform constituency, i.e., individual and collective actors which comprise a significant portion of the population and who are inspired by the confidence that they will ultimately benefit from steps toward political and economic modernization. Given the lack of "transformative" interests which we identified as one of the characteristic traits of the anti-communist changes of 1989, it is obvious that the reform constituency has still to be created in and through the very process of transformation itself.

The obvious (although not sole) candidates for this role are the new owners of private property, the employees of the emerging private sector and the new middle class of self-employed workers in the developing service sector. Thus, the "If" and the "How" of privatization of the huge assets of state-owned properties had a major impact on the formation of a reform constituency. No earlier than in June 1994 did the Bulgarian parliament enact a coherent privatization program. Its implementation was further delayed by the election campaign and the formation of a new government in the fall and winter of 1994, so there are only few privatized enterprises. Moreover, privatization does not necessarily entail the creation of a new class of owners. If former managers and the employees of the enterprises have quasi-property rights in "their" enterprises, they can impede or delay the efficient restructuring or even obstruct a sale altogether. This, in turn, is prone to impede the employees from giving up the attitude of clientilism *vis-à-vis* their company and make them regard their interests as being best served through the perpetuity of the status quo. Under these circumstances it will be difficult to convince them that they must turn into a socio-economic class which promotes its interests in the increase in the economy's productivity and hence in the instigation and sustainability of a dynamic process of technological and economic innovation which will improve their situation and to get them a share in the overall development of the world economy.

Quite consistent with the delay of privatization (as well as the partial reversal of the privatization law, as advocated by the BSP), Bulgaria is also a latecomer in performing the concomitant measures of the marketization, namely the enactment of civil, commercial, company, bank, stock exchange, bankruptcy, and competition laws. This in turn delays the development of manifold financial, legal, commercial and related services and the generation of the concomitant class of individuals who would amplify the reform constituency. Taken together, these omissions account mostly for the non-appearance of a new class of entrepreneurial private owners who could assume the role of modernizers of the production apparatus and create the socio-economic divisions which allow for a translation of social tensions into distributional conflicts under conditions of a dynamic economy. Despite a sad record of ethnic conflicts in the last decade of the communist regime political and social conflicts in Bulgaria have not been conducted as ethnic, linguistic and religious identity conflicts after the regime collapse. But the danger looms over the country.[12]

The vacuum in the sphere of socio-economic interest organization has had other negative consequences. As we stated in our second condition of consolidation, in established democratic societies the political parties are linked with a broad range of interest groups and hence deeply rooted in the texture of the society. Note that even in the elections of December 1994 still the Round Table constellation of BSP vs. UDF applied, while in the other countries under study a differentiated system of political parties with special constituencies had developed. If links with the interests or needs of the communities are weak or missing altogether because the basis of society is still floundering, parties are prone to stylize their political differences based on abstract and irreconcilable ideological doctrines. This tends to make them both unwilling and unable to find compromises. Indeed, we hypothesize that the delayed or even still missing release of a dynamics which is conducive to a reform constituency has played an essential role in the political turmoils and polarizations which have been characteristic of the Bulgarian transition process (Karasimeonov 1995).

Equally damaging for the reform has been Bulgaria's lateness in the creation of the appropriate legal framework for the marketization of the economy. As our account in chapter 5 shows, by the end of 1994 laws about banking, securities, stock exchange and bankruptcy were still lacking. For one thing, the need for these laws was less urgent as long as the government retreated only slowly, if at all, from the subsidization of loss-making enterprises. On the other hand, the continuance of the regulation of the economy through case-by-case intervention rather than through the establishment of a comprehensive legal framework constitutes a significant obstacle to the rise of a culture of legalism which we identified as an important element of a society's social capital. Within the framework of such culture, government is expected to be bound by the law (rather than acting through the discretionary use of its powers), and

---

[12] This is one of the conclusions of a research project reported by Ilchev and Perry 1993.

"everyone else" within civil society is recognized as the holder of legal rights. The failure of the Bulgarian government to start immediately after the collapse of the old regime with profound administrative reforms of the highly centralized state apparatus – which is of course not surprising in view of the electoral victory of the re-named communist party in the founding elections – adds to the picture of a country which seems still largely under the hold of the former regime's inertia and its lack of clearcut lines of functional differentiation.

Given the communist legacy of anti-legalism which may have been nourished by the largely agrarian character of the pre-communist Bulgarian society, the failure to establish modern institutions which create trust under the modern society's conditions of anonymity, the most important being the law, may foster tendencies toward informalism and short-termism which eventually is likely to hinder long-term investments.

Still, it is striking that despite the partially dramatic worsening of the population's living conditions no attempt was made to utilize the newly acquired democratic freedoms to thwart the economic or even the political reform. This may partly be due to the fact that de-communization has not been very profound. Indeed, indications for the successful completion of the first phase of the transition process are still rather weak. The political quandaries of the country may well turn out to have long-lasting damaging effects on its transformation into a consolidated democratic society. The more or less smooth and "positivist," as it were, functioning of the political institution is no evidence that the country has achieved a state of consolidation.

2.2   Czech Republic

In terms of the historical legacies the Czech Republic can be regarded as the straightforward antithesis to Bulgaria. As the most advanced part of one-time Czechoslovakia it shared its properties: it was the only industrialized country of the region and the only one with a, albeit brief, constitutional history of two decades. On the other hand it had to suffer the trauma of the Soviet-led invasion of 1968 and the rule of the most orthodox, rigid and Stalinist-like communist regime in our sample. Moreover, the constitutional and economic consolidation of the country was further hampered by the protracted, almost two years, process of its separation from Slovakia which finally led to its inauguration as an independent state on January 1, 1993. In the view of Prime Minister Klaus the country's first phase of transition has been successfully concluded in that it has emerged "from the operating room of the transformation process" and can now "enter a rehabilitation center, where it is strengthening itself for full parity with Western nations" (cf. Pehe 1995).

In fact, measured by our three criteria of consolidated democratic societies the Czech Republic fares extraordinarily well. However, its political stability is largely due to the "externalization" of the basic factor of instability in Czechoslovakia which arose shortly after the founding elections, namely the split along the Czech-Slovak line and the ensuing dissolution of the country. This event is a striking sign of the overwhelming political significance of national divisions;[13] the founding elections of June 1990 produced a broad anti-communist coalition including the major Slovak political force, which acted resolutely and rapidly in order to start with a thorough reform of the structures of the old regime. This determination, cleverly amalgamated with prudence and caution, was clearly carried on in the Czech Republic after January 1, 1993, because despite the split of the Civic Forum and the multiplication of political parties a stable government under Prime Minister Klaus could be formed. As a side-effect, even the administrative reform of the state made considerable progress.

Although the first figures of voucher privatization in Czechoslovakia do not appear very impressive – as we reported in chapter 5, no more than 20 percent of the enterprises offered in the first round were sold completely – both the pace and the amount of privatization which was basically completed at the end of 1994 (Pehe 1995: 31) went beyond the other countries under study, including Hungary which had started its privatization program already before 1989. Speediness and the rejection of preferential treatment for the managers and employees of the state-owned enterprises were favorable conditions for the creation of a reform constituency which invests its interests and skills in the continuation of the transformation process. Consequently, with the exception of a bankruptcy law, all relevant legal requirements for the operation of a market economy had been established before the dissolution of Czechoslovakia.

Evidently the Czech transformation dynamics focused on the creation of new private enterprises in the production and particularly in the service sectors which were excessively underdeveloped under communism. By mid 1993, the share of the private sector in the Czech Republic's GDP was the second highest in the region;[14] by the end of 1994 more than 65 percent of the economy was privately owned (Pehe 1995: 29f.).

---

[13] A subtle account of the separation is given by Pauer 1993.

[14] Thirty-seven percent, as compared with 50 percent in Poland; in Poland the huge agricultural sector which was never socialized under communism plays a major role; data from UN Economic Commission for Europe, Economic Bulletin for Europe, Vol. 45 (1993), p. 46.

An unemployment rate of 3.5 percent, a growth rate of GNP of about 3 percent, an inflation rate of 11 percent, and an increase in exports (mainly to the West) of about 7 percent (all figures for 1994) show that the newly created private economy performs quite well, although some critical failures, mismanagements, and corruption scandals in the banking and financial sector (Bönker 1993: 55ff.; Pehe 1995: 31f.) have somewhat obscured the bright picture of emerging Czech capitalism. In 1995, there are even signs of a shortage of labor in certain branches and in certain regions (particularly in Prague). Part of this success story is the weakness of the unions which, together with the high employment rate, accounts for the fact that no strikes or major labor disputes occurred in the transition process. In view of the political rhetoric of Prime Minister V. Klaus the Czech path of transformation seems to reflect an unmistakably liberal, i.e., non-interventionist approach to consolidation which restricts the role of the state to setting the institutional framework for a private economy and for the rest counts on the spontaneous emergence of the market forces. In fact, the policies of the Czech government have been far more interventionist than the publicly affirmed doctrine would allow. The apparent economic success of the Czech economy is clearly based on particular government policies and skillfully devised institutional mechanisms: wage controls, which were also conducive to a favorable ratio between public and private sector wages; extended price controls, which continued also after the dissolution of Czechoslovakia and which will be loosened only gradually; a centralized collective bargaining system; embryonic, even not very effective forms of a tripartite corporatist arrangement; and active labor market policies, such as the reduction of the labor supply, artificial employment in state enterprises, and a rather strict approach to benefit provisions in the welfare system.

Yet it is not clear whether the political stability and the social peace will persist if economic growth comes to a halt and the market forces lose their vigor. As we concluded from our comparative analysis of the structures and provisions of the post-communist constitutions, the Czech Republic's highly individualistic conception may rely too much on the ability of the integrative forces of the market and the interest-driven behavior of the individuals to provide the resources of civism which could mitigate social conflicts in times of serious crises. Not accidentally, the debate over the dangers or benefits of a democracy which, quite similar to the French model, consists mainly of a centralized government and free – some would say: atomized – individuals stood on the agenda of the political debates in 1994 which involved both President Havel and Prime Minister Klaus. While the latter insisted that "individual freedom, political pluralism, and a market economy were sufficient prerequisites for a healthy democratic system," Havel was concerned about the possible lack of civic engagement and stressed the necessity for a civil society and its associational infrastructure as a prerequisite of a consolidated democratic order (Pehe 1995: 29). Hence, in the ongoing controversies over the decentralization of the government through the creation of regions, Prime Minister Klaus' party (ODS) has been most reluctant to pursue this goal. The protracted procedure which finally – not earlier than in December 1995 – produced a law and the date for the election of the second Chamber of the parliament, the Senate (now scheduled for November 1996), may also reflect the main political forces' preference for a unitary and individualistic state as the ideal form of a democratic government.[15]

Not surprisingly, the political parties' entrenchment in a web of pluralist interest groups is not strongly developed. Since the intermediary sphere is weak in the Czech Republic and, moreover, dismissed as less important, perhaps even dangerous by the leading political forces of the country, the political parties have thus far remained the predominant actors in the public domain. Yet due to their lack of tradition and, with the exception of the former communists, of organizational resources, their links with society are at best weak, which was manifested in the poor local support for many of them in the last local government elections (Pehe 1995: 30). A striking exception is Vaclav Klaus' ODS. Although it could not benefit from links to any of the traditional political forces of the country, it could establish a robust party organization with a considerable number of party members within a very short timespan (Pauer 1995: 16). Still, the overall weakness of intermediary social forces fosters "overparticization" and, as a consequence, "overparliamentarization"[16] which is indicative of the monopolization of the political roles by the new political class, while other potential social actors have mostly remained silent and submissive. This, then would hardly allow the conclusion that the Czech Republic has reached an undisputable state of consolidation.

This becomes apparent if we look for the mechanisms which provide and sustain trust in the viability and constancy of social relations in the public sphere. While we have no data about the citizens' attitude toward the law and hence cannot assess whether a culture of legalism is emerging, the data reported in chapter 4, section 5 show at least decreasing esteem for the source of the law, the parliament. Other mechanisms of public

---

[15] See the report on the different drafts about the role and the mode of elections of the Senate in EECR Spring 1994 (Vol. III/2), pp. 6–8.
[16] This term was coined by Agh 1995.

trust-generation (corporatist arrangements, class, sectoral, or professional interest groups, cultural and non-partisan political associations and communities) are mostly lacking, and paradoxically even the most important source of trust in a liberal society, the bill of rights, is exposed to some doubts. Being "part of the constitutional order" rather than of the "Constitution" of the Czech Republic, and including a set of positive economic, social and cultural rights which are not in line with the entirely liberal spirit of the constitution, the status and the normative authority of the "Charter of Fundamental Rights and Freedoms" is ambiguous (Sunstein 1995: 50f.; but see also the letter of Lippot 1995: 92).

The current political stability of the Czech Republic seems to rest mostly on the personal qualities of the present political leaders. The two most visible and popular of whom, Prime Minister Vaclav Klaus and Minister of Industry and Trade Vladimir Dlouhy, have had quite similar careers as (economic) technocrats who developed their strong free-market economic beliefs in the shadow of one of the most dogmatic communist regimes[17] (Cf. Pehe 1995: 33; Pauer 1995: 17). Their capacity to skillfully engineer the transition appears to be the most important source of political legitimacy and stability. On the other hand, the charisma of the personality and the personal trustworthiness of President Vaclav Havel may well overshadow the Czech citizens' perception of the presidency. In other words, it is open to question whether trust based on institutions rather than on persons has already become a safe element of the social capital of the post-communist Czech polity.

2.3 Hungary

While the Czech Republic's path of transition is the prototype of a radical and abrupt breach with the communist regime requiring the design of new institutions on an almost white map, Hungary is the paradigm for the opposite constellation. The clear forerunner of the transition process, which in the sensitive field of the transfer of political power from the old regime to the new elites could profit from the experience of their risk-taking Polish predecessors, Hungary could develop its transformation program particularly in the economic sphere based on manifold liberal-izing reforms which had already been set in motion under the old regime. The pragmatic approach to amend the existing communist constitution in a piecemeal manner depending on the requirements of the situation

---

[17] They and several others who joined them were collaborators of the State Bank or of the Academy of Sciences.

furnished the country with a constitution which, as we stated in chapter 3, suffers from several inconsistencies and imbalances. But the authority of the Constitutional Court which made it an accepted arbiter in the political struggles between the other state organs limited the potentially damaging effects on the smooth operation of the machinery of government. Eliminating, for example, capital punishment, banning retroactive justice being brought against the elites of the old regime, limiting the scope of reprivatization (Klingsberg 1993; Morvai 1994; Arato 1994) and declaring even significant parts of the Horn government fiscal reform program (including cuts of sick pay, restrictions of family allowances and child benefits) unconstitutional, it proved strong enough to issue judgments counter to parliamentarian majorities even on extremely divisive issues, and thus preserved the supremacy of the constitution over the vacillations and power plays of the everyday political business. The impression of government stability is confirmed by the fact that the Hungarian parliament is the only one in the whole region which served the whole term. The almost routine change of government from a conservative-national to a left-liberal coalition after the second general elections in May 1994 is another piece of evidence for the political normality of the country.

In the field of economics, the starting conditions were no less favorable. Due to the liberalizing reforms of the Kadar regime in the eighties Hungary was after 1989 fastest in the creation of an equally comprehensive and elaborate legal system which greatly facilitated the attraction of foreign investment.[18] Other favorable starting conditions were the existence of a by and large comprehensive tax system, finished before 1989, and the relatively low share of state subsidies in the GDP, being in 1989 no more than 10.7 percent, as compared with 16.6 percent in Czechoslovakia and 15.5 percent in Bulgaria. Soft wage guidelines (rather than rigid wage controls) and a gradual process of price liberalization promised a smooth adjustment of wages to the inflation rate and to productivity. Thus, the idea of a shock therapy did not arise.

Yet it remains an open question whether the gradualist pattern of transition was a more appropriate approach for the creation of a reform constituency. In the field of privatization, an area of high strategic significance for that goal, the country was only moderately successful although the process had already started in 1988/9. A somewhat erratic

---

[18] Between 1991 and 1994 Hungary was by far ahead of all CEE countries in attracting foreign direct investment (FDI). In 1993 FDI per capita was $558, as compared with $242 in the Czech Republic, $ 83 in Slovakia and $17 in Bulgaria, the average in the CEE region being $99; data from UN Economic Commission for Europe 1994: 119.

(or: experimental) privatization strategy entailed the half-hearted simultaneous or consecutive approach to several quite diverse kinds of privatization – including "spontaneous privatization," near-mass privatization, case-by-case privatization, credit-financed privatization with particular concern for employees, and cash privatization – was not able to trigger the emergence of a strong basis for further economic development. Demands within the ruling Socialist Party, the former communists, to involve employees more in the process, are likely to slow down the process even more and to create disincentives to foreign investors (Oltay 1995). This may be outweighed by the industrial policy which had already been initiated by the conservative government and which is likely to be continued by the socialist-liberal coalition formed in 1994. On the other hand, this is prone to favor a small number of large industrial enterprises rather than foster the creation of a mass of small and medium-sized businesses which would be the basic sources of a reform constituency.

The gradualist approach which has been likewise typical of the national-conservative and the socialist-liberal governments is largely due to both governments' primary concern for the social cushioning of the reform process. In contrast to the other countries under study the state expenditures had not been cut by any considerable amount. Moreover, in 1993 a notably high proportion of GNP, namely more than 22 percent, was allocated to social expenditures (Bulgaria: 12.9 percent, Czech Republic: 14.6 percent, Slovakia: 17 percent). Hence, in March 1995 the Horn government made great efforts to overhaul the whole welfare system, cut unemployment, health care and child care benefits, and announced further reductions, all of which required the revocation of several legal entitlements to social benefits. It is noteworthy that when the Constitutional Court struck down parts of the program it demonstrated, contrary to a widespread opinion, the legal efficiency of the extended catalogue of economic and social rights of the constitution.

This is perhaps paradigmatic of how in Hungary achievements of the past somehow accommodated themselves to the conditions of the new order and survive in a metamorphic shape. To give another consequential example, one of the communist legacies of the many layers of the Hungarian constitution is Article 4 which assigns the trade unions and other interest organizations the task to protect and to represent the interests of employees, members of cooperatives, and entrepreneurs. Consequently, a strike law was already enacted in March 1989, more than a year before the inauguration of the first non-communist government. This can be understood as an exchange of unions' status rights for their moderation in substantive demands; yet due to the constitutional privilege the exchange was biased in favor of the unions. It may not have been purely accidental that a strike or something close to a strike – the taxi drivers' unrest in October 1990 – became the most serious challenge to the government's democratic authority and was solved by the reestablishment of the authority of the already existing Council of Interest Representation which finally developed the formula of compromise (cf. Szabo 1993a). This pattern of conflict is still predominant in Hungary. Efforts to conclude social pacts with workers and employees are likely to stand high on the priority list of any Hungarian government (Oltay 1995: 35).

Still, the ostensibly quite normal Hungarian transformation process displays some strange particularities. Curiously, the aforementioned unions' constitutional task to protect workers and employees was stipulated even before the potentially threatening institution – private property in the form of productive capital – was established. It seems justified to read this as a symbol that concerns for the maintenance of a given social status and for welfare take precedence over considerations of productivity and efficiency. This shifts a great deal of the responsibility for the economic and social well-being of the people to the government and is prone to make the transition process even more difficult. For the failure to achieve privatization (which is the first step toward the restructuration of the relevant enterprises) will not only delay (or prevent) the origination of a capitalist and state-independent democratic reform constituency, but make the government the main object of the manifold economic demands of the different segments of society. Given its limited resources to satisfy them, this is prone to strain its democratic legitimacy.

Paradoxically, this constellation of a caring and socially responsive transformation path is indeed vulnerable to the threat that the economic and the political reform could be voted down by the disenchanted masses through the very democratic means which are part of the reform. Thus, some observers have interpreted the Hungarian election results of 1994 as "the return of the former communists" (this is the title of Oltay's [1995] report). While this does certainly not mean a return of communism to Hungary, it may mean that the bias of the Hungarian political system toward status protection (which in 1995 entailed the Constitutional Court's annulment of several laws which aimed at cutting important social benefits) may weaken its capacity to produce a state-independent reform constituency and to relieve itself from the immediate responsibility for the socio-economic well-being of the citizens.

Although the institutions of the political system operate smoothly, the underdeveloped state of a private economy makes its social foundations appear somewhat insubstantial. The sphere of politics is not only at quite a distance from social reality, but also highly ideologized and fragmented. It is striking that in early 1994 there were no less than about 130 parties, of which 44 registered for the parliamentary elections (Agh and Kurtan 1995: 14). The dogged and protracted struggle for a direct control over the electronic mass media is another symptom. Where both interest groups and parties show weak organization and rootedness in the society, the mass media is (seen to be) the main instrument of mobilizing electoral support. While these media struggles are by no means restricted to Hungary,[19] they have gained here a specific intensity, and they involved likewise the conservative and the socialist-liberal governments (Oltay 1995: 35f.).

A third and perhaps the most significant indication of a still weak democratic structure is the unsettled character of the new democratic elites. Despite the gradualism of the Hungarian transition process less than 4 percent of the MPs of the previous parliament were reelected to parliament in 1990, and no more than 36 percent of the MPs of the first parliament were reelected in 1994; in the parliamentary group of the victorious Hungarian Socialist Party (HSP) 84 percent were newcomers (Agh and Kurtán, 1995: 18, 25). Apparantly the formation of new political elites is still very much in flux; stable patterns of institutionalized recruitment have not yet emerged. Persons appear to be more important for the establishment of a well-ordered polity than institutions. This may explain why political struggles over the filling of posts in important neutral institutions – the public media, the central bank, the Constitutional Court – have played a rather important role in the political process of Hungary since 1990.

These symptoms of institutional fragility are of course not peculiar to Hungary. But they are striking in a country which started a reform process already in the early eighties and in which the free elections of 1990 were the sound conclusion of that process rather than the starting point for a revolutionary overhaul of the entire society. While the political stability of the government is apparant – a first parliament which served the full term of four years, a second parliament which has not more than six factions in the parliament of 386 seats, a coalition which commands a two-thirds majority, a president who in 1995 was reelected to his second term by a broad majority of the quite differently composed second parliament, a Constitutional Court which enjoys high respect in all political sections – institutional consolidation is not yet completed. Remarkably, the Hungarian parliament does not enjoy the level of esteem

[19] See the reports in the special issue on "Media Freedoms in Eastern Europe" in EECR Summer 1993 (Vol. II/3).

from the Hungarian population that is accorded the far less stable parliaments of Bulgaria or Slovakia. Also the other indicators of trust which we reported in chapter 4, section 5 show a low ranking for Hungary. This gap between political stability and institutional weaknesses and the lack of trust of great parts of the population in the institutions may be one of the less favorable consequences of the state's failure to relieve itself from an overload of socio-economic obligations. While this mechanism is more or less operative in all welfare states, it is particularly problematic in polities in which well-functioning interest mediation schemes are not yet entrenched enough so as to be able to mitigate the state's legitimacy burden. Hence, quite paradoxically, the Hungarian transition process appears to be vulnerable to a danger quite similar to that which applies to the Czech Republic, despite the two countries' opposite transformation strategies: their success rests either on the technocratic skills of the political leaders, the case of the Czech Republic, or, as in the Hungarian case, on the good economic and social performance of the government. In both cases the role of institutions in establishing the good quality of the political and economic order is undervalued. This is a major inner frailty of the considerable achievements which both countries have accomplished in their search for a consolidated democratic society.

2.4 Slovakia

By contrast, the transformation in Slovakia has been characterized by many signs of open and conspicuous irregularities. Already the basic criterion of what we called vertical consolidation – the distinction of political struggles under constitutional rules and disputes about such rules – is not safely guaranteed where, as has been claimed with respect to Slovakia, "the evaluation of almost any political proposal for 'constitutionality' or 'unconstitutionality' has become part and parcel of everyday public discourse".[20] Recurrent clashes between the President and the Prime Minister over the boundaries of their respective constitutional powers, walkouts of the parliamentarian minority on the grounds of "unconstitutional acts" of the majority, coalition negotiations in which the position of the sitting president is part of the bargain, more or less unconcealed attempts of the parliamentarian majority to undermine the authority of the president, wholesale cancellations of laws and of acts of the preceding government after the change of the government, dismissals by the parliament (!) of top officials (in the mass media, the judicial

[20] EECR Winter 1995 (Vol. IV/1), pp. 30 ff.

system, the privatization agency) in order to replace them with loyal adherents of the new parliamentarian majority, the involvement of the chairman of the Constitutional Court in a political struggle between majority and minority of the National Council, or, to give a more bizarre example, the "punishment" of the Constitutional Court's President for the Court's opinions through the withdrawal of his state-furnished body guard and automobile[21] all raise serious doubts as to whether the struggle for power in this country follows rules which are sufficiently immune to changes brought about by any one single powerful actor. Unfortunately the bleak assessment seems justified that "every time there is a political change, whether elections or change of government, the entire existence of the democratic structure remains in question" (Abrahám 1995; Mihál.iková 1995).

Contrary to pessimistic forecasts the relevant economic data improved in 1994 notwithstanding the political turmoils and no less than three governments in this year. The inflation rate of 13.4 percent was not only considerably lower than in the previous year (about 23 percent) but fell also short of the projection of 15 percent. Similarly, also the increase in GDP of 4.2 percent was noticeably above the projected 1 percent, and also the negative trade balance of 1993 turned positive in 1994. Unemployment of 14.5 percent (by September 1994) was about 1.5 percent below the OECD projections for this year. However, as the main contributions to these positive results were made in the period between the inauguration of the Moravcik government in March and the elections (September 30/October 1, 1994) they may not indicate a general trend. Although Slovakia was a beneficiary of the rapid legal reforms which had been performed up till the end of 1992 in Czechoslovakia and which set the framework for a market economy, foreign investment remained low, being about one third of the pro-capita rate in the Czech Republic and less than one sixth of Hungary.[22] Although due to a long history of economic backwardness and disadvantages (cf. basic economic data in Johnson 1985: 28ff.; see also Pauer 1993) Slovakia had worse starting conditions than the Czech lands both in 1989 and in 1993, it must be assumed that a major reason for the reluctance of foreign investors has been the stagnant and unclear, in many instances clearly clientelistic character of the Slovak privatization process. Since in the new Meciar

---

[21] For details see EECR Fall 1993/Winter 1994 (Vol. II/4, III/1), pp. 18 f., Spring 1994 (Vol. III/2), pp. 23 f., Summer/Fall 1994 (Vol. III/3, 4), pp. 21 f., Winter 1995 (Vol. IV/1), pp. 30–32, Spring 1995 (Vol. IV/2), pp. 28–31; Fisher 1995.

[22] Data from UN Economic Commission for Europe, *Economic Bulletin for Europe*, 46 (1994), 119.; divergent data, although displaying roughly the same comparative pattern, are reported by Fisher 1995.

coalition government the ZRS[23] (Association of Workers of Slovakia), which is opposed to privatization, has a key role, privatization in Slovakia is likely to stagnate for the next three years.

In Slovakia clearly the threat of a vicious circle of downward dynamics[24] is looming: the unbroken existence of a considerable amount of state-owned enterprises will furthermore spurn foreign investments and delay or prevent the modernization of the production apparatus, sustain the workers' attitude against the uncertainties of the modernization process and perpetuate their demand for economic and social security and equality through the preservation of the status quo; at the same time it will discourage the origination of a domestic reform constituency as an important, if not, in the critical period of transition, the single most important social basis of a democratic society cum market economy. Another imminent consequence of the delayed economic reform is an aggravation of the fiscal crisis owing to the declining tax income of the state and the tendency toward overspending, which in turn is likely to make the necessary economic and social reforms politically ever more costly, because the hardships which have to be imposed on the population are prone to multiply in direct proportion to their delay. On the other hand excessive deficit spending and unbalanced budgets lead foreign creditors such as the IMF and the World Bank to withhold the urgently needed loans. These mutually reinforcing negative causalities may generate an overall feeling of frustration, uniting a growing sense of distrust toward the democratic institutions with the discontent at the failure of the economic and social improvements of the new economic and political order, so that for many Slovaks an authoritarian variant of government could become a tempting alternative to the present order.

In fact, the structure of social conflicts is still quite diffuse. They are not yet unequivocally organized along socio-economic cleavages and the corresponding institutions of interest representations typical of a democratic society. Three obvious facts are striking: first, a coalition government which comprises the extreme right and the extreme left parties of the country; second, the major political force, the HZDS[25] (Movement for a Democratic Slovakia), being even five years after the velvet revolution more a movement than a party, although firmly disciplined by an authoritarian leader, and including as diverse and contradictory tendencies as communism and anti-communism, nationalism and adherence to the idea of participating in European integration, free market ideas and

---

[23] Zdruzenie Robotníkov Slovenska.
[24] Several scenarios of vicious circles are sketched in Bruszt 1993.
[25] Hnutie za demokratické Slovensko.

290 CONSTITUTIONAL POLITICS AND ECONOMIC TRANSFORMATION

interventionism, or pro-Western liberalism and Slavophilism;[26] third, the alliance in the elections of 1994 of the three existing, ideologically quite different Hungarian parties behind the attribute of what they have in common, namely their Hungarian ethnicity. These particulars are indicative of atypical lines of division in the society. Indeed, it has been claimed that the dividing lines in the present Slovak political discourse are predominantly drawn along the different interpretations of the country's recent history (the fascist puppet state 1939–45 and the communist regime 1945–89), and that "the five-year post-communist history of Slovakia can be seen as a struggle among various groups with regard to the legacy of the StB" [= State Secret Police under communism] (Abrahám 1995: 95).

However valid this interpretation may be, the cleavages which determine the organization of social and political actors seem to deal more with issues of collective identity than with questions of how to increase GDP and how to distribute it according to socio-economic patterns of distributive justice developed in the public discourses of a democratic society. Thus far, the identity-oriented conception of social conflict has discouraged the political parties from associating themselves with particular socio-economic groups of society. Therefore, a sense of the plurality of social interests and the necessity to compromise will not easily arise, no less than the distinction between the constitutional framework on the one hand, the political, economic and social struggles with their uncertain outcomes on the other. If the constitution turns into a divisive issue, it cannot become the source of stability and trust, and people will probably look for alternative mechanisms and arrangements which they expect to protect them against the uncertainties of their lives. Since the uncertainties of the market are the most threatening, the absence of a culture of constitutionalism and legalism drives the ruling majority willy-nilly in the position of a protector of socio-economic security of the people. They must assume responsibility for the economy in order to fulfill this obligation and to generate a minimum of trust in the social order. Since this is doomed to fail on mere economic grounds, this is another menacing vicious circle in the Slovak transition process.

This unconsolidated state of the Slovak affairs is puzzling if compared with the situation of the Czech Republic. Having shared a common Czechoslovak history for most of the twentieth century one would expect quite similar post-communist developments in the two successor states. An obviously insufficient explanation of Slovakia's patently less successful

---

[26] Bútorová and Bútora 1995: p. 123; this article was written before the elections of 1994, but this characterization of the HZDS holds still true in 1995.

transition path would be the personality and role of Vladimir Meciar, the charismatic and erratic populist leader of the *Movement for a Democratic Slovakia* (HZDS). The domineering role of a single person in a polity being the *explanandum*, not the explanation, Meciar's role in Slovakia points to structural weaknesses of the country's institutional set-up. A complex causality applies. First, several constitutional flaws may play a certain role, such as the unbalanced construction of the machinery of government or the relatively low requirements for constitutional amendments[27] which tend to blur the boundaries between struggle *about* and *under* rules and which tend to undermine the trust-engendering quality of the constitution. Yet this latter particularity applies also to the Czech Republic whose constitutional framework is stable. The imperfections of the Slovak constitution may have contributed to the failure of consolidation, but it is equally plausible to assume that the vexing political and economic situation in Slovakia in 1992 was the major cause for the inferior quality of the constitution, or that also a more perfect constitutional architecture might not have produced different outcomes of the transition process.

The same ambiguity obtains with respect to the possible economic causes of Slovakia's lag behind the Czech Republic. The economic legacies of the communist regime – the preponderance of huge and technically obsolete factories (with an armaments industry at its core which has been declining worldwide since 1989) – put a heavier burden on Slovakia than on the Czech lands. However, this inequality may not explain entirely the different performances of the two countries. Surprisingly, the basic economic structures of Slovakia and of the Czech Republic are quite similar. By the end of the 1970s the modernization of Slovakia in terms of industrialization, urbanization, standard of life, economic performance, and social stratification had caught up with the Czech lands (Pauer 1993: 15 f.). Consequently, in both countries the share of the agricultural sector in GDP is 9 percent, the respective figures for the industrial sector are 39 percent (Czech Republic) and 38 percent (Slovakia), for the service sector 53 percent (Czech Republic), and 52 percent (Slovakia) (Frankfurter Allgemeine Zeitung / manager magazin / Rödel & Partner 1995).

Moreover, a comparative view of several significant indicators of the economic situation – the annual change of the GDP,[28] inflation rates, changes in real wages, unemployment rates – show that between 1989

---

[27] See chapter 3, section 5.

[28] However, it is striking that in 1994 the increase in GDP in Slovakia was even higher than in the Czech Republic, mostly due to the fact that the economy had started at a low point, having fallen in the previous year by 4.6 percent, see Fisher 1995.

and 1992 the Czech lands and Slovakia had roughly the same starting conditions, with Slovakia only somewhat lagging behind, whereas the respective socio-economic developments of the two countries bifurcated visibly in 1993, the first year after the dissolution of Czechoslovakia. This fact is of course no conclusive evidence for the unfavorable effects of Slovak independence and of Slovak politics on the country's economic conditions. The negative economic data may merely reflect the end of the Czechs' subsidizing Slovak development so that the "true," i.e., "backward," state of the endogeneous economic affairs of Slovakia only came to light after 1992. The divergent developments after 1992 would then simply mirror the normal consequences of the different starting conditions which had been hidden under the benevolent and levelling cover of Czechoslovakism. But it is equally possible that "Slovakism," i.e., endogenous particularities of the Slovak society do largely explain the country's unconsolidated conditions.

In any case it is not possible to explain Slovakia's failure to consolidate its democratic system with the alleged backwardness of its basic economic structures. Obviously politics and culture matter, so much the more since the economic transformation consists mainly in the creation of the appropriate legal institutions, and this is largely a matter of political action. Moreover, Slovakia is the country which is exposed in the purest and most pressing manner to the difficult task which we described in the first chapter, namely to creating simultaneously a new nation, a new economic structure, and new legal and political institutions. While Slovakia's new political elites did not fail to create the institutional framework of a democratic polity cum market economy, first, the corresponding differentiation of the society into a plurality of interests which characterize the cleavages and conflicts of a market society and, second, the spirit of democratic constitutionalism among the currently dominating elites of the country are lacking. This situation is part of the prevalence of identity over interest issues in the social and political organization of the post-communist Slovak society which we analyzed in chapter 7. If Slovakia's alleged socio-economic backwardness cannot account for it, how, then, can the divergent patterns of transition in Slovakia and in the Czech Lands be interpreted? The answer is part of a broader explanation which includes all four countries of our comparative study.

3 How to explain the ranking

Among the four countries of our sample two – the Czech Republic and Hungary – are politically stable, although their institutional stability displays some weaknesses; the two others, Bulgaria and Slovakia, are both politically and institutionally unstable. Also their economies are lagging behind, although the most recent data show that they are slowly recovering from their low level of performance in the first years of transformation. Even in the domain of social policy the Czech Republic performed most successfully, while Bulgaria appears the least advanced. Yet our research clearly displays that the "social net" was not dense or strong enough in any of the countries under study to cushion the painful and often extreme decline of living standards which the losers of the economic reforms – in the short term the majority of the populations – had to suffer.

These findings raise the obvious question: What accounts for the differences between countries and institutional sectors? Why do some countries experience a smoother and more rapid course of social, economic, and political consolidation than others? What is "the" independent variable capable of explaining such observed differences? The following reflections provide the conceptual framework within which we want to suggest an answer.

3.1 A conceptual framework

The burden of explanation can be put on either of three types of variables: legacies, institutions, or decisions. The distinction between the three is to be made both in terms of the temporal structure of determination and the degree of intentionality. Legacies are by definition determinants of present outcomes that stem from the (distant) past, such as inherited endowments of actors with material resources, mentalities, and traditions. The mode in which they affect present outcomes has little (if anything) to do with intentional causation. Legacies generate constraints and opportunities of action that are relatively immune from purposive action. In contrast, institutions are founded, adopted, sanctioned, continuously enacted, and subject to some element of design and alteration. They do not anonymously originate from the "mist of the past," but can be accounted for in terms of actors who have adopted a given set of rules and put them into operation – usually with the purpose in mind of intentionally generating certain outcomes and excluding others. Such determination of outcomes through institutionalized rules, however, is soft, as institutions are associated with some measure of durability. Hence their power of determination pertains to general conditions (such as order, stability, the non-violent resolution of conflict, or some notion of social justice), as institutions are built from behind a "veil of ignorance" concerning who is actually to profit from their operation.

Finally, decisions are most directly concerned with bringing about outcomes most desired by the decision maker, and they can be made – and revised – on short notice in response to changing conditions. In short, durability decreases from "legacies" to "decisions," and intentionality increases, with "institutions" being placed in an intermediate position on both of these dimensions.

Structuralists are virtually defined by their methodically favoring "legacies" as their key variable. "Legacies approaches explain post-communist transformation as a function of the social, cultural and institutional structures created under Leninist regimes and Soviet domination in Eastern Europe that persist in the present period. In this view, the past casts a long shadow on the present" (Crawford and Lijphart 1995: 172). The explanatory model is something like the following. The post-breakdown formation of a new social and political order is largely determined and constrained by the preconditions the old regime has left behind. The long arm of the past shapes the trajectory of transformation events into the indefinite future. Economic patterns such as the type, degree, and timing of industrialization, the territorial organization of the country, as well as internal and external trade relations are seen as lasting determinants of future developments.

The same applies to political, managerial, and administrative elites who control the transition process, as their resources and positions of power within the old regime are easily converted into analogous privileges within the new. And no less does it apply to the heritage of mass attitudes, political culture, and the patterns of identity, cleavages, loyalties, and legitimation. The adoption of this explanatory framework yields the prediction that the transformation process will be slow and highly path-dependent, and lasting differences in the degree of economic, political and cultural modernization must be largely attributed to petrified country-specific historical differences as they were formed before 1989 – and often even before 1945 or before 1918. Transformation is thus seen within the structuralist conceptual framework to be governed by path-dependency, the deadweight of the past, continuity, and inertia – factors which are at best slowly and marginally altered by institutional innovations and rational decisions of actors.

The second explanatory model focuses on institutionalized agency. In a nutshell, the argument is that the course of transformation is critically dependent upon the configuration of actors – as well as procedural rules legitimating and guiding their action – that emerged on the scene in the short period after the breakdown of the old regime, as well as upon the mode of this breakdown itself (e.g., *transicion pactada* with round-table talks vs. *tabula rasa*). True, the newly emerging agents, movements, coalitions, and elites may themselves be shaped by the experience they underwent in their collective past and inspired by institutional patterns remembered and reflexively adopted from the storehouse of their national history. But instead of rigid determination, there are degrees of freedom and spaces for creative institutional innovation to be utilized by the forces that are operative in the proto-constitutional moment of "hour zero." The rules of the game that are being adopted as binding emanate from the particular configuration of post-breakdown actors and the exercise of their "local reason" which is capable of erasing legacies.

Finally, transition outcomes may be also attributed to whether or not the "right" decisions on policy (or investment) have been taken and promising strategic moves made (e.g., concerning the type and pace of privatization or the form of government). Future courses of events will not so much depend on parameters inherited from the past or kinds of agents and rules emerging in the transition, they will rather depend upon enlightened choices and the determination with which they are carried out. And, given the wealth of available knowledge, advice, and tested experience concerning the most promising courses of action that is being supplied by economists, constitutional lawyers, and other experts on modernization and development, it is ultimately a matter of rationality (as well as of the power to implement rational decisions) whether or not the "right" course of action that leads to consolidation is adopted. Here, the strong assumption is that a clear-cut set of "imperatives of liberalization" (Crawford and Lijphart 1995: 172) is available that provides clear guidelines as to what is to be done and what is to be avoided, regardless of the specificities of the local past and the reasoning of local actors.

A balanced account of the transition and the determinants of its outcomes in terms of consolidation will probably have to assess the relative weight of all three of these factors – the residues of the past, the configuration of rule-making actors that emerges at the moment of transition, and future-oriented strategic decision making of key political and economic actors. It might also be observed that choices concerning the preferred type of explanatory variables tend to vary with the academic discipline of authors: social historians are likely to focus upon structures as they path-dependently assert themselves over the *longue durée*, (institutionalist) sociologists and political economists attribute explanatory weight to agents and the rules adopted to govern their interaction, while economists and political scientists focus on actor-specific variables such as choices and decisions, rationality, and power.

The challenge is to arrive at a more synthetic approach. Rather than opting for one of the three types of independent variables, such an approach would have to allow for backward and forward linkages and other forms of complex interaction. Forward linkages occur when structures select agents and institutional settings, and the latter in turn select choices and decisions. Backward linkages would be cases in which choices put agents and institutional rules in their place, and these new arrangements alter or nullify the determining force of structural legacies or replace them with newly created legacies.

A case in point is the take-off of economic growth due to some set of prudent policy and investment decisions which result in setting up a successful accumulation regime, which in turn helps to break inherited constraints that originate from the patterns and structures of the old regime. Another case in point would be the spread of trust, confidence and cooperative virtues that is inculcated by the operation of new institutions. The longer they last, the better they become known, the more they are taken for granted, and the more effectively their hegemonic "spirit" is likely to eradicate, through processes of habituation and socialization, the "mental residues" that were inculcated by the old regime.

We believe that such material and cultural backward linkages – in which newly introduced arrangements serve to relativize the force of legacies and in a way even reverse the temporal structure of causality – are a possible, but by no means the necessary outcome of institutional innovations that occur in the transition process. At the same time it appears that it is the formative impact of new institutions – i.e. their capacity to shape the frames, habits, routines, and expectations (and even memories) of citizens in convergent ways and thereby to render inherited fears, hostilities, and suspicions groundless – that is the critical determinant of consolidation.

How can institutional arrangements manage to exert this beneficial formative effect of endogenously changing preferences and expectations and of putting to rest fear and fundamentalist intransigence? The virtuous circle of new arrangements generating their own foundations in the minds and hearts of citizens who get "used to" them and begin to count on them is contingent, we submit, on their fairness and their potential for performance. In other words, they must be demonstrably impartial and conducive to desired collective outcomes, or legitimate and effective. Through their day-to-day operation, they must earn, as a by-product, the credibility and credit on which their durability eventually depends. It is this capacity for self-consolidation through the sedimentation of the spirit of supportive orientations and attitudes, rather than the inert legacies of the past (or, for that matter, the "right" decisions of the "right" actors), that must be relied upon in accounting for the relative success or failure of national cases of transformation.

3.2 The complex interactions between structures, institutions, and decisions

Our account of the rank order of the four countries under study in terms of consolidation starts with the structural givens. The two stragglers of the transition process display some striking similarities. First, while with the exception of the Czech Lands all CEE countries were agrarian economies which were only industrialized through the communist regimes, Bulgaria and Slovakia made the greatest leaps from economic backwardness in the 1940s to industrialization and urbanization in the 1980s. They gained most from communism. For them, much more than for Hungary which had been more closely linked to Western Europe both economically and culturally, communism was the political force which effectuated their entry into the industrialized world. Therefore communism did not only mould these societies more than the others, but was also largely accepted without hostility, and by a large part of the population even with loyal support. Thus, there was less acutely perceived reason to get rid of the old regime than in Hungary, let alone the Czech Lands.

Second, both in Bulgaria and in Slovakia a considerable number of ethnic minorities exist: in Slovakia their share in the whole population amounts to some 14 percent (almost 11 percent Hungarians, the Gypsies being the second-largest group of about 1.8 percent), in Bulgaria it ranges, depending on the count, between 19 percent and 22 percent (9.5 percent to 12 percent ethnic Turks, 6.5 percent to 7 percent Gypsies, some 3 percent Pomaks) (data from I. Ilchev and D. M. Perry 1993). Apart from the Gypsies, these ethnic minorities settle in coherent territorial spaces in the respective states and can refer their interests and grievances to a neighboring "interested patron state" (Hungary and Turkey, respectively) (Offe 1994: 145 f., 160 f.). Hence they can easily be regarded as a kind of "fifth column" of that patron state, and in fact have been the object of this suspicion several times, particularly as these patron states are also remembered as imperial powers from a long history of oppression suffered by the Slovak and Bulgarian peoples.

Third, in both countries religion and the Church (the Greek Orthodox in Bulgaria, the Roman Catholic in Slovakia) continued to play a certain role even under communism (although much less than the Roman Catholic Church in Poland) (for Slovakia cf. J. Rabas 1984). Moreover, in Bulgaria there was also some form of cooperation with the regime. In contrast to Poland in none of the two countries did the Church symbolize the integrity of the nation against her suppression by foreign or internal usurpers. Given the hierarchical and authoritarian character of both Catholic Churches, particularly the Orthodox, they were no potential candidates for the conceivable task to serve as an antidote against pervasive statism or at least as an embryonic countervailing constituent of an autonomous civil society.

These similarities are legacies of the pre-communist and of the communist pasts. They are paralleled by several remarkable similarities in the transition process itself some of which are indicative of the low degree of consolidation: delayed privatization; a dominant role of former communists in key political positions;[29] the most extremely polarized party systems along ideological lines including expressly ethnic parties compared with the other countries under study; a low degree of differentiation between political representation through parties and functional representation through interest associations (particularly unions and business interest associations); and, last but not least, attempts of the legislative majorities to discipline the courts, including the respective constitutional courts, i.e., to authorize unrestrained majority rule and to undermine the separation of powers. These both pre- and post-communist similarities between Bulgaria and Slovakia suggest, on the one hand, significant correlations between communist-type rapid and precipitous industrialization of a previously agrarian, catholic, and ethnically divided country and on the other, a rather low degree of hostility for the communist regime, tolerance for former communist elites in the top positions of the post-communist order, and strong tendencies to blend political representation and interest lobbying, to evade political compromises due to an extreme ideologization of social and political conflict, and to understand and to practice democracy as a populist-type of unchecked majority rule. Whatever the adequate causal interpretation, these striking affinities seem to amount to a consistent pattern.

There is a notable "forward linkage" between the socio-economic heritage of Bulgaria and Slovakia and the institutional set-up which emerged after 1989. It entailed an incomplete translation of economic, social, and cultural inequality into an institutional and ideological structure of conflict characteristic of modern societies. This failure can be explained as the inheritance of the precipitous changeover of agrarian into industrialized societies. In agrarian societies the perception prevails that the amount of distributable goods is both unalterable and limited, while in industrial societies due to the dynamic character of their

---

[29] "Ex-communists, now members of Meciar's ruling movement for the most part, came to hold all the key posts in the newly independent state . . . Moreover, these were not reform communists who had broken with communism and become dissidents, but mostly people who had remained mentally rooted in communist collectivism"; Bútorová and Bútora 1995: 124; see also Abrahám 1995: 95.

economic systems it is the common view that distributional struggles need not necessarily be zero sum games (Offe 1994: 184). In the two categories of society basic social facts such as inequality, conflict, or power are typically perceived in opposite conceptual frameworks: in the framework of an agrarian society inequality tends to be a "natural" quality of persons which they possess due to the "natural" hierarchy of the society, rather than an attribute of a particular socio-economic structure which is amenable to change; conflict is existential strife in terms of either/or which tends to render the opponents into enemies, rather than a struggle for scarce (but, in principle, augmentable) resources among competitors; power is a means for the control of society rather than a social relation whose skillful design releases its creative and learning capacities. Hence, in agrarian societies there is less tolerance for non-ascriptive, that is, socio-economic inequality than in industrial societies.[30] This entails a stronger tendency to construe the emerging inequalities in "natural", that is, unalterable primordial categories rather than in socio-economic terms. Manifest social conflicts occur less frequently in agrarian than in industrial societies, but due to their predominantly either/or quality they tend to be more vehement, irreconcilable, frequently violent or on the verge of violence, and more doctrinal and ideological than most conflicts in industrial societies because they deal largely with divisible goods (Hirschman 1994: 299ff.). Finally, in agrarian societies power is more likely to be understood as a physical force which due to its irresistibility can reliably effect the causes willed by the power-holder, and therefore its mere, purely quantitative accumulation is considered to be the most efficient use and preservation of (political) power.

Evidently, an abrupt and thorough industrialization authoritatively and largely coercively imposed on an agrarian society generates painful clashes in the life worlds of the individuals who undergo these revolutionary changes. But it does not mean an outright eradication of the old structures and their unqualified replacement with the qualities of industrialism. Rather, in a process of mutual adaptations of the opposite cultures new social structures, modes of behavior, values and institutions arise which partly save, partly transform the agrarian-conservative concepts and perceptions into new worldviews and patterns of behavior which give the newly emerging society the paradoxical character of an industrialized and urbanized peasant society. This oxymoron denotes a society in which the formal institutions of a modern industrial society are

---

[30] Some hints to the underlying rationale of prevailing sense of equality can be found in Moore 1978: 37 ff.

by and large in existence, whereas the spirit in which they are understood and used is still greatly dominated by "agrarian" values, habits, and perceptions. The history of communism in the twentieth century may even suggest the hypothesis that agrarian societies are more receptive to a soviet-type forced industrialization than advanced industrial societies. The inevitable yet deeply disapproved consequences of industrialization can be made compatible with the basic beliefs of an agrarian society with the help of communist tenets. For instance, social inequalities which by necessity come up in the wake of the increased degree of division of labor in an industrializing society is denied because of the "natural" solidarity of the working class. Social conflict, equally a necessary implication of an industrializing society, is translated into the quasi-existential irreconcilable class struggle between the working and the bourgeois class. Power is perceived as the physical capacity of one class to repress and suppress the hostile class. In other words, soviet-type communism which obtained in all CEE countries after World War II, although certainly not congenial with the social, economic, and cultural structures of the mostly agrarian countries of that region, was perhaps best fitting to the most backward agrarian societies in that it facilitated the amalgamation of their conservative values and habits with the institutional and political requirements of rapid industrialization. Soviet-type communism meant industrialization without modernization, or at least modernization at a slower pace and a lower level.

Of course, neither Bulgaria nor Slovakia are agrarian societies any longer; but they are rapidly and coercively industrialized agrarian societies which had not enough time to fully develop the cultural patterns through which a society adapts itself to the conditions of industrialization and undergoes a process of modernization. The soviet-type industrialization did in fact revolutionize these societies, it created radically new social structures and inaugurated unfamiliar institutions: it transformed the spiritual and religious idea of the omnipotence of God into the concept of the secular omnipotence of the people, changed peasants into industrial workers, launched mass education, reduced parochialism by fostering a political, social, and cultural orientation toward the national state or even toward international solidarity, accommodated the popular masses to the integration into and the mobilization through big bureaucratic organizations,[31] concentrated the supreme and unrestrained state power with the leaders of the hegemonic vanguard party, introduced a mode of both agricultural and industrial production in which the peasants – who had been turned into agro-industrial workers – and the

---

[31] See the examples with Beyme 1994: 49.

industrial workers – who were mostly industrialized peasants – were subjected to the functional requirements of authoritatively imposed production plans (mostly five-year plans). However, these were not innovations which were unequivocally modernizing the society in terms of its increased functional differentiation, social stratification, and cultural diversity. While undoubtedly communism *was* an industrial developer of the predominantly agrarian CEE countries,[32] this development was selective; while it promoted industrialization, urbanization, mass education, and the secularization of the society, it did not aim at and in fact accomplish the creation of primarily individualistic values and attitudes such as toleration of inequality, open-mindedness for the diversity and plurality of values, attitudes, and life-styles, the appreciation of competition, individual performance, and other orientations supportive of a pluralist, liberal, and democratic concept of civil society and of a market economy.

This kind of industrialization change had just as little effect on the perceptions of basic social experiences. Under communism scarcity of resources remained to be understood mainly as a consequence of given physical shortages of goods, not as a problem of inappropriate production and incentive structures; inequality was widely accepted insofar as the new quasi-estate of the nomenklatura was now at the top of the social hierarchy, while all other kinds of inequality continued to be illegitimate, this time on the grounds that the human right to equality required the equality of the individuals' socio-economic status. Conflict continued to be denied or regarded as illegitimate; only class conflict was officially acknowledged, but this was not a "conflict" in the modern pluralist society's understanding of the term, but a secular-sacred and existential war among irreconcilable enemies entirely unamenable to compromise. Power continued to be above all a means of control of potential enemies, i.e., predominantly an instrument of discipline and repression. In short, many of the basic perceptions, worldviews, and concepts of an agrarian society could relatively easily survive, if in different forms, under soviet communism and its stiff industrialization program.

Hence, the institutions and behavioral patterns and the spirit of a market economy and of constitutionalism were not simply unknown or not safely rooted in these societies,[33] but almost entirely alien to their

[32] Cf. the general modernization achievements of communism Beyme, 1994: 48 ff.

[33] To be sure, in the time between 1918 and 1938 Slovakia experienced of course as an integral part of Czechoslovakia the structures of a constitutional democracy and of a capitalist industrial economy.

social understanding. If the new changes, the transition to democracy and capitalism, are precipitous, rapid and for the most people also as much imposed from above as the communist regime some 50 years ago, it comes as no surprise that the new institutions – parliaments, political parties, independent unions and interest organizations, commodity, labor, and capital markets – are filled with a spirit which preserved many properties of an agrarian society over the time of communism by amalgamating the compatible elements of both. Although the institutions of the constitutional state and the market economy are flexible enough as to tolerate quite different understandings and political practices, they may be jeopardized in a setting which has not yet fully adopted the political and cultural implications of industrialization, i.e., modernity.

This deficiency has shaped the understanding of the newly created institutions whose devices are not insufficient in themselves. In agrarian societies, traditional modes (in the Weberean sense) of legitimation of political authority predominate; their legitimacy is based on the belief of "the sanctity of time-honored rules and powers" (Weber 1978: 226). Obedience is owed to persons rather than to formal and unpersonal rules, and the master's commands are legitimized either through traditions or "in terms of the master's discretion in that sphere which tradition leaves open to him; this traditional prerogative rests primarily on the fact that the obligations of personal obedience tend to be essentially unlimited" (Weber 1978: 227). There are obvious analogies with the soviet-communist type of domination. Both are inhospitable to what Weber called "legal authority," i.e., a type of domination whose claim to legitimacy rests on the impersonal character of enacted rules which are also imposed on the "master" himself. In both societies domination through the prerogatives of particular persons or group of persons preponderates. In both societies the obligations to obedience are essentially unlimited because they rest on the superior position of the master and thus are only limited through the consideration "of how far master and staff can go in view of the subjects' traditional compliance without arousing their resistance" (Weber 1978: 227). This, then, generates a personalistic view of authority, one which is lastly rooted in the power of the master, not in the overall reasonableness of an order which is governed by rules and embodied in institutions.[34]

Here again, the pre-communist and the communist type of authority could easily amalgamate, and the continuance of the predominantly

[34] One may even raise the question whether the changes of 1989/90 were in all CEE countries what Weber called "traditionalist revolutions," i.e., resistance which was not directed against the system as such but against "the master . . . personally, the accusation being that he failed to observe the traditional limits of his power," Weber 1978: 227.

traditional understanding of authority can be observed in the low estimation which institutions enjoy in Bulgaria and Slovakia: judgments of courts are primarily regarded as personal statements of the judges, and hence dissatisfaction with the courts' decisions is expresssed through actions against them personally; parliament is mainly regarded as the locus of the supreme power which has been assigned to the majority which therefore tends to treat the minority not as a constituent element of the institution but as a near-illegitimate obstacle to its power; a change of government verges on a change of the constitutional order itself because – quite in line with the traditional understanding of authority – the persons who form the government are not recognized as being subject to the impersonal order of the constitution but as masters who possess supreme power due to its delegation through the people whose unrestrained will-power is regarded as the ultimate and entirely unlimited source of political power.

Time and space restrictions do not allow us to undertake a thorough investigation of the myriads of political decisions of the governments of Bulgaria and Slovakia which shaped the transformation process and which may be understood as being selected and shaped by the very institutional settings generated by the objectivity of the historical legacies. Although we believe that "forward linkages" between structures which select institutions which in turn select and shape decisions can be identified, there is of course no determinism which allows a straightforward explanation of each and every single decision as a derivative of a particular institutional device. Obviously this would neglect the role which the contingent factors play and which Macchiavelli termed *fortuna* and *virtú*, i.e., chance and the personal character and quality of political leaders. However, in order to understand why the countries under study display different degrees of consolidation the knowledge of the structural and the institutional conditions which frame characters, chances, and choices yields already abundant insights.

Our conceptual approach allows also a better understanding of the "backward linkages" between choices which create institutions and agents which in turn alter inherited structures. The case in point is the Czech Republic. As we stated earlier, it was mainly the skillful and clever engineering of the process of transition by Vaclav Klaus and the group of economic technocrats around him which created the favorable conditions of the country's successful transition path: inspired by a clear-cut Hayekian-liberalistic world view they struggled uncompromisingly against all residues of communism, created the basic institutions of a pure capitalist market economy and designed their policies according to a mainly individualistic picture of the society (Pauer 1995). Thus, the interventionist and seemingly social-democratic elements of their policies could be pursued in an authoritarian-statist rather than in a "societal corporatist" manner. In the long run the ensuing institutional setting may entail quite novel structures of a capitalist economy without its welfarist underpinnings. In the Czech Republic the legacies of the communist past erected the weakest obstacles to the country's transformation into a constitutional-democratic market society. The obvious explanation is that communism had not succeeded in creating a pervasive web of intermediate institutions, values and attitudes which were able to impose themselves on the society and to survive during the transition period. This in turn may be due to the inhospitability of the society of the Czech lands with the Soviet type of communism, which after 1945 had to be imposed more or less coercively, and to the collective memory of the 1968 invasion.

In sum, whether decisions or structures have a dominant influence on the shape of the societies in transition seems to depend largely upon the robustness of the extant institutions which in turn is mainly determined by the overall structural affinity of the respective societies to the soviet-type communism: while in Bulgaria and Slovakia due to these societies' greater structural openness to the soviet-type communism the spirit of the new democratic institutions is still mixed with a considerable amount of traditional values and perceptions; in the Czech Republic communism could not thoroughly amalgamate with the spirit and the basic institutions of the Czech society which before 1945 had already displayed many signs of a modern, differentiated industrial society. Soviet communism could destroy most elements of that society and create an institutional wasteland, but it was not able to create institutional shelters which were able to preserve considerable elements of a communist legacy. This, then, was the fortunate starting point for determined and strong-willed political actors to cultivate, as it were, the wasteland – by filling the newly created institutions with their liberal spirit without being stymied by strong institutional legacies.

Hungary, ranging somewhere between Bulgaria and Slovakia, on the one hand, the Czech Republic, on the other, represents the rather unique case of a society which endeavored to launch major economic and political reforms under the old regime. This was tantamount to an attempt to reconcile the ideal of socio-economic security (as promised and, at a low level, provided by communism) with the beneficial effects of liberal (economic and political) institutions. However promising or hopeless this undertaking may appear in retrospect, it was consequential in that it created a non-revolutionary spirit of change which tried to keep the "decent" elements of communism within the new institutions of a liberal democracy. Ultimately, this transition path can be read as just another variant of a slow and non-precipitous transformation of this formerly agrarian society into an industrial one.

4 Concluding observations

The comparison of the four countries under study with respect to their achievements in the creation of consolidated democratic societies-cum market economies produced a ranking order in which the Czech Republic ranges first, and Hungary second, being less successful than the Czech Republic but clearly ahead of Slovakia and Bulgaria. This ranking order applies to economic performance, institutional consolidation, political stabilty, and social security. However, in our view institutional consolidation is the key criterion by which success or failure of the transformation of the communist into a democratic society has to be measured.

Our explanation of the rank order amounts to the thesis that Bulgaria and Slovakia have great difficulties in adopting the institutions of a constitutional democracy and a market economy and to apprehend and to internalize their spirit because their precipitously and coercively imposed *industrialization* did not go along with cultural and political *modernization*; hence, or so we have argued, due to the inherently traditional cultural implications of soviet-type communism basic concepts and perceptions of an agrarian society could survive, if mostly in metamorphosed guise, in the behavioral patterns, values and worldviews of the communist era. We believe that the properties of the soviet communist regime served as a congenial host which allowed the endurance of many forms of traditional domination characteristic of agrarian societies even in an industrialized, but not simultaneously modernized society. Although there are as yet no indications to that effect, a regression to some kind of populist-authoritarian rule cannot be excluded. Yet more likely is the persistence of the present state of affairs of unstable governments, intensive political fights, erratic coalitions, and a low degree of political cooperation among the political elites.

While these prospects are not appealing, another conclusion is more comfortable. There are good reasons to assume that the newly acquired political freedom and the means of democratic rule will not be used in any of the countries under study to thwart economic reform. Democratic and economic reforms do not appear as mutually exclusive in any of the countries under study. In the Czech Republic this possibility can be dismissed because of the functional differentiation between the institutional frame and the economic sphere and because protection against undue interventions is firmly established. In Hungary the government's responsibility for the economic and social well-being of the citizens may become and in fact has already turned out to be a serious burden on its authority; still, exactly this burden gives the dissatisfied citizens the chance to vote the government out of office rather than to abolish the basic structures of a market economy altogether. This is what happened in May 1994 and what in fact could be expected on theoretical grounds: the framework of a pluralist democracy clearly displays that different models of a capitalist market economy and, likewise, different paths of transition to such an economic system exist. Moreover, it provides the institutional tools for making collective decisions about the individuals' preferences. Thus, due to the open character of the concept of the market economy democracy is more likely to be an incentive for the striving after the appropriate relationship between the market economy and social demands rather than an instrument for the abolition of the former.

But even in the not yet consolidated Bulgaria and Slovakia democracy is not to be viewed as the problem which adds to the difficulties of economic transition. Democratic rights do not serve the economically deprived and politically disenchanted popular masses as instruments with the help of which they try to get rid of capitalism which many perceive as the cause of their misery. Paradoxically, it is the lack of consolidation which stands in the way of the realization of that potentiality. As our account displays, the degree of socio-economic interest organization in these countries is still rather low, mostly because the cleavage structure of a modern capitalist economy is still lacking. This is part of the democratic weakness which affects the society in two directions: democracy is too weak for unequivocal development toward the structures of a capitalist market economy; and it is equally too impotent for unequivocal regression to a state-controlled economy. A democratic decision for or against a capitalist economy requires coherent collective interests, active and politically skilful minorities, and a high degree of organizational articulation the shortage of which is one of the main causes for the lack of consolidation in Bulgaria and Slovakia. The abolition of the already accomplished development of the capitalist market economy presupposes an active civil society able to allocate the manifold resources and the political support for a goal which, if this support could in fact be mobilized, would no longer be aspired to because the underlying reason – outright misery – would not exist. In other words, the deficiency that has prevented these societies from realizing consolidated democracy is the same which bars them from using democratic instruments for the regression to some kind of authoritarian economy.

However, this does not mean that due to the overall weakness of the

democratic structures authoritarian or semi-authoritarian forms of domination will not arise (which then may easily affect the economy).
Obviously, societies which lack the cleavage structures of a fully developed
capitalist economy and whose basic economic and political institutions
are not yet accustomed to socio-economic interest representation and
mediation can easily fall prey to a populist authoritarianism which
regards the complex web of democratic rules, procedures, institutions
and attitudes as an obstacle to an allegedly direct rule of the people. The
dangerous potentiality of this development cannot be fully dismissed. Yet
the constitutional barriers appear strong enough to prevent a regression
of the current state of democratic affairs to an outright populist-
authoritarian regime (like, e.g., in Croatia or Serbia). In none of the four
countries under study can we find plebiscitarian channels which could
easily open this door. Only in Bulgaria is the president popularly elected,
but his powers are so restricted that the presidency is not likely to serve as
the stepping-stone for a plebiscitarian dictatorship. More likely is the
continuance of a fragmented party structure resting on a poorly developed civic culture and democracy being identified mainly with the
principle of unqualified majority rule.

A final caveat. Our concept of consolidation must not be confused
with economic success. A thriving capitalist economy may go along with
an unconsolidated democracy, and a consolidated democracy may well
suffer from a poorly performing market economy. While we can assume
that "poverty is a principal and probably the principal obstacle to
democratic development" (Huntington 1993: 311), we can be less certain
about the relationship between economic performance and political
consolidation. Although there are some striking positive correlations, the
causal links are far from obvious. We hypothesize that poverty as such
does not necessarily put democracy in jeopardy; on the other hand,
democracy does not necessarily put an end to poverty. What is likely to
endanger democracy is a drastic decline in the standard economic
performance of a society. Our sample provides some hints to this effect:
Bulgaria and Slovakia which lag in terms of consolidation also score
worse economically than the Czech Republic and Hungary. Still, they
perform better than one would expect in view of their problematic
politico-institutional state of affairs. This suggests that political turmoils
have only a limited effect on economic performance. Although we do not
deny that politics matters in that, e.g., the conditions for the accessibility
to loans from international organizations or for the attraction of foreign
investment are likely to be improved if constancy and predictability of the
machinery of government and of its policies obtain, we submit that the
most significant variable for the success of the transformation is the

degree of compatibility of the inherited world views, patterns of behavior and basic social and political concepts with the functional necessities of a modern, partly industrial, partly already post-industrial society. Thus, what matters most is the social and cultural capital and its potential for adjusting the legacies of the past to the requirements of the present.

References

Abel, István and Bonin, John P. (1993) "State Desertion and Convertibility: The Case of Hungary," in Székely, István P. and Newbery, David M. G. (eds.), *Hungary: An Economy in Transition*, Cambridge University Press, pp. 329–41.

Abrahám, S. (1995) "Early Elections in Slovakia: A State of Deadlock," *Government and Opposition*, 30 (Winter), 86–100.

Adam, A. (1990) "Tendances du développement de l'ordre constitutionnel de Hongrie," Studia Juridica Auctoritate Universitatis Pecs Publicata 120, Pecs.

Adam, Jan (1989) *Economic Reforms in the Soviet Union and Eastern Europe since the 1960s*, Basingstoke: Macmillan.

Adams, Bradley F. (1995) "Morality, Wisdom, and Revision: The Czech Opposition of the 1970s and the Expulsion of the Sudeten Germans," *East European Politics and Societies*, 9(2), 234–55.

Agh, Attila (1992a) "The Parliamentary Way to Democracy: The Case of Hungary," in Szoboszlai, György (ed.), *Flying Blind. Emerging Democracies in East-Central Europe*, Budapest: Hungarian Political Science Association, pp. 275–314.

  (1992b) "The Emerging Party Systems in East Central Europe," Budapest Papers on Democratic Transition, No. 13, Hungarian Center for Democracy Studies Foundation, Department of Political Science, Budapest University of Economics.

  (1993) "The 'Comparative Revolution' and the Transition in Central and Southern Europe," *Journal of Theoretical Politics*, 5(2), 231–52.

  (1993a) "The Premature Senility of the Young Democracies: The Central European Experience," Budapest Papers on Democratic Transition,

No. 68, Hungarian Center for Democracy Studies Foundation,
Department of Political Science, Budapest University of Economics.
(1995) "The Role of the First Parliament in Democratic Transition," in
Agh, A. and Kurtán, S. (eds.), *The First Parliament (1990–1994)*,
Budapest: Hungarian Center for Democracy Studies Foundation.
(1995) "Die neuen politischen Eliten in Mittelosteuropa," in Wollmann,
Hellmut, Wiesenthal, Helmut, and Bönker, Frank (eds.),
Transformation sozialistischer Gesellschaften: Am Ende des Anfangs,
Opladen: Westdeutscher Verlag, pp. 422–36.
Agh, A. and Kurtán, S. (1995) "The 1990 and 1994 Parliamentary Elections
in Hungary: Continuity and Change in a Political System," in Agh, A.
and Kurtán, S. (eds.), *The First Parliament (1990–1994)*, Budapest: The
Hungarian Center for Democratic Studies.
Aghion, Philippe and Blanchard, Olivier J. (1994) "On the Speed of
Transition in Eastern Europe," NBER, Working Paper No. 4736,
Cambridge, MA.
Almond, Gabriel A. (1958) "A Comparative Study of Interest Groups and
the Political Process," *American Political Science Review*, 52(1), 270–82.
Almond, Gabriel A. and Verba, Sidney (1963) *The Civic Culture*, Princeton:
Princeton University Press.
Alter, Peter (1995) "Demokratie und ethnische Differenzierung," in
Hatschikjan and Weilemann (eds.), *Nationalismus im Umbruch.
Ethnizität, Staat und Politik im neuen Osteuropa*, Cologne: Verlag
Wissenschaft und Politik, pp. 29–41.
Amsden, Alice, Taylor, Lance, and Kochanowicz, Jacek (1994) *The Market
Meets its Match: Restructuring the Economies of Eastern Europe*,
Cambridge, MA: Harvard University Press.
Andorka, Rudolf (1993) "Regime Transitions in Hungary in the 20th
Century: The Role of National Counter Elites," *Governance*, 6(3),
358–71.
Andorka, Rudolf, Kondratas, Anna and Tóth, Istvan György (1994)
"Hungary's Welfare State in Transition: Structure, Initial Reforms and
Recommendations," Blue Ribbon Commission Policy Study No. 3,
Budapest: Hudson Institute.
Arato, A. (1994) "Constitution and Continuity in the East European
Transitions. Part Two: The Hungarian Case," *Constellations*, 1, 306–25.
(1994a) "Elections, Coalitions, and Constitutionalism in Hungary," *East
European Constitutional Review*, 3 (3/4), 26–32.
Arnason, Johan P. (1993) *The Future That Failed. Origins and Destinies of
the Soviet Model*, London: Routledge.
Arrow, K. *et al.* (eds.) (1995) *Barriers to the Negotiated Resolution of
Conflicts*, New York: Norton.
Ash, Timothy Garton (1990) *The Uses Of Adversity. Essays on the Fate of
Central Europe*, New York: Vintage Books.

Ashley, Stephen (1990) "Bulgaria," *Electoral Studies*, 9(4), 312–18.

Atkinson, Anthony B. and Micklewright, John (1992) *Economic Transformation in Eastern Europe and the Distribution of Income*, Cambridge University Press.

Avineri, Shlomo (1995) "Chancen und Hindernisse auf dem Weg zu einer bürgerlichen Gesellschaft in Mittel- und Osteuropa," inWeidenfeld, Werner (ed.), *Demokratie und Marktwirtschaft in Osteuropa*, Gütersloh: Verlag Bertelsmann Stiftung, pp. 55–64.

Balázs, István (1993) "The Transformation of Hungarian Public Administration," *Public Administration*, 71(1/2), 75–88.

Banac, Ivo (1992) "Post-communism as Post-Yugoslavism: The Yugoslav Non-Revolutions of 1989–1990," in Banac, I. (ed.), *Eastern Europe in Revolution*, Ithaca and London: Cornell University Press, pp. 168–87.

(1992a) "Introduction," in Banac, I. (ed.), *Eastern Europe in Revolution*, Ithaca and London: Cornell University Press, pp. 1–12.

Barbone, Luca and Marchetti, Domenico (1995) "Transition and the Fiscal Crisis in Central Europe," *Economics of Transition*, 3(1), 59–74.

Bartlett, Will (1992) "The Political Economy of Privatization: Property Reform and Democracy in Hungary," *East European Politics and Societies*, 6(1), 73–118.

Barr, Nicholas (1994) "Income Transfers: Social Insurance," in Barr, Nicholas (ed.), *Labor Markets and Social Policy in Central and Eastern Europe. The Transition and Beyond*, London: Oxford University Press, pp. 192–225.

Bates, D. G. (1994) "What's in a Name – Minorities, Identity, and Politics in Bulgaria," *Identities*, 1(2–3), 201–25.

Batt, Judy (1991) *East Central Europe from Reform to Transformation*, London: Pinter.

Bauman, Zygmunt (1993) "A Post-Modern Revolution?" Frentzel-Zagórska, J. (ed.), *From a One-Party State to Democracy: Transitions in Eastern Europe*, Amsterdam and Atlanta: Rodopi.

Baumol, William J. (1986) "Productivity Growth, Convergence, and Welfare: What the Long-Run Data Show," *American Economic Review*, 76(5), 1072–85.

Baylis, Thomas A. (1994) "Plus Ça Change? Transformation and Continuity Among East European Elites," *Communist and Post-Communist Studies*, 27(3), 315–28.

Bellamy, Richard (1993) "Citizenship and rights," in Bellamy, Richard (ed.), *Theories and Concepts of Politics. An Introduction*, Manchester: Manchester University Press, pp. 43–76.

Berend, Ivan T. (1990) *The Hungarian Economic Reforms 1953–1988*, Cambridge University Press.

Berglund, Sten and Dellenbrant, Jan Ake (1991) "Prospects for the New Democracies in Eastern Europe," in Berglund, Sten and Dellenbrant,

Jan Ake (eds.), *The New Democracies in Eastern Europe. Party Systems and Party Cleavages*, Aldershot: Edward Elgar, pp. 211–23.

Berglund, Sten and Dellenbrant, Jan Ake (1994) "The Breakdown of Communism in Eastern Europe," in Berglund, S. and Dellenbrant, J. A. (eds.), *The New Democracies in Eastern Europe*, Cambridge University Press, pp. 1–13.

Bertelsmann Stiftung (ed.) (1994) *Mittel- und Osteuropa auf dem Weg in die Europäische Union. Bericht zum Stand der Integrationsfähigkeit*, Gütersloh: Verlag Bertelsmann Stiftung.

Bertschi, C. C. (1994) "Lustration and the Transition to Democracy – The Cases of Poland and Bulgaria," *East European Quarterly*, 28(4), 435–51.

Besters, Hans (ed.) (1993) *Marktwirtschaft in Osteuropa. Eine Zwischenbilanz*, Baden-Baden: Nomos.

Beyme, Klaus (1988) "The Genesis of Constitutional Review in Parliamentary Systems," in Landfried, Christine (ed.), *Constitutional Review and Legislation. An International Comparison*, Baden-Baden: Nomos, pp. 21–38.

(1993) "Regime Transitions and Recruitment of Elites in Eastern Europe," *Governance*, 6(3), 409–25.

(1994) *Systemwechsel in Osteuropa*, Frankfurt M: Suhrkamp.

Bibó, István (1946) *Die Misere der osteuropäischen Kleinstaaterei*, Frankfurt M: Neue Kritik 1992.

Bihari, Mihály (1994) "Political System and Party System," in Kurtán, Sándor, Sándor, Péter and Vass, László (eds.), *Magyarország politikai évköyve* (Political Yearbook of Hungary), Budapest, pp. 39–49.

Blahoz, Josef (1992) "Human Rights, their Guarantees and the Constitutional Judiciary in the CSFR," *Austrian Journal of Public and International Law*, 43(1), 31–71.

Blanchard, Olivier, Commander, Simon, and Coricelli, Fabrizio (1994) "Unemployment and the Labour Market in Eastern Europe," in Boeri, Tito (ed.), *Unemployment in Transition Countries: Transient or Persistent?* Paris: OECD, pp. 59–76.

Blejer, Mario I. and Gelb, Alan H. (1993) "The Contraction of Eastern Europe's Economies: Introduction to the Conference," in Blejer, Mario I., Calvo, Guillermo A., Coricelli, Fabrizio, and Gelb, Alan H. (eds.), "Eastern Europe in Transition: From Recession to Growth?" World Bank, Discussion Paper No. 196, Washington, DC, pp. 1–7.

Blondel, Jean (1968) "Party Systems and Patterns of Government in Western Democracies," *Canadian Journal of Political Science*, 1(2), 180–201.

Bobeva, Daniela (1994) "Economic Reforms and Labour Market in Bulgaria," unpublished manuscript, Sofia.

Boenker, Frank (1993) "On the Road to a Capitalist Economy: Economic Stabilization and Transformation in Bulgaria, Czechoslovakia, and

Hungary, "Zerp-Diskussionspapier. Papers on East European Constitution Building No. 4, Bremen: Zentrum für Europäische Rechtspolitik an der Universität Bremen.

(1994) "External Determinants of the Patterns and Outcomes of East European Transitions," *Emergo*, 1(1), 34–54.

(1995) "The Dog That Did Not Bark? Politische Restriktionen und ökonomische Reformen in den Visegrád-Ländern," in Wollmann, Hellmut, Wiesenthal, Helmut, and Bönker, Frank (eds.), *Transformation sozialistischer Gesellschaften: Am Ende des Anfangs*, Opladen: Westdeutscher Verlag, pp. 180–206.

Boeri, Tito (1994a) "'Transitional' Unemployment," *Economics of Transition*, 2, 1–25.

(1994b) "Labour Market Flows and the Persistence of Unemployment in Central and Eastern Europe," in Boeri, Tito (ed.), *Unemployment in Transition Countries: Transient or Persistent?* Paris: OECD, pp. 13–56.

Boeri, Tito and Szirácki, György (1993) "Labour Market Policies and Developments in Central and Eastern Europe: A Comparative Analysis," in Fischer, Georg and Standing, Guy (eds.), *Structural Change in Central and Eastern Europe: Labour Market and Social Policy Implications*, Paris: OECD, pp. 241–61.

Bogetic, Zeljko and Hillman, Arye L. (1994) "The Tax Base in Transition: The Case of Bulgaria," *Communist Economies and Economic Transformation*, 6(4), 537–52.

Bogetic, Zeljko and Fox, Louise (1993) "Incomes Policy During Stabilization: A Review and Lessons from Bulgaria and Romania," *Comparative Economic Studies*, 35(1), 39–57.

Bohata, Petr (1990) "Der Wandel des Sozialversicherungssystems in der Tschechoslowakei," *Jahrbuch für Ostrecht*, 31, 397–416.

Bolton, P. and Roland, G. (1992) "Privatization in Central and Eastern Europe," *Economic Policy*, 15, 275–309.

Boycko, Maxim (1991) "Price Decontrol: The Microeconomic Case for the 'Big Bang' Approach," *Oxford Review of Economic Policy*, 7(4), 35–45.

Bozóki, András (1990) "Political Transition and Constitutional Change in Hungary," *Südosteuropa*, 39(9), 538–49.

(1992) "Hungary's Road to Systematic Change: The Opposition Round Table," Working Paper of the Center for the Study of Constitutionalism in Eastern Europe, School of Law, University of Chicago.

Bozóki, András (ed.) (1994) *Democratic Legitimacy in Post-communist Societies*, Budapest: T-Twins Publishers.

Brada, Josef C. (1993) "The Transformation from Communism to Capitalism: How Far? How Fast?" *Post-Soviet Affairs*, 9(2), 87–110.

Brada, Josef C., Singh, Inderjit, and Török, Adám (1994) *Firms Afloat and*

Firms Adrift. Hungarian Industry and the Economic Transition, Armonk, NY and London: Sharpe.

Bren, Pauline (1994) "Czech Restitution Laws Rekindle Sudeten Germans' Grievances," RFE/RL-Research Report, January 14, 17–22.

Brenner, Christine (1995) "Staat, Nation und Minderheiten nach der tschecho-slowakischen Teilung," in Hatschikjan and Weilemann (eds.), *Nationalismus im Umbruch. Ethnizität, Staat und Politik im neuen Osteuropa*, Cologne: Verlag Wissenschaft und Politik, pp. 90–104.

Brom, Karla and Orenstein, Mitchell (1994) "The Privatised Sector in the Czech Republic: Government and Bank Control in a Transition Economy," *Europe-Asia Studies*, 46(6), 893–928.

Brunner, Georg (1991) "Die neue Verfassung der Republik Ungarn: Entstehungsgeschichte und Grundprobleme," *Jahrbuch für Politik*, 1, 297–318.

(1992) "Das Wirtschaftsrecht Osteuropas im Umbruch," in Baur, Jürgen F., Müller-Graff, Peter-Christian, and Zuleeg, Manfred (eds.), *Europarecht – Energierecht – Wirtschaftsrecht. Festschrift für Bodo Börner zum 70. Geburtstag*, Cologne, Berlin, Bonn, and Munich: Heymanns, pp. 39–55.

(1993) *Nationalitätenprobleme und Minderheitenkonflikte in Osteuropa*, Gütersloh: Verlag Bertelsmann Stiftung.

(1995) "Minderheitenkonflikte in Osteuropa – Bestandsaufnahme und Lösungsansätze," in Weidenfeld, Werner (ed.), *Demokratie und Marktwirtschaft in Osteuropa*, Gütersloh: Verlag Bertelsmann Stiftung, pp. 495–520.

Brusis, Martin (1993) "Privatisierungskonflikte in Polen, Ungarn und der ehemaligen CSFR. Überlegungen zu einer vergleichenden Analyse," *Osteuropa*, 43(7), 678–86.

(1994) *Systemtransformation als Entscheidungsprozeß. Eine vergleichende Analyse zur Privatisierungspolitik in Ungarn*. Diss:, FU Berlin.

(1994a) "Korporatismus als Transformationskonsens. Der Fall Ungarn im osteuropäischen Vergleich," Arbeitspapiere AG TRAP 94/3, Berlin.

Bruszt, László (1991) "The Negotiated Revolution of Hungary," in Szoboszlai, György (ed.), *Democracy and Political Transformation. Theories and East-Central European Realities*, Budapest: Hungarian Political Science Association, pp. 213–25.

(1992) "Transformative Politics: Social Costs and Social Peace in East Central Europe," *East European Politics and Societies*, 6 (1), 55–72.

(1993) "Collective Actions, Democracy and the Vicious Circles of Transformative Politics," unpublished paper presented at the Pan Europe Working Group of the SSRC/ACLS, Berlin, May.

Bruszt, László and Simon, János (1992) "The Great Transformation in Hungary and Eastern Europe," in Szoboszlai, György (ed.), *Flying*

Blind. Emerging Democracies in Eastern Central Europe, Budapest: Hungarian Political Science Association, pp. 177–203.

Bruszt, László and Stark, David (1992) "Remaking the Political Field in Hungary: From the Politics of Confrontation to the Politics of Competition," in Banac, I. (ed.), *Eastern Europe in Revolution*, Ithaca and London: Cornell University Press, pp. 13–55.

Bruszt, László and Stark, David (1991) "Remaking the Political Field in Hungary: From the Politics of Confrontation to the Politics of Competition," *Journal of International Affairs*, 45(1), 201–45.

Bryant, Christopher and Mokrzycki, Edmund (eds.) (1994) *The New Great Transformation?* London and New York: Routledge.

Buchtíková, Alena and Flek, Vladislav (1994) "Bargaining Structure and Wage Development in Czechoslovakia," in Krovák, J. (ed.), *Current Economics and Politics of (ex-) Czechoslovakia*, Commack, NY: Nova Science Publishers, pp. 273–97.

Bútarová, Zora and Bútora, Martin (1995) "Political Parties, Value Orientations, and Slovakia's Road to Independence," in Wightman, Gordon (ed.), *Party Formation in East-Central Europe. Post-Communist Politics in Czechoslovakia, Hungary, Poland, and Bulgaria*, Aldershot: Edward Elgar, pp. 107–33.

Bútora, Martin and Bútorová, Zora (1993) "Slovakia – the Identity Challenges of the Newly Born State," *Social Research*, 60(4), 705–36.

Calda, Milos (1992) "The Round Table Talks in Czechoslovakia (November/December 1989)," Working Paper of the Center for the Study of Constitutionalism in Eastern Europe, School of Law, University of Chicago.

Campbell, John L. (1995) "State Building and Postcommunist Fiscal Deficits," *American Behavioral Scientist*, 38(5), 760–87.

Capek, Ales (1994) "The Bad Debts Problem in the Czech Economy," *Moct-Most*, 4(3), 59–70.

Carlin, Wendy, Van Reenen, John and Wolfe, Toby (1994) "Enterprise Restructuring in the Transition: An Analytical Survey of the Case Study Evidence from Central and Eastern Europe," EBRD, Working Paper No. 14, London.

CEC (Commission of the European Communities) (ed.) (1993) *Employment Observatory, Central & Eastern Europe*, No. 5, December, Brussels.
(1995) *Employment Observatory. Central & Eastern Europe*, No. 7, May, Brussels.

Cepl, Vojtech and Gillis, Mark (1993) "Senate, anyone?" EECR, Spring 1993.
(1994) "Survey of Presidential Powers: Formal and Informal – Czech Republic," EECR, Fall 1993/Winter 1994, 64–68.

Charap, Joshua and Zemplinerová, Alena (1993) "Restructuring in the Czech Economy," EBRD, Working Paper No. 2, London.

Chavdarova, Tanya (1994) "The Legal Status of Job in Changing Bulgarian Society," unpublished manuscript, Sofia.

Cichon, Michael (1991) "Health Sector Reforms in Central and Eastern Europe: Paradigm Reversed?" *International Labour Review*, 130, 311–27.

Cichon, Michael (1995) "Social Expenditure in Central and Eastern Europe Under Challenge: Financing A Decent Society Or Cutting Corners?" ILO-CEET Newsletter No. 1, 8–10.

Cichon, Michael (ed.) (1995) "Social Protection in the Visegrád Countries: Four Country Profiles," ILO-CEET Report No. 13, Budapest.

Cichon, Michael and Hagemejer, Krzysztof (1995) "Social Protection Expenditure. A Review of the Macroeconomic Issues," unpublished manuscript, Geneva: ILO.

Cichon, Michael and Samuel, Lenia (eds.) (1995) *Making Social Protection Work. The Challenge of Tripartism in Social Protection Governance for Countries in Transition*, Geneva: ILO.

Comisso, Ellen (1991) "Political Coalitions, Economic Choices," in Szoboszlai, György (ed.), *Democracy and Political Transformation*, Budapest: Hungarian Political Science Association, pp.122–37.

Commander, Simon, Köllö, János and Ugaz, Cecilia (1994) "Labor Market Evolutions in the Transition: Hungary," unpublished manuscript, Washington and Budapest.

Cornia, Giovanni Andrea (1994) "Poverty, Food Consumption, and Nutrition During the Transition to the Market Economy in Eastern Europe," *American Economic Review*, 84(2), 297–302.

Coratelli, Carlo (1993) "Limiting Central Bank Credit to the Government. Theory and Practice," IMF, Occasional Paper No. 110, Washington, DC.

Corbett, Jenny and Mayer, Colin (1991) "Financial Reform in Eastern Europe: Progress with the Wrong Model," *Oxford Review of Economic Policy*, 7(4), 57–75.

Coricelli, Fabrizio and Lane, Timothy D. (1993) "Wage Controls During the Transition from Central Planning to a Market Economy," *World Bank Research Observer*, 8(2), 195–210.

Cotta, Mauricio (1992) "Building New Party Systems after the Dictatorship. The East European Cases in Comparative Perspective," Paper presented at the Workshop: "Between Continuity and Innovation: the rebirth of pluralist party systems after the fall of non-democratic regimes," ECPR Joint Sessions of Workshops, Limerick, March 30 – April 4.

Coulson, Andrew (ed.) (1995) *Local Government in Eastern Europe. Establishing Democracy at the Grassroots*. Aldershot: Edward Elgar.

Crawford, Iain and Thompson, Alan (1994) "Driving Change: Politics and Administration," in Barr, Nicholas (ed.), *Labor Markets and Social*

Policy in Central and Eastern Europe. The Transition and Beyond,
London: Oxford University Press, pp. 322–52.

Cukierman, Alex (1992) *Central Bank Strategy, Credibility, and Independence:
Theory and Evidence*, Cambridge, MA and London: MIT Press.

Daalder, Hans and Mair, Peter (eds.) (1984) *Western European Party
Systems. Continuity and Change*, Beverly Hills: Sage.

Dahl, Robert A. (1971) *Polyarchie: Partizipation and Opposition*, New Haven:
Yale University Press.

   (1991) "Transitions to Democracy," in Szoboszlai, György (ed.),
*Democracy and Political Transformation. Theories and East-Central
European Realities*, Budapest: Hungarian Political Science Association,
pp. 9–20.

Dahrendorf, Ralf (1990) *Betrachtungen über die Revolution in Europa*,
Stuttgart: Deutsche Verlagsanstalt.

Dasgupta, Partha (1988) "Trust as a Commodity," in Gambetta, Diego
(ed.), *Trust. Making and Breaking Cooperative Relations*, Oxford and
New York: Blackwell, pp. 49–72.

Deacon, Bob (1992) "East European Welfare: Past, Present and Future in
Comparative Context," in Deacon, Bob *et al.* (eds.), *The New Eastern
Europe. Social Policy Past, Present and Future*, London: Sage, pp. 1–30.

Dellenbrand, Jan Ake (1993) "Parties and Parety Systems in Eastern Europe,"
in White, Stephen, Batt, Judy, and Lewis, Paul G. (eds.), *Developments in
East European Politics*, Basinstoke: Macmillan, pp. 147–62.

Diamond, Larry and Linz, Juan J. (1989) "Introduction: Politics, Society,
and Democracy in Latin America," in Diamond, Larry, Linz, Juan J.,
and Lipset, Seymour, M. (eds.), *Democracy in Developing Countries,
Vol. IV, Latin America*, Boulder, CO and London: Lynne Rienner
Publishers and Adamanture Press Limited.

Diamond, Larry (1990) "Three Paradoxes of Democracy," *Journal of
Democracy*, 3, 48–60.

Dimitrov, Rumen (1995a) "Türken, Tabak, Politik. Zur Ökonomisierung
ethnischer Konflikte in Bulgarien," in Hatschikjan and Weilemann
(eds.), *Nationalismus im Umbruch. Ethnizität, Staat und Politik im
neuen Osteuropa*, Cologne: Verlag Wissenschaft und Politik, pp. 75–90.

   (1995b) "Sicherheitspolitik und ethnische Konflikte aus bulgarischer
Sicht," in Seewann (ed.), (1995), 174–99.

Dittus, Peter (1994) "Bank Reform and Behavior in Central Europe,"
Journal of Comparative Economics, 19(3), 335–61.

Dobrinsky, Rumen (1994) "The Problem of Bad Loans and Enterprise
Indebtedness in Bulgaria," *Moct-Most*, 4(3), 37–58.

Dornbusch, Rüdiger (1992) "Monetary Problems of Post-Communism:
Lessons from the End of the Austro-Hungarian Empire,"
Weltwirtschaftliches Archiv, 128(3), 391–424.

Drabek, Zdenek, Janacek, Kamil, and Tuma, Zdenek (1994) "Inflation in the Czech and Slovak Republics, 1985–1991," *Journal of Comparative Economics*, 18(2), 146–74.

Duverger, Maurice (1984) "Which is the Best Electoral System?" in Lijphart, A. and Grofman, B. (eds.), pp. 31–9.

   (1992) "A New Political System Model: Semi-Presidential Government," in Lijphart, Arendt (ed.) (1992b), p. 147.

Earle, John S., Frydman, Roman, Rapaczynski, Andrzej, and Turkewitz, Joel (1994) *Small Privatization. The Transformation of Retail Trade and Consumer Services in the Czech Republic, Hungary, and Poland*, Budapest, London, and New York: CEU Press.

EBRD (European Bank for Reconstruction and Development) (1994) Transition Report, London.

   (1995) "Investment and Enterprise Development," Transition report, London.

Edgington, Bella (1994) "To Kill a Romany," *Race and Class*, 35(3), 80–2.

Ehrlich, Éva (1985) "The Size Structure of Manufacturing Establishments and Enterprises: An International Comparison," *Journal of Comparative Economics*, 9(3), 267–95.

   (1991) "Contest Between Countries: 1937–1986," *Soviet Studies*, 43(5), 875–96.

   (1993) "Economic Growth in Eastern Central Europe after World War II," in Szirmai, Adam, van Ark, Bart, and Pilat, Dirk (eds.), *Explaining Economic Growth. Essays in Honour of Angus Maddison*, Amsterdam: North-Holland, pp. 301–25.

Elster, Jon (1990) "When Communism Dissolves," *London Review of Books*, 12 (2), 3–6.

   (1991) "Constitutionalism in Eastern Europe: An Introduction," *The University of Chicago Law Review*, 38(2), 447–82.

   (1993) "Constitution-Making in Eastern Europe: Rebuilding the Boat in the Sea," *Public Administration*, 71, 167–217.

   (1994) "Bargaining over the Presidency," *East European Constitutional Review*, Fall 1993/Winter 1994.

   (1995) "Strategic Uses of Argument," Arrow, K. *et al.* (eds.), *Barriers to the Negotiated Resolution of Conflicts*, New York: Norton.

   (1995a) "Transition, Constitution-Making and Separation in Czechoslovakia," *Archives Européennes de Sociologie*, 36(1), 105–34.

Elster, Jon (ed.) (1996) *The Round Table Talks and the Breakdown of Communism*, Chicago and London: University of Chicago Press.

Engelbrekt, Kjell (1991) "Opposition Narrowly Defeats Socialists in National Elections," *Report on Eastern Europe*, 2 (43), 1–3.

   (1992) "Bulgaria," *Towards the Rule of Law, RFE/RL Research Report*, 1 (27), 4–9.

   (1995) "Political Turmoil, Economic Recovery," *Transition 1*, 19–22.

Estrin, Saul and Takla, Lina (1993) "Competition and Competition Policy in the Czech and Slovak Republics," in Estrin, Saul and Cave, Martin (eds.), *Competition and Competition Policy. A Comparative Analysis of Central and Eastern Europe*, London and New York: Pinter, pp. 44–61.

Evans, Geoffry and Whitefield, Stephen (1993) "Identifying the Bases of Party Competition in Eastern Europe," *British Journal of Political Science*, 23 (4), 521–48.

Fajth, Gáspár and Lakatos, Judith (1995) "The Transformation of Employee Benefits in Hungary," *Economics of Transition*, 3, 255–60.

Fan, Qimiao and Schaffer, Mark E. (1994) "Government Financial Transfers and Enterprise Adjustments in Russia, with Comparisons to Central and Eastern Europe," *Economics of Transition*, 2(2), 151–88.

Fehér, Ferenc (1989) "On Making Central Europe," *East European Politics and Societies*, 3(3), 412–47.

Ferge, Zsuzsa (1989) "Arbeitslosigkeit in Ungarn," *Prokla*, 76, 92–108.

(1992) "Social Policy Regimes and Social Structure. Hypotheses about the Prospects of Social Policy in Central and Eastern Europe," in Ferge, Zsuzsa and Kolberg, Jon Eivind (eds.), *Social Policy in a Changing Europe*, Frankfurt M. and Boulder, CO.: Westview, pp. 201–22.

Filer, Randall K., Veprek, Jaromir, Vyborná, Olga, Papes, Zdenek, and Veprek, Pavel (1995) "Health Care Reform in the Czech Republic," in Svejnar, Jan (ed.), *The Czech Republic and Economic Transition in Eastern Europe*, San Diego: Academic Press, pp. 395–411.

Fischer, Stanley (1995) "Turning Back?" *Transition*, 1(1), 60–3.

Fischer, Stanley and Gelb, Alan (1991) "The Process of Socialist Economic Transformation," *Journal of Economic Perspectives*, 5(4), 91–105.

Fishman, Robert, M. (1990) "Rethinking State and Regime: Southern Europe's Transition to Democracy," *World Politics*, 17(4), 422–40.

de Fougerolles, Jean (1995) "The Latin American Experience with Private Pension Funds: Lessons for Eastern Europe," *Transition*, (newsletter issued by the Transition Economics Division of the World Bank), 6(7–8), 4–7.

Frankfurter Allgemeine Zeitung, manager magazin, Rödel & Partner (eds.) (1995) Investitionsführer Mittel- und Osteuropa. Bd. 3 (Slowakische Republik); Bd. 5 (Tschechische Republik), Frankfurt M.

Freeman, Richard B. (1994) "What Direction for Labor Market Institutions in Eastern and Central Europe?" in Blanchard, Olivier J., Froot, Kenneth A., and Sachs, Jeffrey D. (eds.), *The Transition in Eastern Europe. Vol. II: Restructuring*, Chicago and London: University of Chicago Press, pp. 1–29.

Frentzel-Zagórska, Janina (1990) "Civil Society in Poland and Hungary," *Soviet Studies*, 42(4), 759–77.

(1993) "The Road to a Democratic Political System in Post-Communist

Eastern Europe," in Frentzel-Zagórska, J. (ed.), *From a One-Party State to Democracy*, Amsterdam and Atlanta: Rodopi, pp. 165–94.

Frey, Mária (1994) "The Role of the State in Employment Policy and Labour Market Programmes: The Hungarian Case in International Comparison," unpublished manuscript (prepared for the ILO/Japan Project on Employment Policies for Transition in Hungary), Budapest.

Fromme, Martin and Wolf, Stephan (1995) "Slowakei," in Weidenfeld, Werner (ed.), *Demokratie und Marktwirtschaft in Osteuropa*, Gütersloh: Verlag Bertelsmann Stiftung, pp. 157–70.

Frydman, Roman and Rapaczynski, Andrzej (1994) *Privatization in Eastern Europe: Is the State Withering Away?* Budapest, London, and New York: CEU Press.

Frydman, Roman, Rapaczynski, Andrzej, and Earle, John S. *et al.* (1993) *The Privatization Process in Central Europe*, Budapest, London, and New York: CEU Press.

Gács, János (1994) "Liberalization of Foreign Trade in Eastern Europe: Rush and Reconsideration," in Gács, János and Winckler, Georg (eds.), *International Trade and Restructuring in Eastern Europe*, Heidelberg: Physica, pp. 123–51.

Ganev, Venelin I. (1995) "The Mysterious Politics of Bulgaria's 'Movements for Rights and Freedoms'," *East European Constitutional Review*, 4 (1), 49–53.

Gellner, Ernest (1991) "Nationalism and Politics in Eastern Europe," *New Left Review*, 189, 127–34.

Giaro, Tomasz (1993) "Europa und das Pandektenrecht," *Rechtshistorisches Journal*, 12, 326–45.

Glatz, Ferenc (1995) "Ungarn," in Weidenfeld, Werner (ed.), *Demokratie und Marktwirtschaft in Osteuropa*, Gütersloh: Verlag Bertelsmann Stiftung, pp. 171–90.

Glos, George E. (1992) "The New Czechoslovak Commercial Code," *Review of Central and East European Law*, 18(6), 555–69.

Godfrey, Martin (1994) "Are Hungarian Labour Costs Really so High?" unpublished manuscript (prepared for the ILO/Japan Project on Employment Policies for Transition in Hungary), Budapest.

Goleva, Polja (1995) "Bulgarien: Insolvenzrecht (4. Teil des Handelsgesetzbuches). Einführung," *Wirtschaft und Recht in Osteuropa*, 4(1), 14 f.

Góra, Marek (1993) "Labour Hoarding and its Estimates in Central and Eastern European Economies," in Boeri, Tito and Garonna, Paolo (eds.), *Employment and Unemployment in Economies in Transition. Conceptual and Measurement Issues*, Paris: OECD, pp. 61–84.

Gotovska-Popova, Teodorichka and Engelbrekt, Kjell (1993) "The Tortuous Reform of Bulgarian Television," *RFE/RL Research Report*, 2 (38), 45–9.

Gray, Cheryl W. *et al.* (1993) "Evolving Legal Frameworks for Private Sector Development in Central and Eastern Europe," World Bank, Discussion Paper No. 209, Washington, DC.

Greenberg, D. and Katz, S. N. *et al.* (eds.) (1993), *Constitutionalism and Democracy. Transitions in the Contemporary World*, New York and Oxford: Oxford University Press.

Greskovits, Béla (1994) "Hungerstrikers, the Unions, the Government, and the Parties," unpublished manuscript, Budapest.

Grosfeld, Irene (1994) "Financial Systems in Transition: Is There a Case for a Bank Based System?" CEPR, Discussion Paper No. 1062, London.

Grospic, Jiri and Matula, Milos (1993) "The Central-Local Relation in Czechoslovakia," in Stahlberg, Krister (ed.), *Local Government in Transition. Evolving Local Government in Former Eastern Europe*, Helsinki, pp. 169–94.

Grzybowski, Marian (1994) "The Transition to Competitive Pluralism in Hungary," in Berlund, S. and Dellenbrant, J. A. (eds.), *The New Democracies in Eastern Europe*, Cambridge University Press, pp. 169–202.

Haggard, S. and Kaufmann, R. K. (1994) "The Challenges of Consolidation," *Journal of Democracy*, 5(4), 5–16.

Hall, John A. (1995) "A View of Death: On Communism, Ancient and Modern," unpublished paper, Montreal, McGill University.

Haller, Birgitt, Schaller, Christian, Brokl, Lubomír, Cambáliková, Monika, and Mansfeldová, Zdenka (1993) "Möglichkeiten sozialpartnerschaftlicher Konfliktregelung in der Tschechischen und Slowakischen Republik" (Projekt 4177 des Jubliläumsfonds der Österreichischen Nationalbank), unpublished manuscript, Innsbruck.

Hankiss, Elemer (1993) "The Hungarian Media's War of Independence," Working paper of Analysis, Center for Social Studies, Budapest.

Hatschikjan and Weileman (eds.) (1995) "Nationalismus im Umbruch. Ethnizität, Staat und Politik im neuen Osteuropa," Cologne: Verlag Wissenschaft und Politik.

Hardi, Péter (1992) "Tabula Rasa vs. the Legacy of the Past," in Szoboszlai, György (ed.), *Flying Blind. Emerging Democracies in East-Central Europe*, Budapest: Hungarian Political Science Association. pp. 227–51.

Hardin, Russel (1991) "Trusting Persons, Trusting Institutions," in Zeckhauser, Richard J. (ed.), *Strategy and Choice*, Cambridge, MA and London: MIT Press, pp. 185–209.

Harrison, Mark (1994) "GDPs of the USSR and Eastern Europe: Towards an Interwar Comparison," *Europe-Asia Studies*, 46(2), 243–59.

Hausner, Jerzy and Wojtyna, Andrzej (1993) "Trends and Perspectives in the Development of a System of Interest Representation in Post-Socialist Societies," in Hausner, Jerzy, Jessop, Bob, and Nielson, Klaus (eds.), *Institutional Frameworks Market Economies in Scandinavia and East European Perspectives*, Aldershot, pp. 217–37.

Havel, Vaclav (1992) *Sommermeditationen*, Berlin: Rowohlt.

(1993) *Summer Meditations*, Random House.

Havlik, Peter (1992) "East–West GDP Comparisons: Problems, Methods and Results," in Richter, Sándor (ed.), *The Transition from Command to Market Economies in East-Central Europe*, Boulder, San Francisco, and Oxford: Westview, pp. 185–227.

Hegedus, Eva (1994) "The Hungarian Framework for Bankruptcy and Reorganisation and Its Effect on the National Economy," in *Corporate Bankruptcy and Reorganisation Procedures in OECD and Central and Eastern European Countries*, Paris: OECD, pp. 99–107.

Heitger, Bernhard, Schrader, Klaus, and Bode, Eckhardt (1992) *Die mittel- und osteuropäischen Länder als Unternehmensstandort*, Tübingen: Mohr.

Hellman, Joel (1996) "Constitutions and Economic Reform in Postcommunist Transitions," *EECR*, 5(1), 46–56.

Hendrych, Dusan (1993) "Transforming Czechoslovakian Public Administration: Traditions and New Challenges," *Public Administration*, 71(1/2), 41–54.

Henkin, L. (1985) "Human Rights," *Encyclopedia of Public International Law*, 8, 268–74.

(1989) "Revolutions and Constitutions," *Louisiana Law Review*, 49, 1023–56.

Herczog, László (1994) "The Role of the State in Collective Bargaining in Hungary," unpublished manuscript, Budapest.

Hertel, Hans Hermann (1994) "Die Maueröffnung," *Deutschlandarchiv*, 11, 1136–58 and no. 12.

Hesse, Joachim J. (1993) "From Transformation to Modernization: Administrative Change in Central and Eastern Europe," *Public Administration* (1/2), 219–57.

Hesse, Joachim J. and Johnson, N. (eds.) (1995) *Constitutional Change in Europe*, Oxford University Press.

Hibbing, John R. and Patterson, Samuel C. (1992) "A Democratic Legislative in the Making. The Historic Hungarian Elections of 1990," *Comparative Political Studies*, 24(4), 430–54.

Higley, John and Pakulski, Jan (1995) "Lite Transformation in Central and Eastern Europe," *Australian Journal of Political Research*, 30, 415 – 35.

Hirschman, Albert O. (1993) "Exit, Voice, and the Fate of the German Democratic Republic. An Essay in Conceptual History," *World Politics*, 45, 173–202.

(1994) "Wieviel Gemeinsinn braucht die liberale Gesellschaft?" *Leviathan*, 22, 293–304.

(1995) "Social Conflicts as Pillars of Democratic Market Societies," in

Hirschman, A. O., *A Propensity to Self-subversion*, Cambridge, MA and London: Harvard University Press, pp. 231–48.

Hoekman, Bernard M. and Mavroidis, Petros C. (1995) "Linking Competition and Trade Policies in Central and East European Countries," in Winters, L. Alan (ed.), *Foundations of an Open Economy. Trade Laws and Institutions for Eastern Europe*, London: CEPR, pp. 111–54.

Höpken, Wolfgang (1995) "Bulgarien," in Weidenfeld, Werner (ed.), *Demokratie und Marktwirtschaft in Osteuropa*, Gütersloh: Verlag Bertelsmann Stiftung, pp. 191–226.

Holländer, Pavel (1992) "The New Slovak Constitution: A Critique," *EECR*, Fall, 16–17.

Holmes, Leslie (1992) "Communist and Post-Communist Systems," in Hawskworth, Mary and Kogan, Maurice (eds.), *Encyclopedia of Government and Politics*, Vol. I, London and New York: Routledge, pp. 215–28.

Holzmann, Robert (1991) "Adapting to Economic Change: Reconciling Social Protection with Market Economies," International Labour Organisation CTASS/1991/6, Geneva.

Holzmann, Robert (1994) "Kapitalgedeckte und private Renten für Osteuropa?" unpublished manuscript, Saarbrücken.

Howard, Dick (1993) "How Ideas Travel: Rights at Home and Abroad," in Howard, D. (ed.), *Constitution Making in Eastern Europe*, Baltimore: John Hopkins University Press, pp. 9–20.

Huntington, Samuel P. (1968) *Political Order and Changing Societies*, New Haven and London: Yale University Press.

(1992) "How Countries Democratize," *Political Science Quarterly*, 106(4), 579–616.

(1993) *The Third Wave. Democratization in the Late Twentieth Century*, Norman and London: University of Oklahoma Press.

Hylland, A. (1991) "Proportional Representation without Party Lists," in Malnes, R. and Underdal, A. (eds.), *Rationality and Institutions*, Oslo: Universitetsforlaget.

Ilchev, I. and Perry, D. M. (1993) "Bulgarian Ethnic Groups: Politics and Perceptions," *RFE/RL Research Report*, 2(12), March, 35–41.

ILO (International Labour Organisation) (1927) "Die obligatorische Krankenversicherung. Eine vergleichende Darstellung der Gesetze und Durchführungsbestimmungen," Genf: Internationales Arbeitsamt.

(1993) "Family Benefits and Social Assistance Systems" (Draft Final Report for the Project "Technical Assistance to the Social Security Sector – Czechoslovakia" of the EC PHARE Programme), unpublished manuscript, Geneva.

ILO-CEET (International Labour Organisation – Central and Eastern

European Team) (1994) *The Bulgarian Challenge: Reforming Labour Market and Social Policy*, Budapest: ILO-CEET.

IMF (1994) *World Economic Outlook*, May, Washington, DC.

(1995) "Eastern Europe – Factors Underlying the Weakening Performance of Tax Revenues," *Economic Systems*, 19(2), 101–24.

Ionescu, Ghita (1994) "The Painful Return to Normality," in Parry, G. and Moran, M. (eds.), *Democracy and Democratization*, London and New York: Routledge, pp. 109–28.

Ionin, L. (1994) Kulturelle Modelle der Transformation in Rußland. Theoretische Aspekte, Paper P 94–005, Wissenschaftszentrum Berlin für Sozialforschung, August.

Jackman, Richard and Rutkowski, Michal (1994) "Labor Markets: Wages and Employment," in Barr, Nicholas (ed.), *Labor Markets and Social Policy in Central and Eastern Europe. The Transition and Beyond*, London: Oxford University Press, pp. 121–59.

János, Andrew C. (1994) "Continuity and Change in Eastern Europe: Strategies of Post-Communist Politics," *East European Politics and Societies*, 8(1), 1–31.

Jarvis, Sarah J. and Micklewright, John (1992) "The Targeting of Family Allowance in Hungary," EUI Working Paper ECO No. 92/96, Florence: European University Institute.

Jasiewicz, Krzystof (1993) "Structures of Representation," in White, Stephen, Batt, Judy, and Lewis, Paul G. (eds.), *Developments in East European Politics*, Basinstoke: Macmillan Press, pp. 124–46.

Jellinek, Georg (1963) System der subjektiven öffentlichen Rechte, Darmstadt: Wissenschaftliche Buchgesellschaft.

Jessel-Holst, Christa (1988) "Reformen des Wirtschaftsrechts in Bulgarien," in Westen, Klaus and Schroeder, Friedrich-Christian (eds.), *Sozialistisches Wirtschaftsrecht zwischen Wandel und Bewahrung*, Berlin: Spitz, pp. 253–79.

Jicinsky, Z. and Mikule, V. (1994) *Das Ende der Tschechoslovakei 1992 in verfassungsrechtlicher Sicht, Parts I and II*, Cologne: Bundesinstitut für ostwissenschaftliche und internationale Studien.

Johnson, O. V. (1985) *Slovakia 1918–1938. Education and the Making of a Nation*, Boulder, CO: Columbia University Press.

Jowitt, Ken (1992) "New World Disorder. The Leninist Extinction," Berkeley: University of California Press.

(1992a) "The Leninist Legacy," in Banac, Ivo (ed.), *Eastern Europe in Revolution*, Ithaca and London: Cornell University Press, pp. 207–24.

Juberias, Carlos F. (1992) "The Breakdown of the Czecho-Slovak Party System," in Szoboszlai, György (ed.), *Flying Blind. Emerging Democracies in East-Central Europe*, Budapest: Hungarian Political Science Association, pp. 147–76.

(1994) "Electoral Systems in Eastern Europe. How are they changing? Why are they changing?" Paper for presentation at the XVI International Political Science Association World Congress, Berlin, August 21–5.

Judt, Tony (1990) "The Rediscovery of Central Europe," *Daedalus*, 119(1), 23–54.

Kabaj, Mieczyslaw and Kowalik, Tadeusz (1995) "Letter to the Editor: Who Is Responsible for Postcommunist Successes in Eastern Europe?" *Transition* (newsletter issued by the Transition Economics Division of the World Bank), 6(7–8), 7–8.

Kahler, Miles (1990) "Orthodoxy and its Alternatives: Explaining Approaches to Stabilization and Adjustment," in Nelson, Joan (ed.), *Economic Crisis and Policy Choice: The Politics of Adjustment in the Third World*, Princeton, NJ: Princeton University Press, pp. 33–61.

Karasimeonov, G. (1995) "Differentiation Postponed: Party Pluralism in Bulgaria," in Wightman, G. (ed.), *Party Formation in East-Central Europe*, Aldershot: Edward Elgar.

Karl, Terry Linn and Schmitter, Philippe C. (1991) "Modes of Transition in Latin America, Southern and Eastern Europe," *Journal of International Affairs*, 45, 269–84.

Kasalová, Hana (1994) "Payments for Care: The Case of the Czech Republic," in Evers, Adalbert, Pijl, Marja, and Ungerson, Clare (eds.), *Payments for Care. A Comparative Overview*, Wien: European Center Vienna, pp. 215–25.

Kéri, László and Levendel, Adám (1995) "The First Three Years of a Multi-Party System in Hungary," in Wightman, Gordon (ed.), *Party Formation in East-Central Europe. Post-Communist Politics in Czechoslovakia, Hungary, Poland, and Bulgaria*, Aldershot: Edward Elgar, pp. 134–53.

Kilényi, Géza and Lamm, Vanda (eds.) (1990) *Democratic Changes in Hungary*, Budapest: Public Law Research Center of the Hungarian Academy of Sciences.

Kitschelt, Herbert (1992) "The Formation of Party Systems in East Central Europe," *Politics and Society*, 20(1), 7–50.

(1995) "Die Entwicklung post-sozialistischer Parteiensysteme. Vergleichende Perspektiven," in Wollmann, Hellmut, Wiesenthal, Helmut, and Bönker, Frank (eds.), *Transformation sozialistischer Gesellschaften: Am Ende des Anfangs*, Opladen: Westdeutscher Verlag, pp. 475–508.

Kitschelt, Herbert, Dimitrov, D., and Kanev, A. (1995) "The Structuring of the Vote in Post-Communist Party Systems – The Bulgarian Example," *European Journal of Political Research*, 27(2), 143–60.

Kis, János (1995) "Between Reform and Revolution: Three Hypotheses about the Nature of the Regime Change," *Constellations*, 1/3, 399–421.

Kjellberg, Francesco, Reschova, Jana, Sootla, Georg, and Taylor, John (1994) "The Role of Local Self-Government in Democratic and Democratizing Societies. The New Local Government Acts in Czech Republic, Estonia, and Norway," Paper presented at the XVI. IPSA World Congress, Berlin, August 21–5.

Klingsberg, Ethan (1993) "Hungary: Safeguarding the Transition," *EECR*, 2, Spring, 44–8.

Köllö, János (1994) "Labor Market Developments and Employment Policy in Hungary," unpublished manuscript, Budapest.

Körösényi, Andras (1990) "Hungary," *Electoral Studies*, 9(4), 337–45.

 (1991) "Revival of the Past or New Beginning? The Nature of Post-Communist Politics," in Szoboszlai, György (ed.), *Democracy and Political Transformation. Theories and East-Central Realities*, Budapest: Hungarian Political Science Association, pp. 165–92.

 (1992) "Stable or Fragile Democracy? Political Cleavages and Party System in Hungary," in Szoboszlai, György (ed.), *Flying Blind. Emerging Democracies in East-Central Europe*, Budapest: Hungarian Political Science Association, Budapest, pp. 344–56.

Kolarova, Rumyana (1992) "Tacit Agreements in the Bulgarian Transition to Democracy: Minority Rights and Constitutionalism," unpublished paper, Sofia.

 (1993) "A Self-Restricting Court," *EECR*, Spring, 48–50.

Kolarova, Rumyana and Dimitrov, Dimitr (1991) "Round Table Talks in Bulgaria," Working Paper of the Center for the Study of Constitutionalism in Eastern Europe, School of Law, University of Chicago.

 (1994) "Electoral Laws in Eastern Europe: Bulgaria," *East European Constitutional Review*, 3 (2), 50–5.

 (1996) "The Round Table Talks in Bulgaria," in Elster, Jon (ed.), *The Round Table Talks and the Breakdown of Communism*, Chicago and London: University of Chicago Press, pp. 178–212.

Kommission der Europäischen Gemeinschaften (1995) Vorbereitung der assoziierten Staaten Mittel- und Osteuropas auf die Integration in den Binnenmarkt der Union, KOM (95) 163 endg., Brussels.

Kopecky, Petr (1995) "Factionalism in Parliamentary Parties in the Czech Republic: A Concept and Some Empirical Findings," *Democratization*, 2(1), 138–51.

Korbonski, Andrzej (1989) "The Politics of Economic Reforms in Eastern Europe: The Last Thirty Years," *Soviet Studies*, 41(1), 1–19.

Korkisch, Friedrich (1958) "Das Privatrecht Ost-Mitteleuropas in rechtsvergleichender Sicht," *Rabels Zeitschrift für ausländisches und internationales Privatrecht*, 23(2), 201–30.

Kornai, János (1992) *The Socialist System. The Political Economy of Communism*, Princeton, NJ: Princeton University Press.

(1992a) "The Principles of Privatization in Eastern Europe," *De Economist*, 140(2), 153–76.

(1993) "The Evolution of Financial Discipline under the Postsocialist System," *Kyklos*, 46(3), 315–36.

(1994) "Transformational Recession: The Main Causes," *Journal of Comparative Economics*, 19(1), 39–63.

Kosta, Jiri (1995) "Tschechische Republik," in Weidenfeld, Werner (ed.), *Demokratie und Marktwirtschaft in Osteuropa*, Gütersloh: Verlag Bertelsmann Stiftung, pp. 143–56.

Kostelecky, Thomás (1995) "Changing Party Alliances in an Changing Party System: the 1990 and 1992 Parliamentary Elections in the Czech Republic," in Wightman, Gordon (ed.), *Party Formation in East-Central Europe. Post-Communist Politics in Czechoslovakia, Hungary, Poland, and Bulgaria*, Aldershot: Edward Elgar, pp. 79–106.

Kotrba, Josef and Svejnar, Jan (1994) "Rapid and Multifaceted Privatization: Experience of the Czech and Slovak Republics," *Moct-Most*, 4(2), 147–85.

Kozminski, Andrzej K. (1992) "Transition from Planned to Market Economy: Hungary and Poland Compared," *Studies in Comparative Communism*, 25(4), 315–33.

Krasnodebski, Zdzislaw (1995) "Der Nationalismus in Ostmitteleuropa," in Wollmann, Hellmut, Wiesenthal, Helmut, and Bönker, Frank (eds.), *Transformation sozialistischer Gesellschaften: Am Ende des Anfangs*, Opladen: Westdeutscher Verlag, pp. 235–53.

Krastev, Ivan (1994) "The Postponed Demise of Functional Politics. Party Structure and Party Perspectives in Bulgaria," unpublished manuscript, Sofia.

Krizan, Peter, Durian, Juraj, and Krnac, Peter (1995) "The Reform of the Structure, Management and Financing of the Slovak Health Service from 1989 to 1993," *Sociologia*, 27, 101–6.

Kubiak, Hieronim (1993) "International Consequences of Ethnic Conflicts in Eastern Europe," in Balàsz, Judith *et al.* (eds.), "International Stability: Eastern European Perspectives," WZB, Discussion Paper P 93–305, Berlin, pp. 1–16.

Kukorelli, Istvan (1991) "The Birth, Testing, and Results of the 1989 Hungarian Electoral Law," *Sowjet Studies*, 43(1), 137–56.

Kuron, Jacek (1993) "Man muß träumen. Soziale Gerechtigkeit als soziale Bewegung," *Transit*, 6, 6–24.

Kurtán, Sándor (1993) "Sozialpartnerschaft in Ungarn?" in Tálos, Emmerich (ed.), *Sozialpartnerschaft. Kontinuität und Wandel eines Modells*, Wien: Verlag für Gesellschaftskritik, pp. 267–84.

Kvapilová, Erika (1993) "Social Policy in Independent Slovakia: The Present Situation and Perspectives for the Future," *Czech Sociological Review*, 1, 173–83.

Kymlicka, Will (1995) *Multicultural Citizenship: A Liberal Theory of Minority Rights*, Oxford: Clarendon Press.

Kymlicka, Will and Norman, Wayne (1994) "Return of the Citizen: A Survey of Recent Work on Citizenship Theory," *Ethics*, 104, 352–81.

Laczko, Frank (1993) "Social Policy and the Third Sector in East-Central Europe," in Ringen, Stein and Wallace, Claire (eds.), *Societies in Transition: East-Central Europe Today*, Prague: CEU, pp. 91–104.

(1994) *Older People in Eastern and Central Europe. The Price of Transition to a Market Economy*, London: HelpAge International.

Ladó, Mária (1994) "Workers' and Employers' Interests – as They are Represented in the Changing Industrial Relations in Hungary," UCEMET Working Papers No. 3, Crakow: Academy of Economics.

Laurencie, Jean-Patrice de la (1993) "A European Perspective on the Development of Competition Policy in Transition," in Estrin, Saul and Cave, Martin (eds.), *Competition and Competition Policy. A Comparative Analysis of Central and Eastern Europe*, London and New York: Pinter, pp. 93–108.

Leff, Carol Skalnik (1988) *National Conflict in Czechoslovakia. The Making and Remaking of a State, 1918–1987*, Princeton: Princeton University Press.

Lendvai, Paul (1995) "Nationalitäten- und Minderheitenkonflikte in Mittel- und Osteuropa," in Weidenfeld, Werner (ed.), *Demokratie und Marktwirtschaft in Osteuropa*, Gütersloh: Verlag Bertelsmann Stiftung, pp. 89–104.

Levinson, Sanford (1988) *Constitutional Faith*, Princeton: Princeton University Press.

Lijphart, Arend (1990) "The Political Consequences of Electoral Laws, 1945–85," *American Political Science Review*, 84(2), 481–96.

(1992) "Democratization and Constitutional Choices in Czecho-Slovakia, Hungary, and Poland, 1989–1991," in Szoboszlai, György (ed.), *Flying Blind. Emerging Democracies in East-Central Europe*, Budapest: Hungarian Political Science Association, pp. 99–113.

(1992a) "Democratization and Constitutional Choices in Czecho-Slovakia, Hungary and Poland 1989–1991," *Journal of Theoretical Politics*, 4(2), 207–23.

(1994) *Electoral Systems and Party Systems. A Study of Twenty-Seven Democracies, 1945–1990*, Oxford University Press.

Lijphart, Arend (ed.), (1992b) *Parliamentary versus Presidential Government*, Oxford University Press.

Lijphart, Arend and Grofman, Bernard (eds.) (1984) Choosing an Electoral System. Issues and Alternatives, New York: Praeger.

Linz, Juan J. and Stepan, Alfred (1992) "Political Identities and Electoral Sequences: Spain, the Soviet Union, and Yugoslavia," *Daedalus* 121(2), 123–39.

Lippott, J. (1995) "Letter to the Center," EECR, (4)4, 92.

Lipset, Seymour Martin and Rokkan, Stein (1967) "Cleavage Structures, Party Systems, and Voter Alignments: An Introduction," in Lipset, Seymour Martin and Rokkan, Stein (eds.), *Party Systems and Voter Alignments: Cross National Perspectives*, New York and London: The Free Press, pp. 1–64.

Lipset, Seymour Martin and Bence, Gyorgy (1994) "Anticipations of the Failure of Communism," *Theory and Society*, 23, 169–210.

Lomax, Bill (1995) "Factions and Factionalism in Hungary's New Party System," *Democratization*, 2(1), 125–37.

Machonin, Pavel (1993) "The Social Structure of Soviet-Type Societies, Its Collapse and Leagacy," *Czech Sociological Review*, 1(2), 231–49.

Mänicke-Gyöngyösi, Krisztina (1995) "Ost- und ostmitteleuropäische Gesellschaften zwischen autonomer Gestaltung und Adaptation westlicher Modernisierungsmodelle", in Wollmann, Hellmut, Wiesenthal, Helmut, and Bönker, Frank (eds.), *Transformation sozialistischer Gesellschaften: Am Ende des Anfangs*, Opladen: Westdeutscher Verlag, pp. 30–53.

Mainwaring, Scott (1992) "Presidentialism, Multipartism, and Democracy: The Difficult Combination," in Szoboszlai, György (ed.), *Flying Blind. Emerging Democracies in East-Central Europe*, Budapest: Hungarian Political Science Association. pp. 59–85.

Mair, Peter (1990) "Introduction," in Mair, Peter (ed.), *The West European Party Systems*, Oxford University Press.

    (1991) "Electoral Markets and Stable States," in Moran, Michael and Wright, Maurice (eds.), *The Market and the State. Studies in Interdependence*, London, pp. 119–37.

Major, Iván (1994) "The Constraints on Privatization in Hungary: Insufficient Demand or Inelastic Supply?" *Moct-Most*, 4(2), 107–45.

Majoras, Ferenc (1990) "Ungarns neue Verfassungsordnung: Die Genese einer neuen demokratischen Republik nach westlichen Maßstäben," *Osteuropa-Recht*, 36, 85–99; 161–74.

Malova, Darina (1993a) "The Dimension of Political Culture and Style: The Case of Slovak Republic," Paper prepared for the 3rd meeting on "Europe Agreements," organized by the Institute for European Politics, Bonn, September 27–9.

    (1993b) "Slovakia," unpublished manuscript, Bratislava (to be published in: Political Data Yearbook of the ECPR).

Malova, Darina and Sivakova, Danica (1994) "The National Council of the Slovak Republic: Between Democratic Transition and National State-Building," Paper presented at the Conference on the New Parliaments, Stirin, August 14–17.

Mangott, Gerhard (1993) "Auf dem langen Weg der Konsolidierung.

Mühen und Hindernisse der Parteiensysteme im östlichen Zentraleuropa," in Plasser and Ulram (eds.), pp. 98–112.

Markowski, R. (1994) "Trust in Institutions in East Central Europe at the Beginning of Transformation," in Bozóki, A. (ed.), *Democratic Legitimacy in Post-Communist Societies*, Budapest: T-Twins Publishers.

Markus, György G. (1992) "Parties, Camps, and Cleavages in Post-Communist Hungary: Is the Weakness of the Social Democratic Forces Systemic?" in Szoboszlai, György (ed.), *Flying Blind. Emerging Democracies in East-Central Europe*, Budapest: Hungarian Political Science Association, pp. 331–43.

Mason, David S. (1992) "Attitudes Towards the Market and the State in Post-Communist Europe," unpublished manuscript.

Mates, Pavel (1992) "The New Slovak Constitution," in RFE/RL Research Report, October 30.

Mathernova, Katarina (1993) "Czechoslovakia: Constitutional Disappointments," in Howard, D. (ed.), *Constitution Making in Eastern Europe*, Baltimore: Johns Hopkins University Press, pp. 57–92.

McDermott, Gerald A. (1994) "Renegotiating the Ties That Bind: The Limits of Privatization in the Czech Republic," WZB, Discussion Paper FS I, Berlin, pp. 94–101.

McGregor, James (1993) "How Electoral Laws Shape the Eastern Europe's Parliaments," *RFE/RL Research Report*, 2(4), 11–18.

(1994) "The Presidency in East Central Europe," *RFE/RL Research Report*, 3(2), 23–31.

McIntosh, M. E., Iver, M., Abele, D. G., and Nolle, D. B. (1995) "Minority Rights and Majority Rule – Ethnic Tolerance in Romania and Bulgaria," *Social Forces*, 73(3), 939–67.

McKinnon, Ronald I. (1991) "Financial Control in the Transition from Classical Socialism to a Market Economy," *Journal of Economic Perspectives*, 5(4), 109–22.

Melone, Albert P. (1994) "Bulgaria National Roundtable Talks and the Politics of Accommodation," *International Political Science Review*, 15(3), 257–73.

Messerlin, Patrick A. (1995) "Central and East European Countries' Trade Laws in the Light of International Experience," in Winters, L. Alan (ed.), *Foundations of an Open Economy. Trade Law and Institutions for Eastern Europe*, London: CEPR, pp. 40–63.

Meyer, Klaus E. (1995) "Foreign Direct Investment in the Early Years of Economic Transition: A Survey," *Economics of Transition*, 3(3), 301–20.

Micklewright, John and Nagy, Gyula (1994) "How Does the Hungarian Unemployment Insurance System Really Work?" *Economics of Transition*, 2, 209–32.

Miháliková, Silvia (1995) "Die Slowakei fünf Jahre danach: Die Spaltung von Gesellschaft, Kultur und Politik," in Forschungsstelle Osteuropa an der Universität Bremen (ed.), *Tschechische Republik zwischen Traditionsbruch und Kontinuität*, Bremen: Edition Temmen, pp. 122–39.

Milanovic, Branko, (1994a) "Cash Social Transfers, Direct Taxes, and Income Distribution in Late Socialism," *Journal of Comparative Economics*, 18, 175–97.

(1994b) "A Cost of Transition: 50 Million New Poor and Growing Inequality," *Transition* (newsletter issued by the Transition Economics Division of the World Bank), 5(8), 1–4.

Miller, Petr (1992) *Development in the Sphere of Labour, Wages and Social Affairs Since December 1989 and Other Perspectives*, Bratislava: Research Institute of Labour and Social Affairs.

Miller, Jeffrey B. (1995) "Industrial Planning and the Transition to a Market Economy," *Economics of Transition*, 3(3), 289–99.

Mink, Andras (1994) "Survey of Presidential Powers: Formal and Informal – Hungary," *EECR*, Fall 1993/Winter 1994, 68–71.

Miszlivetz, Ferenc (1991) "Mitteleuropa – Der Weg nach Europa," *Die Neue Gesellschaft / Frankfurter Hefte*, 38(11), 970–83.

Mizsei, Kálmán (1994) "Bankruptcy and Banking Reform in the Transition Economies of Central and Eastern Europe," in Bonin, John P. and Székely, István P. (eds.), *The Development and Reform of Financial Systems in Central and Eastern Europe*, Aldershot and Brookfield: Edward Elgar, pp. 132–51.

MLSW (Ministry of Labour and Social Welfare, National Employment Office) (1994) "Labour Market Strategy," unpublished manuscript, Sofia.

Moerel, Hans (1994) "In Search of Central and Eastern European Labour Relations," WORC, Discussion Paper 94.03.014/1, Tilburg.

Moore, B. (1978) "Injustice. The Social Bases of Obedience and Revolt," New York: M. E. Sharpe.

Morvai, K. (1994) "Retroactive Justice based on International Law: A Recent Decision by the Hungarian Constitutional Court," *EECR*, Fall 1993/Winter 1994, 32–4.

Moynihan, Daniel Patrick (1993) *Pandaemonium. Ethnicity in International Politics*, Oxford University Press.

Murphy, Kevin M., Shleifer, Andrei, and Vishny, Robert W. (1992) "The Transition to a Market Economy: The Pitfalls of Partial Reform," *Quarterly Journal of Economics*, 107(3), 889–906.

Murphy, W. F. (1993) "Constitutions, Constitutionalism, and Democrazy," in Greenberg, D. and Katz, S. N. *et al.* (eds.), *Constitutionalism and Democracy. Transitions in the Contemporary World*, New York and Oxford: Oxford University Press, pp. 3–25.

Murrell, Peter (1992) "Evolution in Economics and in the Economic

Reform of the Centrally Planned Economies," in Clague, Christopher
and Rausser, Gordon C. (eds.), *The Emergence of Market Economies in
Eastern Europe*, Cambridge, MA and Oxford: Blackwell, pp. 35–53.
Myant, Martin (1993) *Transforming Socialist Economies. The Case of Poland
and Czechoslovakia*, Aldershot: Elgar.
   (1993a) "Czech and Slovak Trade Unions," *Journal of Communist Studies*,
   4, 59–84.
Nedelsky, Jennifer (1990) *Private Property and the Limits of American
Constitutionalism. The Madison Framework and Legacy*, Chicago:
Chicago University Press.
Nohlen, Dieter (1984a) "Two Incompatible Principles of Representation,"
in Lijphart, A. and Grofman, B. (eds.), pp. 83–9.
   (1984b) "Changes and Choices in Electoral Systems," in Lijphart, A. and
   Grofman, B. (eds.), pp. 217–24.
Nuti, Domenico M. (1985) "Hidden and Repressed Inflation in Soviet-Type
Economies. Definitions, Measurement and Stabilization," EUI,
Working Paper No. 85/200, Florence.
Nyers, Rezso and Lutz, Gabriella R. (1993) "Restructuring of the Banking
System in Hungary," *Transformation of the Banking System: Portfolio
Restructuring, Privatisation and the Payment System*, Paris: OECD,
pp. 59–68.
Obrman, Jan (1992) "Czechoslovakia: Stage Set for Disintegration?" in *RFE/
RL Research Report*, 1(28), 26–31.
OECD (Organisation for Economic Co-operation and Development) (1991)
"Czech and Slovak Federal Republik," *Economic Survey*, Paris.
   (1992) *Bulgaria. An Economic Assessment*, Paris.
   (1993) *Hungary. Economic Survey*, Paris.
   (1993a) "Competitiveness in Central and Eastern European Countries,"
   Economic Outlook, 53 (June), 125.
   (1994a) "The Czech and Slovak Republics," *Economic Survey*, Paris.
   (1994b) *Industry in the Czech and Slovak Republics*, Paris.
   (1995) *Social and Labour Market Policies in Hungary*, Paris.
   (1995a) *Review of Industry and Industrial Policy in Hungary*, Paris.
   (1995b) *Hungary, Economic Survey*, Paris.
O'Donnell, Guillermo and Schmitter, Phillippe C. (1986) *Transitions from
Authoritarian Rule: Tentative Conclusion about Uncertain Democracies*,
Baltimore and London: Johns Hopkins Unversity Press.
O'Donnell, Guillermo (1992) "Transitions, Continuities, and Paradoxes," in
Mainwaring, S., O'Donnell, Guillermo, and Valenzuela, J. S. (eds.),
*Issues in Democratic Consolidation: The New South American
Democracies in Comparative Perspective*, Notre Dame/Indiana,
pp. 17–56.
   (1993) "On the State, Democratization, and Some Conceptual Problems

(A Latin American View with Glances at some Post-Communist Countries)," *World Politics*, August.

Offe, Claus (1991) "Capitalism by Democratic Design? Democratic Theory Facing the Triple Transition in East Central Europe," *Social Research*, 58(4), 865–92.

(1991a) "Das Dilemma der Gleichzeitigkeit. Demokratisierung und Marktwirtschaft in Osteuropa," *Merkur*, 45(4), 279–92.

(1993) "The Politics of Social Policy in East European Transitions: Antecedents, Agents, and Agenda of Reform," *Social Research*, 60, 649–84.

(1994) *Der Tunnel am Ende des Lichts. Erkundungen der politischen Transformation im Neuen Osten*, Frankfurt M. and New York: Campus.

Olson, David, M. (1993) "Dissolution of the State: Political Parties and the 1992 Elections in Czechoslovakia," *Communist and Post-Communist Studies*, 26(3), 301–14.

Oltay, Edith (1992) "Hungary," in *Towards the Rule of Law*, RFE/RL Research Report, 1(27), 16–24.

(1995) "The Return of the Former Communists," *Transition*, 1, 34–7.

Orenstein, Mitchell (1994a) "The Political Success of Neo-Liberalism in the Czech Republic," unpublished manuscript, Prague and New Haven.

(1994b) "The Czech Tripartite Council and its Contribution to Social Peace," unpublished manuscript, Prague and New Haven.

Orosz, Eva (1994) "Health and Health Care under Socio-Economic Transition in Hungary," unpublished manuscript, Budapest.

Ost, David (1993) "The Politics of Interest in Post-Communist East Europe," *Theory and Society*, 22, 435–86.

(1994) "Class and Democracy. Organizing Antagonism in Post-Communist Eastern Europe," Paper presented at the XVI World Congress of IPSA, Berlin, August 21–5.

Paczolay, Péter (1993) "The New Hungarian Constitutional State: Challenges and Perspectives," in Howard, D. (ed.), *Constitution Making in Eastern Europe*, Baltimore: Johns Hopkins University Press, pp. 21–56.

Palma, Guiseppe Di (1990) *To Craft Democracies. An Essay on Democratic Transitions*, Berkeley and Oxford: University of California Press.

Pataki, Judith (1992) "Reform of the Hungarian Health-Care System," *RFE/RL Research Report*, 1(6), February 7, 59–62.

Pauer, Jan (1993) "Scheidung auf tschecho-slowakisch," *Lutherische Monatshefte*, 32, 13–16.

(1995) "Der tschechische Liberalkonservatismus," in Forschungsstelle Osteuropa an der Universität Bremen (ed.), *Tschechische Republik zwischen Traditionsbruch und Kontinuität*, Bremen: Edition Temmen, pp. 11–69.

Paulus, Christoph, Göpfert, Burkhard, Stuna, Stanislav, and Zoulik,

Frantisek (1993) "Konkurs- und Vergleichsrecht in der Tschechischen und der Slowakischen Republik," in Breidenbach, Stephan *et al.* (eds), *Handbuch Wirtschaft und Recht in Osteuropa*, Munich: Beck.

Pehe, Jiri (1990) "The Electoral Law," *Report on Eastern Europe*, (1)11, 15–8.

(1992a) "Czechoslovak Federal Assembly Adopts Electoral Law," *RFE/RL Research Report*, 1(14), 27–30.

(1992b) "Czechoslovak Elections Create Deadlock," *RFE/RL Research Report*, 1(25), 26–7.

(1995) "A Leader in Political Stability and Economic Growth," *Transition*, 1, 29–33.

Pfaff, Dieter (1993) "Die Rezeption deutschen Rechts in Bulgarien," *Südosteuropa Mitteilungen*, 33(2), 125–8.

Pierson, Paul (1994) *Dismantling the Welfare State? Reagan, Thatcher, and the Politics of Retrenchment*, Cambridge University Press.

(1995) "The New Politics of the Welfare State," ZeS-Arbeitspapier No. 3/95, Bremen: Centre for Social Policy Research.

Plasser, Fritz and Ulram, Peter A. (eds.) (1993) "Transformation oder Stagnation? Aktuelle politische Trends in Osteuropa," Schriftenreihe des Zentrums für angewandte Politikforschung, Bd. 2, Wien: Signum Verlag.

Plasser, Fritz and Ulram, Peter A. (1993) "Zum Stand der Demokratisierung in Ost-Mitteleuropa," in Plasser, Fritz and Ulram, Peter A. (eds.), *Transformation oder Stagnation? Aktuelle politische Trends in Osteuropa*, Wien: Signum Verlag, pp. 9–88.

Pogany, Istvan (1995) "A New Constitutional (Dis)Order for Eastern Europe?" in Pogany, I. (ed.), *Human Rights in Eastern Europe*, London: Edward Elgar.

Pomahac, Richard (1993) "Administrative Modernization in Czechoslovakia between Constitutional and Economic Reform," *Public Administration*, 71(172), 55–63.

Potucek, Martin (1993) "Current Social Policy Developments in the Czech and Slovak Republics," *Journal of European Social Policy*, 3, 209–26.

Poshtov, Georgi and Ganev, Venelin (1994) "Survey of Presidential Powers: Formal and Informal – Bulgaria," EECR, Fall 1993/Winter 1994, 61–4.

Preker, Alexander S. and Feachem, Richard G. A. (1994) "Health and Health Care," in Barr, Nicholas (ed.), *Labor Markets and Social Policy in Central and Eastern Europe. The Transition and Beyond*, London: Oxford University Press, pp. 288–321.

Preuss, Ulrich K. (1995) "Patterns of Constitutional Evolution and Change in Eastern Europe," in Hesse, J. J. and Johnson, N. (eds.), *Constitutional Change in Europe*, Oxford University Press, pp. 95–128.

(1995a) *Constitutional Revolution. The Link Between Constitutionalism and Progress*, New Jersey: Humanities Press.

(1996) "The Political Meaning of Constitutionalism," in Bellamy, Richard (ed.), *Constitutionalism, Democracy and Sovereignty: American and European Perspectives*, Aldershot: Avebury, pp. 11–30.

Pridham, Geoffry (ed.) (1990) *Securing Democracy: Political Parties and Democratic Consolidation in Southern Europe*, London and New York: Routledge.

Pridham, Geoffry (1992) "Coping with the Past, Confronting the Future: Party Strategies in Democratic Transition," Paper presented at the workshop: "Between Continuity and Innovation: The Rebirth of Pluralist Party Systems After the Fall of Non-Democratic Regimes," ECPR Joint Sessions of Workshops, Limerick, March 30 April 4.

Pridham, Geoffry and Vanhanen, Tatu (eds.) (1994) *Democratization in Eastern Europe*, London and New York: Routledge.

Przeworski, Adam (1988) "Some Problems in the Study of Transition to Democracy," in O'Donnell, Guillermo, Schmitter, Ph. C., and Whitehead, L. (eds.), *Transition from Authoritarian Rule. Comparative Perspectives*, Baltimore: Johns Hopkins University Press, pp. 47–63.

(1988a) "Democracy as a Contingent Outcome of Conflicts," in Elster, Jon and Slagstad, R. (eds.), *Constitutionalism and Democracy*, Cambridge University Press, pp. 59–80.

(1991) "Political Dynamics of Economic Reforms: East and South," in Szoboszlai, György (ed.), *Democracy and Political Transformation. Theories and East-Central Realities*, Budapest: Hungarian Political Science Association, pp. 21–74.

(1991a) *Democracy and the Market. Political and Economic Reforms in Eastern Europe and Latin America*, Cambridge University Press.

(1993) "Economic Reforms, Public Opinion, and Political Institutions: Poland in the East European Perspective," in Bresser Pereira, Luiz C., Maravall, José M., and Przeworski, Adam (eds.), *Economic Reforms in New Democracies. A Social-Democratic Approach*, Cambridge University Press, pp. 132–98.

Putnam, R. (1993) *Making Democracy Work. Civic Traditions in Modern Italy*, Princeton: Princeton University Press.

Rabas, J. (1984) "Kirche in Fesseln, Serie Materialien zur Situation der Katholischen Kirche in der CSSR," ed. Sozialwerk der Ackermann-Gemeinde, Munich.

Rae, Douglas W. (1971) *The Political Consequences of Electoral Laws*, 2nd edn, New Haven: Yale University Press.

Regulska, Joanna (1993) "Self-Governance or Central Control? Rewriting Constitutions in Central Europe," in Howard, Dick A. E. (ed.), *Constitution Making in Eastern Europe*, Washington, DC: The Woodrow Wilson Center, Special Studies, pp. 133–61.

Reiner, Thomas A. and Strong, Ann Louise (1995) "Formation of Land and

Housing Markets in the Czech Republic," *Journal of the American Planning Association*, 61, 200–9.

Révész, Gábor (1990) *Perestroika in Eastern Europe. Hungary's Economic Transformation*, Boulder, CO: Westview.

Rhodes, Matthew (1995) "National Identity and Minority Rights in the Constitutions of the Czech Republic and Slovakia," *East European Quarterly*, 29(3), 347–69.

Riese, Hajo (1995) "Transformation als Oktroi von Abhängigkeit," in Wollmann, Hellmut, Wiesenthal, Helmut, and Bönker, Frank (eds.), *Transformation sozialistischer Gesellschaften: Am Ende des Anfangs*, Opladen: Westdeutscher Verlag, pp. 163–79.

Rock, Charles P. (1994) "Interest Representation and the Evolution of the Industrial and Labour Relations System in Bulgaria: 1989–94," *Emergo*, 1(2), 83–99.

Rokkan, Stein (1970) *Citizens, Elections, Parties: Approaches to the Comparative Study of the Processes of Development*, Oslo: Universitätsforlaget.

Roland, Gerard (1994) "The Role of Political Constraints in Transition Strategies," *Economics of Transition*, 2 (1), 27–41.

Rosati, Dariusz K. (1994a) "Endogenous Budget Deficits During Transition: The Mechanism and Policy Response," in Herr, Hansjörg, Tober, Silke, and Westphal, Andreas (eds.), *Macroeconomic Problems of Transformation. Stabilization Policies and Economic Restructuring*, Aldershot and Brookfield: Edward Elgar, pp. 45–76.

(1994b) "Output Decline During Transition from Plan to Market: A Reconsideration," *Economics of Transition*, 2(4), 419–41.

Rose, Richard (1992) "Toward a Civil Economy," *Journal of Democracy*, 3(2), 13–26.

(1994) "Postcommunism and the Problem of Trust," *Journal of Democracy*, 5, 18–30.

Rose, Richard and Mishler, William T. E. (1994) "Mass Reaction to Regime Change: Polarization or Leaders and Laggards," *British Journal of Political Science*, 24, 1–24.

Rose, Richard and Seifert, Wolfgang (1995) "Materielle Lebensbedingungen und Einstellungen gegenüber Marktwirtschaft und Demokratie im Transformationsprozeß. Ostdeutschland und Osteuropa im Vergleich," in Wollmann, Hellmut, Wiesenthal, Helmut, and Bönker, Frank (eds.), *Transformation sozialistischer Gesellschaften: Am Ende des Anfangs*, Opladen: Westdeutscher Verlag, pp. 277–98.

Rosenberger, C. (1993) "Independent Slovakia – a New Country's old Habits," *World Policy Journal*, 10(3), 73–80.

Ross, Lee (1995) "Reactive Devaluation in Negotiation and Conflict," in Arrow, K. *et al.* (eds.), *Barriers to Conflict Resolution*, New York: W. W. Norton, pp. 26–42.

Rostowski, Jacek (1993) "Problems of Creating Stable Monetary Systems in Post-Communist Economies," *Europe-Asia Studies*, 45(3), 445–61.

Rothschild, Joseph (1989) *Return to Diversity: A Political History of East Central Europe since World War II*, New York.

(1993) *Return to Diversity: A Political History of East Central Europe since World War II*, New York (reprinted).

Rüb, Friedbert W. (1993) "Designing Political Systems in East European Transitions. A Comparative Study of Bulgaria, Czecho-Slovakia, and Hungary," ZERP-Diskussionspapier, Papers on East European Constitution Building No. 3, Bremen: Zentrum für europäische Rechtspolitik an der Universität Bremen.

(1994) "Schach dem Parlament! – Über semi-präsaidentielle Regierungssysteme in einigen postkommunistischen Gesellschaften," *Leviathan*, 22, 260–92.

(1995) "Die drei Paradoxien der Konsolidierung der neuen Demokratien in Mittel- und Osteuropa," in Wollmann, Hellmut, Wiesenthal, Helmut, and Bönker, Frank (eds.), *Transformation sozialistischer Gesellschaften: Am Ende des Anfangs*, Opladen: Westdeutscher Verlag, pp. 509–37.

Rutland, Peter (1992/3) "Thatcherism, Czech-style: Transition to Capitalism in the Czech Republic," *Telos*, 94, 103–29.

Rys, Vladimir (1995) "Social Security Developments in Central Europe: Return to Reality," unpublished manuscript, Geneva.

Sachs, Jeffrey D. (1995) "Postcommunist Parties and the Politics of Entitlement," *Transition*, 6(3), 1–4.

Sájo, Andras (1996) "How the Rule of Law Killed Hungarian Welfare Reform," EECR, 5(1), Winter, 31–41.

Salowsky, Heinz (1993) "Soziale Sicherheit, Lohnfindung und Arbeitskosten in den Reformländern Mittel- und Osteuropas," iw-trends 20, 89–100.

Sartori, Giovanni (1976) *Parties and Party Systems: A Framework for Analysis*, Cambridge University Press.

(1994) *Comparative Constitutional Engineering. An Inquiry into Structures, Incentives and Outcomes*, Basinstoke: Macmillan.

Scarpetta, Stefano and Reutersward, Anders (1994) "Unemployment Benefit Systems and Active Labour Market Policies in Central and Eastern Europe: An Overview," in Boeri, Tito (ed.), *Unemployment in Transition Countries: Transient or Persistent?* Paris: OECD, pp. 255–307.

Scarpetta, Stefano and Wörgötter, Andreas (eds.) (1995) *The Regional Dimension of Unemployment in Transition Countries. A Challenge for Labour Market and Social Policies*, Paris: OECD.

Schaffer, Mark E. (1995) "Should We be Concerned About the Provision of Social Benefits by Firms in Transition Economies?" *Economics of Transition*, 3, 247–50.

Schmieding, Holger (1993) "From Plan to Market: On the Nature of the
    Transformation Crisis," *Weltwirtschaftliches Archiv*, 129(2), 216–53.
Schmitter, Phillippe C. (1992) "The Consolidation of Democracy and the
    Representation of Social Groups," *American Behavioral Scientist*, 35(4/
    5), 422–49.
    (1994) "Transition in Europe – Democracy and Its Discontents. Dangers
    and Dilemmas of Democracy," *Journal of Democracy*, 5, published in
    the April edition.
Schöpflin, George (1993) *Politics in Eastern Europe, 1945–1992*, Oxford:
    Blackwell.
Schoukens, Paul (1994) "Die Entwicklung der Gesundheitssysteme in acht
    Ländern Mittel- und Osteuropas," in Internationale Vereinigung für
    Soziale Sicherheit (ed.), *Umstrukturierung der sozialen Sicherheit in
    Mittel- und Osteuropa*, Geneva: ISSA, pp. 125–41.
Schrameyer, K. (1992) "Die neue bulgarische Verfassung," *Osteuropa-Recht*,
    38, 159–80.
Schwartz, Herman (1992) "In Defense of Aiming High," EECR, 1(3), Fall,
    25–8.
    (1993) "The New Courts: An Overview," EECR, 2(2), Spring, 28–32.
    (1993) "The New East European Constitutional Courts," in Howard, D.
    (ed.), *Constitution Making in Eastern Europe*, Baltimore: Johns Hopkins
    University Press, pp. 163–208.
Scully, Gerald W. and Slottje, Daniel J. (1991) "Ranking Economic Liberty
    Across Countries," *Public Choice*, 69(2), 121–52.
Seewann, Gerhard (ed.) (1995) *Minderheiten als Konfliktpotential in
    Ostmittel- und Südosteuropa*, Munich: Oldenbourg.
Segert, Dieter (1995) "Aufstieg der (kommunistischen) Nachfolge-Parteien,"
    in Wollmann, Hellmut, Wiesenthal, Helmut, and Bönker, Frank (eds.),
    Transformation sozialistischer Gesellschaften: Am Ende des Anfangs,
    Opladen: Westdeutscher Verlag, pp. 459–74.
Selbourne, David (1994) *The Principle of Duty*, London: Sinclair
    Stevenson.
Share, Donals and Mainswaring, Scott (1986) "Transitions Through
    Transaction: Democratization in Brazil and Spain," in Selcher, Wayne
    A. (ed.), *Political Liberalisation in Brazil: Dynamics, Dilemmas and
    Future Prospects*, Boulder, CO: Westview Press.
Shentov, Ognian (1991) "The Bulgarian State System at a Crossroads,"
    Center for the Study of Democracy, Report, unpublished manuscript,
    Sofia.
Sik, Endre (1992) "From the Second to the Informal Economy," *Journal of
    Public Policy*, 12(2), 153–75.
Simon, János and Bruszt, Lásló (1992) "The Great Transformation in
    Hungary and Eastern Europe. Theoretical Approaches and Public
    Opinion about Capitalism and Democracy," in Szoboszlai, György

(ed.), *Flying Blind. Emerging Democracies in East-Central Europe,*
Budapest: Hungarian Political Science Association, pp. 177–203.

Sipos, Sándor (1992) "Poverty Measurement in Central and Eastern Europe
Before the Transition to the Market Economy," Innocenti Occasional
Papers, Economic Policy Series No. 29, Florence: UNICEF-ICDC.

(1994) "Income Transfers: Family Support and Poverty Relief," in Barr,
Nicholas (ed.), *Labor Markets and Social Policy in Central and Eastern
Europe. The Transition and Beyond,* London: Oxford University Press,
pp. 226–59.

Skapska, G. (1994) "The Legacy of Anti-Legalism," in Krygier, M. (ed.),
"Marxism and Communism: Posthumous Reflections on Politics,
Society, and Law," *Poznan Studies in Philosophy of Sciences and the
Humanities 1994,* 36, 199–218.

Slapnicka, Helmut (1991) "Das tschechoslowakische
Verfassungsprovisorium," *Osteuropa-Recht,* 258–85.

(1994) "Die Verfassungsordnung der Tschechischen Republik," in:
Osteuropa-Recht, 40, 28–43.

Srinivasan, T. N. (1994) "Human Development: A New Paradigm or
Reinvention of the Wheel?" *American Economic Review. Papers and
Proceedings,* 84, 238–43.

Stahlberg, Krister (ed.) (1993) *Local Government in Transition. Evolving
Local Government in Former Eastern Europe,* Helsinki.

Staniszkis, Jadwiga (1991) *The Dynamics of Break Through in Eastern Europe.
The Polish Experience,* Berkeley, Los Angeles.

Stark, David (1992) "Path Dependence and Privatization Strategies in East
Central Europe," *East European Politics and Societies,* 6(1), 17–54.

(1993) "Recombinant Property in East European Capitalism, WZB,
Discussion Paper FS I 93–102, Berlin.

(1994) "On the Limits of Dual Sector Models of Post-Socialist
Economies: A Comment on Hare," in Herr, Hansjörg, Tober, Silke,
and Westphal, Andreas (eds.), *Macroeconomic Problems of
Transformation. Stabilization Policies and Economic Restructuring,*
Aldeshot: Gower, pp. 215–21.

Stefoi, Elena (1994) "Electoral Law in Eastern Europe: Romania," *East
European Constitutional Review,* 2(2), 55–8.

Stepan, Alfred (1988) "Paths toward Redemocratization: Theoretical and
Comparative Considerations," in O'Donnell, Guillermo, Schmitter, Ph.
C. and Whitehead, L. (eds), *Transition from Authoritarian Rule.
Comparative Perspectives,* Baltimore: Johns Hopkins University Press,
pp. 64–84.

Stiglitz, Joseph E. (1992) "The Design of Financial Systems for the Newly
Emerging Democracies of Eastern Europe," in Clague, Christopher and
Rausser, Gordon C. (eds.), *The Emergence of Market Economies in
Eastern Europe,* Cambridge, MA and Oxford: Blackwell, pp. 161–84.

Stölting, Erhard (1995) "Die Verinnerlichung einer Denkform.
Gemeinsamkeiten und Differenzen des Nationalismus in Osteuropa,"
in Wollmann, Hellmut, Wiesenthal, Helmut, and Bönker, Frank (eds.),
Transformation sozialistischer Gesellschaften: Am Ende des Anfangs,
Opladen: Westdeutscher Verlag, pp. 254–76.

Stokes, Gale (1989) "The Social Origins of East European Politics," in
Chirot, Daniel (ed.), *The Origins of Backwardness in Eastern Europe.
Economics and Politics from the Middle Ages Until the Early Twentieth
Century*, Berkeley and London: University of California Press,
pp. 210–51.

Summers, Lawrence (1993) "Foreword," in Blejer, Mario I., Calvo,
Guillermo A., Coricelli, Fabrizio, and Gelb, Alan H. (eds.), "Eastern
Europe in Transition: From Recession to Growth?" World Bank,
Discussion Paper No. 196, Washington, DC.

Sundhaussen, Holm (1995) "Die 'Transformation' Osteuropas in
historischer Perspektive oder: Wie groß ist der Handlungsspielraum
einer Gesellschaft," in Wollmann, Hellmut, Wiesenthal, Helmut, and
Bönker, Frank (eds.), *Transformation sozialistischer Gesellschaften: Am
Ende des Anfangs*, Opladen: Westdeutscher Verlag, pp. 77–92.

Sunstein, Cass (1992) "Something Old, Something New," EECR, 1(1),
Spring, 18–21.

(1993) "Against Positive Rights," EECR, 2(1), Winter, 35–38.

(1995) "A Constitutional Anomaly in the Czech Republic?" EECR, 4(2),
Spring, 50–1.

(1995a) "A Constitutional Anomaly in the Czech Republic," EECR, 4(2),
Spring, 50–1.

(1995b) "Rights After Communism. Introduction," in EECR, 4(1),
Winter, 61–2.

Svejnar, Jan and Singer, Miroslav (1994) "Using Vouchers to Privatize an
Economy: The Czech and Slovak Case," *Economics of Transition*, 2(1),
43–69.

Svejnar, Jan, Terrell, Katherine, and Münich, Daniel (1995)
"Unemployment in the Czech and Slovak Republics," in Svejnar, Jan
(ed.), *The Czech Republic and Economic Transition in Eastern Europe*,
San Diego: Academic Press, pp. 285–316.

Swain, Geoffrey, Swain, Nigel (1993) *Eastern Europe since 1945*, Basingstoke:
Macmillan.

Swain, Nigel (1991) "Hungary," in Szajkowski, Bogdan (ed.), *New Political
Parties in Eastern Europe and the Soviet Union*, Harlow: Longman,
pp. 129–67.

Szabó, Gábor (1993) "The Role and Function of Local Self-Government in a
Unitary State. The Case of Hungary," in Stahlberg, Krister (ed.), *Local
Government in Transition. Evolving Local Government in Former Eastern
Europe*, Helsinki, pp. 195–215.

(1993a) "Administrative Transition in a Post-Communist Society: The Case of Hungary," *Public Administration*, 71(1/2), 89–103.

(1993b) "Social Protest in a Post-Communist Democracy: The Taxi Drivers' Demonstration in Hungary," in Frentzel-Zagórska, J. (ed.), *From a One-Party State to a Democracy: Transition in Eastern Europe*, Amsterdam and Atlanta: Rodopi, pp. 113–37.

Szajkowski, Bogdan (ed.) (1991) *New Political Parties in Eastern Europe and the Soviet Union*, Harlow: Longman.

(1991) "Bulgaria," in Szajkowski, Bogdan (ed.), *New Political Parties in Eastern Europe and the Soviet Union*, Harlow: Longman. pp. 19–52.

(1992) "Coping with Communist Legacy: The Complexities of the Emerging Party Systems in Bulgaria and Romania," Paper presented to the Workshop, "Between Continuity and Innovation: The rebirth of a pluralist party system after the fall of non-democratic regimes," ECPR Joint Sessions of Workshops, Limmerick, March 30-April 4.

Szelenyi, Ivan and Szelenyi, Balazs (1994) "Why Socialism Failed: Towards a Theory of System Breakdown," *Theory and Society*, 23, 211–31.

Széman, Zsuzsa (1994) "Payments for Care: The Case of Hungary," in Evers, Adalbert, Pijl, Marja, and Ungerson, Clare (eds.), *Payments for Care. A Comparative Overview*, Wien: European Centre Vienna, pp. 227–41.

Sziráczki, György (1990) "Employment Policy and Labour Market in Transition: From Labour Shortage to Unemployment," *Soviet Studies*, 42(4), 701–22.

Szoboszlai, György (1992) "Constitutional Transformation in Hungary," in Szoboszlai, György (ed.), *Flying Blind. Emerging Democracies in East-Central Europe*, Budapest: Hungarian Political Science Association, pp. 315–30.

Szomolányi, Sonja (1993) "Eastern Central Europe 2000: Transformations of Slovak Society and of its Political Scene at the Beginning of 1990s and the Scenario of Changes until 2005," Bratislava.

Szurgacz, Herbert (1991) "Die neueren Entwicklungen auf dem Gebiet des Sozialrechts in Polen," *Zeitschrift für ausländisches und internationales Arbeits- und Sozialrecht*, 5(3), 279–305.

Szücs, Jenö (1988) "Three Historical Regions of Europe," in Keane, John (ed.), *Civil Society and the State. New European Perspectives*, London and New York: Verso, pp. 291–332.

Taagepera, Rein and Shugart, Matthew S. (1989) *Seats and Votes: The Effects and Determinants of Electoral Systems*, New Haven, CO: Yale University Press.

Tang Tsou (1996) "Contribution," in Elster, Jon (ed.), *The Round Table Talks and the Breakdown of Communism*, Chicago and London: University of Chicago Press, pp. 213–40.

Teichova, Alice (1988) *Kleinstaaten im Spannungsfeld der Großmächte.*

Wirtschaft und Politik in Mittel- und Südosteuropa in der Zwischenkriegszeit, Munich: Oldenbourg.

Therborn, Göran (1992) "The Life and Times of Socialism," *New Left Review*, 194.

Thirkell, John, Atasanov, Boyko, and Gradev, Grigor (1993) "Trade Unions, Political Parties, and Governments in Bulgaria, 1989–1992," *Journal of Communist Studies*, 4, 98–115.

Thirkell, John, Scase, Richard, and Vickerstaff, Sarah (1994) "Comparative Labour Relations: Transition and Transformation in Eastern Europe," WORC, Discussion Paper 94.03.008/1, Tilburg.

Thorne, Alfredo (1993) "Eastern Europe's Experience with Banking Reform: Is There a Role for Banks in the Transition?" *Journal of Banking and Finance*, 17, 959–1000.

Tismaneanu, Vladimir (1985) "Ceaucescu's Socialism," *Problems of Communism*, 34(1), 50–66.

Todorova, Maria N. (1992) "Improbable Maverick or Typical Conformist? Seven Thoughts on the New Bulgaria," in Banac, I. (ed.), *Eastern Europe in Revolution*, Ithaca and London: Cornell University Press, pp. 148–67.

Tökés, Rudolf. L. (1993) "Democracy in Hungary: The First Hundred Days and a Mid-Term Assessment," in Volten, Peter M. E. (ed.), *Bound to Change: Consolidating Democracy in East Central Europe*, New York and Prague: Institute for EastWest Studies, pp. 151–90.

Tomes, Igor (1991) "Social Reform: A Cornerstone in Czechoslovakia's New Economic Structure," *International Labour Review*, 130, 191–8.

Toonen, Teo A. J. (1993) "Analysing Institutional Change and Administrative Transformation: A Comparative View," *Public Administration*, 71(1/2), 151–61.

Troebst, Stefan (1990) "Fluchtpunkt San Stefano," *Die neue Gesellschaft*, Frankfurter Hefte, May, 405–14.

Troxel, Juan (1993) "Socialist Persistence in the Bulgarian Elections of 1990–1991," *East European Quarterly*, 26(4), 407–30.

Tzvetkov, Palmen S. (1992) "The Politics of Transition in Bulgaria: Back to the Future," *Problems of Communism*, 41(2), 34–43.

UN Economic Commission for Europe (1994) *Economic Bulletin for Europe*, 46.

UNDP (1990) *Human Development Report*, New York and Oxford: Oxford University Press.

UNICEF (United Nations Children's Fund) (1993) "Central and Eastern Europe in Transition: Public Policy and Social Conditions," Regional Monitoring Report No. 1, Florence: UNICEF-ICDC.

(1995) "Poverty, Children and Policy: Responses for a Brighter Future," Regional Monitoring Report No. 3, Florence: UNICEF-ICDC.

Urbán, László (1991) "Why was the Hungarian Transition Exceptionally Peaceful?" in Szoboszlai, György (ed.), *Democracy and Political Transformation. Theories and East-Central European Realities*, Budapest: Hungarian Political Science Association, pp. 303–09.

Várhegyi, Éva (1993) "The Modernisation of the Hungarian Banking Sector," in Székely, István P. and Newbery, David M. G. (eds.), *Hungary: An Economy in Transition*, Cambridge University Press, pp. 149–62.

Vaughan-Whitehead, Daniel (1993) "Minimum Wage in Central and Eastern Europe: Slippage of the Anchor," ILO-CEET Reports No. 1, Budapest.

Veprek, Jaromir, Papes, Zdenek, and Veprek, Pavel (1994) "Czech Health Care in Economic Transformation," CERGE-EI Working Paper No. 63, Prague.

Verdery, Katherine (1991) "National Ideology Under Socialism. Ideology and Cultural Politics in Ceaucescu's Romania," Berkeley, Los Angeles, and Oxford: University of California Press.

Verdery, Katherine and Kligman, Gail (1992) "Romania after Ceaucescu: Post-Communist Communism," in Banac, Ivo, (ed.), *Eastern Europe in Revolution*, Ithaca and London: Cornell University Press, pp. 117–47.

Vida, Alexander (1994) "Ungarns freiwillige Anpassung an das Europarecht," *Wirtschaft und Recht in Osteuropa*, 3(1), 4–7.

Vidláková, Olga (1993) "Options for Administrative Reform in the Czech Republic," *Public Administration*, 71(1/2), 65–74.

Vörös, Imre (1986) "Neues Wettbewerbsgesetz in Ungarn," *Wirtschaft und Wettbewerb*, 36(6), 476–80.

Voirin, Michel (1993) "Die soziale Sicherheit in den Ländern Mittel- und Osteuropas: Reformen und Kontinuität," *Internationale Revue für Soziale Sicherheit*, 46, 29–71.

Vojtisek, Petr (1993) "Restructuring of the Banks in the Former Czech and Slovak Federal Republic," *Transformation of the Banking System: Portfolio Restructuring, Privatisation and the Payment System*, Paris: OECD, pp. 69–85.

Vyborná, Olga (1994) "The Reform of the Czech Health Care System," CERGE-EI Working Paper No. 64, Prague.

Waller, Michael (1991) "From Party-State to Political Market-Place in Eastern Europe: the Collapse of the Power Monopoly," in Moran, M. and Wright, M. (eds.), *The Market and the State*, London: MacMillan, pp. 100–18.

(1993) "Political Actors and Political Roles in East-Central Europe," *Journal of Communist Studies*, 4, 22–36.

(1994) "Voice, Choice and Loyalty: Democratization in Eastern Europe," in Parry, G. and Moran, M. (eds.), *Democracy and Democratization*, London and New York: Routledge, pp. 129–51.

(1995) "Making and Breaking: Factions in the Process of Party Formation in Bulgaria," *Democratization*, 2(1), 152–67.

Weber, Max (1978) *Economy and Society* (edited by Roth, G. and Wittich, C.), Berkeley, Los Angeles, and London: University of California Press.

Weidenfeld, Werner (ed.) (1995) *Demokratie und Marktwirtschaft in Osteuropa*, Gütersloh: Verlag Bertelsmann Stiftung.

Weingast, Barry R. (1993) "Constitutions as Governance Structures: The Political Foundations of Secure Markets," *Journal of Institutional and Theoretical Economics*, 149(1), 286–311.

Wesolowski, Wlodzimierz (1995) "Destruktion und Konstruktion sozialer Interessen im Zuge der Systemtransformation: Ein theoretischer Ansatz," in Wollmann, Hellmut, Wiesenthal, Helmut, and Bönker, Frank (eds.), *Transformation sozialistischer Gesellschaften: Am Ende des Anfangs*, Opladen: Westdeutscher Verlag, pp. 395–421.

Westen, Klaus (1993) "Das 'sozialistische Zivilrecht' und die Kontinuität europäischer Zivilrechtsentwicklung," *Juristen-Zeitung*, 48(1), 8–16.

White, Stephen (ed.) (1991) *Handbook of Reconstruction in Eastern Europe and the Soviet Union*, Harlow: Longman.

Wieacker, Franz (1990) "Foundations of European Legal Culture," *American Journal of Comparative Law*, 38(1), 1–29.

Wiesenthal, Helmut (1993) "Die 'Politische Ökonomie' des fortgeschrittenen Transformationsprozesses und die (potentiellen) Funktionen intermediärer Akteure (I). Interest Associations as Actors of Transformation (II)," Arbeitspapiere der AG TRAP 93/1, Berlin, Humboldt-Universität.

Wiesenthal, Helmut and Stykow, Petra (1994) "Unternehmerverbände im Systemwechsel. Entwicklung und Status organisierter Wirtschaftsinteressen in den Transformationsprozessen Ostmitteleuropas und Russlands," Arbeitspapiere AG TRAP 94/5, Berlin.

Wightman, Gordon (1990) "Czechoslovakia," *Electoral Studies*, (9)4, 319–26.

(1991) "Czechoslovakia," in Szajkowski, Bogdan (ed.), *New Political Parties in Eastern Europe and the Soviet Union*, Harlow: Longman, pp. 53–92.

(1995a) "The Development of the Party System and the Break-up of Czechoslovakia," in Wightman, Gordon (ed.), *Party Formation in East-Central Europe. Post-Communist Politics in Czechoslovakia, Hungary, Poland, and Bulgaria*, Aldershot: Edward Elgar, pp. 59–78.

Wightman, Gordon (1995b) "Conclusions," in Wightman, Gordon (ed.), *Party Formation in East-Central Europe. Post-Communist Politics in Czechoslovakia, Hungary, Poland, and Bulgaria*, Aldershot: Edward Elgar, pp. 238–51.

WIIW (1995) "Countries in Transition 1995," WIIW Handbook of
    Statistics, Vienna.
Williamson, John (1993) "Why Did Output Fall in Eastern Europe?" in
    Somogyi, Làszlo (ed.), *The Political Economy of the Transition Process in
    Eastern Europe*, Aldershot and Brookfield: Edward Elgar, pp. 25–39.
Winiecki, Jan (1988) *The Distorted World of Soviet-Type Economies*, London
    and New York: Routledge.
Wolchik, Sharon L. (1991) *Czechoslovakia in Transition. Politics, Economics,
    and Society*, London and New York: Pinter.
Wolf-Poweska, Anna (1995) "Politische Kultur in den postkommunistischen
    Gesellschaften," in Weidenfeld, Werner (ed.), *Demokratie und
    Marktwirtschaft in Osteuropa*, Gütersloh: Verlag Bertelsmann Stiftung,
    pp. 35–54.
Wollmann, Hellmut (1994) *Systemwandel und Städtebau in Mittel- und
    Osteuropa* (Forschungsbericht im Auftrag des Bundesministers für
    Raumordnung, Bauwesen und Städtebau), Basel, Boston, and Berlin:
    Birkhäuser.
Wollmann, Hellmut, Wiesenthal, Helmut, and Bönker, Frank (ed.) (1995)
    Transformation sozialistischer Gesellschaften: Am Ende des Anfangs,
    Opladen: Westdeutscher Verlag.
Wyzan, Michael L. (1991) "The Bulgarian Economy in the Immediate Post-
    Zhivkov Era," in Sjöberg, Örjan and Wyzan, Michael L. (eds.),
    *Economic Change in the Balkan States: Albania, Bulgaria, Romania and
    Yugoslavia*, London: Pinter, pp. 83–100.
Yavlinsky, Grigory (1994) *Laissez-Faire versus Policy-Led Transformation.
    Lessons of the Economic Reforms in Russia*, Moscow: Center for
    Economic and Political Research.
Ziebe, Jürgen (1992) "Die Reform des Bankensystems und das neue
    Bankengesetz in der CSFR," *Recht der Internationalen Wirtschaft*, 38(9),
    723–8.

Index